¡APÚNTATE!
Español introductorio

Ana María Pérez-Gironés
Wesleyan University

Thalia Dorwick

Introductory Spanish
101-102

Nassau Community College

Mc Graw Hill **Learning Solutions**

Boston   Burr Ridge, IL   Dubuque, IA   New York   San Francisco   St. Louis
Bangkok   Bogotá   Caracas   Lisbon   London   Madrid
Mexico City   Milan   New Delhi   Seoul   Singapore   Sydney   Taipei   Toronto

¡Apúntate!: español introductorio
Introductory Spanish
101-102
Nassau Community College

This book is a McGraw-Hill Learning Solutions textbook and contains select material from *¡Apúntate!: español introductorio* by Ana María Pérez-Gironés and Thalia Dorwick. Copyright © 2010 by The McGraw-Hill Companies, Inc. Reprinted with permission of the publisher. Many custom published texts are modified versions or adaptations of our best-selling textbooks. Some adaptations are printed in black and white to keep prices at a minimum, while others are in color.

1 2 3 4 5 6 7 8 9 0 DIG DIG 12 11 10

ISBN-13: 978-0-07-746629-9
ISBN-10: 0-07-746629-2

Learning Solutions Manager: Domenic DiNardo
Production Editor: Nina Meyer
Printer/Binder: Digital Impressions
Cover Design: Felicia Cornish

Brief Table of Contents

¡Apúntate!

Contenido

10 La salud 274

Estudiantes (*Students*) en la Plaza Mayor de Madrid, España

As you study Spanish in *¡Apúntate!,* you will also learn about the ethnic, racial, and cultural diversity of the Spanish-speaking world.

Primeros pasos°

 ¡Apúntate! means *Sign up!* or *Get on board!* in Spanish. With *¡Apúntate!* you will begin to learn Spanish and get ready to communicate with Spanish speakers in this country and elsewhere in the Spanish-speaking world.

 To speak a language involves much more than just learning its grammar and vocabulary; to know a language is to know the people who speak it. For this reason *¡Apúntate!* will provide you with cultural information to help you understand and appreciate the traditions and values of Spanish-speaking people all over the world.

 Are you ready for the adventure of learning Spanish? **Pues, adelante** *(Well, let's go),* **¡apúntate!**

°Primeros... *First steps*
*en... *in this chapter*

Saludos° y expresiones de cortesía   *Greetings*

Here are some words, phrases, and expressions that will enable you to meet and greet others appropriately in Spanish.

1. Sevilla, España

1. MANOLO: ¡Hola, Maricarmen!
MARICARMEN: ¿Qué tal, Manolo? ¿Cómo estás?
MANOLO: Muy bien. ¿Y tú?
MARICARMEN: Regular. Nos vemos, ¿eh?
MANOLO: Hasta mañana.

2. ELISA VELASCO: Buenas tardes, señor Gómez.
MARTÍN GÓMEZ: Muy buenas, señora Velasco. ¿Cómo está?
ELISA VELASCO: Bien, gracias. ¿Y usted?
MARTÍN GÓMEZ: Muy bien, gracias. Hasta luego.
ELISA VELASCO: Adiós.

2. Quito, Ecuador

¿Qué tal?, **¿Cómo estás?**, and **¿Y tú?** are expressions used in informal situations with people you know well, on a first-name basis.

¿Cómo está? and **¿Y usted?** are used to address someone with whom you have a formal relationship.

3. La Ciudad de México, México

3. LUPE: Buenos días, profesor.
PROFESOR: Buenos días. ¿Cómo te llamas?
LUPE: Me llamo Lupe Carrasco.
PROFESOR: Mucho gusto, Lupe.
LUPE: Igualmente.

1. **Manolo:** *Hi, Maricarmen!* **Maricarmen:** *How's it going, Manolo? How are you?* **Manolo:** *Very well. And you?* **Maricarmen:** *OK. See you around, OK?* **Manolo:** *See you tomorrow.*

2. **Elisa Velasco:** *Good afternoon, Mr. Gómez.* **Martín Gómez:** *Afternoon, Mrs. Velasco. How are you?* **Elisa Velasco:** *Fine, thank you. And you?* **Martín Gómez:** *Very well, thanks. See you later.* **Elisa Velasco:** *Bye.*

3. **Lupe:** *Good morning, professor.* **Professor:** *Good morning. What's your name?* **Lupe:** *My name is Lupe Carrasco.* **Professor:** *Nice to meet you, Lupe.* **Lupe:** *Likewise.*

¿Cómo se llama usted? is used in formal situations. **¿Cómo te llamas?** is used in informal situations — for example, with other students. The phrases **mucho gusto** and **igualmente** are used by both men and women when meeting for the first time. In response to **mucho gusto**, a woman can also say **encantada**; a man can say **encantado**.

4. La Ciudad de México, México

4. **MIGUEL RENÉ:** ¡Hola! Me llamo Miguel René. ¿Y tú? ¿Cómo te llamas?
     KARINA: Me llamo Karina. Mucho gusto.
     MIGUEL RENÉ: Mucho gusto, Karina. Y, ¿de dónde eres?
     KARINA: Yo soy de Venezuela. ¿Y tú?
     MIGUEL RENÉ: Yo soy de México.

¿De dónde eres? is used in informal situations to ask where someone is from. In formal situations the expression used is **¿De dónde es usted?** To reply to either question, the phrase **(Yo) Soy de _____** is used.

◆ NOTA COMUNICATIVA

Otros saludos y expresiones de cortesía

buenos días	good morning (*used until the midday meal*)
buenas tardes	good afternoon (*used until the evening meal*)
buenas noches	good evening; good night (*used after the evening meal*)
señor (Sr.)	Mr., sir
señora (Sra.)	Mrs., ma'am
señorita (Srta.)	Miss
gracias	thanks, thank you
muchas gracias	thank you very much
de nada, no hay de qué	you're welcome
por favor	please (*also used to get someone's attention*)
perdón	pardon me, excuse me (*to ask forgiveness or to get someone's attention*)
con permiso	pardon me, excuse me (*to request permission to pass by or through a group of people*)

¡OJO!*

There is no Spanish equivalent for *Ms.*; use **Sra.** or **Srta.** as appropriate. Use the titles **profesor** and **profesora** to address your college instructors.

4. **Miguel René:** *Hello! My name is Miguel René. And you? What's your name?* **Karina:** *My name is Karina. Nice to meet you.* **Miguel René:** *Nice to meet you, Karina. And where are you from?* **Karina:** *I'm from Venezuela. And you?* **Miguel René:** *I'm from Mexico.*

*Careful!

Conversación

A. Expresiones de cortesía.
How many different ways can you respond to the following greetings and phrases?

1. Buenas tardes.
2. Adiós.
3. ¿Qué tal?
4. ¡Hola!
5. ¿Cómo está?
6. Buenas noches.
7. Muchas gracias.
8. Hasta mañana.
9. ¿Cómo se llama usted?
10. Mucho gusto.
11. ¿De dónde eres?
12. Buenos días.

B. Situaciones.
If the following people met or passed each other at the times given, what might they say to each other? Role-play the situations with a classmate.

1. Mr. Santana and Miss Pérez, at 5:00 P.M.
2. Mrs. Ortega and Pablo, at 10:00 A.M.
3. Ms. Hernández and Olivia, at 11:00 P.M.
4. you and a classmate, just before your Spanish class.
5. you and your Spanish professor, at 11 A.M.
6. you and your cousin, at 10 P.M.
7. you and the president/rector of your university, at 4 P.M.

—Mucho gusto.
—Igualmente.

C. Más (More) situaciones.
Are the people in these drawings saying **por favor, con permiso,** or **perdón**? **¡OJO!** More than one response is possible for some items.

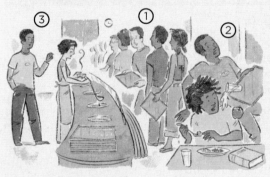

D. Entrevista (Interview)

Paso (Step) 1. Turn to a person sitting next to you and do the following.

- Greet him or her appropriately, that is, with informal forms.
- Ask how he or she is.
- Find out his or her name.
- Ask where he or she is from.
- Conclude the exchange.

Paso 2. Now have a similar conversation with your instructor, using the appropriate formal or familiar forms, according to your instructor's request.

El alfabeto español

There are twenty-nine letters in the Spanish alphabet (**el alfabeto** or **el abecedario**) — three more than in the English alphabet. The three additional letters are the **ch**, the **ll**, and the **ñ**. The letter **ñ** comes after **n** in alphabetized lists in Spanish. The letters **k** and **w** appear only in words borrowed from other languages.

Letters	Names of Letters	Examples		
a	a	Antonio	Ana	(la) Argentina
b	be	Benito	Blanca	Bolivia
c	ce	Carlos	Cecilia	Cáceres
ch*	che	Pancho	Chabela	La Mancha
d	de	Domingo	Dolores	Durango
e	e	Eduardo	Elena	(el) Ecuador
f	efe	Felipe	Francisca	Florida
g	ge	Gerardo	Gloria	Guatemala
h	hache	Héctor	Hortensia	Honduras
i	i	Ignacio	Inés	Ibiza
j	jota	José	Juana	Jalisco
k	ca (ka)	(Karl)	(Karina)	(Kansas)
l	ele	Luis	Lola	Lima
ll*	elle	Guillermo	Estrella	Sevilla
m	eme	Manuel	María	México
n	ene	Nicolás	Nati	Nicaragua
ñ	eñe	Íñigo	Begoña	España
o	o	Octavio	Olivia	Oviedo
p	pe	Pablo	Pilar	Panamá
q	cu	Enrique	Raquel	Quito
r	ere	Álvaro	Rosa	(el) Perú
s	ese	Salvador	Sara	San Juan
t	te	Tomás	Teresa	Toledo
u	u	Agustín	Úrsula	(el) Uruguay
v	ve *or* uve	Víctor	Victoria	Venezuela
w	doble ve, ve doble, *or* uve doble	Oswaldo	(Wilma)	(Washington)
x	equis	Xavier	Ximena	Extremadura
y	i griega	Pelayo	Yolanda	(el) Paraguay
z	ceta (zeta)	Gonzalo	Zoila	Zaragoza

*The **ch** is pronounced with the same sound as in English cherry or chair, as in **nachos** or **muchacho.** The **ll** is pronounced as a type of y sound. Spanish examples of this sound that you may already know are **tortilla** and **Sevilla.**

Práctica

A. ¡Pronuncia! The following letters and letter combinations represent the Spanish sounds that are the most different from English. Pay particular attention to their pronunciation when you see them. Can you match the Spanish letters with their equivalent pronunciation?

EXAMPLES/SPELLING

1. mucho: **ch**
2. Geraldo: **ge** (also: **gi**)
   Jiménez: **j**
3. hola: **h**
4. gusto: **gu** (also: **ga**, **go**)
5. me llamo: **ll**
6. señor: **ñ**
7. profesora: **r**
8. Ramón: **r** (to start a word)
   Monterrey: **rr**
9. nos vemos: **v**

PRONUNCIATION

a. like the *g* in English *garden*
b. similar to *tt* of *butter* when pronounced very quickly
c. like *ch* in English *cheese*
d. like Spanish *b*
e. similar to a "strong" English *h*
f. like *y* in English *yes* or like the *li* sound in *million*
g. a trilled sound, several Spanish **r**'s in a row
h. similar to the *ny* sound in *canyon*
i. never pronounced

B. ¿Cómo se escribe... ? (*How do you write . . . ?*)

Paso 1. Pronounce these U.S. place names in Spanish. Then spell the names aloud in Spanish. All of them are of Hispanic origin: **Toledo, Los Ángeles, Texas, Montana, Colorado, El Paso, Florida, Las Vegas, Amarillo, San Francisco.**

Paso 2. Spell your own name aloud in Spanish, and listen as your classmates spell their names. Try to remember as many of their names as you can.

> **MODELO:** Me llamo María: **M** (eme) **a** (a)
> **r** (ere) **í** (i acentuada) **a** (a).

⟩NOTA COMUNICATIVA

Los cognados

As you begin your study of Spanish, you will probably notice that many Spanish and English words are similar or identical in form and meaning. These related words are called *cognates* (**los cognados**). You will see them used in **Primeros pasos** and throughout *¡Apúntate!* At this early stage of language learning, it's useful to begin recognizing cognates and how they are pronounced in Spanish. Here are some examples of Spanish words that are cognates of English words. These cognates and others will help you enrich your Spanish vocabulary and develop your language proficiency!

WORDS TO NAME OR DESCRIBE PEOPLE, PLACES, AND THINGS

cruel	paciente	banco	hotel
elegante	pesimista	bar	museo
importante	responsable	café	oficina
inteligente	sentimental	diccionario	parque
interesante	terrible	estudiante	teléfono
optimista	tolerante	examen	televisión

¿Cómo eres tú?° (Part 1)*

¿Cómo... *What are you like?*

You can use these forms of the verb **ser** (*to be*) to describe yourself and others.

(yo)	**soy**	I am
(tú)	**eres**	you (*familiar*) are
(usted)	**es**	you (*formal*) are
(él, ella)	**es**	he/she is

—¿Cómo **eres tú**?
—Bueno…° Yo **soy** moderna, independiente, sofisticada…

Well . . .

Conversación

Descripciones

Paso 1. Form complete sentences with the cognates given. Use **no** when necessary.

1. Yo (no) soy...
   estudiante.
   cruel.
   responsable.
   optimista.
   paciente.
2. El/La líder (*leader*) de esta (*this*) nación (no) es…
   importante.
   inteligente.
   pesimista.
   flexible.
   tolerante.
3. Jennifer López (no) es…
   elegante.   egoísta.
   introvertida.   moderna.
   romántica.   espectacular.
   sentimental.   extravagante.

Soy estudiante de esta (*this*) universidad. Soy responsable y realista. ¿Y tú?

Paso 2. Now think of people you might describe with the following additional cognates. Use **es** to express *is*.

MODELO: eficiente ⟶ El profesor / La profesora es eficiente.

1. arrogante
2. egoísta
3. emocional
4. idealista
5. independiente
6. liberal
7. materialista
8. paciente
9. realista
10. rebelde

---

*You will learn more about **ser** in **Gramática 5** (**Capítulo 2**).

Spanish Around the World

Although no one knows exactly how many languages are spoken around the world, linguists estimate that there are between 3,000 and 6,000. Spanish, with 425 million native speakers, is among the top five languages. It is the official language spoken in Spain, in Mexico, in all of South America (except Brazil and the Guianas), in most of Central America, in Cuba, in Puerto Rico, in the Dominican Republic, and in Ecuatorial Guinea (in Africa) — in approximately twenty-one countries in all. It is also spoken by a great number of people in the United States and Canada.

Like all languages spoken by large numbers of people, modern Spanish varies from region to region. The Spanish of Madrid is different from that spoken in Mexico City, Buenos Aires, or Los Angeles. Although these differences are most noticeable in pronunciation ("accent"), they are also found in vocabulary and special expressions used in different geographical areas. Despite these differences, misunderstandings among native speakers are rare, since the majority of structures and vocabulary are common to the many varieties of each language.

You don't need to go abroad to encounter people who speak Spanish on a daily basis. The Spanish language and people of Hispanic descent have been an integral part of life in the United States and Canada for centuries. In fact, the United States has the fifth largest Spanish-speaking population in the world!

There is also great regional diversity among U.S. Hispanics. Many people of Mexican descent inhabit the southwestern part of the United States, including populations as far north as Colorado. Large groups of Puerto Ricans can be found in New York, while Florida is host to a large Cuban and Central American population. More recent immigrants include Nicaraguans and Salvadorans, who have established large communities in many U.S. cities, among them San Francisco and Los Angeles.

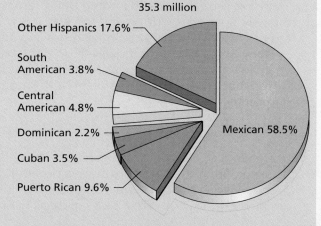

Comparing origins of U.S. Hispanic population
Total population based on U.S. census, 2000 estimate*
35.3 million

Other Hispanics 17.6%
South American 3.8%
Central American 4.8%
Dominican 2.2%
Cuban 3.5%
Puerto Rican 9.6%
Mexican 58.5%

*Source: U.S. Census Bureau. 2006 American Community Survey.

As you will discover in subsequent chapters of *¡Apúntate!,* the Spanish language and people of Hispanic descent have been and will continue to be an integral part of the fabric of this country.

Mural en la Pequeña Habana (Little Havana), *el barrio* (neighborhood) *cubano de* (of) *Miami*

Pronunciación

You have probably already noted that there is a very close relationship between the way Spanish is written and the way it is pronounced. This makes it relatively easy to learn the basics of Spanish spelling and pronunciation.

Many Spanish sounds, however, do not have an exact equivalent in English, so you can't always trust English to be your guide to Spanish pronunciation. Even words that are spelled the same in both languages are usually pronounced quite differently.

Las vocales (*Vowels*): **a, e, i, o, u**

Unlike English vowels, which can have many different pronunciations or may be silent, Spanish vowels are always pronounced, and they are almost always pronounced in the same way. Spanish vowels are always short and tense. They are never drawn out with a *u* or *i* glide as in English: **lo** ≠ *low*; **de** ≠ *day*.

> **a:** pronounced like the *a* in *father,* but short and tense
> **e:** pronounced like the *e* in *they,* but without the *i* glide
> **i:** pronounced like the *i* in *machine,* but short and tense*
> **o:** pronounced like the *o* in *home,* but without the *u* glide
> **u:** pronounced like the *u* in *rule,* but short and tense

¡OJO!

The *uh* sound or schwa (which is how most unstressed vowels are pronounced in English: *canal, waited, atom*) does not exist in Spanish.

A. Sílabas. Pronounce the following Spanish syllables, being careful to pronounce each vowel with a short, tense sound.

1. ma fa la ta pa
2. me fe le te pe
3. mi fi li ti pi
4. mo fo lo to po
5. mu fu lu tu pu
6. mi fe la tu do
7. su mi te so la
8. se tu no ya li

B. Palabras (*Words*). Repeat the following words after your instructor.

1. hasta   tal   nada   mañana   natural   normal   fascinante
2. me   qué   Pérez   Elena   rebelde   excelente   elegante
3. sí   señorita   permiso   terrible   imposible   tímido   Ibiza
4. yo   con   como   noches   profesor   señor   generoso
5. uno   usted   tú   mucho   Perú   Lupe   Úrsula

---

*The word **y** (and) is also pronounced like the letter **i**.

C. Trabalenguas (*Tongue twister*)

Paso 1. Here is a popular nonsense rhyme, the Spanish version of "Eeny, meeny, miney, moe." (Note: The person who corresponds to **fue** is "it.") Listen as your instructor pronounces it.

> Pin, marín
> de don Pingüé
> cúcara, mácara
> títere, fue.

Paso 2. Now pronounce the vowels clearly as you repeat the rhyme.

D. Las naciones

Paso 1. Here is part of a rental car ad in Spanish. Say aloud the names of the countries where you can find this company's offices. Can you recognize all of the countries?

Paso 2. Find the following information in the ad.

1. How many cars does the agency have available?
2. How many offices does the agency have?
3. What Spanish word expresses the English word *immediately*?

ai Ansa International

RENT A CAR

Si necesita un coche para su trabajo o placer, nosotros tenemos el adecuado para Vd.

Con una flota de 40.000 coches y 1.000 oficinas, estamos a su servicio en los siguientes países:

- ALEMANIA
- ARABIA SAUDITA
- ARGENTINA
- AUSTRIA
- BELGICA
- BRASIL
- CHIPRE
- DINAMARCA
- ESPAÑA
- FINLANDIA
- FRANCIA
- GRAN BRETAÑA
- GRECIA
- HOLANDA
- IRLANDA
- ISLANDIA
- ITALIA
- JAMAICA
- LUXEMBURGO
- MALASIA
- MARRUECOS
- MARTINICA
- PARAGUAY
- PORTUGAL
- SUECIA
- SUIZA
- URUGUAY
- U.S.A.

En la mayoría de los casos, podemos confirmar su reserva inmediatamente.

Cuando esto no sea posible, su reserva le será confirmada en un plazo máximo de 48 horas.

Los números del 0 al 30; *Hay*

CANCIÓN INFANTIL

Dos y **dos** son **cuatro,**
cuatro y **dos** son **seis,**
seis y **dos** son **ocho,**
y **ocho dieciséis.**

0	cero				
1	uno	11	once	21	veintiuno
2	dos	12	doce	22	veintidós
3	tres	13	trece	23	veintitrés
4	cuatro	14	catorce	24	veinticuatro
5	cinco	15	quince	25	veinticinco
6	seis	16	dieciséis*	26	veintiséis
7	siete	17	diecisiete	27	veintisiete
8	ocho	18	dieciocho	28	veintiocho
9	nueve	19	diecinueve	29	veintinueve
10	diez	20	veinte	30	treinta

$$1 + 7 = 8$$

Los números del 0 al 30

The number *one* has several forms in Spanish. **Uno** is the form used in counting. The forms **un** and **una** are used before nouns. How will you know which one to use? It depends on the gender of the noun.

noun = a word that denotes a person, place, thing, or idea

   In **Capítulo 1,** you will learn that all Spanish nouns are either masculine or feminine in gender. For example, the noun **señor** is masculine (*m.*) in gender, and the noun **señora** is feminine (*f.*) in gender. (As you will learn, Spanish nouns that are not sex-linked also have gender.) Here is how the word *one* is expressed with these nouns: **un señor, una señora.** Also note that the number **veintiuno** becomes **veintiún** before masculine nouns and **veintiuna** before feminine nouns: **veintiún señores, veintiuna señoras.** Do get used to using **un** and **uno** with nouns now, but don't worry about the concept of gender for the moment.

¡OJO!

uno, dos,... veint**iuno,** veintidós,...
   but
un señor, veint**iún** señores
una señora, veint**iuna** señoras

A children's song *Two and two are four, four and two are six, six and two are eight, and eight (makes) sixteen.*

*The numbers 16 to 19 and 21 to 29 can be written as one word (**dieciséis... veintiuno...**) or as three words (**diez y seis... veinte y uno...**).*

Hay

Use the word **hay** to express both *there is* and *there are* in Spanish. **No hay** means *there is not* and *there are not*. **¿Hay... ?** asks *Is there . . . ?* or *Are there . . . ?*

hay = there is / there are

— ¿Cuántos estudiantes **hay** en la clase?
— **(Hay)** Treinta.

How many students are there in the class?
(There are) Thirty.

— **¿Hay** pandas en el zoológico?
— **Hay** veinte osos, pero **no hay** pandas.

Are there any pandas at the zoo?
There are twenty bears, but there aren't any pandas.

Práctica

A. Los números. Practica los números, según (*according to*) el modelo.

MODELO: 1 señor ⟶ Hay un señor.

1. 4 señoras
2. 12 pianos
3. 1 café (*m.*)
4. 21 cafés (*m.*)
5. 14 días
6. 1 clase (*f.*)
7. 21 ideas (*f.*)
8. 11 personas
9. 15 estudiantes
10. 13 teléfonos
11. 28 naciones
12. 5 guitarras
13. 1 león (*m.*)
14. 30 señores
15. 20 oficinas

B. Problemas de matemáticas. Express the following simple mathematical equations in Spanish. Note: + (**y**), − (**menos**), = (**son**).

MODELOS: $2 + 2 = 4$ ⟶ Dos y dos son cuatro.
$4 - 2 = 2$ ⟶ Cuatro menos dos son dos.

1. $2 + 4 = 6$
2. $8 + 17 = 25$
3. $11 + 1 = 12$
4. $3 + 18 = 21$
5. $9 + 6 = 15$
6. $5 + 4 = 9$
7. $1 + 13 = 14$
8. $15 - 2 = 13$
9. $9 - 9 = 0$
10. $13 - 8 = 5$
11. $14 + 12 = 26$
12. $23 - 13 = 10$
13. $1 + 4 = 5$
14. $1 - 1 + (\textbf{más})3 = 3$
15. $8 - 7 = 1$
16. $13 - 9 = 4$
17. $2 + 3 + 10 = 15$
18. $28 - 6 = 22$
19. $30 - 17 = 13$
20. $28 - 5 = 23$
21. $19 - 7 = 12$

Conversación

Preguntas (*Questions*)

1. ¿Cuántos (*How many*) estudiantes hay en la clase de español? ¿Cuántos estudiantes hay en clase hoy (*today*)? ¿Hay tres profesores o un profesor / una profesora?
2. ¿Cuántos días hay en una semana (*week*)? ¿Hay seis? (No, no hay...) ¿Cuántos días hay en un fin de semana (*weekend*)? ¿Cuántos días hay en el mes (*month*) de febrero? ¿en el mes de junio? ¿Cuántos meses hay en un año (*year*)?
3. En una universidad, hay muchos edificios (*many buildings*). En esta (*this*) universidad, ¿hay una cafetería? (Sí, hay... / No, no hay...) ¿un teatro? ¿un laboratorio de lenguas (*languages*)? ¿un bar? ¿una clínica? ¿un hospital? ¿un museo? ¿muchos estudiantes? ¿muchos profesores?

¿Te gusta el fútbol? ⟶ ■ Sí, **me gusta** mucho el fútbol.
■ No, **no me gusta** el fútbol.

To indicate you like something:	**Me gusta** ____.
To indicate you don't like something:	**No me gusta** ____.
To ask a classmate if he or she likes something:	**¿Te gusta** ____?
To ask your instructor the same question:	**¿Le gusta** ____?

En español, **fútbol** = *soccer* y **fútbol americano** = *football*

> **infinitive** = a verb form that indicates action or state of being without reference to person, time, or number

In the following activities, you will use the word **el** with masculine nouns and the word **la** with feminine nouns to express *the*. Don't try to memorize which nouns are masculine and which are feminine. Just get used to using the words **el** and **la** before nouns.

You will also be using a number of Spanish verbs in the infinitive form, which always ends in **-r.** Here are some examples: **estudiar** = *to study;* **comer** = *to eat.* Try to guess the meaning of the infinitives used in these activities from context. If someone asks you, **¿Te gusta *beber* Coca-Cola?**, it is a safe guess that **beber** means *to drink*.

Conversación

A. Los gustos y las preferencias

Paso 1. Make a list of six things you like and six things you don't like, following the model. You may choose items from the **Vocabulario útil** box. All words are provided with the appropriate definite article **el** or **la,** depending on the gender of the noun.

> **MODELO:** Me gusta *la clase de español.* No me gusta *la clase de matemáticas.*

1. Me gusta ____. No me gusta ____.
2. _____ 3. _____ 4. _____
5. _____ 6. _____

Vocabulario útil†

el actor ____, **la actriz** ____
el café, el té, la limonada
el/la cantante (singer) ____
  (**¡OJO!** The word **cantante** is used for both men *and* women.)
el cine (movies), **el teatro, la ópera, el arte abstracto, el fútbol**
la música moderna, la música clásica, el rap, la música *country*
la pizza, la pasta, la comida (food) **mexicana, la comida de la cafetería**

Paso 2. Now ask a classmate if he or she shares your likes and dislikes.

> **MODELO:** ESTUDIANTE 1: ¿Te gusta la clase de español?
> ESTUDIANTE 2: Sí, me gusta (la clase de español).
> ESTUDIANTE 1: ¿Y la clase de matemáticas?
> ESTUDIANTE 2: Sí, también (*also*) me gusta (la clase de matemáticas).

Do you like soccer? ⟶ • *Yes, I like soccer very much.* • *No, I don't like soccer.*

*You will learn more about **gustar** in **Gramática 21** (**Capítulo 7**).

†*The material in **Vocabulario útil** lists is not active; that is, it is not part of what you need to focus on learning at this point. You may use these words and phrases to complete exercises or to help you converse in Spanish, if you need them.*

B. ¿Qué hora es? Express the time in full sentences in Spanish.

1. 1:00 P.M.
2. 6:00 P.M.
3. 11:00 A.M.
4. 1:30
5. 3:15

6. 6:45
7. 4:15
8. 11:45 exactly
9. 9:10 on the dot
10. 9:50 sharp

Conversación

A. Entrevista

Paso 1. Ask a classmate at what time the following events or activities take place. He or she will answer according to the cue or will provide the necessary information.

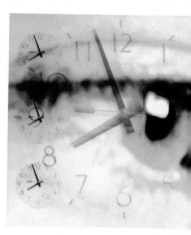

> MODELO: la clase de español (10:00 A.M.) →
> ESTUDIANTE 1: ¿A qué hora es la clase de español?
> ESTUDIANTE 2: A las diez de la mañana… ¡en punto!

1. la clase de francés (1:45 P.M.)
2. la sesión de laboratorio (3:10 P.M.)
3. la excursión (8:45 A.M.)
4. el concierto (7:30 P.M.)
5. la clase de física (11:50 A.M.)
6. la fiesta (10:00 P.M.)

Paso 2. Now ask at what time your partner likes to perform these activities. He or she will provide the necessary information.

> MODELO: cenar (*to have dinner*) →
> ESTUDIANTE 1: ¿A qué hora te gusta cenar?
> ESTUDIANTE 2: Me gusta cenar a las ocho de la noche.

1. almorzar (*to have lunch*)
2. mirar (*to watch*) la televisión
3. ir (*to go*) al (*to the*) gimnasio
4. ir al cine
5. estudiar
6. ir a una fiesta

B. Situaciones. How might the following people greet each other if they met at the indicated time? With a classmate, create a brief dialogue for each situation.

> MODELO: Jorge y María, a las once de la noche →
> JORGE: Buenas noches, María.
> MARÍA: ¡Hola, Jorge! ¿Cómo estás?
> JORGE: Bien, gracias. ¿Y tú?
> MARÍA: ¡Muy bien!

1. el profesor Martínez y Gloria, a las diez de la mañana
2. la Sra. López y la Srta. Luna, a las cuatro y media de la tarde
3. tú y tu (*your*) profesor(a) de español, en la clase de español

Need more practice?
- Workbook/Laboratory Manual
- Online Learning Center
  [www.mhhe.com/apuntate]

Estrategia: Guessing Meaning from Context

You will recognize the meaning of a number of cognates in the following reading about the geography of the Hispanic world. In addition, you should be able to guess the meaning of the underlined words from the context (the words that surround them); they are the names of geographical features. The photo captions will also be helpful.

Note also that a series of headings divides the reading into brief parts. It is always a good idea to scan such headings before starting to read, in order to get a sense of a reading's overall content.

La geografía del mundo[a] hispánico

Introducción

La geografía del mundo hispánico es impresionante y muy variada. En algunas[b] regiones hay de todo.[c]

En América

En la Argentina hay <u>pampas</u> extensas en el sur[d] y la <u>cordillera</u> de los Andes en el oeste. En partes de Venezuela, Colombia y el Ecuador, hay regiones tropicales de densa <u>selva</u>. En el Brasil (donde se habla portugués) está[e] el famoso <u>río</u> Amazonas. En el centro de México y también en El Salvador, Nicaragua, Colombia y otros países,[f] hay <u>volcanes</u> activos. A veces[g] producen erupciones catastróficas. El Perú y Bolivia comparten[h] el enorme <u>lago</u> Titicaca, situado en una <u>meseta</u> entre los dos países.

La <u>cordillera</u> de los Andes, Chile

La <u>isla</u> de Caja de Muertos, Puerto Rico

En el Caribe

Cuba, Puerto Rico y la República Dominicana son tres <u>islas</u> situadas en el <u>mar</u> Caribe. Las bellas playas[i] del mar Caribe y de la <u>península</u> de Yucatán son populares entre[j] los turistas de todo el mundo.

[a]*world* [b]*some* [c]*de... a bit of everything* [d]*south* [e]*is* [f]naciones
[g]*A... Sometimes* [h]*share* [i]bellas... *beautiful beaches* [j]*among*

EN LA PENÍNSULA IBÉRICA

España comparte[k] la Península Ibérica con Portugal. También tiene[l] una geografía variada. En el norte están los Pirineos, la cordillera que separa a España del[m] resto de Europa. Madrid, la capital del país, está situada en la meseta central. En las costas del sur y del este hay playas tan hermosas como las de[n] Latinoamérica y del Caribe.

Una meseta de La Mancha, España

La ciudad de Montevideo, Uruguay

¿Y LAS CIUDADES?

Es importante mencionar también la gran[ñ] diversidad de las ciudades del mundo hispánico. En la Argentina está la gran ciudad de Buenos Aires, que[o] muchos consideran como[p] «el París» o «la Nueva York» de Sudamérica. En Venezuela está Caracas, y en el Perú están Lima, la capital, y Cuzco, una ciudad indígena antigua.

CONCLUSIÓN

En fin,[q] el territorio del mundo hispánico es muy diverso. ¿Y el de[r] este país?

[k]shares [l]it has [m]from the [n]tan... as beautiful as those of [ñ]great [o]which [p]as [q]En... In short [r]el... that of

COMPRENSIÓN

Ejemplos (*Examples*). Give examples of similar geographical features found in this country or close to it. Then give examples from the Spanish-speaking world.

MODELO: un río ⟶ *the Mississippi*, el río Orinoco

1. un lago
2. una cordillera
3. un río
4. una isla
5. una playa
6. una costa
7. un mar
8. un volcán
9. una península

En resumen

See the Workbook/Laboratory Manual and Online Learning Center (www.mhhe.com/apuntate) for self-tests and practice with the grammar and vocabulary presented in this chapter.

Vocabulario

Although you have used and heard many words in this preliminary chapter of *¡Apúntate!,* the following words are the ones considered to be active vocabulary. Be sure that you know all of them, including the meaning of the group titles, before beginning **Capítulo 1.**

Saludos y expresiones de cortesía

Buenos días. Buenas tardes. Buenas noches.
   Muy buenas.
¡Hola! ¿Qué tal? ¿Cómo está(s)?
Regular. (Muy) Bien.
¿Y tú? ¿Y usted?
Adiós. Hasta mañana. Hasta luego. Nos vemos.

¿Cómo te llamas? ¿Cómo se llama usted?
   Me llamo _____ .
¿De dónde eres? ¿De dónde es usted?
   (Yo) Soy de _____ .

señor (Sr.), señora (Sra.), señorita (Srta.)

(Muchas) Gracias.
De nada. No hay de qué.
Por favor. Perdón. Con permiso.
Mucho gusto. Igualmente. Encantado/a.

¿Cómo eres tú?

soy, eres, es

Los números del 0 al 30

cero	diez	veinte
uno	once	treinta
dos	doce	
tres	trece	
cuatro	catorce	
cinco	quince	
seis	dieciséis	
siete	diecisiete	
ocho	dieciocho	
nueve	diecinueve	

Los gustos y las preferencias

¿Te gusta _____ ? ¿Le gusta _____ ?
(Sí,) Me gusta _____ . (No,) No me gusta _____ .

¿Qué hora es?

es la... , son las...
y/menos cuarto (quince)
y media (treinta)
en punto
de la mañana (tarde, noche)
¿a qué hora... ?, a la(s)...

Las palabras interrogativas

¿cómo?	how?; what?
¿dónde?	where?
¿qué?	what?

Palabras adicionales

sí/no	yes/no
hay	there is/are
no hay	there is not / are not
hoy/mañana	today/tomorrow
y/o	and/or
a	to; at (*with time*)
de	of; from
en	in; on; at
pero	but
también	also
los gustos	likes
la palabra	word
el saludo	greeting

◄►) VOCABULARIO PERSONAL

Use this space for other words and phrases you learn in this chapter.

Español   **Inglés**

Los Estados Unidos

According to the latest United States census information, approximately 28 million people speak Spanish at home in the United States.* Does that make the United States a Spanish-speaking country? It depends on your definition of "Spanish-speaking." The entire population of Ecuador is almost 14 million. The population of Chile is just over 16 million. The population of Venezuela is about 26 million . . . In other words, there are more Spanish speakers in the United States than citizens in each of these three Spanish-speaking countries.

Spanish speakers in the United States come from a wide variety of backgrounds. Some are recent immigrants, while others' families have been here for many generations, some since before the Mayflower arrived in Massachusetts. They come from all over the world, from every country where Spanish is spoken, and they live all over the United States. They are part of the fabric of society.

According to census information, most live in the southern and western states; however, there are large populations of Spanish speakers in places like New York and Chicago as well.

*Of those 28 million people, about 20 million reported they also speak English "very well" or "well."

A bookstore in the Pilsen neighborhood of Chicago

Dancers from the Ballet Folklórico de San Antonio

On the New York City subway

A Cuban American family in Miami

Unos estudiantes universitarios hablan de (*talk about*) las clases

1. Are there many Hispanic students on your campus? Where are they from?

2. Is there an organization for Spanish-speaking students on your campus? What is it called?

3. What languages are taught on your campus? Which language is the most popular?

En la universidad

En el salón de clase

la profesora
la pizarra
el profesor
la ventana
la puerta
la estudiante
el estudiante
Rosa
Javier
la silla
el libro de texto
el diccionario
el libro
la mesa
el cuaderno
Paco
el lápiz
Nina
el bolígrafo
el papel
el dinero
la calculadora
el escritorio
la mochila

¿DÓNDE? LUGARES EN LA UNIVERSIDAD

la biblioteca	the library
la cafetería	the cafeteria
el edificio	the building
la librería	the bookstore *or La papelería*
la oficina	the office
la residencia	the dormitory
el salón de clase	the classroom

or Sala de clase

¿QUIÉN? PERSONAS

el bibliotecario	the (male) librarian
la bibliotecaria	the (female) librarian

el compañero (de clase)	the (male) classmate
la compañera (de clase)	the (female) classmate
el compañero de cuarto	the (male) roommate
la compañera de cuarto	the (female) roommate
el consejero	the (male) advisor
la consejera	the (female) advisor
el hombre	the man
la mujer	the woman
el secretario	the (male) secretary
la secretaria	the (female) secretary

¿QUÉ? OBJETO

la computadora	the computer

Conversación

A. Identificaciones. ¿Es hombre o mujer?

> **MODELO:** ¿La consejera? ⟶ Es mujer.

1. ¿El profesor?
2. ¿La estudiante?
3. ¿El secretario?
4. ¿El estudiante?
5. ¿La bibliotecaria?
6. ¿El compañero de cuarto?

B. ¿Dónde están *(are they)*? _where_ **Tell where these people are and identify the numbered people and things: 1 = la consejera, 2 = la estudiante,** and so on. Refer to the drawing and vocabulary lists on page 26 as much as you need to.

> **MODELO:** El dibujo 1: Están en el salón de clase.
> 1 = la profesora, 2 = la estudiante,...

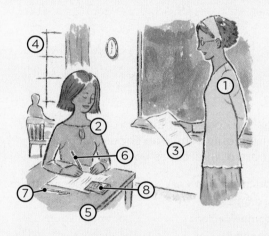

1. Están en _____ .

2. Están en _____ .

3. Están en _____ .

4. Están en _____ .

⟐ NOTA CULTURAL

Las universidades en el mundo[a] hispánico

Universities have a long history in the Spanish-speaking world. The very first university in the western hemisphere was **la Universidad de Santo Domingo,** founded in 1538 in what is now the Dominican Republic. Other early universities in this hemisphere include **la Real y Pontificia Universidad de América** (Mexico City, 1553) and **la Universidad de San Marcos** (Lima, Peru, 1571). Early Spanish colonial cities were meticulously designed and planned, and it is no accident that these universities were established in three of the most important cities. The Spaniards already had almost 300 years of experience with university-level education. **La Universidad de Salamanca,** one of the oldest universities in the world, was founded in 1220 in Salamanca, Spain.

[a]world

Esta (*This*) estatua de Fray Luis de León está en la Universidad de Salamanca. La Universidad, que data del año 1220 (mil doscientos veinte), es una de las más antiguas (*oldest*) del mundo.

Las materias°

Las... *Subject areas*

The names for most of these subject areas are cognates. See if you can recognize their meaning without looking at the English equivalent. You should learn in particular the names of subject areas that are of interest to you.

la computación
el arte
la sicología
la química
la física
$E=MC^2$
la historia
el inglés
ENGLISH 101
Rosa
Javier

la administración de empresas	business administration
las comunicaciones	communications
la economía	economics
el español	Spanish
la filosofía	philosophy
las humanidades	humanities
las lenguas (extranjeras)	(foreign) languages
la literatura	literature
las matemáticas	mathematics
la sociología	sociology
las ciencias	sciences
naturales	natural
políticas	political
sociales	social

Conversación

A. Asociaciones. ¿Qué materia(s) asocias con las siguientes (*following*) personas y cosas (*things*)?

1. el nitrógeno, el hidrógeno
2. la doctora Joyce Brothers, el doctor Sigmund Freud
3. NBC, CBS
4. Sócrates, Platón
5. Mark Twain, Toni Morrison, J. K. Rowling
6. Frida Kahlo, Pablo Picasso
7. Microsoft, IBM
8. la civilización azteca, una guerra (*war*) civil

B. ¿Qué estudias? Tell about your academic interests by creating sentences using one word or phrase from each column. You can tell what you *are* studying (1), *want* to study (2), *need* to study (3), and *like* to study (4). Using the word **no** makes the sentence negative.

1. (No) Estudio _____ .
2. (No) Deseo estudiar _____ .
3. (No) Necesito estudiar _____ .
4. (No) Me gusta estudiar _____ .

+

español, francés, inglés
arte, filosofía, literatura, música
ciencias políticas, historia
antropología, sicología, sociología
biología, física, química
matemáticas, computación
¿ ?

¿Recuerdas?°

Do you remember?

In **Primeros pasos,** you used a number of interrogative words and phrases to get information: **¿cómo?, ¿dónde?,** and **¿qué?** What do those words mean in the following sentences?

1. ¿Cómo estás?
2. ¿Cómo es usted?
3. ¿De dónde eres?
4. ¿Qué hora es?

You will learn more about interrogatives in the following **Nota comunicativa.**

interrogative = a word, phrase, or sentence used to ask a question

⟩ NOTA COMUNICATIVA

Las palabras interrogativas (Part 1)

Use **¿qué?** to mean *what?* when you are asking for a definition or an explanation. Use **¿cuál?** to mean *what?* in all other circumstances. You will learn more about using these words in **Gramática 28** (**Capítulo 9**).

¿**Qué** es un hospital?   ¿**Cuál** es la capital de Colombia?
¿**Qué** es esto (*this*)?

Guess the meaning of the following interrogatives from the context in which they appear.

1. —¿**Cuándo** es la clase? —Es mañana, a las nueve.
2. —¿**Cuánto** cuesta (*costs*) el cuaderno? —Dos dólares.
3. —¿**Cuántos** estudiantes hay en la clase? —Hay quince.
4. —¿**Cuántas** naciones hay en Centroamérica? —Hay siete.
5. —¿**Quién** es la consejera? —Es la señora Arana.

Note that in Spanish the voice falls at the end of questions that begin with interrogative words.

¿Qué es un tren?   ¿Cómo estás?

C. Anuncio (*Ad*) de una universidad

Paso 1. Answer the following questions based on the ad.

1. ¿Cómo se llama la universidad?
2. ¿Dónde está la universidad?
3. ¿Cuál es el número de teléfono de la universidad? ¿y la dirección (*address*)?
4. ¿Cuándo hay clases, por (*in*) la mañana o por la noche (*at night*)? ¿Hay clases los fines de semana (*weekends*)?
5. ¿Eres «un estudiante tradicional»? ¿Qué palabras asocias con los estudiantes tradicionales?
6. ¿En cuántas ciudades (*cities*) hay un programa acelerado?
7. ¿Cómo es la universidad? (¿flexible, exclusiva, interesante, urbana, rural?)

POST UNIVERSITY

Cada Estudiante, Cada Día

- Diplomas de bachiller y grado asociado
- Totalmente acreditado
- Clases tradicionales
- Programa acelerado de clases nocturnas y fines de semana alternados
- Clases a través de la Internet
- Campus residencial ubicado en Waterbury para estudiantes tradicionales
- Programa acelerado con clases en las siguientes ciudades de Connecticut: Waterbury, Meriden, y Danbury
- Becas y ayuda financiera disponibles
- División II del NCAA

Llame para fijar una cita y visitar el campus o solicite vía Internet:

1 (888) 801-7448
LaVoz.Post.edu

POST 1890
UNIVERSITY

Office of Admissions
800 Country Club Road
P.O. Box 2540
Waterbury, CT 06723-2540

Paso 2. Now answer the questions in **Paso 1** but about your university, referring to it as **esta** (*this*) **universidad.** For item 5, also tell whether or not you are "**un(a) estudiante tradicional.**"

D. Entrevista (*Interview*).

Work with a classmate and use the following questions to interview each other. Find out as much as possible about each other's classes and schedules. Follow up your answers by returning the question or asking for more information.

> **MODELO:** **ESTUDIANTE 1:** ¿Qué estudias este semestre/trimestre (*this term*)?
> **ESTUDIANTE 2:** Estudio matemáticas, historia, literatura y español. Y tú, ¿qué estudias?

1. ¿Qué estudias este semestre/trimestre?
2. ¿Cuántas horas estudias por semana (*per week*)?
3. ¿Cuándo te gusta estudiar, por la mañana, por la tarde o por la noche?
4. ¿Dónde estudias?
5. ¿Quién es tu profesor favorito (profesora favorita)? (Mi profesor...)
6. ¿Cuál es tu clase favorita? (Mi clase...)

Need more practice?
- Workbook/Laboratory Manual
- Online Learning Center [www.mhhe.com/apuntate]

Review what you already know about the pronunciation of Spanish vowels by saying the following names and nicknames aloud.

1. Ana   **2.** Pepe   **3.** Pili   **4.** Momo   **5.** Lulú

You will learn more about Spanish vowels in **Pronunciación.**

Pronunciación

Diphthongs and Linking

Two successive weak vowels (**i** or **u**) or a combination of a strong vowel (**a, e,** or **o**) and a weak vowel (**i** or **u**) are pronounced as a single syllable in Spanish, forming a *diphthong* (**un diptongo**): *Luis, siete, cuaderno.*

When words are combined to form phrases, clauses, and sentences, they are linked together in pronunciation. In spoken Spanish, it is often difficult to hear the word boundaries — that is, where one word ends and another begins.

> **diphthong** = a combination of two vowel sounds in one syllable

A. Vocales. Más práctica con las vocales.

1. hablar	regular	reservar	compañera
2. trece	clase	papel	general
3. pizarra	oficina	bolígrafo	libro
4. hombre	profesor	dólares	los
5. universidad	gusto	lugar	mujer

B. Diptongos. Practica las siguientes (*following*) palabras.

1. historia	secretaria	gracias	estudiante	materia
2. bien	Oviedo	siete	ciencias	diez
3. secretario	biblioteca	adiós	diccionario	Antonio
4. cuaderno	Eduardo	el Ecuador	Guatemala	Managua
5. bueno	nueve	luego	pueblo	Venezuela

C. Frases y oraciones (*sentences*). Practice saying each phrase or sentence as if it were one long word, pronounced without a pause.

1. el papel y el lápiz
2. la profesora y la estudiante
3. las ciencias y las matemáticas
4. la historia y la sicología
5. la secretaria y el profesor
6. el inglés y el español
7. la clase en la biblioteca
8. el libro en la librería
9. Es la una y media.
10. Hay siete estudiantes en la oficina.
11. No estoy muy bien.
12. No hay consejero aquí (*here*).
13. Hay siete edificios en la universidad.
14. Estudio historia y comercio.
15. Deseo estudiar computación y matemáticas.
16. Necesito un diccionario y una mochila.

Los Estados Unidos

DATOS ESENCIALES

NOMBRE OFICIAL: *United States of America* (los Estados Unidos de América)

CAPITAL: Washington, D.C.

POBLACIÓN HISPÁNICA TOTAL DE LOS ESTADOS UNIDOS: más de 40 (cuarenta) millones de habitantes

FÍJATE[a]

- La presencia hispánica en los Estados Unidos precede a[b] la Declaración de la Independenc de los Estados Unidos.
- Los españoles originalmente ocuparon[c] el continente americano en los siglos XV y XVI.[d] Después, a través de[e] los siglos, varios grupos de hispan inmigraron[f] a los Estados Unido por una razón u otra.[g]
- Hoy día sólo,[h] México y España tienen[i] una población más grande que[j] la población hispánica de los Estados Unido
- Los principales grupos hispánicos en los Estados Unidos son[k] los mexicanos, los puertorriqueños y los cubanos, pero claro,[l] hay hispanos de todas partes del mundo[m] hispánico.
- Las palabras **hispano/a** e[n] **hispánico/a** se refieren al[ñ] idioma y a la cultura, no a la raza[o] o grupo étnico.

[a]*Check it out* [b]*precede... predates* [c]*occupied* [d]*siglos... 15th and 16th centuries* [e]*Después... Later, throughout* [f]*immigrated* [g]*por... for one reason or another* [h]*Hoy... Today only* [i]*have* [j]*más... larger than* [k]*are* [l]*pero... but of course* [m]*world* [n]*y* [ñ]*se... refer to the* [o]*race*

¡MÚSICA!

La música hispánica ha tenido gran[a] impacto en los Estados Unidos. Entre[b] los artistas hispanos de mayor[c] fama están Jennifer López,

La salsa, una forma de música y danza hispana muy popular en los Estados Unidos

Los Lonely Boys, Marc Anthony, Ricky Martin, Gloria Estefan y Shakira. ¿Puedes nombrar otros?[d] Los ritmos[e] hispánicos también han influido en[f] la música de artistas estadounidenses no hispanos.

[a]*ha... has had a great* [b]*Among* [c]*greatest, most* [d]*¿Puedes... Can you name any others?* [e]*rhythms* [f]*han... have influenced*

 ## LOS LONELY BOYS

Los Lonely Boys son de San Ángelo, Texas. Definen[a] su[b] música como *Texican Rock n'Roll*, porque[c] tiene influencias de[d] la música tejana, del rock, del *blues, soul* y del *country*. La canción «Dime mi amor»[e] es de su[f] álbum *Los Lonely Boys*.

[a]*They define* [b]*their* [c]*because* [d]*tiene... it has influences from* [e]*La... The song "Tell Me My Love"* [f]*their*

Los Lonely Boys en concierto

paso 2 Gramática

¿Recuerdas?

As you know, in English and in Spanish, a noun is the name of a person, place, thing, or idea. You have been using nouns since the beginning of *iApúntate!* Remember that **el** and **la** mean *the* before nouns. If you can change the Spanish words for *the* to *one* in the following phrases, you already know some of the material in **Gramática 1.**

1. el libro   **2.** la mesa   **3.** el profesor   **4.** la estudiante

1 Identifying People, Places, Things, and Ideas (Part 1) • Singular Nouns: Gender and Articles*

Gramática en acción: La lista de José María

¡OJO!

Note the use of colored text in the dialogues and other brief readings that appear in **Gramática en acción** sections. The color will call your attention to examples of the grammar point of focus.

Comprensión. ¿Cierto o falso?

	CIERTO	FALSO
1. La profesora de matemáticas es la profesora Durán.	❑	❑
2. El cuaderno es para (*for*) la clase de literatura.	❑	❑
3. La agenda es para la clase de matemáticas.	❑	❑

To name people, places, things, and ideas, you need to use nouns. In Spanish, all *nouns* (**los sustantivos**) have either masculine or feminine *gender* (**el género**). This is a purely grammatical feature; it does not mean that Spanish speakers perceive things or ideas as having male or female attributes.

Since the gender of all nouns must be memorized, it is best to learn the definite article along with the noun; that is, learn **el lápiz** rather than just **lápiz.** The definite article is given with nouns in vocabulary lists in this book.

José María's list   *For Spanish 30 / Professor Durán • a Spanish-English dictionary • the novel* Don Quijote *• a notebook. For Calculus 2 / Professor Lifante • the textbooks (2) • a calculator • the access card for the online workbook • a notebook. And • a calendar/datebook • a few ballpoint pens*

*The grammar sections of ¡Apúntate! *are numbered consecutively throughout the book. If you need to review a particular grammar point, the index will refer you to its page number.*

	Masculine Nouns		Feminine Nouns	
Definite	**el hombre**	the man	**la mujer**	the woman
Articles	**el libro**	the book	**la mesa**	the table
Indefinite	**un hombre**	a (one) man	**una mujer**	a (one) woman
Articles	**un libro**	a (one) book	**una mesa**	a (one) table

¡OJO!

The grammar explanations in *¡Apúntate!* are arranged in a two-column format. Explanations are on the left, and examples, with important material to be learned, are on the right. In many grammar charts, colored text is used to highlight specific letters or words.

Gender

1. **Masculine Nouns** Nouns that refer to male beings and most other nouns that end in **-o** are *masculine* (**masculino**) in gender.	**sustantivos masculinos:** hombre, libro
2. **Feminine Nouns** Nouns that refer to female beings and most other nouns that end in **-a, -ión, -tad,** and **-dad** are *feminine* (**femenino**) in gender.	**sustantivos femeninos:** mujer, mesa, nación, libertad, universidad
3. **Other Endings** Nouns that have other endings and that do not refer to either male or female beings may be masculine or feminine. The gender of these words must be memorized.	el lápiz, la clase, la tarde, la noche
4. **Spelling Changes** Many nouns that refer to people indicate gender . . . • by changing the last vowel OR, • by adding **-a** to the last consonant of the masculine form to make it feminine.	el compañero ⟶ la compañer**a** el bibliotecario ⟶ la bibliotecari**a** un profesor ⟶ una profesor**a**
5. **Articles** Many other nouns that refer to people have a single form for both masculine and feminine genders. Gender is indicated by an article. However, a few nouns that end in **-e** also have a feminine form that ends in **-a.**	**MASCULINO** **FEMENINO** **el estudiante** **la estudiante** **el dentista** **la dentista** **el presidente** **la presidenta** **el cliente** **la clienta** **el dependiente** (*clerk*) **la dependienta**

¡OJO!

A common exception to the normal rules of gender is the word **el día,** which is masculine in gender. Many words ending in **-ma** are also masculine: **el problema, el programa, el sistema,** and so on. Watch for these exceptions as you continue your study of Spanish.

Articles

1. Definite Articles In English, there is only one *definite article* (**el artículo definido**): *the*. In Spanish, the definite article for masculine singular nouns is **el**; for feminine singular nouns it is **la**.	**definite article:** *the* *m. sing.* ⟶ **el** *f. sing* ⟶ **la**
2. Indefinite Articles In English, the singular *indefinite article* (**el artículo indefinido**) is *a* or *an*. In Spanish, the indefinite article, like the definite article, must agree with the gender of the noun: **un** for masculine nouns, **una** for feminine nouns. **Un** and **una** can mean *one* or *a/an*.	**indefinite article:** *a, an* *m. sing.* ⟶ **un** *f. sing* ⟶ **una**

AUTOPRUEBA

Give the correct definite article: **el** or **la**.

1. _____ el _____ libro
2. _____ la _____ mujer
3. _____ la _____ oficina

4. _____ el _____ escritorio
5. _____ la _____ libertad
6. _____ la _____ acción

Answers: 1. *el* 2. *la* 3. *la* 4. *el* 5. *la* 6. *la*

¡OJO!

Autoprueba means *self-quiz*. These brief tests appear at the end of **Gramática** explanations. They will help you determine if you understand the basics of the grammar point.

Práctica

A. Los artículos

Paso 1. Da (*Give*) el artículo definido apropiado (**el, la**).

1. escritorio *el*
2. biblioteca *la*
3. bolígrafo *el*
4. mochila *la*
5. hombre *el*
6. diccionario *el*
7. universidad *la*
8. dinero *el*
9. mujer *la*
10. nación *la*
11. bibliotecario
12. calculadora
13. fiesta
14. clase
15. puerta
16. amigo
17. apartamento
18. cuarto
19. lengua
20. física

Paso 2. Ahora (*Now*) da el artículo indefinido apropiado (**un, una**).

1. día *un/unos*
2. mañana *una*
3. problema *un*
4. lápiz *un*
5. clase *una*
6. papel *un*
7. condición *una*
8. programa *un*

¿Qué hay en el salón de clase?

B. Escenas de la universidad

Paso 1. Haz una oración (*Form a sentence*) con las palabras indicadas.

> **MODELO:** estudiante / librería ⟶ Hay un estudiante en la librería.

1. consejero / oficina
2. profesora / salón de clase
3. lápiz / mesa
4. cuaderno / escritorio
5. libro / mochila
6. bolígrafo / silla
7. palabra / papel
8. oficina / residencia
9. compañero / biblioteca
10. diccionario / librería

Need more practice?
- Workbook/Laboratory Manual
- Online Learning Center
  [www.mhhe.com/apuntate]

Paso 2. Now create new sentences by changing one of the words in each item in **Paso 1.** Try to come up with as many variations as possible.

> **MODELOS:** Hay un estudiante en *la residencia.* Hay *una profesora* en la librería.

Conversación

A. Definiciones. En parejas (*pairs*), definan las siguientes palabras en español, según (*according to*) el modelo.

> **MODELO:** biblioteca / ¿ ? ⟶ **ESTUDIANTE 1:** ¿La biblioteca?
> **ESTUDIANTE 2:** Es un edificio.

Categorías: edificio, materia, objeto, persona

1. cliente / ¿ ?
2. bolígrafo / ¿ ?
3. residencia / ¿ ?
4. dependienta / ¿ ?
5. hotel (*m.*) / ¿ ?
6. computadora / ¿ ?
7. computación / ¿ ?
8. inglés / ¿ ?
9. ¿ ?

B. Nuestra (*Our*) universidad. With a classmate, take turns using the cues to form complete sentences with information about your university.

> **MODELOS:** consejero/a ⟶ En nuestra universidad el profesor Márquez es consejero.
> cafetería ⟶ En nuestra universidad hay una cafetería. Se llama (*It's called*) Foster Hall.

En nuestra universidad...

1. consejero/a
2. profesor(a) de _____ (materia)
3. edificio de _____ (materia)
4. biblioteca principal
5. cafetería
6. edificio de clases

¡OJO!

Use the article **el** or **la** when referring to someone with a title: **el profesor Márquez.**

2 Identifying People, Places, Things, and Ideas (Part 2) • Nouns and Articles: Plural Forms

Gramática en acción: Un anuncio de una escuela (*school*) de idiomas

- You can find many nouns in this ad. Can you guess the meaning of most of them?
- Some of the nouns in this ad are plural. Can you tell how to make nouns plural in Spanish, based on these nouns?
- Look for the Spanish equivalent of the following words.
  adult   preparation   program
  courses
- **Idioma** is another word for *language,* and it is a false cognate. It never means *idiom.*
- Based on the words and graphics in the ad, guess what **en el extranjero** means.

Singular		Plural	
Nouns Ending in a Vowel	el **libro**	los **libros**	the books
	la **mesa**	las **mesas**	the tables
	un **libro**	unos **libros**	some books
	una **mesa**	unas **mesas**	some tables
Nouns Ending in a Consonant	la **universidad**	las **universidades**	the universities
	un **papel**	unos **papeles**	some papers

1. **Plural Endings** Spanish nouns that end in a vowel form plurals by adding **-s.** Nouns that end in a consonant add **-es.** Nouns that end in the consonant **-z** change the **-z** to **-c** before adding **-es: lápiz** ⟶ **lápices.**	Plurals in Spanish: vowel + **-s** consonant + **-es** **-z** ⟶ **-ces**
2. **Plural of Articles** The definite and indefinite articles also have plural forms: **el** ⟶ **los, la** ⟶ **las, un** ⟶ **unos, una** ⟶ **unas. Unos** and **unas** mean *some, several,* or *a few.*	**el** ⟶ **los** **un** ⟶ **unos** **la** ⟶ **las** **una** ⟶ **unas**
3. **Groups of People** In Spanish, the masculine plural form of a noun is used to refer to a group that includes both males and females.	**los** amig**os** *the friends* (both male and female) **unos** extranjer**os** *some foreigners* (both male and female)

Práctica

A. Singular ⟶ plural. Da la forma plural.

1. la mesa
2. el papel
3. el amigo
4. la oficina
5. un cuaderno
6. un lápiz
7. una universidad
8. un bolígrafo
9. un edificio

B. Plural ⟶ singular. Da la forma singular.

1. los profesores
2. las computadoras
3. las bibliotecarias
4. los estudiantes
5. unos hombres
6. unas tardes
7. unas residencias
8. unas sillas
9. unos escritorios

Las mesas de un café en España

Need more practice?
- Workbook/Laboratory Manual
- Online Learning Center
  [www.mhhe.com/apuntate]

Conversación

A. Identificaciones. Nombra (*Name*) las personas, los objetos y los lugares.

> **MODELO:** Hay _____ en _____. ⟶ Hay *unos estudiantes* en *el salón de clase.*

Vocabulario útil

la computadora
el experimento
la planta
el teléfono

1.

2.

B. ¡Ojo alerta!*

Paso 1. ¿Cuáles son las semejanzas (*similarities*) y las diferencias entre (*between*) los dos cuartos (*rooms*)? Hay por lo menos (*at least*) seis diferencias.

> **MODELO:** En el dibujo A, hay _____.
> En el dibujo B, hay sólo (*only*) _____.
> En el escritorio del dibujo A, hay _____.
> En el escritorio del dibujo B, hay _____.

Vocabulario útil

la alfombra rug
la almohada pillow
la cama bed
el cuadro picture
el espejo mirror
la lámpara lamp
el monitor

A

B

Paso 2. Ahora indica qué hay en tu propio (*own*) cuarto. Usa palabras del **Paso 1**.

> **MODELO:** En mi cuarto hay _____. En mi escritorio hay _____.

---

*In Spanish, activities like this one are often called **¡Ojo alerta!** = Eagle Eye!*

1. La Misión San José de Laguna, Nuevo México

Las misiones españolas se encuentran[a] en la Florida, Texas, Nuevo México, Arizona, Colorado y California. La Misión San José de Laguna, por ejemplo,[b] se construyó[c] en Nuevo México, cerca de[d] Albuquerque, a finales de siglo XVII.[e] Hoy es una iglesia[f] activa y un centro para bailes[g] y fiestas de la comunidad durante todo el año.[h]

[a]se... are found   [b]por... for example   [c]se... was built
[d]cerca... near   [e]a... at the end of the 17th century
[f]church   [g]dances   [h]durante... all year long

2. Un puesto de comida[a] de la Calle[b] Ocho

La famosa Calle Ocho está en el barrio[c] de la Pequeña[d] Habana en Miami, donde viven[e] muchos cubanoamericanos y se habla más español que inglés.[f] En marzo,[g] se celebra[h] el Festival Calle Ocho. Con numerosos puestos de comida, múltiples actuaciones musicales diarias[i] y más de un millón de participantes, es la fiesta callejera más grande del mundo.[j]

[a]puesto... food stand   [b]Street   [c]neighborhood
[d]Little   [e]live   [f]se... more Spanish than English is
spoken   [g]March   [h]se... is celebrated   [i]actuaciones...
daily musical acts   [j]fiesta... largest street party in the
world

Casi el mismo número[a]

Casi el mismo número[a] de puertorriqueños que vive[b] en los Estados Unidos vive en Puerto Rico (unos[c] 4 millones). La mayor[d] concentración de puertorriqueños es en Nueva York. Los puertorriqueños son ciudadanos[e] estadounidenses de nacimiento[f] y han contribuido[g] mucho a su nación. Una de sus contribuciones más populares hoy en día es la salsa. La salsa se baila[h] hoy en casi todos los rincones[i] del mundo.[j]

[a]Casi... Almost the same number   [b]que...
that live   [c]some   [d]largest   [e]citizens
[f]de... by birth   [g]han... they have
contributed   [h]se... is danced   [i]casi...
almost every corner   [j]world

4. John Leguizamo

La presencia hispánica se nota[a] en todos los campos[b] de los Estados Unidos: la política, la literatura, la música, el cine, el teatro, los deportes,[c] etcétera. ¿Cuántos hispanos famosos puedes nombrar?[d] Por ejemplo, John Leguizamo, de madre colombiana y padre puertorriqueño,[e] es cómico y actor.

[a]se... is found   [b]todos... all fields   [c]sports
[d]puedes... can you name   [e]de... with a Colombian
mother and Puerto Rican father

Latina, una revista bilingüe dirigida a[a] la mujer hispana en los Estados Unidos

Todos los medios de comunicación ofrecen[b] publicaciones y programación en español. Univisión y Telemundo son canales[c] de televisión con programación en español las veinticuatro horas del día.[d] Periódicos[e] populares como *La Opinión* de Los Ángeles y *El Nuevo Herald* de Miami se publican[f] en español. Muchas revistas publican sus propias[g] versiones en español también, como *People en español* y *NewsWeek en español.*

[a]revista... bilingual magazine whose target
audience is   [b]Todos... All media offer
[c]channels   [d]las... twenty-four hours a
day   [e]Newspapers   [f]se... are published
[g]own

¿Recuerdas?

You already know (from **Primeros pasos**) that a verb describes an action or a state of being. The following sentences contain Spanish verbs that you have already used. Pick them out.

1. Soy estudiante en la Universidad de _____ .
2. Este (*This*) semestre/trimestre, estudio español.
3. En el futuro, deseo estudiar francés.

If you selected **estudiar** in addition to three other words, you did very well! You will learn more about Spanish verbs and how they are used in **Gramática 3**.

3 Expressing Actions • Subject Pronouns (Part 1); Present Tense of **-ar** Verbs; Negation

Gramática en acción: Una escena en la biblioteca

- Dos estudiantes trabajan hoy en esta sección de la biblioteca.
- Yo no trabajo en la biblioteca.
- Hoy Manuel y yo estudiamos para un examen de historia.
- Un profesor habla por teléfono ahora con un amigo.
- ¿Hablas tú por teléfono en la biblioteca? No se permite, ¿verdad?

Comprensión. En la escena...

1. ¿cuántos estudiantes trabajan?
2. ¿cuántos estudiantes estudian?
3. ¿quién habla?
4. ¿quién habla por teléfono?

Subject Pronouns (Part 1)

	Subject Prounouns		
Singular		**Plural**	
yo	I	**nosotros/nosotras**	we
tú	you (*fam.*)	**vosotros/vosotras**	you (*fam. Spain*)
usted (Ud.)*	you (*form.*)	**ustedes (Uds.)***	you (*form.*)
él	he	**ellos**	they (*m., m. + f.*)
ella	she	**ellas**	they (*f.*)

subject = the person or thing that performs the action in a sentence
pronoun = a word that takes the place of a noun or represents a person

A scene at the library • Two students are working in this section of the library today. • I don't work at the library. • Today Manuel and I are studying for a history test. • A professor is talking to a friend on the phone now. • Do you talk on the phone in the library? It's not allowed, is it?

*****Usted** and **ustedes** *are frequently abbreviated in writing as* **Ud.** *or* **Vd.***, and* **Uds.** *or* **Vds.***, respectively.*

1. **Subject Pronouns** The person that performs the action in a sentence is expressed by *subject pronouns* (**los pronombres personales**).
 	
In Spanish, several subject pronouns have masculine and feminine forms. The masculine plural form is used to refer to a group of males as well as to a group of males and females.
	Mark ⟶ *he*
	Martha ⟶ *she*
	Mark and Paul ⟶
	  they
	Mark and Martha ⟶
	  they
	Martha and Emily ⟶
	  they
		Marcos ⟶ **él**
		Marta ⟶ **ella**
		Marcos y Pablo ⟶
		  ellos (*all male*)
		Marcos y Marta ⟶
		  ellos (*male and female*)
		Marta y Emilia ⟶
		  ellas (*all female*)

2. **Words for *you*** Spanish has different words for *you*. In general, **tú** is used to refer to a close friend or a family member, while **usted** is used with people with whom the speaker has a more formal or distant relationship. The situations in which **tú** and **usted** are used also vary among different countries and regions.	**tú** ⟶ close friend, family member **usted (Ud.)** ⟶ formal or distant relationship	
3. ***Ustedes* vs. *vosotros*** In Latin America and in the United States and Canada, the plural for both **usted** and **tú** is **ustedes**. In Spain, however, **vosotros/vosotras** is the plural of **tú**, while **ustedes** is used as the plural of **usted** exclusively.	**LATIN AMERICA, NORTH AMERICA** **tú** **usted (Ud.)** ⟶ **ustedes (Uds.)** **SPAIN** **tú** ⟶ **vosotros/vosotras** **usted (Ud.)** ⟶ **ustedes (Uds.)**	
4. **Omitting Subject Pronouns** Subject pronouns are not used as frequently in Spanish as they are in English, and they may usually be omitted. You will learn more about the uses of Spanish subject pronouns in **Gramática 7** (**Capítulo 2**).		

Present Tense of -ar Verbs

1. **Infinitives** As you know, the *infinitive* (**el infinitivo**) of a verb indicates the action or state of being, with no reference to who or what performs the action or when it is done (present, past, or future). In Spanish, all infinitives end in **-ar, -er,** or **-ir.** Infinitives in English are indicated by *to*: *to* speak, *to* eat, *to* live.	**-ar:** **hablar** to speak **-er:** **comer** to eat **-ir:** **vivir** to live

tense = the quality of a verb form that indicates time: present, past, or future

La mamá habla por teléfono.

2. **Conjugating Verbs** To *conjugate* (**conjugar**) a verb means to give the various forms of the verb with their corresponding subjects: *I speak, you speak, she speaks,* and so on. All regular Spanish verbs are conjugated by adding *personal endings* (**las terminaciones personales**) that reflect the subject doing the action. These are added to the *stem* (**la raíz** or **el radical**), which is the infinitive minus the infinitive ending.

INFINITIVE		STEM
hablar	→	**habl-**
comer	→	**com-**
vivir	→	**viv-**

3. **Present Tense Endings** The right-hand column shows the personal endings that are added to the stem of all regular **-ar** verbs to form the *present tense* (**el presente**).

Regular present tense *-ar* endings

-o	-amos
-as	-áis
-a	-an

---

hablar (*to speak; to talk*): habl-

Singular			Plural		
(yo)	**hablo**	I speak	**(nosotros)** **(nosotras)**	**hablamos**	we speak
(tú)	**hablas**	you speak	**(vosotros)** **(vosotras)**	**habláis**	you speak
(Ud.) **(él)** **(ella)**	**habla**	you speak he speaks she speaks	**(Uds.)** **(ellos)** **(ellas)**	**hablan**	you speak they (*m., m.+f.*) speak they (*f.*) speak

---

4. **Important -ar Verbs** Some important *-ar* verbs in this chapter include those in the list at right.

ganar to earn (handwritten)

bailar	to dance
buscar	to look for
cantar	to sing
comprar	to buy
desear	to want
enseñar	to teach
escuchar	to listen (to)
estudiar	to study
hablar	to speak; to talk
necesitar	to need
pagar	to pay (for)
practicar	to practice
regresar	to return (*to a place*)
tocar	to play *+ to touch* (handwritten) (*a musical instrument*)
tomar	to take *(transportation)* (handwritten)
3 meanings (handwritten)	to drink *to take pictures* (handwritten)
trabajar	to work

¡OJO!

Note that in Spanish the meaning of the English word *for* is included in the verbs **buscar** (*to look for*) and **pagar** (*to pay for*); *to* is included in **escuchar** (*to listen to*).

5. Conjugated Verb + Infinitive As in English, when two Spanish verbs are used in sequence and there is no change of subject, the second verb is usually in the infinitive form.	**Necesito llamar** a mi familia. *I need to call my family.* **Me gusta bailar.** *I like to dance.*	

6. Tense In both English and Spanish, conjugated verb forms also indicate the *time* or *tense* (**el tiempo**) of the action: *I speak* (present), *I spoke* (past). Some English equivalents of the present tense forms of Spanish verbs are shown at the right.	**hablo**	I speak — *Simple present tense* I am speaking — *Present progressive (indicates an action in progress)* I will speak — *Near future action*

Negation

In Spanish the word **no** is placed before the conjugated verb to make a negative sentence.	El estudiante **no habla** español. *The student doesn't speak Spanish.* No, **no necesito** dinero. *No, I don't need money.*

Práctica

A. Asociaciones. Give at least one **-ar** infinitive whose meaning you associate with the following words and phrases.

1. español
2. mucho dinero
3. en la librería
4. en el salón de clase
5. un coche (*car*)
6. a la residencia
7. Coca-Cola o café
8. la música

B. ¡Anticipemos! Mis compañeros y yo

Paso 1. Tell whether or not the following statements are true for you and your classmates. If any statement is not true for you or your class, make it negative or change it in another way to make it correct.

> **MODELO:** Toco el piano ⟶ Sí, toco el piano.
> (No, no toco el piano. Toco la guitarra.)

1. Necesito más (*more*) dinero.
2. Trabajo en la biblioteca.
3. Canto en un coro (*choir*) de la universidad.
4. Tomamos ocho clases cada (*every*) semestre / trimestre.
5. Bailamos salsa en el salón de clase.
6. Deseamos hablar español correctamente.
7. El profesor / La profesora enseña italiano.
8. El profesor / La profesora habla muy bien el alemán (*German*).

¡OJO!

¡Anticipemos! (*Let's look ahead!*) activities show you new structures in context before you begin to use them. As you do these activities, think about the structure that you are studying (e.g., -ar verbs) and how it is used in the activity.

Paso 2. Now turn to a partner and restate each sentence as a question, using **tú** forms of the verbs in all cases. Your partner will indicate whether or not the sentences are true for him or her.

> **MODELO:** ¿Tocas el piano? ⟶ Sí, toco el piano. (No, no toco el piano.)

C. Una o más personas

Paso 1. Change the following sentences to reflect a plural subject.

> MODELOS: Él no desea tomar café. ⟶ Ellos no desean tomar café.
> Yo no deseo tomar café. ⟶ Nosotros no deseamos tomar café.

1. Ella no desea estudiar francés.
2. Ud. baila muy bien el tango.
3. ¿Hablas con la dependienta?
4. Escucho la radio con frecuencia.

Paso 2. Now change the following sentences to reflect a singular subject. More than one option may be possible in some cases.

1. Ellas no buscan el dinero.
2. Los estudiantes no necesitan seis clases.
3. Pagamos mucho (*a lot of*) dinero de matrícula (*tuition*).
4. ¿Compran Uds. muchos libros?

D. En una fiesta.

The following paragraphs describe a party. First scan the paragraphs to get a general sense of their meaning. Then complete the paragraphs with the correct form of the numbered infinitives.

Unos amigos en la fiesta de Marcos y Julio

Esta noche[a] hay una fiesta en el edificio de apartamentos de Marcos y Julio. Todos[b] los estudiantes (cantar[1]) y (bailar[2]). Una persona (tocar[3]) la guitarra y otras personas (escuchar[4]) la música.

Jaime (buscar[5]) una Coca-Cola. Marta (hablar[6]) con un amigo. María José (desear[7]) enseñarles a todos[c] un baile[d] de Colombia. Todas las estudiantes desean (bailar[8]) con el estudiante mexicano —iél (bailar[9]) muy bien!

La fiesta es estupenda, pero todos (necesitar[10]) regresar a casa[e] o a su[f] cuarto temprano.[g] ¡Hay clases mañana!

[a]Esta... *Tonight* [b]*All* [c]enseñarles... *to teach everyone* [d]*dance* [e]a... *home* [f]*their* [g]*early*

Comprensión. ¿Cierto o falso?

	CIERTO	FALSO
1. Marcos es profesor de español.	☐	☐
2. A Jaime le gusta el café.	☐	☐
3. María José es de Colombia.	☐	☐
4. Los estudiantes desean bailar.	☐	☐

Need more practice?
- Workbook/Laboratory Manual
- Online Learning Center
  [www.mhhe.com/apuntate]

Conversación

A. Oraciones lógicas.

Form at least eight complete logical sentences by using one word or phrase from each column. The words and phrases may be used more than once, in many combinations. Be sure to use the correct form of the verbs. Make any of the sentences negative, if you wish.

MODELO: Yo no estudio francés.

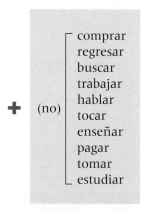

yo
tú (estudiante)
nosotros (los miembros de esta clase)
los estudiantes de aquí
el extranjero
un secretario
una profesora de español
una dependienta

+ (no) [comprar / regresar / buscar / trabajar / hablar / tocar / enseñar / pagar / tomar / estudiar] **+**

la guitarra, el piano, el violín
el edificio de ciencias
en la cafetería, en la universidad
en una oficina, en una librería
a casa por la noche
a la biblioteca a las dos
francés, alemán, italiano, inglés
bien el español
un poco de (*a little bit of*) café
los libros de texto con un cheque
libros y cuadernos en la librería

¡OJO!

Remember that the verb form that follows **desear** or **necesitar** is the infinitive, just as in English

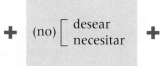

+ (no) [desear / necesitar] **+**

tomar una clase de computación
hablar bien el español
estudiar más
comprar una calculadora, una mochila
pagar la matrícula en septiembre

¡OJO!

Remember that **de la mañana (tarde, noche)** are used when a specific hour of the day is mentioned, like the English *A.M.* and *P.M.* Also, remember to use **a la una / a las dos (tres...)** to express a specific time of day.

Generalmente estudio en casa **por** la mañana.

Hoy estudio con Javier en la biblioteca a las diez **de** la mañana.

⬡ NOTA COMUNICATIVA

Expressing the Time of Day

You can use the preposition **por** to mean *in* or *during* when expressing the time of day.

Estudio **por** la mañana y trabajo **por** la tarde. **Por** la noche, estoy en casa.
I study in the morning and I work in the afternoon. At night I'm at home.

B. Entrevista.

Use the following questions as a guide to interview a classmate and take notes on what he or she says. (Write down what your partner says using the **él/ella** form of the verbs.)

MODELO: ESTUDIANTE 1: Karen, ¿estudias filosofía?
ESTUDIANTE 2: No, no estudio filosofía. Estudio música.
ESTUDIANTE 1: (escribe [*writes*]): Karen no estudia filosofía. Estudia música.

1. ¿Estudias mucho o poco (*a little*)? ¿Dónde estudias, en casa, en la residencia o en la biblioteca? ¿Cuándo te gusta estudiar, por la mañana, por la tarde o por la noche?
2. ¿Cantas bien o mal (*poorly*)? ¿Tocas un instrumento musical? ¿Cuál es? (el piano, la guitarra, el violín...)
3. ¿Trabajas? ¿Dónde? ¿Cuántas horas a la semana (*per week*) trabajas? ¿Trabajas todos los días (*every day*) de la semana? ¿Trabajas hasta muy tarde (*late*)?
4. ¿Quiénes pagan los libros de texto, tú o los profesores? ¿Qué más necesitas pagar? ¿diccionarios? ¿el alquiler (*rent*)? ¿la matrícula? ¿ ?

⟳ NOTA COMUNICATIVA

The Verb *estar*

Estar is another Spanish **-ar** verb. It means to *be*, and you have already used forms of it to ask how others are feeling or to tell where things are located. Here is the complete present tense conjugation of **estar**. Note that the **yo** form is irregular. The other forms take regular **-ar** endings, and some have an accented **á** to maintain the stress pattern.

yo	**est**o**y**	nosotros/as	**est**amos
tú	**est**á**s**	vosotros/as	**est**á**is**
Ud., él, ella	**est**á	Uds., ellos, ellas	**est**á**n**

You will learn the uses of the verb **estar**, along with those of **ser** (the other Spanish verb that means *to be*) gradually, over the next several chapters. In the following questions, **estar** is used to inquire about location or feelings.

1. ¿Cómo estás en este momento (*right now*)?
2. ¿Cómo están tus (*your*) compañeros? (Mis compañeros...)
3. ¿Dónde estás en este momento?

C. ¿Qué hacen (*are they doing*)? Tell where these people are and what they are doing. Remember to use the definite article with titles when you are talking about a person: **el señor, la señora, la señorita, el profesor, la profesora.**

MODELO: La Sra. Martínez _____. →
 La Sra. Martínez está en la oficina.
 Busca un documento, trabaja…

Vocabulario útil

hablar por teléfono
preparar la lección
pronunciar las palabras

tomar apuntes to take notes
trabajar en la caja at the register
usar una computadora

1. Estas (*These*) personas _____.

 La profesora Gil *enseña*
 Casi (*Almost*) todos los estudiantes *escuchan*.
 Un estudiante _____.

2. Estas personas _____.
 El Sr. Miranda _____.
 La bibliotecaria _____.
 El estudiante _____.

3. Estas personas *esen libreria*
 El cliente *pagar*
 La dependienta *compra los libros*

Lengua y cultura: Dos universidades fabulosas... y diferentes. Complete the following description of two well-known universities. Give the correct form of the verbs in parentheses, as suggested by context. When the subject pronoun is in *italics,* don't use it in the sentence. When two possibilities are given in parentheses, select the correct word.

¿**B**uscas la universidad perfecta? (Hay/Es[1]) dos (universidad/universidades[2]) muy famosas en los Estados Unidos. La primera[a] es (el/la[3]) Universidad de Texas, en Austin. ¡Es (un/una[4]) universidad muy grande[b]! Hay veinticuatro grupos sociales para estudiantes hispanos y una (librería/biblioteca[5]) con una colección latinoamericana fantástica, la Colección Latinoamericana Benson. (Los/Las[6]) materias más populares en la UT son: administración de empresas, ingeniería, humanidades y comunicaciones. Muchos estudiantes (tomar[7]) cursos en (el/la[8]) Instituto de Estudios Latinoamericanos y en (el/la[9]) Centro para Estudios Mexicoamericanos.

La Colección Latinoamericana Benson es una colección comprensiva de libros, documentos, revistas (*magazines*) y periódicos (*newspapers*) relacionados con (*related to*) Latinoamérica.

Stanford, en (el/la[10]) estado de California, es una universidad menos grande.[c] Tiene[d] una residencia para estudiantes de español, la Casa Zapata. Allí,[e] (los/las[11]) estudiantes (practicar[12]) español y (participar[13]) en celebraciones hispanas. Las materias más populares en Stanford son[f]: biología, economía, inglés y ciencias políticas. (El/La[14]) problema en Stanford es que los estudiantes (pagar[15]) mucho por[g] la matrícula.

¿Prefieres la UT o Stanford? ¿(*Tú:* Desear[16]) (estudia/estudiar[17]) en California o en Texas?

[a]La... *The first one* [b]*big* [c]*menos... smaller* [d]*It has* [e]*There* [f]*are* [g]*for*

Comprensión. ¿Cierto o falso? Which of these statements is true, based on the **Lengua y cultura** passage? Change false statements to make them true.

	CIERTO	FALSO
1. En la Universidad de Texas hay dos grupos sociales para estudiantes hispanos.	❏	❏
2. En el Instituto de Estudios Latinoamericanos hay pocos (*few*) estudiantes.	❏	❏
3. La Universidad de Stanford está en Texas.	❏	❏
4. La Casa Zapata es una biblioteca importante.	❏	❏

En resumen

Gramática en breve

1. Singular Nouns: Gender and Articles

Noun Endings

Masculine: **-o**

Feminine: **-a, -ión, -dad, -tad**

Masculine or Feminine: **-e**

2. Nouns and Articles: Plural Forms

Plural Endings	**Definite Articles**
-o ⟶ -os	Masculine: **el** ⟶ **los**
-a ⟶ -as	Feminine: **la** ⟶ **las**
-e ⟶ -es	**Indefinite Articles**
consonant + **-es**	Masculine: **un** ⟶ **unos**
	Feminine: **una** ⟶ **unas**

3. Subject Pronouns: Present Tense of **-ar** Verbs; Negation

Regular –ar Verb Endings, Present Tense

-o, -as, -a, -amos, -áis, -an

Subject Pronouns

yo, tú, Ud., él, ella, nosotros/as, vosotros/as, Uds., ellos/as

Vocabulario

Infinitives listed in colored text in **Vocabulario** lists are conjugated in their entirety (all tenses and moods) in Appendix 4 on the Online Learning Center. **Repaso** (*Review*) indicates vocabulary words and phrases listed as active in this chapter that you have already learned in previous chapters. **Cognado(s)** lists vocabulary words whose meaning you should be able to recognize because they are close cognates of English. Be sure that you know the meaning of the group headings in addition to the meaning of the words in each group. (If the word or words in a group heading are not close cognates, their meaning will be given elsewhere in the **Vocabulario** section. If you are not sure of the meaning of a word, you can always look it up in the end-of-book Spanish-English Vocabulary.)

Los verbos

bailar	to dance
buscar	to look for
cantar	to sing
comprar	to buy
desear	to want
enseñar	to teach
escuchar	to listen (to)
estar (estoy, estás,...)	to be
estudiar	to study
hablar	to speak; to talk
hablar por teléfono	to talk on the phone
necesitar	to need
pagar	to pay (for)
practicar	to practice
regresar	to return (*to a place*)
regresar a casa	to go home

tocar	to play (*a musical instrument*)
tomar	to take; to drink
trabajar	to work

Los lugares

el apartamento	apartment
la biblioteca	library
la cafetería	cafeteria
el cuarto	room
el edificio	building
la fiesta	party
la librería	bookstore
la oficina	office
la residencia	dormitory
el salón de clase	classroom
la universidad	university

Las personas

el/la amigo/a	friend
el/la bibliotecario/a	librarian
el/la cliente/a	client
el/la compañero/a (de clase)	classmate
el/la compañero/a de cuarto	roommate
el/la consejero/a	advisor
el/la dependiente/a	clerk
el/la estudiante	student
el/la extranjero/a	foreigner
el hombre	man
la mujer	woman
el/la profesor(a)	professor
el/la secretario/a	secretary

Los objetos

el bolígrafo	pen
la calculadora	calculator
la computadora	computer
el cuaderno	notebook
el diccionario	dictionary
el dinero	money
el escritorio	desk
el lápiz (pl. lápices)	pencil
el libro (de texto)	(text)book
la mesa	table
la mochila	backpack
el papel	paper
la pizarra	chalkboard
la puerta	door
la silla	chair
la ventana	window

Las materias

la administración de empresas	business administration
la ciencia	science
la computación	computer science
la física	physics
las lenguas (extranjeras)	(foreign) languages
la química	chemistry
la sicología	psychology

Cognados: el arte, las ciencias naturales/políticas/ sociales, las comunicaciones, la economía, la filosofía, la historia, las humanidades, la literatura, las matemáticas, la sociología

Las lenguas (extranjeras)

el alemán	German
el español	Spanish
el francés	French
el inglés	English
el italiano	Italian

Otros sustantivos

el café	coffee
la clase	class (of students); class, course (academic)
el día	day
el lugar	place
la materia	subject area
la matrícula	tuition

Las palabras interrogativas

¿cuál?	what?; which?
¿cuándo?	when?
¿cuánto?	how much?
¿cuántos/as?	how many?
¿quién?	who?; whom?

Repaso: ¿cómo?, ¿dónde?, ¿qué?

¿Cuándo?

ahora	now
con frecuencia	frequently
el fin de semana	weekend
por la mañana/tarde	in the morning/afternoon
por la noche	at night, in the evening
tarde/temprano	late/early
todos los días	every day

Los pronombres personales

yo, tú, usted (Ud.), él/ella, nosotros/nosotras, vosotros/vosotras, ustedes (Uds.), ellos/ellas

Palabras adicionales

aquí	here
con	with
en casa	at home
mal	poorly
más	more
mucho	much; a lot
muy	very
poco	little
un poco (de)	a little bit (of)
sólo	only

⟩⟩ VOCABULARIO PERSONAL

Remember to use this space for other words and phrases you learn in this chapter.

Español   **Inglés**

México y Centroamérica

Long before Mexico and the Central American countries of Guatemala, Honduras, El Salvador, Nicaragua, Costa Rica, and Panama became Spanish-speaking, vibrant indigenous civilizations and peoples lived and flourished in this area. The arrival of the Spanish and their religion and culture profoundly changed the existing cultures, but the Spanish culture changed as well. Today, Mexico and the Central American countries are proud of both their indigenous and Spanish cultural heritages, which have fused together to create something unique. The past, present, and future of Mexico and Central America are intimately connected to the convergence of these varied cultures.

A traditional gourd marimba in Chichicastenango, Guatemala

Mexican music is much more than just the well-known **mariachi** sound. The amazing variety of Mexican music blends European traditions (such as the polka) with indigenous sounds. Mexican music also has evolved on the U.S. side of the border. **Tejano** music is immensely popular in the Southwest. In Central America, there are even more types of music, too many to list here. Of special note is the use of the **marimba** throughout the entire region. The **marimba,** an instrument similar to the xylophone, is of African origin; it was introduced in Latin America in the 16th century.

A canopy cable ride in, Monteverde, Santa Elena, Costa Rica

Guatemalan women wearing traditional clothing

Temple of the Great Jaguar at Tikal, Guatemala

Una familia mexicana
que (*that*) celebra el cumpleaños
(*birthday*) del abuelo (*grandfather*)

1. How does your family celebrate birthdays and other special occasions?

2. What do you know about Mexican celebrations?

3. Why do you think that multiple generations of a family are almost always involved in Mexican celebrations?

La familia

2

LA FAMILIA DE PATRICIA

los abuelos maternos de Patricia

el abuelo   **la abuela**

Pedro   Eliana

abuelo/a Grandma/pa

hermana – Sister

hermano – brother

hermana – sister

los padres de Patricia   **los tíos de Patricia**

el padre   **la madre**   **el tío**   **la tía**

Aunt Uncle

Felipe   Gloria   Luis   Isabel

los hermanos de Patricia   **los primos de Patricia**

la hermana   **el hermano**   **el primo**   **la prima**

Patricia   Rita   José   Pícaro   Carlos   Ana

la madre (mamá)	mother (mom)	**la nieta**	granddaughter
el padre (papá)	father (dad)	**el nieto**	grandson
la hija	daughter	**la sobrina**	niece
el hijo	son	**el sobrino**	nephew
los hijos	children		
la esposa	wife		
el esposo	husband		

LAS MASCOTAS°   Las... *Pets*

el gato	cat
el pájaro	bird
el perro	dog

Vocabulario útil

el padrastro / la madrastra stepfather / stepmother

el hijastro / la hijastra stepson / stepdaughter

el hermanastro / la hermanastra stepbrother / stepsister

el medio hermano / la media hermana half-brother / half-sister

el suegro / la suegra father-in-law / mother-in-law

el yerno / la nuera son-in-law / daughter-in-law

el cuñado / la cuñada brother-in-law / sister-in-law

...(ya) murió . . . has (already) died

Conversación

A. ¿Cierto o falso? Look at the drawings of the family that appear on page 54. Decide whether each of the following statements is true (**cierto**) or false (**falso**) according to the drawings. Correct the false statements.

	CIERTO	FALSO
1. José es el hermano de Ana.	❑	❑
2. Eliana es la abuela de Patricia.	❑	❑
3. Ana es la sobrina de Felipe y Gloria.	❑	❑
4. Patricia y José son primos.	❑	❑
5. Gloria es la tía de José.	❑	❑
6. Carlos es el sobrino de Isabel.	❑	❑
7. Pedro es el padre de Luis y Gloria.	❑	❑
8. Isabel y Gloria son las esposas de Luis y Felipe, respectivamente.	❑	❑

B. ¿Quién es?

Paso 1. Completa las siguientes (*following*) oraciones lógicamente.

1. La madre de mi (*my*) padre es mi _Abuela_
2. El hijo de mi tío es mi _____.
3. La hermana de mi padre es mi _____.
4. El esposo de mi abuela es mi _____.

Paso 2. Ahora define la relación de estas (*these*) personas, según (*according to*) el modelo de las oraciones del **Paso 1**.

MODELOS: El _____ de mi _____ es mi _____.
La _____ de mi _____ es mi _____.

1. prima
2. sobrino
3. tío
4. abuelo

Vocabulario útil

tengo I have
tienes you (*fam.*) have
¿tienes? do you (*fam.*) have?

¿cuántos? (*with male relatives*)
¿cuántas? (*with female relatives*)

C. Entrevista. Find out as much as you can about the family of a classmate, using the following dialogue as a guide.

MODELO: E1:* ¿Cuántos hermanos tienes?
E2: Bueno (*Well*), tengo seis hermanos y una hermana.
E1: ¿Y cuántos primos?
E2: ¡Uf! Tengo un montón (*bunch*). Más de (*than*) veinte.

---

*From this point on in the text, ESTUDIANTE 1 *and* ESTUDIANTE 2 *will be abbreviated as* E1 *and* E2, *respectively.*

Handwritten notes in left margin:

cien
ciento dos
ciento tres
200 - doscientos
300 - trescientos
400 - cuatrocientos
500 - quinientos
600 - seiscientos
700 - setecientos
800 - ochocientos ~~cientos~~
900 - novecientos
1000 - Mil
1,000,000 un millón

Continúa las secuencias:

treinta y uno, treinta y dos…
ochenta y cuatro, ochenta y cinco…

El abuelito Pedro tiene 85

La abuelita Eliana tiene

31	treinta y uno	40	cuarenta
32	treinta y dos	50	cincuenta
33	treinta y tres	60	sesenta
34	treinta y cuatro	70	setenta
35	treinta y cinco	80	ochenta
36	treinta y seis	90	noventa
37	treinta y siete	100	cien, ciento
38	treinta y ocho		
39	treinta y nueve		

Beginning with 31, Spanish numbers are *not* written in a combined form; **treinta y uno,** * **cuarenta y dos, sesenta y tres,** and so on, must be three separate words.

Cien is used before nouns and in counting.

cien casas	*a (one) hundred houses*
noventa y ocho, noventa y nueve, **cien**	*ninety-eight, ninety-nine, one hundred*

Conversación

A. **Más problemas de matemáticas.** Recuerda (*Remember*): + **y,** – **menos,** = **son.**

1. $30 + 50 = 80$ **2.** $45 + 45 = 90$ **3.** $32 + 58 = 90$ **4.** $77 + 23 = 100$ **5.** $100 - 40 = 60$

NOTA CULTURAL

Los apellidos hispánicos

In most Hispanic countries, people are given two last names (**apellidos**). The custom is demonstrated in this wedding invitation. The names of the bride's parents are in the top left corner: Ramón Ochoa Benítez and Ana Márquez Blanco de Ochoa. Their daughter's name, before her marriage, is Ana Luisa Ochoa Márquez. Her first last name (Ochoa) is her father's first last name, and her second last name (Márquez) is her mother's first last name. The groom's parents are in the top right corner. What do you think his full name (with both last names) is? If you said Antonio Lázaro Pérez, you are correct. Some Spanish-speaking women take their husband's first last name as their new second last name, dropping the second last name they had before marriage. Ana Luisa Ochoa Márquez's name may change to Ana Luisa Ochoa de Lázaro.

Ramón Ochoa Benítez	Antonio Lázaro Aguirre
Ana Márquez Blanco de Ochoa	Susana Pérez de Lázaro

tienen el gusto de anunciar la boda de sus hijos

Ana Luisa y Antonio

La ceremonia tendrá lugar
el 2 de julio, a las 12 del mediodía
en la Iglesia de la Candelaria

Almuerzo en Restaurante Don Paco	Lista de bodas: El Corte Inglés
Avda. de la Constitución, 7	

---

*Remember that when **uno** is part of a compound number (**treinta y uno,** and so on), it becomes **un** before a masculine noun and **una** before a feminine noun: **setenta y un** coches; **cincuenta y una** mesas.*

B. Los números de teléfono

```
LAZARO AGUIRRE, A. -Schez Pacheco, 17    415 0046
LAZCANO DEL MORAL, A. -E. Larreta, 14     215 8194
LAZCANO DEL MORAL, A. -Ibiza, 8 .....     274 6868
LEAL ANTON, J. -Pozo, 8 .............     222 3894
LIEBANA RODRIGUEZ, A.
    Guadarrama, 10 ..................     463 2593
LOPEZ BARTOLOME, J. -Palma, 69 .....      232 2027
LOPEZ CABRA, J. -E. Solana, 118 ....      407 5086
LOPEZ CABRA, J. -L. Van, 5 .........      776 4602
LOPEZ GONZALEZ, J. A. -Ibiza, 27 ...      409 2552
LOPEZ GUTIERREZ, G. -S. Cameros, 7 ...    478 8494
LOPEZ LOPEZ, J. -Alamedilla, 21 ....      227 3570
LOPEZ MARIN, V. -Illescas, 53 ......      218 6630
LOPEZ MARIN, V. -N. Rey, 7 .........      463 6873
LOPEZ MARIN, V. -Valmojado, 289 ...       717 2823
LOPEZ NUÑEZ, J. -Pl. Pinazo, s/n ...      796 0035
LOPEZ NUÑEZ, J. -Rocafort, Bl. 321 ...    796 5387
LOPEZ RODRIGUEZ, C. -Pl. Jesús, 7 ...     429 3278
LOPEZ RODRIGUEZ, J. -Pl. Angel, 15 ...    239 4323
LOPEZ RODRIGUEZ, M. E.
    B. Murillo, 104 .................     233 4239
LOPEZ TRAPERO, A. -Cam. Ingenieros, 1 .   462 5392
LOPEZ VAZQUEZ, J. -A. Torrejón, 17 ...    433 4646
LOPEZ VEGA, J. -M. Santa Ana, 5 ...       231 2131
LORENTE VILLARREAL, G. -Gandia, 7 .       252 2758
LORENZO MARTINEZ, A. -Moscareta, 5 .      479 6282
LORENZO MARTINEZ, A. -P. Laborde, 21      778 2800
LORENZO MARTINEZ, J.
    Av. S. Diego, 116 ...............     477 1040
LOSADA MIRON, M. -Padilla, 31 ......      276 9373
LOSADA MIRON, M. -Padilla, 31 ......      431 7461
LOZANO GUILLEN, E.
    Juan H. Mendoza, 5 .............      250 3884
LOZANO PIERA, F. J. -Pinguino, 8 ...      466 3205
LUDEÑA FLORES, G. -Lope Rueda, 56 ...     273 3735
LUENGO CHAMORRO, J.
    Gral Ricardos, 99 ..............      471 4906
LUQUE CASTILLO, J. -Pto Arlaban, 121 .    478 5253
LUQUE CASTILLO, L. -Cardeñosa, 15 ...     477 6644
```

Paso 1. Here is part of a page from an Hispanic telephone book. What can you tell about the names? (See the **Nota cultural** on page 56.)

Paso 2. With a classmate, practice giving telephone numbers at random from the list. Your partner will listen and identify the person. **¡OJO!** In many Hispanic countries phone numbers are said differently than in this country. Follow the model.

MODELO: 4–15–00–46 ⟶
    E1: Es el *cuatro-quince-cero cero-cuarenta y seis.*
    E2: Es el número de *A. Lázaro Aguirre.*

Paso 3. Now give your classmate your phone number and get his or hers.

MODELO: Mi número es el...

◆》NOTA COMUNICATIVA

Expressing Age

NORA: ¿Cuántos años tienes, abuela?

ABUELA: Setenta y tres, Nora.

NORA: ¿Y cuántos años tiene el abuelo?

ABUELA: Setenta y cinco, mi amor (*love*). Y ahora, dime (*tell me*), ¿cuántos años tienes tú?

NORA: Yo tengo cuatro.

In Spanish, age is expressed with the phrase tener... **años** (literally, *to have . . . years*). You have now seen all the singular forms of tener (*to have*): **tengo, tienes, tiene.**

C. ¡Lógico! Completa las siguientes oraciones lógicamente.

(handwritten: nueve mese, 9 months)

1. Una persona de *ochenta* años es muy vieja (*old*).
2. Un niño (*small child*) que tiene sólo *uno* año es muy joven (*young*).
3. La persona mayor (*oldest*) de mi familia es mi *suegra*. Tiene *setenta y siete* años.
4. La persona más joven (*youngest*) de mi familia es mi *sobrina*. Tiene *siete* años. Es el hijo/la hija de mi *hermano*.
5. En mi opinión, es ideal tener *50* años.
6. Si (*If*) una persona tiene _____ años, ya (*already*) es adulta.
7. Para (*In order to*) tomar alcohol en este estado (*state*)/esta provincia, es necesario tener _____ años.
8. Para mí (*For me*), ¡la idea de tener *cienta* años es inconcebible (*inconceivable*)!

guapo	handsome; good-looking	
bonito	pretty	
feo	ugly	
grande	large, big	
pequeño	small	
casado	married	
soltero	single	
simpático	nice, likeable	
antipático	unpleasant	
corto	short (*in length*)	
largo	long	
bueno	good	
malo	bad	
listo	smart; clever	
tonto	silly, foolish	
trabajador	hardworking	
perezoso	lazy	
rico	rich	
pobre	poor	
delgado	thin, slender	
gordo	fat	

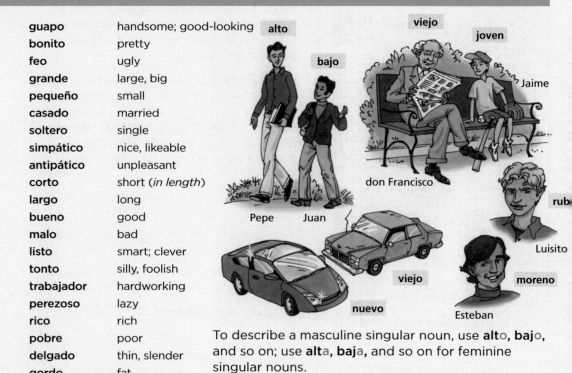

To describe a masculine singular noun, use **alt**o, **baj**o, and so on; use **alt**a, **baj**a, and so on for feminine singular nouns.

Conversación

A. **Preguntas** (*Questions*). Contesta (*Answer*) según los dibujos.

1. Einstein es listo. Y el chimpancé, ¿en comparación con Einstein?

2. Roberto es trabajador. ¿Y José?

3. Pepe es bajo. ¿Y Pablo?

4. Jaime es bueno y simpático. También es guapo. ¿Y Memo?

5. Ramón Ramírez es casado. ¿Y Paco Pereda?

6. El libro es viejo. ¿Y el lápiz?

B. ¿Cómo es? Describe a famous personality, using as many adjectives as possible so that your classmates can guess who the person is. Don't forget to use cognate adjectives that you have seen in **Primeros pasos** and **Capítulo 1**.

Need more practice?
- Workbook/Laboratory Manual
- Online Learning Center
  [www.mhhe.com/apuntate]

MODELO: Es un hombre importante; controla una compañía de *software* muy importante. Es muy trabajador y muy rico. ⟶ Bill Gates

Pronunciación

Stress and Written Accent Marks (Part I)

Some Spanish words have *written accent marks* over one of the vowels. That mark is called **el acento (ortográfico)**. It means that the syllable containing the accented vowel is stressed when the word is pronounced, as in the word **bolígrafo (bo-LÍ-gra-fo),** for example.

Although all Spanish words of more than one syllable have a stressed vowel, most words do not have a written accent mark. Most words have the spoken stress exactly where native speakers of Spanish would predict it. These two simple rules tell you which syllable is accented when a word does not have a written accent.

> In this chapter you will learn predictable patterns of stress. In **Capítulo 3,** you will learn when the written accent mark is needed.

- Words that end in a vowel, or **-n,** or **-s** are stressed on the *next-to-last syllable* (**la penúltima sílaba**).

co-sa	e-**xa**-men	i-ta-**lia**-no
gra-cias	**e**-res	**len**-guas

- Words that end in any other consonant are stressed on the *last syllable* (**la última sílaba**).

us-**ted**	es-pa-**ñol**	doc-**tor**
na-tu-**ral**	pro-fe-**sor**	es-**tar**

A. Sílabas. The following words have been separated into syllables for you. Read them aloud, paying careful attention to where the stress falls

1. Stress on the next-to-last syllable

chi-no	me-sa	li-bro	cien-cias
ar-te	si-lla	con-se-je-ra	o-ri-gen
cla-se	Car-men	li-te-ra-tu-ra	com-pu-ta-do-ra

2. Stress on the last syllable

se-ñor	co-lor	sen-ti-men-tal
mu-jer	po-pu-lar	lu-gar
fa-vor	li-ber-tad	u-ni-ver-si-dad
ac-tor	ge-ne-ral	con-trol

B. Vocales. Indicate the stressed vowel in the following words.

1. mo-chi-la	**4.** i-gual-men-te	**7.** li-be-ral
2. me-nos	**5.** E-cua-dor	**8.** hu-ma-ni-dad
3. re-gu-lar	**6.** e-le-gan-te	

México

DATOS ESENCIALES

NOMBRE OFICIAL: Estados Unidos Mexicanos
CAPITAL: Ciudad de México, «México, Distrito Federal», «México, D.F.» o «el D.F.»
POBLACIÓN: más de 107 (ciento siete) millones de habitantes

FÍJATE

- El nombre «México» viene[a] de los mexicas, el nombre original de los aztecas. Los mexicas eran[b] una tribu[c] nomada que estableció[d] su capital, Tenochtitlán, en el centro del antiguo Lago[e] Texcoco. Tenochtitlán era[f] una de las ciudades más grandes del mundo[g] en el siglo XVI.[h] Hoy d[i] la Ciudad de México cubre los restos[j] de Tenochtitlán.
- México tiene la población hispanohablante más grande d[ ] mundo.
- México tiene 31 estados y el Distrito Federal.
- Se hablan[k] aproximadamente sesenta idiomas indígenas en México todavía,[l] y hay zonas[m] rurales donde los indígenas no hablan español.

[a]comes [b]were [c]tribe [d]established [e]antiguo... *former Lake* [f]*was* [g]ciudades... *largest cities in the world* [h]siglo... *16th century* [i]Hoy... *Today* [j]cubre... *covers the remains* [k]Se... *Are spoken* [l]*still* [m]*areas*

¡MÚSICA!

La música mexicana tiene gran diversidad de estilos y ritmos.[a] De los géneros[b] tradicionales, la música ranchera, interpretada por mariachis, es la más conocida.[c] También hay variación en cuanto a[d] los instrumentos musicales que se usan[e] de una región a otra. Por ejemplo, la música norteña,[f] influida por[g] la polka alemana, usa mucho el acordeón, y la música folclórica de la costa caribeña se caracteriza[h] por la marimba.

[a]estilos... *styles and rhythms* [b]genres [c]la... *the most well-known* [d]en... *in terms of* [e]se... *are used* [f]northern [g]by [h]se... *is characterized*

 ## JULIETA VENEGAS

La cantante[a] de música pop Julieta Venegas nació[b] en California, pero se crió[c] en Tijuana, México. Además de cantar,[d] toca varios instrumentos musicales (guitarra, acordeón y teclados[e]). Su canción «Algo está cambiando»[f] es del álbum *Sí*.

[a]singer [b]was born [c]se... *was raised* [d]Además... *In addition to singing* [e]keyboards [f]Su... *Her song "Something Is Changing"*

Julieta Venegas en concierto en México, D.F.

4 Describing • Adjectives: Gender, Number, and Position

Gramática en acción: Un poema sencillo

Amigo
Fiel
Amable
Simpático
¡Lo admiro!

Amiga
Fiel
Amable
Simpática
¡La admiro!

¿Y tú? According to their form, which of the following adjectives can be used to describe each person? Which can refer to you?

Marta:
Mario: fiel   amable   simpática   simpático

Adjectives (**Los adjetivos**) are words used to talk about nouns or pronouns. Adjectives may describe or tell how many there are.

You have been using adjectives to describe people since **Primeros pasos**. In this section, you will learn more about describing the people and things around you.

large desk   **few** desks
tall woman   **several** women

> **adjective** = a word used to describe a noun or pronoun

Adjectives with *ser*

In Spanish, forms of **ser** are used with adjectives that describe basic, inherent qualities or characteristics of the nouns or pronouns they modify. **Ser** establishes the "norm," that is, what is considered basic reality: *snow is cold, water is wet.*

Tú **eres** **amable**.
You're nice. (You're a nice person.)

El diccionario **es** **barato**.
The dictionary is inexpensive.

Mi hermana **es** **trabajadora**.
My sister is hardworking.

A simple poem   *Friend Loyal Kind Nice I admire him/her!*

Forms of Adjectives

Spanish adjectives agree in gender and number with the noun or pronoun they modify. Each adjective has more than one form.

1. Adjectives Ending in -*o* Adjectives that end in **-o** (**alto**) have four forms, showing gender and number.

	Masculine	Feminine
Singular	amigo alto	amiga alta
Plural	amigos altos	amigas altas

2. Adjectives Ending in -*e* or a Consonant Adjectives that end in **-e** (**amable**) or in most consonants (**fiel**) have only two forms, a singular and a plural form. The plural of these adjectives is formed in the same way as that of nouns, by adding **-s** or **-es**.

[Práctica A – B]

	Masculine	Feminine
Singular	amigo amable amigo fiel	amiga amable amiga fiel
Plural	amigos amables amigos fieles	amigas amables amigas fieles

¡OJO!

Notes in brackets, like [**Práctica A–B**] here, let you know that you are now ready to do all of the indicated activities, in this case, **Práctica A–B** (page 64). Then, after you read grammar point 4, you will be prepared to do **Práctica C** on page 65, as the bracketed reference in 4 indicates.

3. Nationality Adjectives Most adjectives of nationality have four forms.

¡OJO!

Nationality adjectives ending in **-e** generally have only two forms: **estadounidense(s)** (from the U.S.), **canadiense(s).**

	Masculine	Feminine
Singular	el doctor mexicano español inglés	la doctora mexicana española inglesa
Plural	los doctores mexicanos españoles ingleses	las doctoras mexicanas españolas inglesas

4. Names of Languages The names of many languages—which are masculine in gender—are the same as the masculine singular form of the corresponding adjective of nationality.

[Práctica C]

Language	Adjective
el italiano	italiano/a/os/as
el alemán*	alemán, alemana/es/as

¡OJO!

Note that in Spanish the names of languages and adjectives of nationality are not capitalized, but the names of countries are: **el español, española,** but **España.**

---

*Adjectives that end in **-dor, -ón, -án,** and **-ín** also have four forms: **trabaja**dor, **trabaja**dora, **trabaja**dores, **trabaja**doras.*

Position of Adjectives

As you have probably noticed, adjectives do not always precede the noun in Spanish as they do in English. Note the following rules for adjective placement.

1. **Adjectives of Quantity** Like numbers, adjectives of quantity *precede* the noun, as do the interrogatives **¿cuánto/a?** and **¿cuántos/as?**

   ¡OJO!

   Otro/a by itself means *another* or *other*. The indefinite article is never used with **otro/a**.

   Hay **muchas** sillas y **dos** escritorios.
   There are many chairs and two desks.

   ¿Cuánto dinero necesitas?
   How much money do you need?

   Busco **otro** coche.
   I'm looking for another car.

2. **Adjectives of Quality** Adjectives that describe the qualities of a noun and distinguish it from others generally *follow* the noun. Adjectives of nationality are included in this category.

   un perro **listo**
   un dependiente **trabajador**
   una mujer **delgada** y **morena**
   un profesor **español**

3. *Bueno and malo* The adjectives **bueno** and **malo** may precede or follow the noun they modify. When they precede a masculine singular noun, they shorten to **buen** and **mal**, respectively.

   un **buen** perro / un perro **bueno**
   una **buena** perra / una perra **buena**
   un **mal** día / un día **malo**
   una **mala** noche / una noche **mala**

4. *Grande* The adjective **grande** may also *precede* or *follow* the noun. When it precedes a singular noun—masculine or feminine—it shortens to **gran** and means *great* or *impressive*. When it follows the noun, it means *large* or *big*.

   [Conversación A–B]

   Nueva York es una ciudad **grande**.
   New York is a large city.

   Nueva York es una **gran** ciudad.
   New York is a great (impressive) city.

Forms of *this/these* (Part 1)

1. *This/These* The demonstrative adjective *this/these* has four forms in Spanish.* Learn to recognize them when you see them.

este hijo	this son
esta hija	this daughter
estos hijos	these sons
estas hijas	these daughters

2. *Esto* You have already seen the neuter demonstrative **esto**. It refers to something that is as yet unidentified.

   ¿Qué es **esto**?
   What is this?

Hamburgo es una ciudad alemana.

*You will learn all forms of the Spanish demonstrative adjectives (this, that, these, those) in **Gramática 8 (Cap. 3).**

Práctica

A. ¿Cierto o falso?

Paso 1. Make complete sentences with the adjectives that describe you, using the masculine or feminine form as necessary.

(No) Soy...

1.	alto	**6.**	fiel
2.	trabajadora	**7.**	simpático
3.	estadounidense	**8.**	europeo
4.	rico	**9.**	soltero
5.	rubia	**10.**	hispana (latina)*

Paso 2. Now make sentences with the adjectives in **Paso 1** that describe your father or mother, your husband or wife, or your best friend (**mi mejor amigo/a**).

B. La familia de Carlos.
The following incomplete sentences describe some members of the family of Carlos, the cousin of Patricia. Their family tree is on page 54. Scan the adjectives to see which ones can complete the statements. Then complete each statement with only the adjectives that fit the context.

1. El tío Felipe es _____. (trabajador / alto / nueva / grande / fea / amable)

2. Los abuelos son _____. (rubio / antipático / inteligentes / viejos / religiosos / sinceras)

3. Mi tía Gloria, la madre de Patricia, es _____. (rubio / elegante / sentimental / buenas / casadas / simpática)

4. Mis primos son _____. (solteros / morenos / lógica / bajas / mala)

◆) NOTA COMUNICATIVA

Más nacionalidades

CENTROAMÉRICA		SUDAMÉRICA		ASIA	
costarricense	nicaragüense	argentino/a	ecuatoriano/a	chino/a	pakistaní (pl.
guatemalteco/a	panameño/a	boliviano/a	paraguayo/a	coreano/a	pakistaníes)
hondureño/a	salvadoreño/a	brasileño/a	peruano/a	indio/a	tailandés,
		chileno/a	uruguayo/a	japonés,	tailandesa
		colombiano/a	venezolano/a	japonesa	vietnamita

*_____

*__*Hispano/a*__ is a general term used by most Hispanics to refer to themselves. The term **latino/a** is often used by Hispanics born in this country.

C. ¿Cuál es su (their) nacionalidad?

Paso 1. Di (*Tell*) la nacionalidad de las siguientes (*following*) personas.

1. Monique es de Francia; es _____.
2. Piero y Andri son del Uruguay; son _____.
3. Indira y su (*her*) hermana son de la India; son _____.
4. Ronaldo y Ronaldinho son del Brasil; son _____.
5. Saji es un hombre del Japón; es _____.
6. La familia Musharraf es de Pakistán; son (*they are*) _____.
7. Paul es de Liverpool; es _____.
8. Samuel y su (*his*) hermana son de Guatemala; son _____.

Sunisa y Mai son de Tailandia. Son tailandesas.

Paso 2. En parejas (*pairs*), hagan (*form*) oraciones con las nacionalidades hispánicas, según el modelo. Busquen (*Look for*) los nombres de las naciones hispánicas en el mapa de la página 10.

> **MODELO:** **E1:** La mujer es de Costa Rica.
> **E2:** Es costarricense. El hombre es de Panamá.
> **E1:** Es panameño. La mujer...

Need more practice?
■ Workbook/Laboratory Manual
■ Online Learning Center
[www.mhhe.com/apuntate]

Conversación

A. Asociaciones.
With several classmates, talk about people or things you associate with the following phrases. Use the model as a guide. To express agreement or disagreement, use **(No) Estoy de acuerdo**.

> **MODELO:** un gran hombre ⟶
> **E1:** Creo que (*I believe that*) el presidente es un gran hombre.
> **E2:** No estoy de acuerdo.

1. un mal restaurante
2. un buen programa de televisión
3. una gran mujer, un gran hombre
4. un buen libro (¿una novela?), un libro horrible
5. un buen coche

B. Descripciones.
En parejas, describan a sus (*your*) familias, haciendo (*forming*) oraciones completas con estas palabras, con cualquier (*any*) otro adjetivo que conozcan (*that you may know*) y con los adjetivos de nacionalidad. **¡OJO!** Cuidado (*Be careful*) con la forma de los adjetivos.

> **MODELO:** Mi familia no es grande. Es pequeña. Mi padre tiene 50 años.
> Es pakistaní de nacimiento (*by birth*).

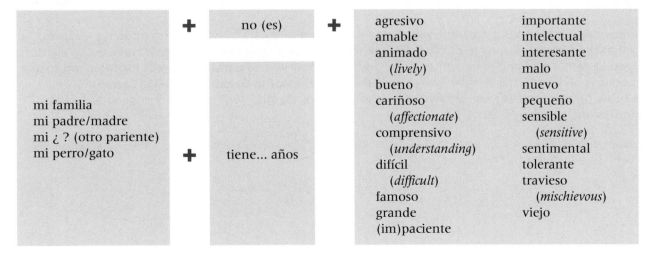

| mi familia <br> mi padre/madre <br> mi ¿ ? (otro pariente)
 mi perro/gato | **+** no (es)

 + tiene... años | **+** | agresivo <br> amable <br> animado (*lively*)
 bueno <br> cariñoso (*affectionate*)
 comprensivo (*understanding*)
 difícil (*difficult*)
 famoso <br> grande
 (im)paciente | importante <br> intelectual <br> interesante <br> malo <br> nuevo <br> pequeño <br> sensible (*sensitive*)
 sentimental <br> tolerante <br> travieso (*mischievous*)
 viejo |

¿Recuerdas?

Before beginning **Gramática 5,** review the forms and uses of **ser** that you know already by answering these questions.

1. ¿Eres estudiante o profesor(a)?
2. ¿Cómo eres? ¿Eres una persona sentimental? ¿inteligente? ¿paciente? ¿elegante?
3. ¿Qué hora es? ¿A qué hora es la clase de español?
4. ¿Qué es un hospital? ¿Es una persona? ¿un objeto? ¿un edificio?

5 Expressing *to be* • Present Tense of **ser,** Summary of Uses (Part 2)

Gramática en acción: Presentaciones

— ¡Hola! Me llamo Francisco Durán, pero todos me llaman Pancho.

- Soy profesor de la universidad.
- Soy alto y moreno.
- Soy de Guanajuato, México.

— ¿Y Lola Benítez, mi esposa?

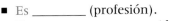

- Es _____ (profesión).
- Es _____ y _____ (descripción).
- Es de _____ (origen).

bonita doctora muy inteligente Mérida, México

ser (*to be*)			
(yo)	soy	(nosotros/as)	somos
(tú)	eres	(vosotros/as)	sois
(Ud.)		(Uds.)	
(él)	es	(ellos)	son
(ella)		(ellas)	

As you know, there are two Spanish verbs that mean *to be:* **ser** and **estar**. They are not interchangeable; the meaning that the speaker wishes to convey determines their use. In this chapter, you will review the uses of **ser** that you already know and learn some new ones. Remember to use **estar** to express location and to ask how someone is feeling. You will learn more about the uses of **estar** in **Gramática 14–15 (Cap. 5).**

Some basic functions of **ser** are presented on the following pages. You have used or seen all of them already in this and previous chapters.

Introductions *Hello! My name is Francisco Durán, but everyone calls me Pancho. • I'm a university professor. • I'm tall and brunet. • I'm from Guanajuato, Mexico. And Lola Benítez, my wife? • She's ____. • She's ____ and ____. • She's from ____.*

Identification

To *identify* people and things [Práctica A]	Yo **soy estudiante.**
	Alicia y yo **somos hermanas.**
Remember that the notes in brackets refer you to activities that practice the grammar point.	La doctora Ramos **es profesora.**
	Esto **es un libro.**

Description

To *describe* people and things*	**Soy sentimental.**
	I'm sentimental (a sentimental person).
	El coche es muy viejo.
	The car is very old.

Origin

With **de,** to express *origin* [Práctica B – C]	**Somos de los Estados Unidos,** pero nuestros padres **son de la Argentina. ¿De dónde es** Ud.?
	We're from the United States, but our parents are from Argentina. Where are you from?

Generalizations

To express *generalizations* (only **es**) [Conversatión B]	**Es necesario** estudiar, pero no **es posible** estudiar todos los días.
	It's necessary to study, but it's not possible to study every day.

Here are two basic functions of **ser** that you have not yet practiced.

Possession

With **de,** to express *possession* [Práctica D]	**Es** el perro **de Carla.**
	It's Carla's dog.
Note that there is no **'s** to mark possession in Spanish.	**Son** las gatas **de Jorge.**
	They're Jorge's (female) cats.
¡OJO!	**de + el ⟶ del**
The masculine singular article **el** contracts with the preposition **de** to form **del.** No other article contracts with **de.**	**Es** la casa **del** abuelito.
	It's grandpa's house.
	Es la casa **de la** abuelita.
	It's grandma's house.

---

*You practiced this language function of **ser** in **Gramática 4** in this chapter.

Destination

With **para,** to tell *for* whom or what something *is intended*	¿*Romeo y Julieta?* **Es para** la clase de inglés. *Romeo and Juliet? It's for English class.*
[Conversación A]	— ¿**Para** quién **son** los regalos? — **(Son) Para** mi nieto. *Who are the presents for?* *(They're) For my grandson.*

Práctica

A. ¡Anticipemos! Los parientes de Gloria. Look back at the family drawings on page 54. Then tell whether the following statements are true (**cierto**) or false (**falso**) from Gloria's standpoint. Correct the false statements.

	CIERTO	FALSO
1. Felipe y yo somos hermanos.	❏	❏
2. Pedro es mi esposo.	❏	❏
3. Pedro y Eliana son mis (*my*) padres.	❏	❏
4. Carlos es mi sobrino.	❏	❏
5. Mi hermano es el esposo de Isabel.	❏	❏
6. El padre de Felipe no es abuelo todavía (*yet*).	❏	❏
7. Mi familia no es muy grande.	❏	❏

Naciones

Alemania
China
El Salvador
los Estados Unidos
Francia
Inglaterra
Italia
Portugal
Tailandia

B. Nacionalidades

Paso 1. ¿De dónde son, según los nombres, apellidos y ciudades?

MODELO: João Gonçalves, Lisboa ⟶ João Gonçalves es de Portugal.

1. John Doe, Nueva York
2. Karl Lotze, Berlín
3. Graziana Lazzarino, Roma
4. Mongkut, Bangkok
5. María Gómez, San Salvador
6. Claudette Moreau, París
7. Timothy Windsor, Londres
8. Hai Chow, Beijing

Paso 2. Ahora, ¿de dónde eres tú? ¿De este estado / esta provincia? ¿de una metrópoli? ¿de un área rural? ¿Eres de una ciudad de nombre hispánico? ¿Eres de otro país (*country*)?

C. Personas extranjeras

Paso 1. ¿Quiénes son, de dónde son y dónde trabajan ahora?

MODELO: Teresa: actriz / de Madrid / en Cleveland ⟶ Teresa es actriz. Es de Madrid. Ahora trabaja en Cleveland.

1. Carlos Miguel: médico (*doctor*) / de Cuba / en Milwaukee
2. Pilar: profesora / de Burgos / en Miami
3. Mariela: dependienta / de Buenos Aires / en Nueva York
4. Juan: dentista* / de Lima / en Los Ángeles

Paso 2. Ahora habla sobre (*talk about*) un amigo o pariente según el modelo del **Paso 1.**

---

*A number of professions end in **-ista** in both masculine and feminine forms. The article indicates gender: **el/la dentista, el/la artista,** and so on.

D. Usemos (*Let's use*) la lógica. ¿De quién son estas cosas (*things*)? En parejas, hagan y contesten preguntas (*ask and answer questions*). Las respuestas pueden variar (*can vary*).

> **MODELO:** E1: ¿De quién es el perro?
> E2: Es de…

¿De quién es/son… ?

1. la casa en Beverly Hills
2. la casa en Bombay
3. la camioneta (*station wagon*)
4. el perro
5. las fotos de la Argentina
6. las mochilas con todos los libros

Vocabulario útil
la actriz
el estudiante extranjero
las estudiantes
la familia con cuatro hijos
el niño
los Sres. Sarma

¿De quién es el perro?

E. ¡Somos como una familia! Completa el párrafo con las formas correctas de **ser**.

Me llamo Antonia y _____¹ de Chicago. (Yo) _____² estudiante de ingeniería en la Universidad de Illinois, y tengo muchos amigos en Chicago. Mis amigos _____³ de todas partesᵃ y muchos de ellos _____ ⁴ hispanos. Mi familia _____⁵ de origen mexicano y aunque nunca he vividoᵇ en México, hablo bastante bienᶜ el español. Me gusta hablar español con mi amigo Javier. Javier _____ ⁶ de Costa Rica y estudia ingeniería también. Javier y yo _____⁷ los asistentes del profesor Thomas; por esoᵈ pasamos mucho tiempo juntos.ᵉ Javier _____⁸ muy guapo y simpático, pero nosotros sólo _____ ⁹ buenos amigos. Javier _____¹⁰ el novioᶠ de mi mejorᵍ amiga.

ᵃplaces   ᵇaunque… *although I have never lived*   ᶜbastante… *rather well*   ᵈpor… *for that reason*   ᵉpasamos… *we spend a lot of time together*   ᶠ*boyfriend*   ᵍ*best*

Need more practice?
☐ Workbook/Laboratory Manual
☐ Online Learning Center [www.mhhe.com/apuntate]

Conversación

⬦❯ NOTA COMUNICATIVA

Explaining Your Reasons

In conversation, it is often necessary to explain a decision, tell why someone did something, and so on. Here are some simple words and phrases that speakers use to offer explanations.

porque   because   **para**   in order to

— ¿Por qué necesitamos una televisión nueva?   *Why do we need a new TV set?*
—Pues… **para** mirar el partido de fútbol…   *Well . . . (in order) to watch the*
    ¡Es el campeonato!   *soccer game . . . It's the championship!*

— ¿Por qué trabajas tanto?   *Why do you work so much?*
— **¡Porque** necesitamos dinero!   *Because we need money!*

Note the differences between **porque** (one word, no accent) and the interrogative **¿por qué?** (two words, accent on **qué**), which means *why?*

A. El regalo (*gift*) ideal

Paso 1. Look at Diego's list of gifts and what his family members like. With a partner, decide who receives each gift and why. The first one is done for you.

> **MODELO:** 1. la novela de J. K. Rowling ⟶
> **E1:** ¿Para quién es la novela de J. K. Rowling?
> **E2:** Es para la prima.
> **E1:** ¿Por qué?
> **E2:** Porque le gustan las novelas.

LOS REGALOS DE DIEGO
2. la calculadora
3. los libros de literatura clásica
4. los discos compactos de Bach
5. la televisión
6. el perro
7. el dinero

LOS MIEMBROS DE LA FAMILIA DE DIEGO
a. el padre: Le gusta mirar las noticias (*news*).
b. los abuelos: Les gusta mucho la música clásica.
c. la madre: Le gustan los animales.
d. el hermano: Le gustan mucho las historias viejas.
e. la hermana: Necesita pagar la matrícula.
f. el primo: Le gustan las matemáticas.
g. la prima: Le gustan las novelas.

Paso 2. With a partner, exchange ideas about good gifts for members of your family and also about good gifts for you.

> **MODELO:** Para mi mamá, deseo comprar ropa, porque ella necesita ropa nueva. Yo necesito ropa nueva también.

Vocabulario útil
el coche
el radio
la ropa clothing

B. ¿Qué opinas?
Expresa opiniones originales, afirmativas o negativas, con estas palabras.

> **MODELO:** En mi opinión, es importante hablar español en la clase de español.

(no) es importante
(no) es muy práctico
(no) es necesario
(no) es absurdo
(no) es fascinante
(no) es una lata (*pain, drag*)
(no) es posible

\+

mirar la televisión todos los días
hablar español en la clase
tener muchas mascotas
llegar (*to arrive, get*) a clase puntualmente
tomar café en el salón de clase
hablar con los animales / las plantas
tomar mucho café y fumar cigarrillos
trabajar dieciocho horas al día
tener muchos hermanos
ser amable con todos los miembros de la familia
estar mucho tiempo (*a lot of time*) con la familia

¿Crees que es bueno mirar mucho la tele?

Lectura cultural 2 México

❶ La Quebrada[a] en Acapulco La geografía de México es variada, con montañas, selvas,[b] desiertos y volcanes. Tiene playas blancas[c] en el este[d] y costas rocosas[e] en el oeste.[f] Este acantilado[g] en la costa de Acapulco se llama «La Quebrada». Es famoso por los clavadistas que hacen saltos[h] de treinta y cinco metros[i] al agua.

[a]Gorge [b]jungles [c]playas... white beaches [d]east [e]costas... rocky coasts [f]west [g]cliff [h]clavadistas... divers that dive [i]treinta... 35 meters (115 feet)

Un chac mool, en Chichén Itzá El chac mool es la escultura de una figura reclinada con la cabeza levantada.[a] Es de origen tolteca, una de las culturas indígenas más antiguas[b] de México, pero fue adoptado por[c] otras culturas, como los mayas. Chichén Itzá está en el estado mexicano de Yucatán.

[a]figura... reclined figure with a raised head [b]más... oldest [c]fue... it was adopted by

❸ En un cementerio durante[a] el Día de los Muertos[b] Muchos mexicanos visitan los cementerios el 2 de noviembre para celebrar el Día de los Muertos. Preparan altares con las comidas[c] y posesiones favoritas de sus seres fallecidos.[d] En el cementerio, decoran las tumbas con velas y flores.[e] La flor tradicional de esta celebración es la maravilla.[f]

[a]during [b]Día... Day of the Dead [c]foods [d]seres... loved ones who have passed away [e]velas... candles and flowers [f]marigold

La Basílica de Nuestra Señora del Rosario, en Guanajuato Guanajuato es una ciudad colonial en el centro de México que se hizo famosa[a] por las ricas venas de plata y oro que se encontraron allí[b] en el siglo XVI.[c] Hoy día[d] Guanajuato es famoso por sus iglesias[e] y edificios coloniales, como la Basílica de Nuestra Señora del Rosario, que atraen a[f] turistas de todo el mundo.

[a]se... became famous [b]ricas... rich veins of silver and gold that were found there [c]siglo... 16th century [d]Hoy...Today [e]churches [f]atraen... attract

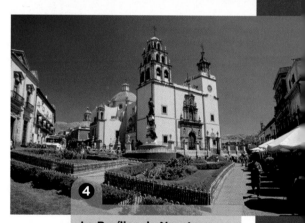

❺ Una cabeza[a] olmeca La civilización olmeca es la más antigua[b] de las civilizaciones que han ocupado[c] una parte de lo que[d] hoy es México y Centroamérica. Los olmecas crearon[e] estatuas de cabezas gigantescas. Se han encontrado por lo menos[f] diecisiete de estas cabezas desde[g] México hasta[h] El Salvador, y algunas de ellas[i] pesan hasta[j] once toneladas.[k]

[a]head [b]la... the oldest [c]han... have occupied [d]lo... what [e]created [f]Se... They have found at least [g]from [h]to [i]algunas... some of them [j]pesan... weigh up to [k]tons

Lectura cultural 2   **setenta y uno** ▪ 71

6 Expressing Possession • (Unstressed) Possessive Adjectives*

Gramática en acción: Invitación y posesión

los Sres. Ortega

Comprensión

1. En el dibujo A, ¿de quién es la casa?
2. ¿Quiénes llegan a la casa?
3. En el dibujo B, ¿de quién son los juguetes?
4. ¿Quién desea jugar (*to play*) con los juguetes?

A. «¡Pasen, por favor! Nuestra casa es su casa».

B. «¡No son tus juguetes! ¡Son mis juguetes!»

---

possessive adjective = an adjective that shows who owns or has something

Possessive adjectives (**Los adjetivos posesivos**) are words that tell to whom or to what something belongs: *my* (book), *his* (sweater). You have already seen and used several possessive adjectives in Spanish. Here is the complete set.

(Unstressed) Possessive Adjectives			
my	mi **hijo/hija** mis **hijos/hijas**	our	nuestro **hijo** nuestra **hija** nuestros **hijos** nuestras **hijas**
your (*fam.*)	tu **hijo/hija** tus **hijos/hijas**	your (*fam, Sp.*)	vuestro **hijo** vuestra **hija** vuestros **hijos** vuestras **hijas**
your, his, her, its	su **hijo/hija** sus **hijos/hijas**	your, their	su **hijo/hija** sus **hijos/hijas**

¡OJO!

The forms **vuestro/a/os/as** are used extensively in Spain, but are not common in Latin America.

1. **Agreement with Person or Thing Possessed** In Spanish, the ending of a possessive adjective agrees in form with the person or thing possessed, not with the owner or possessor. Note that these possessive adjectives are placed before the noun.

   The possessive adjectives **mi(s), tu(s)**, and **su(s)** show agreement in number only. **Nuestro/a/os/as** and **vuestro/a/os/as**, like all adjectives that end in **-o,** show agreement in both number and gender.

Son ⎡ **mis**
     tus   hermanos.
     sus ⎦

Es ⎡ **nuestra**
   vuestra   familia
   su ⎦

Another kind of possessive is called the stressed possessive adjective. It can be used as a noun. For information on them, see the Online Learning Center Appendix 2, Using Adjectives as Nouns.

2. Using *su(s)* The possessive form **su(s)** can have several different equivalents in English: *your (sing.)*, *his, her, its, your (pl.)*, and *their*. Usually its meaning will be clear in context. When the meaning of **su(s)** is not clear, **de** and a pronoun are used instead to indicate the possessor.

el padre
la madre   de él (de ella, de Ud., de
los abuelos   ellos, de ellas, de Uds.)
las tías

¿Son jóvenes los hijos **de él?**
Are his children young?

¿Dónde vive el abuelo **de ellas?**
Where does their grandfather live?

Práctica

A. Las posesiones. Which nouns can these possessive adjectives modify without changing form?

1. su: problema   primos   dinero   tías   escritorios   familia
2. tus: perro   idea   hijos   profesoras   abuelo   examen
3. mi: ventana   médicos   cuarto   coche   abuela   gatos
4. sus: animales   oficina   nietas   padre   hermana   abuelo
5. nuestras: guitarra   libro   materias   lápiz   sobrinas   tía
6. nuestros: gustos   consejeros   parientes   puerta   clase   residencia

B. La familia de Maribel

Paso 1. Change the following sentences, spoken by Maribel, to reflect a plural noun. The noun is indicated in blue. Note that the possessive adjective itself does not change; only its form changes.

> **MODELO:** «Mi hermano es alto.» ⟶
> «*Mis* hermanos *son altos.*»

1. «Mi hermana es lista.»
2. «Mi primo está en California.»
3. «Mi tío habla español.»
4. «Mi abuela mira mucho la tele (televisión).»

Paso 2. Now restate the sentences in **Paso 1** to quote what Maribel said. The possessive adjective itself will change.

> **MODELO:** «Mi hermano es alto.» ⟶
> «*Su* hermano es alto.»

Paso 3. Now restate the sentences in **Paso 1** to make them express what Maribel and her brother Julio would say about their family. The possessive adjective itself will change.

> **MODELO:** «Mi hermano es alto.» ⟶
> «*Nuestro* hermano es alto.»

Mi familia
es grande.

C. ¿Cómo es la familia de David?

Paso 1. Mira a* (*Look at*) la familia de David en el dibujo. Completa las oraciones según el modelo.

David

MODELO: familia / pequeño ⟶ Su familia es pequeña.

1. hijo pequeño / guapo
2. perro / feo
3. hija / rubio

4. abuelo / viejito (*very old*)
5. esposa / bonito

Paso 2. Imagina que eres David y modifica (*change*) las respuestas (*answers*).

MODELO: familia / pequeño ⟶ Mi familia es pequeña.

Paso 3. Imagina que eres la esposa de David. Habla por ti (*Speak for yourself*) y por tu esposo. Modifica sólo las respuestas del 1 al 4.

MODELO: familia / pequeño ⟶ Nuestra familia es pequeña.

Need more practice?
- Workbook/Laboratory Manual
- Online Learning Center [www.mhhe.com/apuntate]

Conversación

A. En nuestro salón de clase. Use the following phrases to describe aspects of your classroom at this moment. If the phrases can't be used to describe the classroom, explain why not.

MODELOS: mi computadora ⟶ Mi computadora está en mi mochila. (Mi computadora no está en el salón de clase; está en casa.)
nuestras computadoras ⟶ Nuestras computadoras están en los escritorios del salón de clase. (Nuestras computadoras no están en el salón de clase hoy; están en casa.)

1. mi computadora
2. nuestras computadoras
3. nuestro profesor / nuestra profesora de español
4. su computadora (la computadora del profesor / de la profesora)
5. nuestros libros de texto
6. nuestras calculadoras
7. mi silla
8. mis lápices
9. su mochila (la mochila de otro/a estudiante de la clase)
10. mi dinero (la cartera = *wallet*)

B. Entrevista. Take turns asking and answering questions about your families. Talk about what family members are like, their ages, some things they do, and so on. Use the model as a guide. Take notes on what your partner says. Then report the information to the class.

MODELO: tu abuela ⟶ **E1:** Mi abuela es alta. ¿Y tu abuela? ¿Es alta?
E2: Bueno, no. Mi abuela es baja.
E1: ¿Cuántos años tiene?...

1. tu familia en general
2. tus padres
3. tus abuelos

4. tus hermanos / hijos
5. tu esposo/a / compañero/a de cuarto

---

*Note the use of **a** here. In this context, the word **a** has no equivalent in English. It is used in Spanish before a direct object that is a specific person. You will learn more about this use of **a** in **Capítulo 6**. Until then, the exercises and activities in ¡Apúntate! will indicate when to use it.*

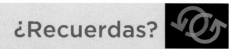

¿Recuerdas?

The personal endings used with **-ar** verbs share some characteristics with **-er** and **-ir** verbs which you will learn in **Gramática 7**. Review the present tense endings of **-ar** verbs by telling which subject pronoun(s) you associate with each of these endings.

1. -amos   2. -as   3. -áis   4. -an   5. -o   6. -a

7 Expressing Actions • Present Tense of -er and -ir Verbs; Subject Pronouns (Part 2)

Gramática en acción: Un estudiante típico

- Se llama Samuel Flores Toledo.
- Estudia en la UNAM (Universidad Autónoma de México).
- Vive con su familia en la Ciudad de México, el D.F. (Distrito Federal).
- Come pizza y tacos con frecuencia.
- Bebe cerveza en las fiestas.
- Recibe muchos e-mails y cartas de sus primos del Canadá.
- Lee y escribe mucho para su especialización.
- Aprende inglés porque desea visitar a su familia en Ontario.

¿Y tú? Contesta estas preguntas de Samuel.

1. ¿Dónde vives tú?
2. ¿Comes muchos tacos?
3. ¿Recibes muchos e-mails?
4. ¿Lees y escribes mucho para tu especialización? ¿O no tienes especialización todavía (*yet*)?

Verbs That End in -er and -ir

1. **Present Tense Endings** The present tense of **-er** and **-ir** verbs is formed by adding personal endings to the stem of the verb (the infinitive minus its **-er/-ir** ending). The personal endings for **-er** and **-ir** verbs are the same except for the first and second person plural.

comer (*to eat*)		vivir (*to live*)	
como	comemos	vivo	vivimos
comes	coméis	vives	vivís
come	comen	vive	viven

Regular present tense -er and -ir endings			
	-er		**-ir**
Yo -o	-emos nosotros -o		-imos
Tú -es	-éis vosotros -es		-ís
Ud/Ello/Ella -e	-en ellos/ellas uds/ -e		-en

A typical student • *His name is Samuel Flores Toledo.* • *He studies at UNAM (the Autonomous University of Mexico).* • *He lives with his family in Mexico City,* **el D.F.** *(Federal District).* • *He frequently eats pizza and tacos.* • *He drinks beer at parties.* • *He gets a lot of e-mails and letters from his cousins in Canada.* • *He reads and writes a lot for his major.* • *He's learning English because he wants to visit his family in Ontario.*

2. Important -er/-ir Verbs These are the frequently used **-er** and **-ir** verbs you will find in this chapter.

-er verbs		-ir verbs	
aprender	to learn	**abrir**	to open
beber	to drink	**asistir**	to attend, go to
comer	to eat		*(a class function)*
comprender	to understand	**escribir**	to write
creer (en)	to think; to believe	**recibir**	to receive
	(in)	**vivir**	to live
deber + *inf.*	should, must, ought		
	to *(do something)*		
leer	to read		
vender	to sell		

Remember that the Spanish present tense has a number of present tense equivalents in English. It can also be used to express future meaning.	**como** = *I eat, I am eating, I will eat*
Deber, like **desear** and **necesitar**, is followed by an infinitive.	**Debes leer** tus e-mails todos los días. *You should read your e-mails on a daily basis.*
Aprender + **a** + *infinitive* means *to learn how to (do something)*.	Muchos niños **aprenden a hablar** español con sus abuelos. *Many children learn to speak Spanish with their grandparents.*

Subject Pronouns (Part 2): Use and Omission

In English, a verb must have an expressed subject (a noun or pronoun): ***the train*** *arrives,* ***she*** *says.* In Spanish, however, as you have probably noticed, an expressed subject is not required. Verbs are accompanied by a subject pronoun only for clarification, emphasis, or contrast.

- *Clarification:* When the context does not make the subject clear, the subject pronoun is expressed. This happens most frequently with third person singular and plural verb forms.

- *Emphasis:* Subject pronouns are used in Spanish to emphasize the subject when in English you would stress it with your voice.

- *Contrast:* Contrast is a special case of emphasis. Subject pronouns are used to contrast the actions of two individuals or groups.

Ud. / él / ella vende
nosotros / nosotras vendemos
vosotros / vosotras vendéis
Uds. / ellos / ellas venden

— ¿Quién debe pagar?   *Who should pay?*
— ¡**Tú** debes pagar!   ***You*** *should pay!*

Ellos leen mucho; **nosotros** leemos poco.
They *read a lot; we read little.*

AUTOPRUEBA

Give the correct verb forms.

1. Elena (comer) _____   **4.** José (escribir) _____
2. yo (beber) _____   **5.** Uds. (vivir) _____
3. nosotros (leer) _____   **6.** tú (abrir) _____

Answers: 1. come 2. bebo 3. leemos 4. escribe 5. viven 6. abres

Práctica

A. Asociaciones. Give at least one **-er** or **-ir** infinitive whose meaning you associate with the following words and phrases.

1. un libro o una revista (*magazine*)
2. una composición, un ensayo (*essay*), una carta
3. un café o una Coca-Cola
4. en la cafetería
5. las materias
6. la opinión de un pariente
7. una librería o un supermercado
8. una puerta o una ventana
9. clases y conciertos
10. en la residencia o en una casa
11. estudiar más
12. regalos

¿Para quién son estos regalos?

B. En la clase de español

Paso 1. Tell whether the following statements are true for your classroom environment. Make untrue statements negative or change them in another way to make them correct.

> **MODELO:** Bebemos café en el salón de clase. ⟶ Sí, bebemos café en el salón de clase. (No, no bebemos café en el salón de clase. Bebemos café en casa.)

1. Debemos estudiar más esta materia.
2. Leemos los capítulos completos de *¡Apúntate!*
3. Todos comprendemos bien el español de nuestro profesor / nuestra profesora.
4. Asistimos al laboratorio de computadoras con frecuencia.
5. Abrimos los libros con frecuencia en esta clase.
6. En esta clase escribimos mucho.
7. En esta clase aprendemos a hablar y comprender español.
8. Vendemos nuestros libros al final del año.
9. Recibo muchos paquetes de mi familia.
10. Como en casa/_____ (*dining facility*) por la noche.
11. Vivo con mi familia este semestre/trimestre.
12. Mi profesor(a) cree que yo debo asistir a clase con más frecuencia.
13. Debo aprender a leer más rápido.

Paso 2. Now turn to the person next to you and rephrase each sentence, using **tú** forms of the verbs. Your partner will indicate whether the sentences are true for him or her.

> **MODELO:** Bebemos café en el salón de clase. ⟶
> **E1:** Bebes café en el salón de clase, ¿verdad (*right*)?
> **E2:** Sí, bebo café en el salón de clase. (No, no bebo café en el salón de clase. Bebo café en la cafetería.)

C. Diego habla de su padre. Completa el siguiente párrafo con la forma correcta de los verbos entre paréntesis.

Mi padre (vender[1]) coches y trabaja mucho. Mis hermanos y yo (aprender[2]) mucho de papá. Según mi padre, los jóvenes (deber[3]) (asistir[4]) a clase todos los días, porque es su obligación. Papá también (creer[5]) que no es necesario mirar la televisión por la noche. Es más interesante (leer[6]) el periódico,[a] una revista o un buen libro. Por eso nosotros (leer[7]) o (escribir[8]) por la noche y no miramos la televisión. Yo admiro a mi papá y (creer[9]) que él (comprender[10]) la importancia de la educación.

[a]*newspaper*

Comprensión. ¿Cierto o falso? Corrige (*Correct*) las oraciones falsas.

	CIERTO	FALSO
1. Diego y sus hermanos venden coches.	❏	❏
2. Diego mira mucho la televisión.	❏	❏
3. El padre de Diego lee mucho.	❏	❏

D. Este domingo (*Sunday*), tamalada. Form complete sentences based on the words given, in the order given. Conjugate the verbs and add other words if necessary. Don't use the subject pronouns in parentheses.

Una tamalada consiste en hacer (*making*) y comer tamales, una comida (*food*) típica de México y Centroamérica. Hay ocasiones en que hacer tamales es una fiesta familiar. Este domingo es un día especial para la familia de la pintura. Habla Luis.

Tamalada (Making Tamales), por (*by*) Carmen Lomas Garza (estadounidense)

1. hay / tamalada / hoy / por / tarde
2. todo / familia / asistir / tamalada / en / nuestro / casa
3. mi / padres / celebrar / su / aniversario de boda (*wedding*)
4. la / mujeres / de / familia / y / un / hombres / preparar / comida
5. mi / tíos / beber / café / y / mirar / tele
6. mi / primas / pequeño / leer / revistas / para niños
7. mi / hermano / deber / estudiar / pero / leer / noticias (*news*) del fútbol de México / en el Internet
8. (él) no / comprender / todo / porque / su / español / no / ser / perfecto
9. yo / preparar / comida / con / mi mamá / y / abuela
10. (nosotros) comer / comida (*meal*) / grande / a / tres
11. (yo) creer / que / mi / mamá / y / tías / ser / cocineras (*cooks*) / excelente
12. (yo) desear / ser / uno / bueno / cocinero / también

Conversación

Telling How Frequently You Do Things

Use the following words and phrases to tell how often you perform an activity. Some of them will already be familiar to you.

todos los días, siempre	every day, always	**una vez a la semana**	once a week
con frecuencia	frequently	**casi nunca**	almost never
a veces	at times	**nunca**	never

Hablo con mis amigos **todos los días.** Hablo con mis padres **una vez a la semana. Casi nunca** hablo con mis abuelos. Y **nunca** hablo con mis tíos que viven en Italia.

For now, use the expressions **casi nunca** and **nunca** only at the beginning of a sentence. You will learn more about how to use them in **Gramática 18** (**Cap. 6**).

A. ¿Con qué frecuencia?

Paso 1. How frequently do you do the following things?

	CON FRECUENCIA	A VECES	CASI NUNCA	NUNCA
1. Asisto al laboratorio de computadoras.	❑	❑	❑	❑
2. Recibo e-mails y cartas.	❑	❑	❑	❑
3. Escribo poemas.	❑	❑	❑	❑
4. Leo novelas románticas.	❑	❑	❑	❑
5. Como en una pizzería.	❑	❑	❑	❑
6. Recibo y leo revistas.	❑	❑	❑	❑
7. Aprendo palabras nuevas en español.	❑	❑	❑	❑
8. Asisto a todas las clases.	❑	❑	❑	❑
9. Compro regalos para los amigos	❑	❑	❑	❑
10. Vendo los libros al final del semestre/trimestre.	❑	❑	❑	❑

Paso 2. Now compare your answers with those of a classmate. Then answer the following questions. **¡OJO! los/las dos** = *both* (*of us*); **ninguno/a** = *neither*

	YO	MI COMPAÑERO/A	LOS/LAS DOS	NINGUNO/A
1. ¿Quién es muy estudioso/a?	❑	❑	❑	❑
2. ¿Quién come mucha pizza?	❑	❑	❑	❑
3. ¿Quién compra muchas cosas?	❑	❑	❑	❑
4. ¿Quién es muy romántico/a?	❑	❑	❑	❑
5. ¿Quién recibe muchos e-mails?	❑	❑	❑	❑
6. ¿Quién escribe mucho?	❑	❑	❑	❑
7. ¿Quién lee mucho?	❑	❑	❑	❑

B. Entrevista. Use the following cues to interview a classmate. Include expressions of frequency when appropriate.

MODELO: leer + novelas de horror ⟶
Carmen, ¿lees novelas de horror?

| (nombre de estudiante), tú tus padres/hijos tus abuelos tu mejor (*best*) amigo/a | **+** | abrir leer escribir beber vender comprender recibir vivir ¿ ? | **+** | mucho / poco la situación / los problemas de los estudiantes Coca-Cola / café antes de (*before*) la clase mi ropa (*clothing*), un estéreo viejo la puerta a (*for*) las mujeres / los hombres novelas de ciencia ficción / de horror el periódico / una revista todos los días muchas / pocas cartas, novelas, revistas muchos / pocos ejercicios, libros, regalos en una casa / un apartamento / una residencia en otra ciudad / en otro estado / país en un cuaderno / con un bolígrafo / con un lápiz |
| deber | | | | mirar mucho la televisión llegar a casa temprano |

¿Qué bebe Nora?

Lengua y cultura: Las familias Complete the following paragraphs about families. Give the correct form of the words in parentheses, as suggested by context.

¿**E**xiste la familia hispana típica? Muchas personas (creer[1]) que (todo[2]) las familias (hispano[3]) son (grande[4]). Pero el concepto de la familia (ser[5]) diferente ahora, sobre todo[a] en las ciudades (grande[6]).

(Ser[7]) cierto que la familia rural (típico[8]) es grande, pero es así[b] en casi (todo[9]) las sociedades rurales del mundo.[c] Muchos hijos (trabajar[10]) la tierra[d] con sus padres. Por eso es bueno y (necesario[11]) tener muchos niños.

Pero en los grandes centros (urbano[12]) las familias con sólo dos o tres hijos (ser[13]) más comunes. Es difícil[e] tener (mucho[14]) hijos en una sociedad (industrializado[15]). Y cuando los padres (trabajar[16]) fuera de[f] casa, ellos (pagar[17]) a quien cuide a[g] los niños. Esto pasa especialmente en las familias de la clase media.[h]

Pero no es fácil[i] (hablar[18]) de una familia (hispano[19]) típica. ¿Hay una familia (norteamericano[20]) típica?

[a]sobre... *especially* [b]es... *that's the way it is* [c]*world* [d]*land* [e]*difficult* [f]fuera... *outside of the* [g]a quien... *someone to care for* [h]*middle* [i]*easy*

Comprensión ¿Cierto o falso? Corrige (*Correct*) las oraciones falsas.

	CIERTO	FALSO
1. Todas las familias hispanas son iguales.	❑	❑
2. Las familias rurales son grandes en casi todo el mundo.	❑	❑
3. Las familias rurales necesitan tener muchos niños.	❑	❑
4. Por lo general (*Generally*), las familias urbanas son más pequeñas.	❑	❑
5. Las madres urbanas típicamente cuidan a los hijos durante el día.	❑	❑

La familia, por (*by*) Fernando Botero, de Colombia

En resumen

See the Workbook/Laboratory Manual and Online Learning Center (www.mhhe.com/apuntate) for self-tests and practice with the grammar and vocabulary presented in this chapter.

Gramática en breve

4. Adjectives: Gender, Number, and Position

Adjective Endings

SINGULAR	PLURAL
-o	-os
-a	-as
-e	-es
–[consonant]	–[consonant] + -es
-í	-íes

5. Present Tense of **ser,** Summary of Uses (Part 2)

ser: **soy, eres, es, somos, sois, son**

6. (Unstressed) Possessive Adjectives (Part 1)

Possessive Adjectives

SINGULAR: **mi(s), tu(s), su(s)**

PLURAL: **nuestro/a(s), vuestro/a(s), su(s)**

7. Present Tense of **-er** and **-ir** Verbs; Subject Pronouns (Part 2)

Regular -*er* endings

PRESENT TENSE: **-o, -es, -e, -emos, -éis, -en**

Regular -*ir* endings

PRESENT TENSE: **-o, -es, -e, -imos, -ís, -en**

Vocabulario

Los verbos

abrir	to open
aprender	to learn
aprender a + *inf.*	to learn how to (*do something*)
asistir (a)	to attend, go to (*a class, function*)
beber	to drink
comer	to eat
comprender	to understand
creer (en)	to think; to believe (in)
deber + *inf.*	should, must, ought to (*do something*)
escribir	to write
leer	to read
llegar	to arrive
mirar	to look at, watch
mirar la tele(visión)	to watch television
recibir	to receive
ser (soy, eres,...)	to be
vender	to sell
vivir	to live

La familia y los parientes

el/la abuelo/a	grandfather/grandmother
los abuelos	grandparents
el/la esposo/a	husband/wife

el/la hermano/a	brother/sister
el/la hijo/a	son/daughter
los hijos	children
la madre (mamá)	mother (mom)
el/la nieto/a	grandson/granddaughter
el/la niño/a	small child; boy/girl
el padre (papá)	father (dad)
los padres	parents
el pariente	relative
el/la primo/a	cousin
el/la sobrino/a	nephew/niece
el/la tío/a	uncle/aunt

Las mascotas

el gato	cat
la mascota	pet
el pájaro	bird
el perro	dog

Otros sustantivos

la carta	letter
la casa	house, home
la ciudad	city
el coche	car
el estado	state
el/la médico/a	(medical) doctor
el país	country

el periódico	newspaper
el regalo	present, gift
la revista	magazine

Los adjetivos

alto/a	tall
amable	kind; nice
antipático/a	unpleasant
bajo/a	short (*in height*)
bonito/a	pretty
buen, bueno/a	good
casado/a	married
corto/a	short (*in length*)
delgado/a	thin, slender
este/a	this
estos/as	these
feo/a	ugly
fiel	faithful
gordo/a	fat
gran, grande	large, big; great
guapo/a	handsome; good-looking
inteligente	intelligent
joven	young
largo/a	long
listo/a	smart; clever
mal, malo/a	bad
moreno/a	brunet(te)
mucho/a	a lot (of)
muchos/as	many
necesario/a	necessary
nuevo/a	new
otro/a	other, another
pequeño/a	small
perezoso/a	lazy
pobre	poor
posible	possible
rico/a	rich
rubio/a	blond(e)
simpático/a	nice, likeable
soltero/a	single (*not married*)
todo/a	all; every
tonto/a	silly, foolish
trabajador(a)	hardworking
viejo/a	old

talentosa   *talented*

Los adjetivos de nacionalidad

alemán/alemana	German
español(a)	Spanish
estadounidense	U.S.
inglés/inglesa	English
mexicano/a	Mexican

Los adjetivos posesivos

mi(s)	my
tu(s)	your (*fam. sing.*)
nuestro/a(s)	our
vuestro/a(s)	your (*fam. pl. Sp.*)
su(s)	his, hers, its, your (*form sing.*); their, your (*form. pl.*)

Los números del 31 al 100

treinta, cuarenta, cincuenta, sesenta, setenta, ochenta, noventa, cien (ciento)

¿Con qué frecuencia... ?

a veces	sometimes, at times
casi nunca	almost never
nunca	never
siempre	always
una vez a la semana	once a week

Repaso: con frecuencia, todos los días

Palabras adicionales

bueno...	well . . .
¿de quién?	whose?
del	of the, from the
esto	this
(no) estoy de acuerdo	I (don't) agree
para	(intended) for; in order to
por eso	for that reason
¿por qué?	why?
porque	because
que	that, which; who
según	according to
si	if
tener... años (tengo, tienes, tiene)	to be . . . years old

⏩ VOCABULARIO PERSONAL

Use this space to write down other words and phrases you learn in this chapter.

Español   **Inglés**

Un mercado callejero (*street*), en Antigua, Guatemala

1. What do you know about the woven goods of Guatemala or other Latin American countries?

2. Are there craft markets in your area? What kinds of crafts are sold?

3. Where do you prefer to shop for various items (e.g., clothing, food, household items)? Do you go to a mall, supermarket, farmer's market, boutique, . . . ?

3

De compras°

°De… *Shopping*

De compras: La ropa°

La... *Clothing*

las chanclas
la sudadera · $42
la chaqueta · $81
los pantalones · $57

las botas · $74
la camisa · $33
el traje de baño · $65
los calcetines · $12

el abrigo · $100
el vestido · $99
los zapatos de tenis · $48
la bolsa · $76

la falda · $49
el suéter · $97
el reloj · $28
el cinturón · $19

LOS VERBOS

comprar	to buy
llevar	to wear; to carry; to take
regatear	to haggle, bargain
usar	to wear; to use
vender	to sell
venden de todo	they sell (have) everything

LOS LUGARES

el almacén	department store
el centro	downtown
el centro comercial	shopping mall
el mercado	market(place)
la plaza	plaza
la tienda	shop, store

¿CUÁNTO CUESTA(N)?

la ganga	bargain
el precio	price
el precio fijo	fixed (set) price
las rebajas	sales, reductions
barato/a	inexpensive
caro/a	expensive
cómodo/a	comfortable

OTRAS PALABRAS Y EXPRESIONES ÚTILES

la blusa	blouse
la camiseta	T-shirt

la cartera	wallet; handbag	de cuadros	plaid
la corbata	tie	**(lunares, rayas)**	(polka-dot, striped)
la gorra	baseball cap	**es de (algodón,**	it is made of (cotton,
el impermeable	raincoat	**cuero, lana, oro,**	leather, wool, gold,
los *jeans**	blue jeans	**plata, seda)**†	silver, silk)
las medias	stockings		
la ropa interior	underwear	**Es de última**	
las sandalias	sandals	**moda.**	It's trendy (hot).
el sombrero	hat	**Está de moda.**	
el traje	suit		

Conversación

A. La ropa

Paso 1. ¿Qué ropa llevan estas personas?

1. El Sr. Rivera lleva
_____.

2. La Srta. Alonso
lleva _____.
El perro lleva _____.

3. Sara lleva _____.

4. Alfredo lleva _____.
Necesita comprar
_____.

Paso 2. De estas personas, ¿quién trabaja hoy? ¿Quién va a (*is going to*) una fiesta? ¿Quién no trabaja en este momento?

B. Las compras y la ropa. Completa las siguientes oraciones lógicamente con palabras de **De compras: La ropa.**

1. Un _____ es una tienda grande.
2. No es posible _____ cuando hay precios fijos.
3. En la librería, _____ de todo: textos y otros libros, cuadernos, lápices, … Hay grandes _____ al final del semestre/trimestre, en las cuales (*in which*) todo es muy barato.
4. Siempre hay *boutiques* en los _____.
5. El _____ de una ciudad es la parte céntrica.
6. Esta ropa no es para hombres: _____.
7. Esta ropa es para hombres y mujeres: _____.
8. La ropa de _____ (material) es muy elegante.

---

*The influx of U.S. goods to Latin America and Spain has affected common language. **Jeans** is one example of an English word that is commonly used in Spanish-speaking countries.
†Note another use of **ser** + **de**: to tell what material something is made of.

Vocabulario útil

The preposition **para** can be used to express *in order to*, followed by an infinitive.

Para ir al centro, me gusta llevar pantalones, una camiseta y sandalias.
(*In order*) *To go downtown, I like to wear pants, a T-shirt, and sandals.*

C. El estilo personal. Completa las siguientes oraciones lógicamente para hablar de tus preferencias con relación a la ropa.

1. Para ir a la universidad, llevo _____ .
2. Para ir a las fiestas con los amigos, llevo _____ .
3. Para pasar un día en la playa (*beach*), me gusta llevar _____ .
4. Para estar en casa todo el día, me gusta llevar _____ .
5. Nunca uso _____ .
6. No puedo vivir sin (*I can't live without*) _____ y _____ .

▶ NOTA COMUNICATIVA

More About Getting Information

Tag phrases can change statements into questions.

Aquí venden de todo, { **¿no?** / **¿verdad?** }   *They sell everything here, right? (don't they?)*

No necesito impermeable hoy, **¿verdad?** *I don't need a raincoat today, do I?*

¿Verdad? is found after affirmative or negative statements; **¿no?** is usually found after affirmative statements only. **¡OJO!** The inverted question mark comes immediately before the tag question, not at the beginning of the statement.

D. Entrevista. Using tag questions, ask a classmate questions based on the following statements. He or she will answer based on general information or as truthfully as possible .

MODELO E1: Estudias en la biblioteca por la noche, ¿verdad? (¿no?)
E2: No. Estudio en la biblioteca por la mañana. (No, no estudio en la biblioteca. Me gusta estudiar en casa.)

1. Los almacenes tienen precios fijos.
2. Regateamos mucho en este país.
3. No hay muchos mercados en esta ciudad.
4. Los *jeans* de Gap son muy baratos.
5. Es necesario llevar traje y corbata a clase.
6. Te gusta mucho la ropa elegante.
7. Tienes mucha ropa.
8. No hay rebajas en la librería.

▶ NOTA CULTURAL

La ropa en el mundo[a] hispánico

In Hispanic countries, people tend to dress more formally than do people in this country. As a rule, Hispanics consider neatness and care for one's appearance to be very important.

In the business world, women wear dressy pants, skirts, or dresses, and many wear high-heeled shoes. Men generally dress in trousers, shirts, and ties. Jeans, T-shirts, and tennis shoes are considered inappropriate in traditional business environments. Students at some business schools, like **ESAN (la Escuela de Administración de Negocios)** in Peru, are even required to wear formal business attire to attend classes, as if they were already working at a company. Shorts and sweatpants are considered very casual and are reserved almost exclusively for use at home, for a day at the beach, or for sports.

Young adults generally dress casually in social situations and, as in other countries, are often concerned with dressing according to current styles. As a rule, what is considered stylish in this country is also in style in Europe and Latin America.

[a]*world*

Ropa diseñada por (*designed by*) la famosa diseñadora venezolana Carolina Herrera

¿De qué color es?

Here are colors you can use to describe clothing and other objects.

rosado · amarillo · negro · anaranjado · gris · morado · azul · (de) color café* · verde · blanco · rojo

Conversación

A. Muchos colores. ¿Cuántos colores hay en este cuadro (*painting*) de Gonzalo Endara Crow? ¿Cuáles son?

Después de (After) *la noche*, por (*by*) Gonzalo Endara Crow, de Ecuador

---

*The expression **(de) color café** is invariable: **el sombrero (de) color café, la falda (de) color café, los pantalones (de) color café.**

B. ¡Ojo alerta! ¿Escaparates (*Window displays*) **idénticos?** These window displays are almost alike . . . but not quite! Can you find at least eight differences between them?

MODELO: En el dibujo A hay _____ , pero en el dibujo B hay _____.

A.

B.

C. Asociaciones. ¿Qué colores asocias con... ?

1. el dinero
2. la una de la mañana
3. una mañana bonita
4. una mañana fea
5. el demonio
6. este país
7. una jirafa
8. un pingüino
9. un limón
10. una naranja
11. un elefante
12. las flores (*flowers*)

¿De qué color es la jirafa? ¿Y el pingüino?

D. ¿De qué color es?

Paso 1. Tell the color of things in your classroom, especially the clothing your classmates are wearing.

MODELO: El bolígrafo de Anita es amarillo. Roberto lleva calcetines azules, una camisa de cuadros morados y azules, *jeans*…

Paso 2. Now describe what someone in the class is wearing, without revealing his or her name. Can your classmates guess whom you are describing?

MODELO: **E1:** Lleva botas negras, una camiseta blanca y *jeans*.
E2: Es Anne.

Más allá del° número 100

Más... *Beyond the*

Continúa las secuencias:

noventa y nueve, cien, ciento uno…
mil, dos mil…
un millón, dos millones…

100	cien, ciento	**700**	setecientos/as
101	ciento uno/una	**800**	ochocientos/as
200	doscientos/as	**900**	novecientos/as
300	trescientos/as	**1.000**	mil
400	cuatrocientos/as	**2.000**	dos mil
500	quinientos/as	**1.000.000**	un millón
600	seiscientos/as	**2.000.000**	dos millones

¡Doscientos quince dólares!

- **Ciento** is used in combination with numbers from 1 to 99 to express the numbers 101 through 199: **ciento uno, ciento dos, ciento setenta y nueve,** and so on. **Cien** is used in counting and before numbers greater than 100: **cien mil, cien millones.**

- When the numbers 200 through 900 modify a noun, they must agree in gender: **cuatrocientas niñas, doscientas dos casas.**

- **Mil** means *one thousand* or *a thousand*. It does not have a plural form in counting, but **millón** does. When followed directly by a noun, **millón** (**dos millones**, and so on) must be followed by **de.**

mil gracias	un millón **de** gracias
3.000 habitantes	tres mil habitantes
14.000.000 **de** habitantes	catorce millones **de** habitantes

- Note how years are expressed in Spanish.

1899	mil ochocientos noventa y nueve
2008	dos mil ocho

¡OJO!

In many parts of the Spanish-speaking world, a period in numerals is used where English uses a comma, and a comma is used to indicate the decimal where English uses a period: **$1.500; $1.000.000; $10,45; 65,9%.**

Conversación

A. ¿Cuánto cuesta(n)? En parejas, expresen los siguientes precios en dólares en español. Luego (*Then*) calculen los precios en quetzales y en lempiras, las monedas (*currency*) de Guatemala y Honduras, respectivamente (*respectively*).

Vocabulario útil

1 dólar estadounidense	= 8 quetzales (*m.*) (aproximadamente)
	= 20 lempiras (aproximadamente)

1. unos *jeans* de moda: $100
2. unos zapatos de tenis tipo NBA: $150
3. un anillo (*ring*) de diamantes: $1.200
4. unos aretes (*earrings*) de oro: $225
5. una tela (*fabric*) de artesanía local de excelente calidad: $400
6. un cinturón de cuero de un diseñador (*designer*) famoso: $330
7. un coche europeo: $75.000
8. una casa grande en una zona residencial muy exclusiva: $2.000.000
9. un edificio de apartamentos: $15.800.000

B. ¿Cuánto pesan? (*How much do they weigh?*)

Paso 1. Estos son los animales terrestres más grandes. ¿Cuánto pesan en kilos? **¡OJO!** Usa el artículo masculino para todos los nombres, menos para (*except for*) **jirafa** y **gorila.**

MODELO: El elefante pesa cinco mil kilos.

Paso 2. Pregúntale (*Ask*) a un compañero o compañera cuánto pesan aproximadamente en libras los siguientes animales y objetos.

1. un perro/gato
2. su mochila con los libros
3. un coche
4. su libro de español
5. el animal más grande del mundo

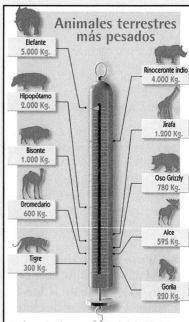

Animales terrestres más pesados

Elefante 5.000 Kg.
Hipopótamo 2.000 Kg.
Bisonte 1.000 Kg.
Dromedario 600 Kg.
Tigre 300 Kg.
Rinoceronte indio 4.000 Kg.
Jirafa 1.200 Kg.
Oso Grizzly 780 Kg.
Alce 595 Kg.
Gorila 220 Kg.

De los animales terrestres, el elefante, con sus 5.000 kilos de peso medio entre todas sus especies, es sin duda el mamífero más pesado. El hipopótamo y el rinoceronte son los siguientes en la lista, y el hombre, ni aparece.

Need more practice?
- Workbook/Laboratory Manual
- Online Learning Center
  [www.mhhe.com/apuntate]

Pronunciación

Stress and Written Accent Marks (Part 2)

¿Recuerdas?

In the **Pronunciación** section of **Capítulo 2,** you learned that most Spanish words do not need a written accent mark because their pronunciation is completely predictable by native speakers. Review the two basic rules of Spanish word stress by looking at the examples and completing the rules. The stressed syllable is underlined.

- Examples: **li**bro, **me**sa, e**xa**men, i**ma**gen, **e**res, **gra**cias

  A word that ends in a _____ , _____ , or _____ is stressed on the next-to-last syllable.

- Examples: bai**lar,** us**ted,** pa**pel,** es**toy**

  A word that ends in _____ is stressed on the last syllable.

The written accent mark is used in the following situations.

- A written accent mark is needed when a word does not follow the two basic rules reviewed in **¿Recuerdas?**
- Look at the words in this group.

  ta-bú   ca-fé   a-le-mán   na-ción   in-glés   es-tás

The preceding words end in a vowel, **-n**, or **-s**, so one would predict that they would be stressed on the next-to-last syllable. But the written accent mark shows that they are in fact accented on the last syllable.

- Now look at the words in this group.

  lá-piz   dó-lar   ál-bum   á-gil   dó-cil

  The preceding words end in a consonant (other than **-n** or **-s**), so one would predict that they would be stressed on the last syllable. But the written accent mark shows that they are in fact accented on the next-to-last syllable.

- All words that are stressed on the third-to-last syllable must have a written accent mark, regardless of which letter they end in.

  bo-lí-gra-fo   ma-trí-cu-la   ma-te-má-ti-cas

- When two consecutive vowels do not form a diphthong (see **Pronunciación, Cap. 1**), the vowel that receives the spoken stress will have a written accent mark. This pattern is very frequent in words that end in **-ía**.

  Ma-rí-a   po-li-cí-a   as-tro-no-mí-a

  dí-a   bio-lo-gí-a

- Some one-syllable words have accents to distinguish them from other words that sound like them. For example:

  él (*he*)/el (*the*)   tú (*you*)/tu (*your*)

  sí (*yes*)/si (*if*)   mí (*me*)/mi (*my*)

- Interrogative and exclamatory words have a written accent on the stressed vowel. For example:

  ¿quién?   ¿dónde?   ¡Qué ganga! (*What a bargain!*)

¡OJO!

Contrast the pronunciation of those words with the following words in which the vowels **i** and **a** *do* form a diphthong: **Patricia, Francia, infancia, distancia.**

A. Sílabas. The following words have been separated into syllables for you. Read them aloud, paying careful attention to where the spoken stress should fall. Don't worry about the meaning of words you haven't heard before. The rules you have learned will help you pronounce them correctly.

1. a-quí   pa-pá   a-diós   bus-qué
2. prác-ti-co   mur-cié-la-go te-lé-fo-no   ar-chi-pié-la-go
3. Ji-mé-nez   Ro-drí-guez   Pé-rez   Gó-mez
4. si-co-lo-gí-a so-cio-lo-gí-a sa-bi-du-rí-a   e-ner-gí-a
5. his-to-ria   te-ra-pia   Pre-to-ria   me-mo-ria

B. Reglas (*Rules*). Indicate the stressed vowel of each word in the following list. Give the rule that determines the stress of each word.

1. exámenes
2. lápiz
3. necesitar
4. perezoso
5. actitud
6. acciones
7. dólares
8. francés
9. están
10. hombre
11. peso
12. mujer
13. plástico
14. María
15. Rodríguez
16. Patricia

Un lápiz corto

Guatemala y Honduras

MAR CARIBE

MÉXICO · BELICE

HONDURAS

GUATEMALA

Ciudad de Guatemala ✯ · ✯Tegucigalpa

NICARAGUA

EL SALVADOR

COSTA RICA

PANAMÁ

OCÉANO PACÍFICO

DATOS ESENCIALES

GUATEMALA

NOMBRE OFICIAL: República de Guatemala
CAPITAL: Ciudad de Guatemala
POBLACIÓN: más de (*more than*) 12 millones de habitantes

HONDURAS

NOMBRE OFICIAL: República de Honduras
CAPITAL: Tegucigalpa
POBLACIÓN: más de 7 millones de habitantes

FÍJATE

GUATEMALA

- Guatemala es el país centroamericano más poblado[a] y el corazón[b] de la civilización maya.
- Esta civilización antigua tenía[c] un sistema de escritura jeroglífica que usaba[d] para documentar su historia, sus costumbres religiosas y su mitología.
- El calendario maya era[e] el calendario más exacto de su época.
- Hoy día, los maya-quichés componen[f] más del 40 por ciento de la población del país y son famosos por sus tejidos[g] y otras artesanías.[h]

HONDURAS

- El nombre indígena de la capital, Tegucigalpa, significa «cerros de plata».[i] Honduras recibió[j] este nombre en español por la profundidad[k] de sus aguas del Caribe.
- La zona arqueológica de Copán es hoy un parque nacional que tiene ruinas mayas impresionantes.
- La riqueza[l] de la ecología y los recursos[m] naturales de Honduras contrastan con la suma pobreza[n] de dos tercios[o] de su población.

[a]*populous* [b]*heart* [c]*had* [d]*it used* [e]*was* [f]*make up* [g]*woven goods* [h]*crafts* [i]*cerros... hills of silver* [j]*received* [k]*depth* [l]*richness* [m]*resources* [n]*suma... extreme poverty* [o]*dos... two thirds*

¡MÚSICA!

La música de Guatemala y Honduras es una mezcla[a] de tradiciones indígenas, africanas y europeas. Los instrumentos típicos de la música folclórica son la marimba y la caracola.[b] La marimba, el instrumento musical más característico de la región, es también el instrumento nacional de Guatemala. La música tradicional se conserva en algunos grupos indígenas de Honduras, como los lencas con su baile «el guancasco» y los garífunas con su música y su baile «la punta».

[a]*mixture* [b]*conch shell*

★ LA MÚSICA DE LOS GARÍFUNAS

La población garífuna deja[a] su marca musical con «la punta», un tipo de música y baile de tradición claramente africana. Los garífunas, un pueblo[b] de origen africano e indígena, vive a lo largo de la Bahía[c] de Honduras, desde[d] Belice hasta Nicaragua.

[a]*leaves, makes* [b]*people* [c]*Bay* [d]*from*

Un grupo garífuna que toca y baila «la punta»

¿Recuerdas?

You learned the four forms of the demonstrative adjective **este** in **Gramática 4** (**Cap. 2**). Review them now by completing these phrases.

1. est____ pantalones
2. est____ falda
3. est____ blusas
4. est____ abrigo

8 Pointing Out People and Things • Demonstrative Adjectives (Part 2) and Pronouns

Gramática en acción: Suéteres a buenos precios

Susana busca un suéter en el mercado con su amigo Jorge.

SUSANA: ¿Cuánto cuesta este suéter?

VENDEDOR: Bueno, ese que Ud. tiene en la mano cuesta 800 quetzales. Este aquí cuesta 700 quetzales.

SUSANA: ¡Qué caros!

VENDEDOR: Es que todos son de pura lana. Mire aquellos suéteres de rayas sobre aquella mesa. Sólo cuestan 300 quetzales. Son acrílicos.

SUSANA: Muchas gracias.

Comprensión. ¿Quién habla, Susana, su amigo Jorge o el vendedor?

1. «Estos suéteres de rayas son bonitos. ¡Y sólo cuestan 300 quetzales!»
2. «Los suéteres en aquella mesa no son de pura lana.»
3. «Compro este suéter. Me gusta la ropa de lana.»
4. «Estos suéteres acrílicos son más baratos que aquellos de lana.»

Sweaters at good prices Susana is looking for a sweater in the market with her friend Jorge. **Susana:** How much is this sweater? **Salesman:** Well, that one that you have in your hand costs 800 quetzales. This one here costs 700 quetzales. **Susana:** (They're) So expensive! **Salesman:** It's because they're all pure wool. Take a look at those striped sweaters on that table (over there). They only cost 300 quetzales. They're acrylic. **Susana:** Thanks a lot.

Demonstrative Adjectives (Part 2)

	Demonstrative Adjectives				
	Singular			**Plural**	
this	este abrigo	esta gorra	these	estos abrigos	estas gorras
that	ese abrigo (allí)	esa gorra (allí)	those	esos abrigos (allí)	esas gorras (allí)
	aquel abrigo (allá)	aquella gorra (allá)		aquellos abrigos (allá)	aquellas gorras (allá)

¡OJO!

Note that the final **-e** in the singular forms **este** and **ese** changes to an **-o-** in the plural: **estos, esos**.

1. **Agreement** To indicate a specific noun or nouns, *demonstrative adjectives* (**los adjetivos demostrativos**) are used. In Spanish, demonstrative adjectives precede the nouns they modify. They also agree in number and gender with the nouns.

2. **Using *ese* and *aquel*** In the chart above, the word **allí** (*there*) is provided as a clue that forms of **ese** refer to something that is distant from the speaker, and **allá** (*way over there*) is a clue that forms of **aquel** refer to something even farther away. However, it is not at all obligatory to use these words when using forms of **ese** and **aquel**.

   There are two ways to say *that/those* in Spanish. Forms of **ese** refer to nouns that are not close to the speaker in space or in time. Forms of **aquel** refer to nouns that are even farther away.

demonstrative adjective = an adjective used to indicate a particular person, place, thing, or idea

Este niño es mi hijo. **Ese** joven allí es mi hijo también. Y **aquel** señor allá es mi esposo.
This boy is my son. That young man there is also my son. And that man way over there is my husband.

Demonstrative Pronouns

1. **Demonstrative Pronouns** To point out or indicate people, places, things, or ideas when omitting the noun they refer to (remember that pronouns replace nouns), *demonstrative pronouns* (**los pronombres demostrativos**) are used. Demonstrative pronouns are the same as demonstrative adjectives, except that the noun is not used.* In English, the demonstrative pronouns are *this (one), that (one), these,* and *those.*

2. **Agreement of Demonstrative Pronouns** In Spanish, demonstrative pronouns agree in gender and number with the noun they are replacing (as in the preceding examples).

   [Práctica A–B]

—¿Te gusta **aquella casa** allá?
Do you like that house way over there?
—¿Cuál?
Which one?
—**Aquella**, con las ventanas grandes.
***That one**, with the big windows.*
—¡Ah, **aquella** me gusta mucho!
*Oh, I like **that** one a lot!*

---

*Some Spanish speakers prefer to use accents on these forms: **este coche y ése, aquella casa y ésta**. However, it is acceptable in modern Spanish, per the **Real Academia Española** in Madrid, to omit the accent on these forms when context makes the meaning clear and no ambiguity is possible. To learn more about these forms, consult the Online Learning Center, Appendix 2, Using Adjectives as Nouns.*

3. **Neuter Demonstratives** The neuter demonstratives **esto, eso,** and **aquello** are used to refer to as yet unidentified objects or to a whole idea, concept, or situation.

[Práctica C–D]

¿Qué es **esto**?
What is this?

Eso es todo.
That's it. That's all.

¡Aquello es terrible!
That's terrible!

¡OJO!

Esto es una mochila.
(to identify in general)
This is a backpack.

Esta es mi mochila.
(to identify one out of a group)
This (one) is my backpack.

Práctica

A. Cambios (*Changes*)

Paso 1. Restate the sentences, changing forms of **este** to **ese** and adding **también**, following the model.

> **MODELO:** Este abrigo es muy grande. ⟶
> *Ese* abrigo también es muy grande.

1. Esta falda es muy pequeña.
2. Estos pantalones son muy largos.
3. Este libro es muy bueno.
4. Estas corbatas son muy feas.

Paso 2. Now change the forms of **este** to **aquel.**

> **MODELO:** Este abrigo es muy grande. ⟶
> *Aquel* abrigo allí también es muy grande.

B. Más or menos

Paso 1. With a classmate, determine how much the following items cost, using **¿Cuánto cuesta(n)... ?** and the correct form of **aquel.** Keep track of the prices that you decide on. Follow the model.

> **MODELO:** una chaqueta de cuero ⟶
> **E1:** ¿Cuánto cuesta aquella chaqueta de cuero?
> **E2:** Cuesta doscientos dólares.

1. una calculadora pequeña
2. un coche nuevo/usado
3. una computadora Mac/IBM
4. un reloj Timex / de oro
5. unos zapatos de tenis (**¡OJO!** cuesta**n**)

Paso 2. Now compare the prices you selected with those of others in the class. What is the most expensive thing on the list? (**¿Cuál es el objeto más caro?**) What is the least expensive? (**¿Cuál es el más barato?**)

C. Situaciones. Find an appropriate response for each situation.
1. Aquí hay un regalo para ti (*you*).
2. Ocurre un accidente de coche.
3. No hay clases mañana.
4. La matrícula cuesta más este semestre/trimestre.
5. Tienes A en tu examen de español.

AUTOPRUEBA

Match each word with the corresponding meaning in English.

1. _____ estas   **a.** that
2. _____ aquellos   **b.** those (*over there*)
3. _____ ese   **c.** these
4. _____ esas   **d.** this
5. _____ este   **e.** those

Answers: 1. c 2. b 3. a 4. e 5. d

Vocabulario útil

¡Eso es un desastre!
¡Eso es magnífico!
¿Qué es esto?
¡Eso es terrible!

D. En una tienda

Paso 1. Completa el siguiente diálogo con los demostrativos apropiados. (**¡OJO!** *Imagine that the client and the salesman are standing next to you and that you are all looking at the mannequins from your point of view. Thus, the mannequin with the red sweater and blue slacks is closest to you.*)

VENDEDOR: ¿Qué suéter le gusta? ¿_____¹ rojo que está aquí?

CLINETE: No, el rojo no.

VENDEDOR: ¿_____² suéter amarillo?

CLIENTE: No, tampocoª el amarillo. ¡Me gusta _____³ anaranjado de allá!

ªNo... *No, not [the yellow one] either*

Paso 2. Empareja (*Match*) el color de los pantalones con el demostrativo apropiado, según la distancia.

1. _____ los pantalones negros
2. _____ los pantalone azules
3. _____ los pantalones color kaki

a. estos
b. esos
c. aquellos

Need more practice?
- Workbook/Laboratory Manual
- Online Learning Center [www.mhhe.com/apuntate]

Conversación

En la alcoba (*bedroom*) **de Ernesto.** Working with a partner, imagine that you are the person depicted in the drawing, who is looking into Ernesto's bedroom. Some objects and items of clothing are close to you, some are a bit farther away, and some are at the other end of the room. Describe them as accurately as you can, using the appropriate demonstrative adjectives and all of the vocabulary you have learned so far.

MODELOS: Esta mesa es de madera.
Ese gato es blanco.
Aquel gato está en la silla.

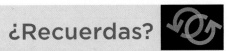

You began using the singular forms of the verb **tener** in **Capítulo 2**. Review them by completing the following verb forms.

1. tú t____nes   **2.** yo te____o   **3.** Julio t____ne

You will learn about similar patterns in **Gramática 9**.

9 Expressing Actions and States • Tener, venir, preferir, querer, and poder; Some Idioms with tener

Gramática en acción: Un mensaje telefónico

Hola, Jorge, soy yo, Jaqui.

Como tú sabes, yo siempre prefiero comprar la ropa en los grandes almacenes. Pero hoy no tengo tiempo de ir al centro. Quiero comprar una camisa para Juan Miguel para su cumpleaños mañana. Creo que puedo encontrar algo aquí en una *boutique*.

¿Puedes ayudarme?

¡¡Llámame!! O mejor todavía… ¿por qué no vienes a mi casa?

Un millón de gracias, Jorge. Hasta pronto.

Comprensión. Ahora vuelve a contar (*retell*) la conversación de Jaqui. Todos los infinitivos terminan en **-er** o **-ir**.

1. Jaqui prefier_____ comprar en un almacén.
2. Pero hoy no tien_____ tiempo de ir al centro.
3. Quier_____ comprar algo para un amigo.
4. Cree que pued_____ encontrar una camisa en una *boutique*.
5. Su amigo Jorge, ¿vien_____ a ayudarla (*help her*) a hacer la compra (*shop*)?
¿Qué crees?

Tener, venir, preferir, querer, and poder

tener (to have)		venir (to come)		preferir (to prefer)		querer (to want)		poder (to be able, can)	
tengo	tenemos	vengo	venimos	prefiero	preferimos	quiero	queremos	puedo	podemos
tienes	tenéis	vienes	venís	prefieres	preferís	quieres	queréis	puedes	podéis
tiene	tienen	viene	vienen	prefiere	prefieren	quiere	quieren	puede	pueden

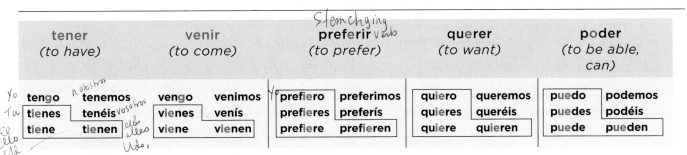

A phone message Hello, Jorge, it's me, Jaqui. As you know, I always like to buy clothes in big department stores. But today I don't have time to go downtown. I want to buy a shirt for Juan Miguel for his birthday tomorrow. I think (that) I can find something here in a boutique. Can you help me? Call me!!! Or better yet . . . why don't you come to my house? Thanks a lot (lit. a million thanks), Jorge. See you soon.

- The **yo** forms of **tener** and **venir** are irregular.
- In other forms of **tener** and **venir**, and in **preferir** and **querer**, when the stem vowel **e** is stressed, it becomes **ie**.
- Similarly, the stem vowel **o** in **poder** becomes **ue** when stressed.
- In vocabulary lists these changes are shown in parentheses after the infinitive: **poder (puedo)**. Verbs of this type are called stem-changing verbs. You will learn more verbs of this type in **Gramática 12 (Cap. 4)**.
- The verbs **poder, preferir,** and **querer** can be followed by an infinitive, like **deber, desear,** and **necesitar**.

tener: yo **tengo,** tú **tienes** (e $\longrightarrow$ ie)…
venir: yo **vengo,** tú **vienes** (e $\longrightarrow$ ie)…

preferir, querer: (e $\longrightarrow$ ie)

poder: (o $\longrightarrow$ ue)

¡OJO!

The **nosotros** and **vosotros** forms of these verbs do not have changes in the stem vowel because it is not stressed.

¿Puedes correr muy rápido?
Can you run very fast?

¿Qué **quieres/prefieres hacer** hoy?
What do you want/prefer to do today?

¡OJO!

You will learn to use the verb **hacer** (*to do* or *to make*) in **Gramática 11 (Cap. 4).** Learn to recognize it in questions and direction lines.

Some Idioms with **tener**

1. **Conditions or States** Many ideas expressed in English with the verb *to be* are expressed in Spanish with *idioms* (**los modismos**) using **tener.** You already know one: **tener… años.** At right and below are some more. They describe a condition or state.

idiom = an expression whose meaning cannot be inferred from the meaning of the words that make it up

Idiomatic expressions are often different from one language to another. For example, in English, *to pull Mary's leg* usually means *to tease her,* not *to grab her leg and pull it.* In Spanish, *to pull Mary's leg* is **tomarle el pelo a Mary** (lit. *to take hold of Mary's hair*).

tener **miedo (de)**

tener **sueño**

tener **prisa**

tener **razón**

no tener **razón**

2. *Tener* Idioms + Infinitive Other **tener** idioms include **tener ganas de** (*to feel like*) and **tener que** (*to have to*). The infinitive is always used after these two idiomatic expressions.

Note that the English translation of one of these examples results in a verb ending in *-ing*, not the infinitive.

Tengo ganas de comer.
I feel like eating.

¿No tiene Ud. que leer este capítulo?
Don't you have to read this chapter?

AUTOPRUEBA

Give the missing letters in each verb.

1. p____des
2. pref____re
3. ve____o

4. t____nemos
5. qu____ro
6. t____nen

Answers: **1.** puedes **2.** prefiere **3.** vengo **4.** tenemos **5.** quiero **6.** tienen

Práctica

A. ¡Sara tiene mucha tarea (*homework*)!

Paso 1. Haz (*Form*) oraciones completas con las palabras indicadas. Añade (*Add*) palabras si es necesario.

> **MODELO:** Sara / tener / que / estudiar / mucho / hoy →
> Sara tiene que estudiar mucho hoy.

1. Sara / tener / muchos exámenes
2. (ella) venir / a / universidad / todos los días
3. hoy / trabajar / hasta / nueve / de / noche
4. preferir / estudiar / en / biblioteca
5. querer / leer / más / pero / no poder
6. por eso / regresar / a / casa
7. tener / ganas de / leer / más
8. pero / unos amigos / venir a mirar / televisión
9. Sara / decidir / mirar / televisión / con ellos

Paso 2. Now retell the same sequence of events, first as if they had happened to you, using **yo** as the subject of all but item 8, then as if they had happened to you and your roommate, using **nosotros/as**.

Sara tiene que estudiar mucho hoy. Yo también tengo que estudiar mucho.

B. Situaciones. Match each statement with the appropriate response.

SITUACIONES
1. El niño es muy joven.
2. En esa casa, hay un perro grande y furioso.
3. Son las tres de la mañana.
4. Pablito dice (*says*): «Dos y dos son… seis».
5. Ahora Pablito dice: «Buenos Aires es la capital de la Argentina».
6. Tenemos que estar en el centro a las tres y ya son (*it's already*) las tres menos cuatro.
7. Los exámenes de la clase de español son muy fáciles (*easy*).

RESPUESTAS
a. Tengo mucho sueño.
b. Yo tengo miedo del perro.
c. Sólo tiene dos años.
d. Tiene razón.
e. Por eso no tengo que estudiar mucho.
f. No tiene razón.
g. Por eso tenemos mucha prisa.

Need more **practice?**
- Workbook/Laboratory Manual
- Online Learning Center [www.mhhe.com/apuntate]

Conversación

A. Los estereotipos.
Draw some conclusions about Isabel based on this scene. Think about things that she has, likes, needs to or has to do or buy, and so on. When you have finished, compare your predictions with those of a classmate. Did you reach the same conclusions?

MODELO: Isabel tiene cuatro gatos. Tiene que…

Vocabulario útil

los aretes
el juguete toy
los muebles furniture
el sofá

hablar por télefono
tener alergia a to be allergic to

⊕ NOTA COMUNICATIVA

Using *mucho* and *poco*

In the first chapters of *¡Apúntate!* you have used the words **mucho** and **poco** as both adjectives and adverbs. *Adverbs* (**Los adverbios**) are words that modify verbs, adjectives, or other adverbs: *quickly*, *very* smart, *very* quickly. In Spanish and in English, adverbs are invariable in form. However, in Spanish adjectives agree in number and gender with the word they modify.

ADVERBS

Rosario estudia **mucho** hoy.	*Rosario is studying a lot today.*
Julio come **poco**.	*Julio doesn't eat much.*

ADJECTIVES

Rosario tiene **mucha** ropa. Sobre todo tiene **muchos** zapatos.	*Rosario has a lot of clothes. She especially has a lot of shoes.*
Julio come **poca** carne. Come **pocos** postres.	*Julio doesn't eat much meat. He eats few desserts.*

B. Las circunstancias personales

Paso 1. Choose a partner, but before working with him or her, try to predict the choices he or she will make in each of the following cases.

> **MODELO:** Tiene muchos / pocos libros. ⟶
> Mi compañero tiene pocos libros.

1. Tiene mucho / poco trabajo académico este semestre/trimestre.
2. Tiene mucho / poco dinero. Es muy rico/a / pobre.
3. Viene en coche / en autobús / a pie (*on foot*) a la universidad todos los días.
4. Prefiere estudiar en la biblioteca / en casa / en la residencia.
5. Quiere comprar un abrigo de cuero / una sudadera con el logo de la universidad.
6. Puede correr (*run*) una milla en menos / más de (*than*) cinco minutos.
7. Tiene muchas ganas de estudiar / bailar esta noche.
8. Tiene mucha / poca ropa.

Paso 2. Now, using tag questions, ask your partner questions to find out if you guessed correctly in **Paso 1**.

> **MODELO:** E1: Tienes muchos libros, ¿verdad?
> E2: Sí, tengo muchos libros. (No, tengo pocos libros.)

C. Entrevista.
En parejas, túrnense (*take turns*) para entrevistarse sobre los siguientes temas. Deben añadir una pregunta original para cada (*each*) verbo.

1. preferir: ¿los gatos o los perros? ¿mirar una película (*movie*) en casa o ir al cine (*theater*)? ¿la ropa elegante o la ropa cómoda? ¿ ?
2. tener: ¿mucho dinero o muchas deudas (*debts*)? ¿una familia grande o pequeña? ¿sueño en clase con frecuencia? ¿ ?
3. venir: ¿a clase tarde o temprano? ¿de una familia anglosajona, hispana o de otro origen? ¿ ?
4. (¿qué?) querer: ¿comprar esta semana? / ¿ser en el futuro (profesión)? ¿ ?
5. poder: ¿hablar una lengua extranjera? ¿hacer algo especial? ¿ ?

1 **El Templo del Gran Jaguar en las ruinas de Tikal, Guatemala** Tikal, en Guatemala, es la ciudad maya antigua más grande. Tiene quince kilómetros cuadrados[a] y más de 3.000 estructuras que incluyen[b] acrópolis,[c] plazas, templos y palacios. Tikal tiene la estructura indígena más alta del continente americano. El Templo del Gran Sacerdote[d] mide aproximadamente 69,8 metros.[e]

[a]quince... *5.8 square miles*   [b]*include*
[c]*elevated terraces*   [d]*Gran... High Priest*   [e]mide... *measures about 229 feet tall*

3 **Volcanes al oeste[a] de Guatemala** En el oeste de Guatemala hay más de treinta volcanes, algunos de los cuales[b] son activos. La mayoría de[c] los maya-quichés vive en esta zona montañosa.[d]

[a]*west*   [b]algunos... *some of which*   [c]La... *Most of*   [d]*mountainous*

4 **Una estela[a] de Copán, Honduras** Las ruinas de Copán son más pequeñas que otras ruinas mayas, pero tienen gran importancia por su cantidad[b] de jeroglíficos. En la Gran Plaza de Copán hay dieciséis estelas. Estos monumentos representan a líderes[c] mayas y están cubiertos[d] de muchos jeroglíficos.

[a]*carved stone column*   [b]*quantity*
[c]*leaders*   [d]*covered*

2 **Máscaras en un mercado de Chichicastenango, Guatemala** En los coloridos[a] mercados de Guatemala venden una variedad[b] de tejidos[c] de lana, artículos de cuero y otras artesanías.

[a]*colorful*   [b]*variety*   [c]*woven objects*

5 **La Bahía[a] de Honduras** Esta bahía caribeña,[b] que está al sur[c] de la Península de Yucatán, limita con[d] Belice, Guatemala y Honduras. Aquí se encuentran[e] las Islas de la Bahía de Honduras, que por muchos años fueron habitadas por[f] piratas.

[a]*Bay*   [b]*Caribbean*   [c]al... *to the south*   [d]limita... *borders*   [e]se... *are found*
[f]fueron... *were inhabited by*

10 Expressing Destination and Future Actions • Ir; Ir + a + *Infinitive*; The Contraction al

Gramática en acción: ¿Adónde vas?

Rosa y Casandra son compañeras de cuarto.

CASANDRA: ¿Adónde vas?
ROSA: Voy al centro.
CASANDRA: ¿Qué vas a hacer en el centro?
ROSA: Voy a comprar un vestido para la fiesta de Javier. ¿No vas a ir a su fiesta este fin de semana?
CASANDRA: ¡Claro que voy!

Comprensión. ¿Cierto o falso? Corrige las oraciones falsas.

	CIERTO	FALSO
1. Rosa va a estudiar.	☐	☐
2. Rosa va a comprar algo.	☐	☐
3. Casandra va a asistir a la fiesta.	☐	☐

The Verb ir

Ir is the irregular Spanish verb used to express *to go*.

ir *(to go)*	
voy	vamos
vas	vais
va	van

The first person plural of **ir**, **vamos** (*we go, are going, do go*), is also used to express *let's go*.

Vamos a clase ahora mismo.
Let's go to class right now.

Ir + a + *infinitive*

Ir + a + *infinitive* is used to describe actions or events in the near future.

Van a venir a la fiesta esta noche.
They're going to come to the party tonight.

¡OJO!

This structure is like **aprender + a + *infinitive***, which you learned in **Gramática 7 (Cap. 2).**

Where are you going? Rosa and Casandra are roommates. **Casandra:** Where are you going? **Rosa:** I'm going downtown. **Casandra:** What are you going to do downtown? **Rosa:** I'm going to buy a dress for Javier's party. Aren't you going to go to his party this weekend? **Casandra:** Of course I'm going!

The Contraction al

In **Capítulo 2** you learned about the contraction **del** (**de** + **el** ⟶ **del**). The only other contraction in Spanish is **al** (**a** + **el** ⟶ **al**).

a + **el** ⟶ **al**

Voy **al** centro comercial.
I'm going to the mall.

Vamos **a la** tienda.
We're going to the store.

¡OJO!

Both **del** and **al** are obligatory contractions.

Práctica

A. ¿Adónde van de compras?
Haz oraciones completas, usando (*using*) **ir**. Recuerda: **a** + **el** ⟶ **al**.

MODELO: Marta / el centro ⟶ Marta *va al* centro.

1. nosotros / una boutique
2. Francisco / el almacén Goya
3. Juan y Raúl / el centro comercial
4. tú / un mercado
5. Ud. / una tienda pequeña
6. yo / ¿ ?

B. Mañana

Paso 1. Usa las siguientes frases para expresar lo que (*what*) vas a hacer o no hacer mañana.

MODELO: ir de compras ⟶ Mañana no *voy a ir* de compras.

1. ir a un centro comercial
2. comer en la cafetería de la universidad
3. estudiar en la biblioteca
4. escribir e-mails
5. venir a la clase de español
6. poder hacer toda mi tarea (*homework*)
7. bailar en una discoteca

Paso 2. Ahora usa las frases del **Paso 1** para entrevistar a un compañero o compañera.

MODELO: ir de compras ⟶ ¿Vas a ir de compras mañana?

Vocabulario útil

el cine movie theater
el mercadillo flea market

Conversación

A. ¿Adónde vas? ¿Cuántas oraciones puede hacer?

MODELO: Me gusta leer novelas. Por eso voy a una librería.

Me gusta **+**
leer.
ir de compras.
buscar gangas y regatear.
hablar con mis amigos.
comer en restaurantes.
mirar programas de detectives.
ver películas (*movies*)
+ Por eso voy a _____.

B. Entrevista: Este fin de semana.

Entrevista a un compañero o compañera sobre sus planes para el fin de semana. Aquí hay unas actividades posibles. Traten de obtener (*Try to get*) mucha información. **¡OJO! ¿adónde?** = *where to?*

MODELO: ir de compras ⟶ ¿Vas a ir de compras este fin de semana? ¿Adónde vas a ir? ¿Por qué vas a ese centro comercial? ¿Qué vas a comprar?

¿Vas a... ?

1. ir de compras
2. leer una novela
3. asistir a un concierto
4. estudiar para un examen
5. ir a una fiesta

6. escribir una carta
7. ir a bailar
8. escribir la tarea
9. practicar un deporte (*sport*)
10. mirar mucho la televisión

UN POCO DE TODO

Lengua y cultura: Pero, ¿no se puede* (*can't one*) regatear? Complete the following paragraphs about shopping. Give the correct form of the words in parentheses, as suggested by context. When two possibilities are given in parentheses, select the correct word.

¿**T**e gusta ir de compras? ¿Te gusta regatear? En (los/las[1]) ciudades hispánicas, hay una (grande[2]) variedad de tiendas para (ir[3]) de compras. Hay almacenes, centros comerciales y *boutiques* (elegante[4]), como en (este[5]) país, en donde los precios son siempre (fijo[6]).

También hay tiendas (pequeño[7]) que venden un solo[a] producto. Por ejemplo,[b] en una zapatería sólo hay zapatos. En español el sufijo **-ería** se usa[c] para (formar[8]) el nombre de la tienda. ¿Dónde (creer[9]) tú que venden papel y (otro[10]) artículos de escritorio? ¿A qué tienda (ir[11]) a ir a comprar fruta?

Si (poder[12]) pagar el precio que piden,[d] (deber[13]) comprar los recuerdos[e] en (los/las[14]) almacenes o *boutiques*. Pero si (tener[15]) ganas o necesidad de regatear, tienes (de/que[16]) ir a un mercado: un conjunto[f] de tiendas o puestos[g] donde el ambiente[h] es más (informal[17]) que[i] en los (grande[18]) almacenes. No (deber[19]) pagar el primer[j] precio que pide el vendedor.[k] ¡Casi siempre va (a/de[20]) ser muy alto!

[a]*single* [b]*Por... For example* [c]*se... is used* [d]*they ask* [e]*souvenirs* [f]*group* [g]*stalls* [h]*atmosphere* [i]*than* [j]*first* [k]*que... that the seller asks for*

Una frutería en Sevilla, España

Comprensión. ¿Cierto o falso? Corrige las oraciones falsas.

	CIERTO	FALSO
1. En el mundo hispánico, todas las tiendas son similares.	❏	❏
2. Uno puede regatear en un almacén hispánico.	❏	❏
3. Es posible comprar limones en una papelería.	❏	❏
4. En un mercado, el vendedor siempre pide un precio bajo al principio (*beginning*).	❏	❏

Note that placing the word **se before a verb changes its meaning slightly: **puede** = he/she/you can; **se puede** = one can. You will learn how to use this structure in **Capítulo 7**.*

See the Workbook/Laboratory Manual and Online Learning Center (www.mhhe.com/apuntate) for self-tests and practice with the grammar and vocabulary presented in this chapter.

Gramática en breve

8. Pointing Out People and Things — Demonstrative Adjectives (Part 2) and Pronouns

Demonstrative Adjectives and Pronouns

this	these	that	those	that *(over there)*	those *(over there)*
este	**estos**	**ese**	**esos**	**aquel**	**aquellos**
esta	**estas**	**esa**	**esas**	**aquella**	**aquellas**

Neuter Demonstratives

esto	**eso**	**aquello**

9. Expressing Actions and States — **Tener, venir, preferir, querer,** and **poder;** Some Idioms with **tener**

tener: tengo, tienes, tiene, tenemos, tenéis, tienen

venir: vengo, vienes, viene, venimos, venís, vienen

preferir: prefiero, prefieres, prefiere, preferimos, preferís, prefieren

querer: quiero, quieres, quiere, queremos, queréis, quieren

poder: puedo, puedes, puede, podemos, podéis, pueden

10. Expressing Destination and Future Actions — **Ir; Ir + a +** *Infinitive*; The Contraction **al**

ir: **voy, vas, va, vamos, vais, van**

Vocabulario

[handwritten: los tacones / zepatos de taco alto } hi-heels]

Los verbos

ir (voy, vas,...)	to go
ir a + *inf.*	to be going to *(do something)*
ir de compras	to go shopping
llevar	to wear; to carry; to take
poder (puedo)	to be able, can
preferir (prefiero)	to prefer
querer (quiero)	to want
regatear	to haggle, bargain
tener (tengo, tienes,...)	to have
usar	to wear; to use
venir (vengo, vienes,...)	to come

Repaso: comprar, vender

La ropa

[handwritten: rijos – est. price]

el abrigo	coat
los aretes	earrings
la blusa	blouse
la bolsa	purse
las botas	boots
los calcetines	socks
la camisa	shirt
la camiseta	T-shirt
la cartera	wallet; handbag
las chanclas	flip-flops
la chaqueta	jacket
el cinturón	belt
la corbata	tie
la falda	skirt
la gorra	baseball cap
el impermeable	raincoat
los *jeans*	blue jeans
las medias	stockings
los pantalones	pants
el reloj	watch
la ropa	clothing
la ropa interior	underwear
las sandalias	sandals
el sombrero	hat
la sudadera	sweatshirt
el suéter	sweater
el traje	suit
el traje de baño	swimsuit
el vestido	dress
los zapatos (de tenis)	(tennis) shoes

De compras

la ganga	bargain
el precio (fijo)	(fixed, set) price

las rebajas	sales, reductions
¿cuánto cuesta(n)?	how much does it (do they) cost?
de todo	everything
Es de última moda.	
Está de moda.	It's trendy (hot).

Los materiales

de...	
cuadros	plaid
lunares	polka-dot
rayas	striped
es de...	it is made of . . .
algodón (m.)	cotton
cuero	leather
lana	wool
oro	gold
plata	silver
seda	silk

Los lugares

el almacén	department store
el centro	downtown
el centro comercial	shopping mall
el mercado	market(place)
la tienda	shop, store
Cognado: la plaza	

Los colores

amarillo/a	yellow
anaranjado/a	orange
azul	blue
blanco/a	white
(de) color café	brown
gris	gray
morado/a	purple
negro/a	black
rojo/a	red
rosado/a	pink
verde	green

azul — claro (lt.) obscuro (dk)

Otro sustantivo

el examen	exam, test

Los adjetivos

barato/a	inexpensive
caro/a	expensive
cómodo/a	comfortable
poco/a	little, few
Repaso: mucho/a	

Más allá del número 100

doscientos/as, trescientos/as, cuatrocientos/as, quinientos/as, seiscientos/as, setecientos/as, ochocientos/as, novecientos/as, mil, un millón (de)

Repaso: cien(to)

Las formas demostrativas

aquel, aquella, aquellos/as	that, those ([way] over there)
ese/a, esos/as	that, those
eso, aquello	that, that ([way] over there)

Repaso: este/a, esto, estos/as

Palabras adicionales

¿adónde?	where (to)?
al	to the
algo	something
allá	(way) over there
allí	there
tener...	
ganas de + inf.	to feel like (doing something)
miedo (de)	to be afraid (of)
prisa	to be in a hurry
que + inf.	to have to (do something)
razón	to be right
sueño	to be sleepy
no tener razón	to be wrong
¿no?, ¿verdad?	right? don't they (you, and so on)?

Repaso: mucho (adv.), poco (adv.), tener... años

 VOCABULARIO PERSONAL

Unas casas en la ciudad de Granada, Nicaragua

1. What kind of housing would you expect to find in cities like Granada (pop. 116,000)?

2. What is housing like in your area? What types of housing are available (houses, apartments, high-rise condominiums, new, old, large, small, and so on)? What are the advantages and disadvantages of the different kinds of housing in your area?

3. What do you think the houses in the photo are like inside? Do you think that these homes have gardens or patios? Do you have similar buildings in your area?

4

En casa

lunes

1. Javier asiste a clase el lunes a las ocho.

martes

2. Javier mira la televisión el martes.

miércoles

3. Javier va al gimnasio el miércoles.

jueves

4. Javier trabaja cuatro horas el jueves.

viernes

5. El viernes va al mercado con unos amigos.

el fin de semana (sábado y domingo)

6. El fin de semana juega al basquetbol con sus amigos.

Hoy es viernes (domingo...).	Today is Friday (Sunday . . .).
Mañana es sábado (lunes...).	Tomorrow is Saturday (Monday . . .).
Ayer fue martes (miércoles...).	Yesterday was Tuesday (Wednesday . . .).
el fin de semana	the weekend
pasado mañana	the day after tomorrow
el próximo jueves (viernes,...)	next Thursday (Friday, . . .)
la semana (el lunes...) que viene	next week (Monday . . .)

- In Spanish-speaking countries, the week usually starts with **lunes.**
- The days of the week are not capitalized in Spanish.
- Except for **el sábado / los sábados** and **el domingo / los domingos,** all the days of the week use the same form for the plural as they do for the singular: **el lunes / los lunes.**

Expressing *on* with Days of the Week

The definite article (singular or plural) is used to express *on* with the days of the week in Spanish.

Esta semana, tengo que ir al mercado **el** lunes.

This week, I have to go to the market on Monday.

Por lo general voy al gimnasio **los** domingos.

I generally go to the gym on Sundays.

As in the preceding examples, use **el** before a day of the week to refer to a specific day (**el lunes** = *on Monday*), and **los** to refer to that day of the week in general (**los lunes** = *on Mondays*).

Conversación

A. Entrevista. En parejas, hagan y contesten las siguientes (*following*) preguntas.

1. ¿Qué día es hoy? ¿Qué día es mañana? Si hoy es sábado, ¿qué día es mañana? Si hoy es jueves, ¿qué día es mañana? ¿Qué día fue ayer?
2. ¿Qué días de la semana tenemos clase? ¿Qué días no hay clases?
3. ¿Estudias mucho durante (*during*) el fin de semana? ¿y los domingos por la noche?
4. ¿Qué te gusta hacer los viernes por la tarde? ¿Te gusta salir (*to go out*) con los amigos los sábados por la noche?

B. Mi semana. Expresa una actividad para cada (*each*) día de la semana, según el modelo. **¡OJO!** Usa uno de los siguientes verbos o expresiones + un infinitivo en tu respuesta: **deber, desear, ir a, necesitar, poder, preferir, querer, tener ganas de, tener que.**

MODELO: El lunes tengo que ir al gimnasio.

Vocabulario útil

descansar (to rest) **hasta muy tarde**
estar en la cama (bed)
ir al bar (al parque, al museo, a…)
ir al cine (movies)
jugar (to play) **(juego) al tenis (al golf, al voleibol, al…)**

la cama · la cómoda · el armario · la bañera · el lavabo · el estante · la pared · la lámpara · la alcoba† · el baño · el escritorio · la cocina · el comedor · la sala · los platos · el sofá · la silla · la mesa · la televisión · la alfombra · la mesita · el sillón

el garaje	garage
el jardín	garden
el patio	patio; yard
la piscina	swimming pool

Conversación

A. Asociaciones

Paso 1. ¿Qué muebles o partes de la casa usas para hacer las siguientes actividades?

1. estudiar para un examen
2. dormir la siesta (*to take a nap*) por la tarde
3. pasar (*to spend*) una noche en casa con la familia
4. celebrar con una comida (*meal*) especial
5. tomar el sol (*to sunbathe*)
6. hablar de temas (*topics*) serios con los amigos (padres, hijos)

Paso 2. Ahora compara tus respuestas con las (*those*) de otros estudiantes. ¿Tienen todos las mismas costumbres (*same customs*)?

---

*This is the first group of words you will learn for talking about where you live and the things found in your house or apartment. You will learn additional vocabulary for those topics in **Capítulos 9** and **12**.

†Other frequently used words for bedroom include **el dormitorio** and **la habitación**.

B. ¿Qué hay en esta casa? En parejas, digan (*say*) los nombres de las partes de esta casa y lo que (*what*) hay en cada cuarto.

MODELO: 7 →

E1: El número 7 es el patio.
E2: ¿Qué hay en el patio? ¿Hay piscina?
E1: No, sólo hay plantas.

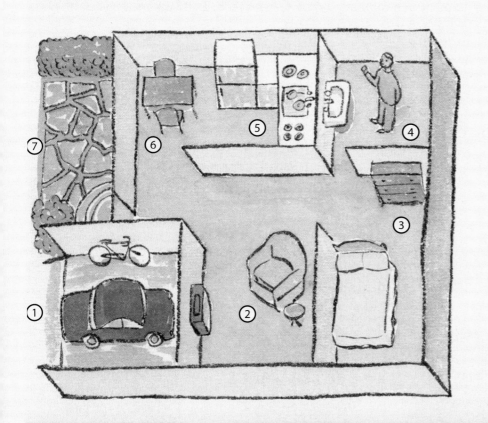

♦) NOTA CULTURAL

Las casas en el mundo hispánico

There is no such thing as a typical Hispanic house. Often, the style of housing depends on geographic location. For example, in hot regions such as southern Spain, traditional houses are built around a central interior patio. These patios are filled with plants, and some even have a fountain.

The population in Hispanic countries tends to be centered in urban areas. Due to population density in cities, many people live in apartments, like people in larger cities in this country.

While the Spanish word **hogar** literally means *home*, the word **casa** is often used to mean *home*.

Voy a casa.   *I'm going home.*
Estoy en casa.   *I'm at home.*

In Spain, people use the word **piso** or **apartamento** to refer to an apartment; in some Hispanic countries, the word **departamento** is used.

In big Latin American cities, especially in more modern homes, a small front yard with ornamental plants and/or small trees is called **un jardín**. Large backyards are uncommon (except in rural areas and small towns) because the lots where houses are built are rather small. If a house has a back area, it is generally referred to as **el patio**.

El patio interior de una casa en Sevilla, España

C. Diseño (*Design*) y decoración

Paso 1. En parejas, dibujen (*draw*) el plano de una casa con al menos (*at least*) dos alcobas y un baño. Luego (*Then*) amueblen (*furnish*) la casa con los muebles necesarios.

Paso 2. Ahora describan su casa a otra pareja de compañeros. Ellos deben dibujar el plano de la casa que Uds. describen sin (*without*) mirar el dibujo de Uds.

Mesas, sillas, armarios, camas y todo lo que necesitas para vestir tu casa está en la sección de decoración.

EL PAIS

Vocabulario útil

a la derecha (de) to the right (of)

a la izquierda (de) to the left (of)

¿Cuándo? • Las preposiciones (Part 1)*

1. Antes de la fiesta, Rosa prepara la ensalada.

2. Durante la fiesta, Rosa baila.

3. Después de la fiesta, Rosa limpia la sala.

The prepositions (as well as the words that they link) are indicated in the first two sentences below. Pick out the prepositions in the last two.

> **preposition** = a word or phrase that specifies the relationship, usually in space or time, of one word to another

1. The book is *on* the table.

2. The homework is *for* tomorrow.

3. We're going to the store for milk.

4. Voy a estar con la familia de mi esposo este fin de semana.

---

*You will learn prepositions that express spatial relationships in **Paso 1: Vocabulario** of **Capítulo 5**.

Some common Spanish prepositions you have already used include **a, con, de, en, para,** and **por** (*in, during,* as in **por la mañana**). Some prepositions that express time relationships include **antes de** (*before*), **después de** (*after*), **durante** (*during*), and **hasta** (*until*).

¡OJO!

As you know, the infinitive is the only verb form that can follow a preposition.

¿Adónde vas **después de estudiar?**

Where are you going after studying (after you study)?

Conversación

A. ¿Cuándo?

Paso 1. Completa las siguientes oraciones lógicamente. Puedes usar sustantivos, infinitivos, días de la semana, etcétera.

1. Por lo general, prefiero estudiar antes de / después de mirar la tele.
2. Siempre tengo mucho sueño durante la clase de _____.
3. Voy a la clase de español antes de / después de la clase de _____.
4. Los _____ (día o días), estoy en la universidad hasta _____ (hora).
5. No puedo ir a fiestas durante la semana. Voy los _____ (día o días).
6. Tengo que estudiar en esta universidad hasta el año (*year*) _____, para poder graduarme.

Paso 2. Ahora entrevista a un compañero o compañera, usando (*using*) las oraciones del **Paso 1.**

> **MODELOS:** ¿Prefieres estudiar antes de mirar la tele?
> ¿Prefieres estudiar antes o después de mirar la tele?
> ¿Cuándo prefieres estudiar, antes o después de mirar la tele?

B. Entrevista. En parejas, túrnense para entrevistarse. Hagan sus preguntas, usando una palabra o frases de cada columna.

estudiar
hablar por
  teléfono
leer
trabajar
¿ ?
	antes de
	después de
	durante
	hasta
		tu programa favorito de televisión
		las clases
		las conferencias (*lectures*) de _____
		los viernes por la noche, los
		  domingos por la mañana...
		estudiar, mirar la tele,...
		las tres de la mañana, medianoche
		  (*midnight*), muy tarde,...
		¿ ?

Need more **practice?**
- Workbook/Laboratory Manual
- Online Learning Center (www.mhhe.com/apuntate)

¿Usas tu celular durante la clase?

El Salvador y Nicaragua

DATOS ESENCIALES

EL SALVADOR

NOMBRE OFICIAL: República de El Salvador
CAPITAL: San Salvador
POBLACIÓN: más de 6 millones de habitantes

NICARAGUA

NOMBRE OFICIAL: República de Nicaragua
CAPITAL: Managua
POBLACIÓN: más de 5 millones de habitantes

Fíjate

EL SALVADOR

- El Salvador se conoce como[a] «el Pulgarcito[b] de América» por su tamaño[c] y la forma del país. Es el país más pequeño d continente americano, pero tie la densidad de población más alta de Centroamérica.
- Los salvadoreños viven entre[d] veinte volcanes, cuatro de los cuales[e] son activos.
- El volcán de Izalco se conoce como «el faro[f] del Pacífico» porque se mantuvo[g] activo en 1770 y 1966 y servía de guía[h] los navegantes.[i]

NICARAGUA

- Se dice que[j] Nicaragua es tierr de lagos[k] y volcanes por[l] sus diecisiete volcanes y dos gran lagos: el Lago de Nicaragua y Lago de Managua.
- Como sus vecinos[m] centroamericanos, Nicaragua tiene una rica biodiversidad, y bosque lluvioso[n] es el segundo más grande[ñ] del hemisferio occidental.[o]

[a]se... is known as [b]Little Thumb [c]size [d]among [e]de... of which [f]lighthouse [g]se it stayed [h]servía... served as a guide [i]sailo [j]Se... It's said that [k]tierra... land of lakes [l]because of [m]neighbors [n]bosque... rain f [ñ]segundo... second largest [o]western

¡MÚSICA!

Como en otros países centroamericanos, la música folclórica de El Salvador y Nicaragua es una fusión de la música española y la música indígena. No se sabe mucho de[a] la música indígena de El Salvador antes de la colonización, pero algunos[b] de los instrumentos musicales importantes fueron[c] los tambores,[d] las flautas[e] y la chirimía.[f] En Nicaragua, el instrumento musical folclórico más típico es la marimba.

[a]No... Little is known about [b]some [c]were [d]drums [e]flutes [f]clarinet-type wind instrument

---

 ## YOLOCAMBA I TA Y LUIS ENRIQUE

Yolocamba I Ta es un grupo salvadoreño de música popular con mensaje[a] social. El nombre del grupo significa «La rebelión de la siembra[b]», y viene de dos lenguas indígenas del sureste[c] del país, el lenca y el chorti. La canción «Podría ser[d]» es de su álbum *Cara o cruz*.[e]

El grupo salvadoreño Yolocamba I Ta

El cantante nicaragüense Luis Enrique es también llamado[f] El príncipe de la salsa. Su canción «Así es la vida[g]» es del álbum *Luis Enrique*.

[a]message [b]La... The Crop Rebellion [c]southeast [d]Podría... It Could Be [e]Cara... Heads or Tails [f]called [g]Así... That's Life

Luis Enrique durante un concierto en Nueva York

¿Recuerdas?

Most of the verbs presented in **Gramática 11** share a first person singular irregularity with two verbs that you learned in **Capítulo 3**. Review what you know about those two verbs by completing their first person forms.

(yo) ven_____o   (yo) ten_____o

11 Expressing Actions • Hacer, oír, poner, salir, traer, and ver

Gramática en acción: Aspectos de la vida de Rigoberto

1. Traigo muchos libros al salón de clase.

2. No oigo bien. Por eso hago muchas preguntas en clase.

3. Los viernes pongo la tele y veo mi programa favorito.

4. Salgo con Elena los fines de semana.

Comprensión

1. ¿Qué trae Rigoberto al salón de clase? ¿Qué tiene en la mochila?
2. ¿Por qué hace muchas preguntas en clase? ¿Ve bien? ¿Oye bien?
3. ¿A qué hora pone la tele los viernes? ¿Por qué prefiere mirar la tele a esa hora?
4. ¿Con quién sale? ¿Es una relación nueva o vieja?

hacer (to do; to make)		oír (to hear)		poner (to put; to place)		salir (to leave; to go out)		traer (to bring)		ver (to see)	
hago	hacemos	oigo	oímos	pongo	ponemos	salgo	salimos	traigo	traemos	veo	vemos
haces	hacéis	oyes	oís	pones	ponéis	sales	salís	traes	traéis	ves	veis
hace	hacen	oye	oyen	pone	ponen	sale	salen	trae	traen	ve	ven

Aspects of Rigoberto's life **1.** *I bring a lot of books to class.* **2.** *I don't hear well. That's why I ask a lot of questions in class.* **3.** *On Fridays, I turn on the TV and watch my favorite program.* **4.** *I go out with Elena on the weekends.*

1. **Hacer** Some common idioms with **hacer:**

   hacer un viaje *(to take a trip)*
   hacer una pregunta *(to ask a question)*

   Hacer is used to express *to do* physical and academic exercises. To express *to do exercises* for a Spanish or math class, for example, the plural **ejercicios** is used. To express *to exercise* in a gym, the singular is used, except for aerobics.

   ¿Por qué no **haces** la tarea?
   Why aren't you doing the homework?

   Quieren **hacer un viaje** al Perú.
   They want to take a trip to Peru.

   Los niños siempre **hacen muchas preguntas.**
   Children always ask a lot of questions.

   Alicia **hace los ejercicios** en el cuaderno.
   Alicia does the exercises in the notebook.

   Hace ejercicio en el gimnasio, pero **hace ejercicios aeróbicos** en casa.
   She exercises in the gym but does aerobics at home.

2. **Oír** The command forms of **oír** are used to attract someone's attention in the same way that English uses *Listen!* or *Hey!*

   oye (tú)   **oiga** (Ud.)   **oigan** (Uds.)

   Oír means *to hear.* In **Capítulo 1,** you learned the verb **escuchar,** which means *to listen (to).* Some speakers use **oír** for *to listen to* when referring to things like music or the news. **Escuchar** never means *to hear.*

   Oye, Juan, ¿vas a la fiesta?
   Hey, Juan, are you going to the party?

   ¡Oigan! ¡Silencio, por favor!
   Listen! Silence, please!

   No **oigo** bien a la profesora.
   I can't hear the professor well.

   Oímos/Escuchamos música en clase.
   We listen to music in class.

   No **oigo** bien por el ruido *(noise).*

3. **Poner** Many Spanish speakers use **poner** with appliances to express *to turn on.*

   Voy a **poner** la televisión.
   I'm going to turn on the TV.

   Siempre **pongo** leche y mucho azúcar en el café.

4. **Salir** Note that **salir** is always followed by **de** to express leaving a place.

   Salir con can mean *to go out with, to date.*

   Use **salir para** to indicate destination.

   Another useful expression with **salir** is **salir bien/mal,** which means *to turn/come out well/poorly, to do well/poorly.*

   Salgo con el hermano de Cecilia.
   I'm going out with Cecilia's brother.

   Salimos para la sierra pasado mañana.
   We're leaving for the mountains the day after tomorrow.

   Todo va a **salir bien.**
   Everything is going to turn out OK (well).

   No quiero **salir mal** en esta clase.
   I don't want to do poorly in this class.

   Salen de la clase ahora.

5. Traer ¡OJO! la televisión (*set, medium*) but **el radio** (*set*), **la radio** (*medium*)	¿Por qué no **traes** ese radio a la cocina? *Why don't you bring that radio to the kitchen?*
6. Ver The verb **ver** means *to see* or *to watch*. In **Capítulo 2**, you learned that **mirar** means *to look (at)* or *to watch* something. Some speakers use **ver** interchangeably with **mirar** for *to watch* (**veo/miro la televisión**), but **mirar** can never mean *to see*. **Buscar** (from **Capítulo 1**) expresses *to look for* something, but it never means *to look at* or *to watch*.	No **veo** bien sin mis lentes. *I don't see well without my glasses.* Los niños **ven/miran** una película. *The kids are watching a movie.* **Busco** los platos nuevos. *I'm looking for the new plates.*

Oigo música entre las clases.

Práctica

A. ¡Anticipemos! Cosas rutinarias

Paso 1. ¿Cierto o falso?

	CIERTO	FALSO
1. Hago ejercicio en el gimnasio con frecuencia.	❏	❏
2. Veo a mis amigos los viernes por la tarde.	❏	❏
3. Nunca salgo con mis primos.	❏	❏
4. Siempre hago los ejercicios para la clase de español.	❏	❏
5. Salgo para la universidad a las ocho de la mañana.	❏	❏
6. Nunca pongo la ropa en la cómoda o en el armario.	❏	❏
7. Siempre traigo todos los libros necesarios a clase.	❏	❏
8. Siempre oigo la radio durante el camino (*on the way*) a la universidad.	❏	❏

Paso 2. Now rephrase each sentence in **Paso 1** as a question and interview a classmate. Use the **tú** form of the verb. **¡OJO!** Es necesario hacer otros cambios también. Para los números 3 y 6: **Nunca...** ⟶ **¿Siempre...**

> **MODELO:** Hago ejercicio en el gimnasio con frecuencia. ⟶
> ¿Haces ejercicio en el gimnasio con frecuencia?

B. Del periódico: Publicidad. Lee (*Read*) el siguiente anuncio (*ad*) de un periódico de Venezuela y contesta las preguntas.

1. ¿Cómo se expresan en inglés las primeras dos líneas del anuncio?
2. Los sujetos pronominales **yo, tú** y **nosotros** no se usan siempre en español, ya que (*since*) la terminación del verbo (**-o, -s, -mos**) expresa la persona. ¿Por qué crees que sí se usan los pronombres en el titular (*headline*)?
3. ¿Qué palabras inglesas hay en el anuncio?
4. ¿Cuál es la dirección (*address*) del sitio web de esta compañía? (**.com** = «punto com»)
5. ¿Cuál es la dirección de e-mail de la oficina en Puerto Ordaz? (@ = «arroba»)

Vocabulario útil

hacer (hago) un viaje / una pregunta
oír (oigo) al profesor / a la profesora*
poner (pongo) la televisión / el radio
salir (salgo) con/de/ para...
traer (traigo) el libro a clase
ver (veo) mi programa favorito

Conversación

A. Consecuencias lógicas. En parejas, indiquen una acción lógica para cada situación.

MODELO: No tengo tarea. Por eso... → pongo la televisión.

1. Me gusta esquiar en las montañas. Por eso...
2. Todos los días usamos este libro en la clase de español. Por eso...
3. Mis compañeros de cuarto hacen mucho ruido en la sala. Por eso...
4. La televisión no funciona. Por eso...
5. Hay mucho ruido en la clase. Por eso...
6. Estoy en la biblioteca y ¡no puedo estudiar más! Por eso...
7. Queremos bailar y necesitamos música. Por eso...
8. No comprendo la lección. Por eso...

*Remember that the word **a** is necessary in front of a human direct object. You will study this usage of **a** in **Capítulo 6**. For now, you can answer following the pattern in **Vocabulario útil.***

B. Entrevista

Paso 1. En parejas, hagan y contesten las siguientes preguntas.

EN CASA

1. ¿Qué pones en el armario? ¿y en la cómoda? ¿en el cajón (*drawer*) del escritorio?
2. ¿Pones la televisión con frecuencia cuando estás en casa? ¿Qué programa(s) ves todos los días? ¿Qué programa muy popular no ves nunca? (Nunca veo...) ¿Cuál es el canal de televisión que más miras? ¿Por qué te gusta tanto (*so much*)?
3. ¿Pones el radio con frecuencia? ¿Prefieres oír las noticias (*news*) por radio o verlas (*to see them*) en la televisión? ¿Cuál es la estación de radio que más escuchas? ¿Por qué te gusta tanto?

MIS ACTIVIDADES

4. ¿Qué haces los _____ (día) por la noche? ¿Cuándo sales con los amigos? ¿Adónde van cuando salen juntos (*together*)?
5. ¿Te gusta hacer ejercicio? ¿Haces ejercicios aeróbicos? ¿Dónde haces ejercicio? ¿en casa? ¿en el gimnasio? ¿en la piscina?

PARA LAS CLASES

6. Generalmente, ¿qué traes a clase todos los días? ¿Crees que traes más cosas (*things*) que tus compañeros o menos? ¿Sales a veces para la clase sin tu libro de texto? ¿sin dinero? ¿Qué trae tu profesor(a) de español a clase?
7. ¿A qué hora sales para las clases los lunes? ¿A qué hora sales de clase los viernes?
8. ¿Cuándo haces la tarea? ¿Por la mañana? ¿por la tarde? ¿por la noche? ¿Dónde haces la tarea? ¿En casa? ¿en la biblioteca? ¿Haces la tarea mientras (*while*) ves la televisión? ¿mientras oyes música?
9. ¿Siempre sales bien en los exámenes? ¿En qué clase no sales bien? ¿Qué haces si sales mal en un examen? ¿Hablas con tu profesor(a)?

Paso 2. Ahora digan a la clase dos o tres cosas que Uds. tienen en común.

> **MODELO:** Jim y yo nunca ponemos la ropa en el armario. Hacemos ejercicio todos los días: Jim hace ejercicios aeróbicos y yo voy al gimnasio. Los dos vemos el programa *24* los lunes por la noche; es nuestro programa favorito.

¿Dónde haces la tarea?

The change in the stem vowels of **preferir, querer,** and **poder** follows the same pattern as that of the verbs presented in **Gramática 12**. Review the forms of **preferir, querer,** and **poder** before beginning **Gramática 12**.

preferir: e → ?		querer: e → ?		poder: o → ?	
pref__ro	preferimos	qu__ro	queremos	p__do	podemos
pref__res	preferís	qu__res	queréis	p__des	podéis
pref__re	pref__ren	qu__re	qu__ren	p__de	p__den

12 Expressing Actions • Present Tense of Stem-Changing Verbs (Part 2)

Gramática en acción: ¿Una fiesta exitosa?

- Aurora duerme en el sofá.
- Samuel juega a las cartas… a solas.
- Ernesto sirve las bebidas. Kevin pide una Coca-Cola.
- Noemí sale y vuelve con más amigas.
- ¿Es una fiesta exitosa? ¿Qué piensas tú? ¿Por qué?

¿Y tú? ¿Qué haces en las fiestas?

Yo (no)…

1. dormir en el sofá
2. jugar a las cartas
3. servir las bebidas
4. pedir Coca-Cola
5. volver con más amigos

e → ie pensar (*to think*)		o → ue volver (*to return*)		e → i pedir (*to ask for; to order*)	
pienso	pensamos	vuelvo	volvemos	pido	pedimos
piensas	pensáis	vuelves	volvéis	pides	pedís
piensa	piensan	vuelve	vuelven	pide	piden

A successful party? ■ *Aurora is sleeping on the couch.* ■ *Samuel is playing cards . . . alone.* ■ *Ernesto is serving beverages. Kevin asks for a Coke.* ■ *Noemí leaves and comes back with more friends.* ■ *Is it a successful party? What do you think? Why?*

1. **Stem-Changing Verbs** You have already learned five *stem-changing verbs* (**los verbos que cambian el radical**).

quérer preférir tener venir póder

In these verbs the stem vowels **e** and **o** become **ie** and **ue**, respectively, in stressed syllables. There is also another group of stem-changing verbs in which the stem vowel **e** becomes **i** in stressed syllables. The stem-change pattern of all three groups is shown at the right. The stem vowels are stressed in all present tense forms except **nosotros** and **vosotros**. All three classes of stem-changing verbs follow this regular "boot" pattern in the present tense.

In vocabulary lists, the stem change for the **yo** form will always be shown in parentheses after the infinitive: **pensar (pienso)**, **volver (vuelvo)**, **pedir (pido)**.

Stem vowel changes:

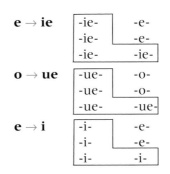

e → ie	-ie-	-e-
	-ie-	-e-
	-ie-	-ie-

o → ue	-ue-	-o-
	-ue-	-o-
	-ue-	-ue-

e → i	-i-	-e-
	-i-	-e-
	-i-	-i-

¡OJO!

Nosotros and **vosotros** forms *do not* have a stem vowel change.

2. **Important Stem-Changing Verbs** Some stem-changing verbs practiced in this chapter include the following.

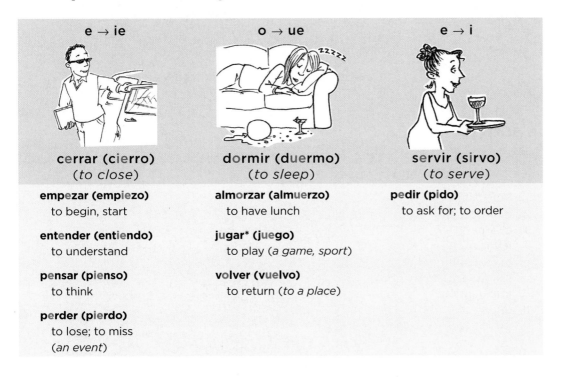

e → ie	**o → ue**	**e → i**
cerrar (cierro) *(to close)*	**dormir (duermo)** *(to sleep)*	**servir (sirvo)** *(to serve)*
empezar (empiezo) to begin, start	**almorzar (almuerzo)** to have lunch	**pedir (pido)** to ask for; to order
entender (entiendo) to understand	**jugar* (juego)** to play (*a game, sport*)	
pensar (pienso) to think	**volver (vuelvo)** to return (*to a place*)	
perder (pierdo) to lose; to miss (*an event*)		

***Jugar** *is the only* **u → ue** *stem-changing verb in Spanish.* **Jugar** *is usually followed by* **al** *when used with the name of a sport:* **Juego al tenis.** *Some Spanish speakers, however, omit the* **al**.

3. Present Tense Equivalents Remember that the Spanish present tense has a number of present tense equivalents in English. It can also be used to express future meaning.	**cierro** = *I close, I am closing, I will close*
4. Verb + *a* **+ Infinitive** Like **aprender** and **ir**, the stem-changing verbs **empezar** and **volver** are followed by **a** before an infinitive. The meaning of **empezar** does not change in this structure, but **volver a** + *infinitive* expresses *to do (something) again.*	Uds. **empiezan a hablar** muy bien el español. *You're starting to speak Spanish very well.* ¿Cuándo **vuelves a jugar** al tenis? *When are you going to play tennis again?*
5. Conjugated Verb + Infinitive Like other verbs you already know (**desear, necesitar, deber,...**), **pensar** can be followed directly by an infinitive. In that case, it expresses *to intend, plan.* The phrase **pensar en** can be used to express *to think about.*	¿Cuándo **piensas** almorzar? *When do you plan to eat lunch?* —¿**En qué piensas**? *What are you thinking about?* —**Pienso en** las cosas que tengo que hacer el domingo. *I'm thinking about the things I have to do on Sunday.*

STEM-CHANGE SUMMARY

empezar (empiezo)
volver (vuelvo)
jugar (juego)
pedir (pido)

Práctica

A. Asociaciones. Give at least one infinitive whose meaning you associate with the following words and phrases.

1. una bebida
2. una lección
3. a casa
4. las llaves (*keys*)
5. una hamburguesa
6. las cartas (*cards*)
7. una opinión
8. una siesta
9. una puerta

Una pelota de tenis
(*tennis ball*)

B. ¡Anticipemos!

Paso 1. ¿Cierto o falso? Si la declaración es cierta, di en qué lugar de la casa o de la universidad haces las siguientes cosas.

	CIERTO	FALSO
1. Duermo la siesta casi todos los días.	❏	☑
2. Cierro la puerta para dormir la siesta.	☑	❏
3. Almuerzo solo/a (*alone*) con frecuencia.	☑	❏
4. Juego a las cartas con mis padres (mis hijos).	☑	❏
5. Por la mañana, pienso en las cosas que tengo que hacer.	☑	❏
6. Con frecuencia pido una pizza para almorzar.	☑	❏
7. Pierdo mis llaves con frecuencia.	❏	☑
8. Vuelvo a leer la lección de español antes de la clase.	☑	❏
9. Hay mucho que no entiendo en la clase de matemáticas.	❏	☑

Paso 2. En parejas, túrnense para entrevistarse, usando las declaraciones del **Paso 1.**

> **MODELO:** ¿Duermes la siesta casi todos los días?

Paso 3. Ahora digan a la clase dos cosas que Uds. tienen en común.

> **MODELO:** Nosotras dormimos la siesta casi todos los días. Dormimos en un sofá en una sala del centro estudiantil.

C. Una tarde típica en casa.
¿Cuáles son las actividades de todos? Haz oraciones completas, usando una palabra o frase de cada columna.

yo mi padre/madre mi esposo/a los niños mi amigo/a _____ y yo el perro/gato mi compañero/a	(no)	almorzar dormir empezar a entender jugar a pedir pensar perder preferir volver volver a ¿ ?

+ ... +

descansar, dormir
en un sillón / en la cocina
toda la tarde / la siesta
su pelota (*ball*), sus llaves, su mochila
tarde / temprano a casa
en el patio / en la piscina / afuera (*outside*)
el golf (tenis, voleibol...), las cartas
las películas viejas / recientes
la lección, la oración
hablar bien el español
ver una película con frecuencia
¿ ?

¿Qué hacen esta madre y su hija?

Need more practice?
■ Workbook/Laboratory Manual
■ Online Learning Center
[www.mhhe.com/apuntate]

Conversación

A. Una semana ideal... ¡y posible!

Paso 1. ¿Qué vas a hacer la semana que viene? ¿Qué prefieres hacer? Organiza la semana que viene en la siguiente agenda. Incluye actividades que tienes que hacer pero también algunas (*some*) que te gustaría (*you would like*) hacer. Usa el **Vocabulario útil,** pero inventa por lo menos tres actividades que no están en la lista. **¡OJO! e → ie, o → ue, e → i.**

Vocabulario útil

almorzar (almuerzo) en un restaurante con _____
dormir (duermo) una siesta
empezar (empiezo) un proyecto para _____
hacer ejercicio
hacer la tarea de _____
jugar (juego) al tenis/ golf/basquetbol con _____
servir (sirvo) una comida (*meal*) en casa
ver la televisión
volver (vuelvo) a ver a _____

	por la mañana	por la tarde	por la noche
lunes			
martes			
miércoles			
jueves			
viernes			
sábado			
domingo			

Paso 2. En parejas, hablen de su horario (*schedule*) para esta semana, basándose (*based on*) en la agenda del **Paso 1.**

> **MODELO: E1:** ¿Qué piensas hacer el domingo por la tarde?
> **E2:** Pienso ver la televisión. Y tú, ¿qué haces el domingo?
> **E1:** El domingo juego al tenis con mi amigo Alex.

B. Preguntas

1. ¿A qué hora cierran la biblioteca? ¿A qué hora cierran la cafetería? ¿Y a qué hora cierran durante la época de los exámenes finales?
2. ¿A qué hora almuerzas por lo general? ¿Dónde te gusta almorzar? ¿Con quién? ¿Dónde piensas almorzar hoy? ¿mañana?
3. ¿Eres un poco olvidadizo/a? Es decir (*That is*), ¿pierdes las cosas con frecuencia? ¿Qué cosa pierdes? ¿el dinero? ¿el cuaderno? ¿la mochila? ¿las llaves?

❶

El Lago de Coatepeque y el volcán de Santa Ana, El Salvador El Salvador tiene dos filas[a] de volcanes que forman un arco[b] en el oeste[c] del país. La depresión[d] que forma el Lago de Coatepeque es el cráter volcánico más grande del país: 6,4 kilómetros de ancho[e] por 122 metros de profundidad.[f]

[a]rows   [b]arc   [c]west   [d]hollow   [e]6,4... four miles wide   [f]122... 400 feet deep

❷

La pirámide principal de las ruinas de Tazumal, El Salvador La civilización maya se extendía hasta[a] el territorio de El Salvador. Las ruinas de Tazumal, con una pirámide principal y un campo de juego de pelota,[b] son pequeñas en comparación con las ruinas de otras regiones, pero la variedad[c] de construcción y la evidencia de comercio[d] entre[e] las comunidades son importantes para entender la civilización maya.

[a]se... extended into   [b]campo... ball court   [c]variety   [d]trade   [e]among

❸

El cráter Santiago del volcán Masaya, Nicaragua El volcán Masaya está cerca de[a] Managua y es uno de los dos volcanes activos del mundo que tienen un camino pavimentado[b] que lleva[c] a la cumbre.[d] De hecho,[e] hace cientos de años,[f] los indígenas de la zona también mantenían[g] un camino que llevaba[h] al cráter Santiago. Este gran volcán ha dado origen[i] a varias leyendas.[j]

[a]cerca... close to   [b]camino... paved road   [c]leads   [d]summit   [e]De... In fact   [f]hace... hundreds of years ago   [g]maintained   [h]led   [i]ha... has given rise   [j]legends

El Lago de Nicaragua, la isla Ometepe y el volcán Maderas (al fondo[a]) El Lago de Nicaragua, el segundo[b] más grande de Latinoamérica, tiene muchas islas. La isla Ometepe, formada por[c] los volcanes Maderas y Concepción, es la isla volcánica de agua dulce[d] más grande del mundo. El Lago de Nicaragua, o «el Mar Dulce[e]» como algunos lo llaman,[f] tiene muchas características oceánicas, como olas[g] grandes, tiburones[h] y otros animales y plantas que normalmente se encuentran[i] en un mar de agua salada.[j]

[a]al... in the background   [b]second   [c]formada... formed by   [d]de... fresh water   [e]Mar... Fresh Water Sea   [f]como... as some call it   [g]waves   [h]sharks   [i]se... are found   [j]salt

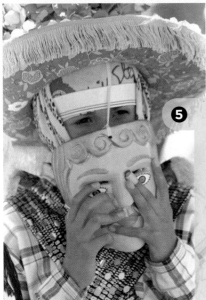

❺

Un danzante[a] güegüense de Nicaragua El teatro y la danza güegüenses son una fusión de tradiciones indígenas y españolas. También llamado «Macho Ratón»,[b] es un baile[c] teatral con máscara[d] que proviene de[e] la tradición picaresca[f] de España. Se representa[g] en Diriamba, Nicaragua, en enero,[h] durante el Festival de San Sebastián.

[a]dancer   [b]llamado... called "Brave Mouse"   [c]dance   [d]mask   [e]proviene... comes from   [f]rogue, picaresque   [g]Se... It's performed   [h]January

❹

13 Expressing *-self/-selves* • Reflexive Pronouns (Part 1)

Gramática en acción: La rutina diaria de Andrés

La rutina de Andrés empieza a las siete y media.

1.   2.   3.   4.

5.   6.   7.

(1) Me despierto a las siete y media y me levanto en seguida. Primero, (2) me ducho y luego (3) me cepillo los dientes. (4) Me peino, (5) me pongo la bata y (6) voy al cuarto a vestirme. Por fin, (7) salgo para la universidad. No tomo nada antes de salir porque, por lo general, ¡tengo prisa!

¿Y tú? ¿Cómo es tu rutina diaria?

1. Yo me levanto a las _____.
2. Me ducho por la (mañana/noche).
3. Me visto en (el baño/mi cuarto).
4. Me peino (antes de/después de) vestirme.
5. Antes de salir para las clases, (tomo/no tomo) el desayuno.

Andrés's daily routine   *Andrés's routine begins at seven-thirty. (1) I wake up at seven-thirty and I get up right away. First, (2) I take a shower and then (3) I brush my teeth. (4) I comb my hair, (5) I put on my robe, and (6) I go to my room to get dressed. Finally, (7) I leave for the university. I don't eat or drink anything before leaving because I'm generally in a hurry!*

Uses of Reflexive Pronouns*

bañarse (to take a bath)					
(yo)	**me baño**	I take a bath	(nosotros/as)	**nos bañamos**	we take baths
(tú)	**te bañas**	you take a bath	(vosotros/as)	**os bañáis**	you take baths
(Ud.)		you take a bath	(Uds.)		you take baths
(él)	**se baña**	he takes a bath	(ellos)	**se bañan**	they take baths
(ella)		she takes a bath	(ellas)		they take baths

1. **Reflexive Pronouns** The pronoun **se** at the end of an infinitive indicates that the verb is used reflexively. The reflexive pronoun in Spanish reflects the subject doing something to or for himself, herself, or itself. When the verb is conjugated, the reflexive pronoun that corresponds to the subject must be used.

bañarse = to take a bath (to bathe oneself)
me baño = I take a bath (bathe myself)
te bañas = you take a bath (bathe yourself)

Reflexive Pronouns			
me	myself	**nos**	ourselves
te	yourself (*fam., sing.*)	**os**	yourselves (*fam. pl. Sp.*)
se	himself, herself, itself; yourself (*form. sing.*)	**se**	themselves; yourselves (*form. pl.*)

¡OJO!

Many English verbs that describe parts of one's daily routine — to get up, to take a bath, and so on — are expressed in Spanish with a reflexive construction.

2. **Important Reflexive Verbs** Here and on the following page are some reflexive verbs that you will find useful as you talk about daily routines. Note that some of these verbs are also stem-changing:

e → ie, o → ue, e → i

despertarse (me despierto) (*to wake up*)	**ducharse** (*to take a shower*)	**afeitarse** (*to shave*)	**vestirse (me visto)** (*to get dressed*)	**sentarse (me siento)** (*to sit down*)

*You will learn more about using reflexive pronouns to express each other in **Gramática 30** (**Cap. 10**).

acostarse (me acuesto)	to go to bed
bañarse	to take a bath
cepillarse los dientes	to brush one's teeth
divertirse (me divierto)	to have a good time, enjoy oneself
dormirse (me duermo)	to fall asleep
levantarse	to get up (out of bed); to stand up
peinarse	to brush/comb one's hair
ponerse (me pongo)	to put on (*an article of clothing*)
quitarse	to take off (*an article of clothing*)

Note also the verb **llamarse**, which you have been using since **Primeros pasos: Me llamo _____. ¿Cómo se llama Ud.?**

llamarse = to be called

3. **Nonreflexive Use of Verbs** All of these verbs can also be used nonreflexively, often with a different meaning. Some examples of this appear on the right.

dormir = to sleep **dormirse** = to fall asleep

poner = to put, place **ponerse** = to put on

¡OJO!

After **ponerse** and **quitarse**, the definite article, not the possessive as in English, is used with articles of clothing.

Se pone el abrigo.
He's putting on his coat.

Se quitan el sombrero.
They're taking off their hats.

¡OJO!

The reflexive pronoun must be repeated with each verb in a series of verbs.

Me levanto a las siete, **me ducho** y **me visto** antes de **peinarme.**

Mi esposo **se baña,** yo **me ducho** y los dos **nos peinamos** antes de las seis.

[Práctica A – C]

Placement of Reflexive Pronouns

Reflexive pronouns are placed before a conjugated verb. In a negative sentence, they are placed between the word **no** and the conjugated verb: **No** se **bañan.** When a conjugated verb is followed by an infinitive, the pronouns may either precede the conjugated verb or be attached to the infinitive.

[Práctica D]

Me tengo que levantar temprano.
Tengo que **levantarme** temprano.
I have to get up early.

Debo **acostarme** más temprano.
Me debo acostar más temprano.
I should go to bed earlier.

Práctica

A. Asociaciones. Give as many words as you can think of that form a logical association with the following infinitives. **¡OJO!** Think about vocabulary groups that you already know: rooms of the house, furniture, articles of clothing, verbs of many types, and so on.

1. llamarse
2. levantarse
3. bañarse
4. sentarse
5. vestirse
6. despertarse

B. ¡Anticipemos! Su rutina diaria

Paso 1. ¿Haces lo mismo (*the same thing*) todos los días? Indica los días que haces las siguientes cosas.

	LOS LUNES	LOS SÁBADOS
1. Me levanto antes de las ocho.	❑	❑
2. Siempre me baño o me ducho.	❑	❑
3. Siempre me afeito.	❑	❑
4. Me pongo un traje / una falda.	❑	❑
5. Me quito los zapatos después de llegar a casa.	❑	❑
6. Me acuesto antes de las once de la noche.	❑	❑

Paso 2. ¿Es diferente tu rutina los sábados? ¿Qué día prefieres? ¿Por qué?

⟩ NOTA COMUNICATIVA

Sequence Expressions

The following adverbs and expressions will help you indicate the sequence of actions or events.

primero	first	**finalmente**	finally
después	then, later	**por fin**	finally
luego	then, afterward, next		

Primero, me ducho y me visto. **Luego,** tomo un café y leo el periódico. **Después,** me cepillo los dientes. **Por fin,** salgo para el trabajo.

C. Mi rutina diaria

Paso 1. ¿Qué acostumbras a hacer en un día típico? Usa las siguientes frases para describir tu rutina diaria. Añade (*Add*) otras ideas si quieres. Usa las palabras de la **Nota comunicativa** en tus oraciones.

MODELO: despertarse a (hora) → Me despierto a las siete. Luego...

1. despertarse a (hora)
2. levantarse a (hora)
3. (no) ducharse / bañarse por la mañana
4. vestirse antes o después de tomar algo
5. ir a la universidad y asistir a (número) clases
6. almorzar a (hora) y sentarse en (lugar) para estudiar
7. volver a (lugar) a (hora)
8. comer con (persona[s] o solo/a)
9. acostarse tarde/temprano
10. dormirse a (hora)

Paso 2. Usa las oraciones del **Paso 1** para indicar lo que vas a hacer mañana. Añade información si puedes.

MODELO: despertarse a (hora) → Primero, voy a despertarme (me voy a despertar) a las diez. ¡Es sábado! Pienso... Debo... pero no voy a hacerlo (*do it*).

D. Un día típico

Paso 1. Completa las siguientes oraciones lógicamente para describir tu rutina diaria. Usa el pronombre reflexivo cuando sea (*it's*) necesario. **¡OJO!** Usa el infinitivo después de las preposiciones.

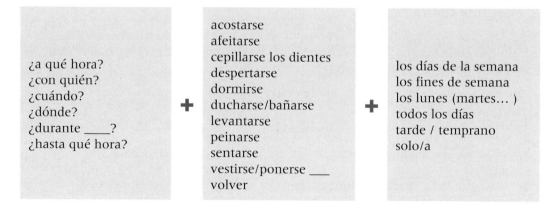

1. Me levanto después de _____.
2. Primero (yo) _____ y luego _____.
3. Me visto antes de / después de _____.
4. Luego me siento a la mesa para _____.
5. Me gusta estudiar antes de _____ o después de _____.
6. Por la noche me divierto y luego _____.
7. Me acuesto antes de / después de _____ y finalmente _____.

Me acuesto después de hacer la tarea.

Need more practice?
- Workbook/Laboratory Manual
- Online Learning Center
  [www.mhhe.com/apuntate]

Paso 2. Con las oraciones del **Paso 1,** describe los hábitos de tu esposo/a, tu compañero/a de cuarto/casa, tus hijos...

Conversación

A. Hábitos.
Indica en qué cuarto o parte de la casa haces cada actividad. Debes indicar también los muebles y otros objetos que usas.

> **MODELO:** estudiar →
> Por lo general, estudio en la alcoba. Uso el escritorio, una silla, los libros y la computadora.

1. estudiar
2. dormir la siesta
3. quitarse los zapatos
4. bañarse o ducharse
5. despertarse
6. tomar el desayuno
7. sentarse a almorzar
8. vestirse
9. divertirse
10. acostarse

B. Entrevista: Tu rutina

Paso 1. En parejas, túrnense para entrevistarse. Hagan preguntas, usando las ideas de las tres columnas y otras de su imaginación. Traten de usar (*Try to use*) una palabra o frase de cada columna.

¿a qué hora? ¿con quién? ¿cuándo? ¿dónde? ¿durante ____? ¿hasta qué hora?	acostarse afeitarse cepillarse los dientes despertarse dormirse ducharse/bañarse levantarse peinarse sentarse vestirse/ponerse ___ volver	los días de la semana los fines de semana los lunes (martes...) todos los días tarde / temprano solo/a

Paso 2. Ahora digan a la clase un detalle (*detail*) interesante, raro o indiscreto de la vida (*life*) de su compañero/a.

> **MODELO:** Sebastián duerme con su perro y con sus dos gatos. ¡Debe tener una cama muy grande!

UN POCO DE TODO

Lengua y cultura: Una tradición extendida—El Día de la Cruz (*Cross*).
Complete the following paragraphs about a special holiday. Give the correct form of the words in parentheses, as suggested by context. When two possibilities are given in parentheses, select the correct word.

Por su extensión,[a] Nicaragua es el país más grande de Centroamérica. El Salvador es el país más pequeño, pero el más densamente poblado.[b] (Este[1]) países (centroamericano[2]), como toda Latinoamérica, reflejan una mezcla[c] de (diverso[3]) influencias étnicas y culturales. (*Ellos:* Tener[4]) (un/una[5]) clima tropical, costas marítimas, (grande[6]) volcanes y muchas fiestas de interés para los turistas de todas partes del mundo.[d]

Una de estas fiestas es la[e] (del/de la[7]) Día de la Cruz. Es una fiesta religiosa que se celebra (el/la[8]) 3 de mayo en El Salvador, en Nicaragua y en otros países hispanohablantes, incluyendo España. ¿(Por qué/Porque[9]) es una tradición tan[f] extendida la celebración del Día de la Cruz? Porque todos son países en donde muchas personas (pero no todas) observan las (tradición[10]) católicas.

En algunos[g] pueblos y (ciudad[11]) hay procesiones[h] que (salir[12]) por los barrios.[i] Muchas familias salvadoreñas (poner[13]) una cruz en su patio. Las (cruz[14]) están adornadas con mucha fruta y con fruta y flores[j] (con/de[15]) papel. Las personas (vestirse[16]) con ropa especial y (celebrar[17]) el día con comidas y bebidas típicas, con (su[18]) familia y con sus amigos.

En El Salvador la celebración del 3 de mayo (unir[k][19]) el culto a la cruz de los cristianos con el culto a la tierra[l] de los indígenas. En el mes de mayo se cosecha[m] la fruta y también (empezar[20]) las lluvias.[n] (Por/Para[21]) eso es un (bueno[22]) momento para dar gracias[ñ] a la tierra. Además,[o] los campesinos (pedir[23]) una buena cosecha para el año entrante,[p] según la tradición indígena. Esto es sólo *un* ejemplo de cómo la influencia indígena y la española se unen en las tradiciones latinoamericanas.

El Día de la Cruz en Panchimalco, El Salvador

[a]Por... *Because of its size* [b]*populated* [c]reflejan... *show a mixture* [d]*world* [e]*that* [f]*so* [g]*some* [h]*religious parades, processions* [i]por... *out of (individual) neighborhoods* [j]*flowers* [k]*to join, unite* [l]*earth* [m]se... *is harvested* [n]*rains* [ñ]dar... *to thank* [o]*Besides* [p]*coming*

Comprensión ¿Cierto o falso? Corrige las oraciones falsas.

	CIERTO	FALSO
1. Nicaragua y El Salvador tienen mucho en común, aunque (*although*) Nicaragua es más grande que El Salvador.	☐	☐
2. Pocos turistas internacionales visitan estos países.	☐	☐
3. El Día de la Cruz es una celebración política.	☐	☐
4. Todos los nicaragüenses y salvadoreños son católicos.	☐	☐
5. Hay pocas tradiciones indígenas en estos dos países.	☐	☐

Resources for Review
and Testing
Preparation

- Workbook/Laboratory Manual
- Online Learning Center
  [www.mhhe.com/apuntate]

En resumen

Gramática en breve

11. Expressing Actions — **Hacer, oír, poner, salir, traer,** and **ver**

hacer: **hago, haces, hace, hacemos, hacéis, hacen**
oír: **oigo, oyes, oye, oímos, oís, oyen**
poner: **pongo, pones, pone, ponemos, ponéis, ponen**
salir: **salgo, sales, sale, salimos, salís, salen**
traer: **traigo, traes, trae, traemos, traéis, traen**
ver: **veo, ves, ve, vemos, veis, ven**

12. Expressing Actions — Present Tense of Stem-Changing Verbs (Part 2)

Stem-Changing Pattern

e → ie

-ie-	-e-
-ie-	-e-
-ie-	-ie-

e → i

-i-	-e-
-i-	-e-
-i-	-i-

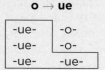

o → ue

-ue-	-o-
-ue-	-o-
-ue-	-ue-

13. Expressing -self/-selves — Reflexive Pronouns (Part 1)

Reflexive Pronouns

me, te, se, nos, os, se

Vocabulario

Los verbos

almorzar (almuerzo)	to have lunch
cerrar (cierro)	to close
descansar	to rest
dormir (duermo)	to sleep
dormir la siesta	to take a nap
empezar (empiezo)	to begin, start
empezar a + *inf.*	to begin to (*do something*)
entender (entiendo)	to understand
hacer (hago)	to do; to make
hacer ejercicio	to exercise
hacer un viaje	to take a trip
hacer una pregunta	to ask a question
jugar (juego) (a, al)	to play (*a game, sport*)
oír (oigo, oyes,...)	to hear; to listen to (*music, the radio*)
pedir (pido)	to ask for; to order
pensar (pienso) (en)	to think (about)
pensar + *inf.*	to intend, plan to (*do something*)
perder (pierdo)	to lose; to miss (*an event*)
poner (pongo)	to put; to place; to turn on (*an appliance*)
salir (salgo) (de/con/para)	to leave (*a place*); to go out (with); to leave (for) (*a place*)
salir bien/mal	to turn/come out well/badly; to do well/poorly
servir (sirvo)	to serve

traer (traigo)	to bring
ver (veo)	to see
volver (vuelvo)	to return (*to a place*)
volver a + *inf.*	to (*do something*) again

Los verbos reflexivos

acostarse (me acuesto)	to go to bed
afeitarse	to shave
bañarse	to take a bath
cepillarse los dientes	to brush one's teeth
despertarse (me despierto)	to wake up
divertirse (me divierto)	to have a good time, enjoy oneself
dormirse (me duermo)	to fall asleep
ducharse	to take a shower
levantarse	to get up (out of bed); to stand up
llamarse	to be called
peinarse	to brush/comb one's hair
ponerse (me pongo)	to put on (*an article of clothing*)
quitarse	to take off (*an article of clothing*)
sentarse (me siento)	to sit down
vestirse (me visto)	to get dressed

Los cuartos y otras partes de una casa

la alcoba	bedroom
el baño	bathroom
la cocina	kitchen
el comedor	dining room
el jardín	garden
la pared	wall
el patio	patio; yard
la piscina	swimming pool
la sala	living room

Cognado: el garaje

Repaso: el cuarto

Los muebles y otras cosas de una casa

la alfombra	rug
el armario	armoire, free standing closet
la bañera	bathtub
la cama	bed
la cómoda	bureau; dresser
el estante	bookshelf
la lámpara	lamp
el lavabo	(bathroom) sink
la mesita	end table
los muebles	furniture
los platos	dishes; plates
el sillón	armchair

Cognado: el sofá

Repaso: el escritorio, la mesa, la silla, la televisión

Otros sustantivos

la bebida	drink
el cine	movies; movie theater
la cosa	thing
el ejercicio	exercise
la llave	key
la película	movie
el ruido	noise
la rutina diaria	daily routine
la tarea	homework

Los adjetivos

cada (inv.)*	each, every
diario/a	daily
siguiente	following
solo/a	alone

Las preposiciones

antes de	before
después de	after
durante	during
hasta	until
sin	without

Repaso: a, con, de, en, para, por (in, during)

¿Qué día es hoy?

los días de la semana
- lunes
- martes
- miércoles
- jueves
- viernes
- sábado
- domingo

ayer fue (miércoles...)	yesterday was (Wednesday . . .)
el lunes (martes...)	on Monday (Tuesday . . .)
los lunes (los martes...)	on Mondays (Tuesdays . . .)
pasado mañana	the day after tomorrow
el próximo (martes...)	next (Tuesday . . .)
la semana (el lunes...) que viene	next week (Monday . . .)

Repaso: el día, el fin de semana, hoy, mañana

Palabras adicionales

lo que	what, that which
luego	then, afterward, next
por fin	finally
por lo general	generally
primero	first

 VOCABULARIO PERSONAL

The abbreviation inv. *means* invariable (*in form*). *The adjective* **cada** *is used with masculine and feminine nouns* (**cada libro, cada mesa**), *and it is never used in the plural.*

La playa (*beach*) de Manuel Antonio, en Costa Rica

1. What kind of weather would you expect on the coasts of Costa Rica?

2. What do you know about the seasons in Costa Rica?

3. What are the seasons like in your area? What kind of weather do you associate with each season?

5

Las estaciones y el tiempo°

°Las... *Seasons and the weather*

¿Qué tiempo hace hoy?°

¿Qué... *What's the weather like today?*

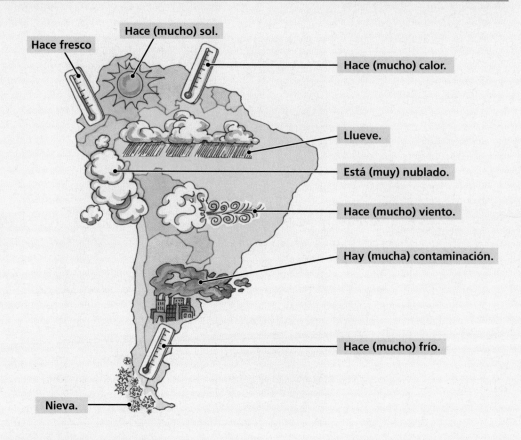

Hace fresco

Hace (mucho) sol.

Hace (mucho) calor.

Llueve.

Está (muy) nublado.

Hace (mucho) viento.

Hay (mucha) contaminación.

Hace (mucho) frío.

Nieva.

Hace (muy) buen/mal tiempo.
It's (very) good/bad weather. The weather is (very) good/bad.

In Spanish, many weather conditions are expressed with **hace,** and there is no literal English equivalent for it. The adjective **mucho** is used with the nouns **frío, calor, viento,** and **sol** to express *very*.

Pronunciation hint: Remember that, in most parts of the Spanish-speaking world, **ll** is pronounced exactly like **y: llueve**. Also remember that the letter **h** is silent in Spanish.

Conversación

A. El tiempo y la ropa. Di qué tiempo hace, según la ropa de cada persona. Luego di dónde están estas personas.

> **MODELO:** Todos llevan traje de baño y chanclas. →
> Hace calor. (Hace buen tiempo.) Están en Miami.

1. María lleva pantalones cortos y una camiseta.
2. Juan lleva suéter, pero no lleva chaqueta.
3. Roberto lleva sudadera y chaqueta.
4. Ramón lleva impermeable y botas y también tiene paraguas (*umbrella*).
5. Todos llevan abrigo, botas y sombrero.

B. El clima en el mundo (*world*)

Paso 1. ¿Qué clima asocias con estas ciudades de los Estados Unidos?

1. Seattle, Washington
2. Los Ángeles, California
3. Phoenix, Arizona
4. Buffalo, Nueva York
5. Honolulu, en las Islas Hawai
6. Chicago, Illinois

Paso 2. ¿Qué clima asocias con los siguientes países?

1. el Canadá
2. Costa Rica
3. Chile
4. México
5. el Perú
6. Vietnam
7. el Brasil
8. España

C. El tiempo y las actividades. Haz oraciones completas, indicando una actividad apropiada para cada situación.

cuando hace buen/mal tiempo cuando hace calor cuando hace frío cuando hay mucha contaminación cuando llueve cuando nieva		me quedo (*I stay*) en cama / en casa juego al basquetbol/voleibol con mis amigos almuerzo afuera (*outside*) / en el parque me divierto en el parque / en la playa (*beach*) con mis amigos no salgo de casa vuelvo a casa y trabajo o estudio

⏩ NOTA COMUNICATIVA

More *tener* Idioms

Several other conditions are expressed in Spanish with **tener** idioms — not with *to be*, as in English — including the following.

tener (mucho) calor	to be (very) warm, hot
tener (mucho) frío	to be (very) cold

These expressions are used to describe people or animals only. *To be comfortable* — neither hot nor cold — is expressed with **estar bien.**

D. ¿Tienen frío o calor? ¿Están bien? With a partner, describe the following weather conditions, and tell how the people depicted are feeling.

1.   **2.**    **3.**   **4.**   **5.**   **6.**   **7.**

Los meses y las estaciones del año

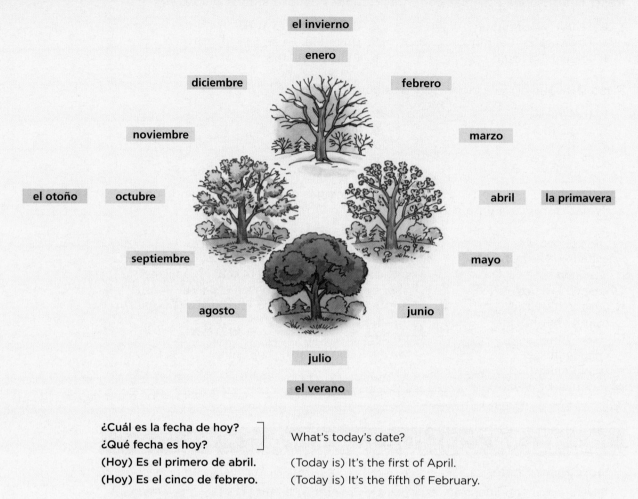

el invierno

enero

diciembre · febrero

noviembre · marzo

el otoño · octubre · abril · la primavera

septiembre · mayo

agosto · junio

julio

el verano

¿Cuál es la fecha de hoy?	
¿Qué fecha es hoy?	What's today's date?
(Hoy) Es el primero de abril.	(Today is) It's the first of April.
(Hoy) Es el cinco de febrero.	(Today is) It's the fifth of February.

- The ordinal number **primero** (**1°**) is used to express the first day of the month. Cardinal numbers (**dos, tres,** and so on) are used for other days.
- The definite article **el** is used before the date. However, when the day of the week is expressed, **el** is omitted: **Hoy es jueves, 3 de octubre.**
- As you know, **mil** is used to express the year (**el año**) after 999.

1950 mil novecientos cincuenta   2008 dos mil ocho

Conversación

A. Un poema. Completa el siguiente poema sobre los meses del año. ¿Cuál es el equivalente del poema en inglés?

_____¹ (número) días tiene noviembre,

con abril, junio y _____².

De veintiocho sólo hay uno,

Y los demás,° treinta y _____³.

°los… *the rest*

B. Las fechas

Paso 1. Expresa estas fechas en español. ¿En qué estación caen (*do they fall*)?

1. March 7
2. August 24
3. December 1
4. June 5
5. September 19, 1997
6. May 30, 1842
7. January 31, 1660
8. July 4, 1776

Paso 2. ¿Cuándo se celebran?* ¿Y en qué día de la semana caen este año?

1. el Día del Año Nuevo
2. el Día de los Enamorados (de San Valentín)
3. la Navidad (*Christmas*)
4. el Día de los Inocentes (*Fools*), en los Estados Unidos
5. tu cumpleaños (*birthday*)
6. el cumpleaños de tu novio/a (*boyfriend/girlfriend*), esposo/a, mejor (*best*) amigo/a,...

⬍ NOTA CULTURAL

El Niño

Most people have heard of El Niño, a weather phenomenon that is often associated with devastating climatic events. But why is it called El Niño?

The name El Niño dates from the end of the nineteenth century, when Peruvian fishermen noticed the periodic appearance of an abnormally warm ocean current off the coast of Peru. This warm current made its appearance around Christmas time. The name El Niño is a reference to the Christ Child, or El Niño Jesús, whose birth is celebrated by Christians at Christmas. At that time the name only referred to the current. Nowadays, it refers to the meteorological phenomenon as a whole. Torrential rains, flooding, and landslides can occur from the southwestern United States to Peru, whereas in Australia, Indonesia, and southeast Africa, the opposite may happen: severe droughts and the potential for destructive fires.

Destrucción causada por (*caused by*) El Niño en California

C. Entrevista

Paso 1. En parejas, túrnense para entrevistarse sobre los siguientes temas. Deben obtener detalles interesantes y personales de su compañero/a.

> **MODELO:** la fecha de su cumpleaños ⟶
> ¿Cuál es la fecha de tu cumpleaños? ¿Qué tiempo hace, generalmente, ese día? ¿Cómo celebras tu cumpleaños?

1. la fecha de su cumpleaños
2. su signo del horóscopo
3. su estación favorita
4. una estación que no le gusta

LOS SIGNOS DEL HORÓSCOPO	
Aries	Libra
Tauro	Escorpión
Géminis	Sagitario
Cáncer	Capricornio
Leo	Acuario
Virgo	Piscis

Paso 2. Digan a la clase lo que Uds. tienen en común.

> **MODELO:** Nosotras tenemos el cumpleaños en abril. La fecha de María es el 16 y mi fecha es el 18. Nuestro signo es Aries. Las dos (*Both of us*) preferimos la primavera. ¿Por qué? Porque nuestro cumpleaños es en primavera y es una estación muy bonita.

---

*Note that the word **se** *before a verb changes the verb's meaning slightly.* **¿Cuándo se celebran?** = When are they celebrated? *You will see this construction throughout* ¡Apúntate!

Pablito está a la derecha de Teresa.

Teresa está entre Carmen y Pablito.

El libro está encima de la mesa.

La mochila está debajo de la mesa.

cerca de	close to	**delante de**	in front of
lejos de	far from	**detrás de**	behind
debajo de	below	**a la derecha de**	to the right of
encima de	on top of	**a la izquierda de**	to the left of
al lado de	alongside of	**al norte/sur/**	to the north/south/
entre	between, among	**este/oeste de**	east/west of

◆》NOTA COMUNICATIVA

Los pronombres preposicionales

In Spanish, the pronouns that serve as objects of prepositions are identical in form to the subject pronouns, except for **mí** and **ti**.

Julio está delante de **mí.**	*Julio is in front of me.*
María está detrás de **ti.**	*María is behind you.*
Me siento a la izquierda de **ella.**	*I sit on her left.*

Mí and **ti** combine with the preposition **con** to form **conmigo** (*with me*) and **contigo** (*with you*), respectively.

¿Vienes **conmigo**?	*Are you coming with me?*
Sí, voy **contigo**.	*Yes, I'll go with you.*

¡OJO!

Note that **mí** has a written accent, but **ti** does not. This is to distinguish the object of a preposition (**mí**) from the possessive adjective (**mi**).

Conversación

A. ¿Quién o qué? Escoge (*Choose*) a una persona o un objeto en el salón de clase. Luego, sin nombrarlo/la (*without naming him/her/it*), usa las preposiciones de lugar para explicar dónde está. La clase va a adivinar (*guess*) qué persona, objeto o mueble es.

> **MODELO:** Está a la derecha de Paul ahora, pero generalmente se sienta detrás de mí. Siempre llega a clase con Paul.

B. Entrevista: ¿De dónde eres? Find out as much information as you can about the location of each others' hometown or state, or about the country you are from. You should also tell what the weather is like, and ask if the other person would like to go there with you.

> **MODELO:** **E1:** ¿De dónde eres?
> **E2:** Soy de Tylertown.
> **E1:** ¿Dónde está Tylertown?
> **E2:** Está cerca de…

C. ¿De qué país se habla?

Paso 1. Escucha (*Listen to*) la descripción de un país de Sudamérica que da (*gives*) tu profesor(a). ¿Puedes decir (*tell*) cuál es ese país?

Paso 2. Ahora describe un país de Sudamérica. Tus compañeros de clase van a decir cuál es. Sigue (*Follow*) el modelo, usando todas las frases que sean (*are*) apropiadas.

> **MODELO:** Este país está al norte/sur/este/oeste de _____. También está cerca de _____. Pero está lejos de _____. Está entre _____ y _____. ¿Cómo se llama?

Paso 3. A la derecha hay una lista de los nombres de las capitales de varios países de Sudamérica. Sin mirar el mapa, empareja (*match*) los nombres con el país correspondiente.

> **MODELO:** _____ es la capital de _____.

LAS CAPITALES

Asunción	La Paz
Bogotá	Lima
Brasilia	Montevideo
Buenos	Quito
Aires	Santiago
Caracas	

Need more practice?
- Workbook/Laboratory Manual
- Online Learning Center
  [www.mhhe.com/apuntate]

Costa Rica

Map showing MÉXICO, BELICE, GUATEMALA, HONDURAS, EL SALVADOR, NICARAGUA, COSTA RICA, San José, PANAMÁ, COLOMBIA, JAMAICA, MAR CARIBE, OCÉANO PACÍFICO

DATOS ESENCIALES

NOMBRE OFICIAL: República de Costa Rica

CAPITAL: San José

POBLACIÓN: más de 4 millones de habitantes

FÍJATE

- El ecoturismo es importante para la economía de Costa Rica y para la preservación de la biodiversidad y la belleza[a] natural que existe en el país. El ecoturismo tiene como propósito[b] controlar la entrada[c] de turistas en regiones protegidas[d] y, a la vez,[e] obtener fondos[f] para continuar con la protección de las regiones naturales. Aproximadamente el 30 por ciento del territorio costarricense está cubierto de selvas o bosques.[g] En total, más de un cuarto[h] del territorio del país ha sido destinado[i] para la preservación.
- Costa Rica es una de las primeras democracias de América. En 1821, convocaron[j] las primeras elecciones. El gobierno de Costa Rica tiene tres poderes:[k] el ejecutivo (un presidente y dos vicepresidentes), el legislativo y el judicial.
- Costa Rica no tiene fuerzas armadas.[l] De hecho,[m] la Constitución prohíbe la organización de un ejército.[n]
- Muchos consideran a Costa Rica como «la Suiza[ñ] de Centroamérica» porque es un país «amistoso[o]» que se mantiene neutral durante conflictos internacionales. A menudo[p] los líderes de Costa Rica intervienen para negociar paz[q] durante tales[r] conflictos.

[a]beauty [b]purpose [c]entrance [d]protected [e]a... at the same time [f]funds [g]está... is covered with jungles or forests [h]quarter [i]ha... has been set aside [j]they held [k]powers, branches [l]fuerzas... military forces [m]De... In fact [n]army [ñ]Switzerland [o]friendly [p]A... Often [q]peace [r]such

¡MÚSICA!

Los instrumentos musicales tradicionales de Costa Rica son la marimba, la ocarina,[a] el quijongo[b] y la chirimía.[c] La provincia de Guanacaste es conocida[d] por su música y sus bailes, entre ellos «la cajeta», «la flor de caña» y «el punto guanacasteco», tal vez el baile folclórico más conocido. Su música se toca[e] con marimba de calabaza[f] y guitarra.

[a]potato-shaped wind instrument [b]single-bow with gourd resonator [c]clarinet-type wind instrument [d]known [e]se... is played [f]gourd

LA COMPAÑÍA FOLCLÓRICA MATAMBÚ

La Compañía Folclórica Matambú es un grupo de variada formación[a] artística y profesional. Los miembros del grupo se dedican a fomentar[b] y cultivar el folclore[c] costarricense. La canción «¡Cállate, hombre![d]» sigue[e] el estilo de la cimarrona, una banda musical local que toca en las fiestas del pueblo y en otras ocasiones, como las bodas.[f] Es del álbum *Música de Costa Rica*.

Hugo Castillo Castro, músico (*musician*) de la Compañía Folclórica Matambú

[a]de... with many kinds of backgrounds [b]encouraging [c]native tradition [d]¡Cállate.... Shut up, Man! [e]is done in, follows [f]como... such as weddings

14 ¿Qué están haciendo? • Present Progressive: *Estar + -ndo*

Gramática en acción: ¿Qué está haciendo Elisa?

Elisa es periodista. Por eso escribe y habla mucho por teléfono en su trabajo. Pero ahora no está trabajando. Está descansando en casa. Está oyendo música, leyendo una novela y tomando un café.

¿Y Uds.? En el salón de clase, ¿quién está haciendo las siguientes cosas en este momento? **¡OJO! nadie** = *nobody*.

1. descansando
2. leyendo un periódico
3. tomando un café
4. trabajando
5. escuchando al profesor / a la profesora con mucha atención

Uses of the Progressive

1. Progressive Forms In Spanish, you can use special verb forms to describe an action in progress—that is, something actually happening at the time it is being described. These Spanish forms, called **el progresivo,** correspond in form to the English *progressive* (*I am walking, we are driving, she is studying*), but their use is not identical. Compare the Spanish and English verb forms in the sample sentences in **2.**	**progressive** = a verb form that expresses continuing or developing action

2. Uses of the Progressive English uses the present progressive (*I am -ing*) to tell what is happening right now (sentence 1), what is going to happen (sentence 2), and what someone is doing over a period of time (sentence 3). However, in Spanish the present progressive is used *only* to express an action that is currently in progress (sentence 1). The simple Spanish present tense is used to express sentences 2 and 3. Sentence 2 can also be expressed with **ir** + **a** + *infinitive*.	1. *Ramón is eating right now.*
	   Ramón **está comiendo** ahora mismo.
	
	2. *We're buying the house tomorrow.*
	   Compramos (Vamos a comprar) la casa mañana.
	
	3. *Adelaida is studying chemistry this semester.*
	   Adelaida **estudia** química este semestre.

What's Elisa doing? *Elisa is a journalist. That's why she writes and talks a lot on the phone in her job. But she's not working now. She's resting at home. She's listening to music, reading a novel, and having a cup of coffee.*

Formation of the Present Progressive

1. Spanish Present Progressive The Spanish present progressive is formed with **estar** plus the *present participle* (**el gerundio**).

The present participle is formed by adding **-ando** to the stem of **-ar** verbs and **-iendo** to the stem of **-er** and **-ir** verbs.*

The present participle never varies; it always ends in **-o**.

estar + *present participle*

tomar →	**tom**ando	taking; drinking
comprender →	**comprend**iendo	understanding
abrir →	**abr**iendo	opening

¡OJO!

Unaccented **i** represents the sound [y] in the participle ending **-iendo: comiendo, viviendo.**

Unaccented **i** between two vowels becomes the letter **y:**

leer: le + iendo ⟶ le**y**endo
oír: o + iendo ⟶ o**y**endo

2. Present Participle of *ir* Verbs The stem vowel in the present participle of **-ir** stem-changing verbs also changes. From this point on in *¡Apúntate!* that stem change will be shown in parentheses.

pr**e**f**e**rir (pref**ie**ro) (**i**) ⟶	pref**i**riendo
p**e**dir (p**i**do) (**i**) ⟶	p**i**diendo
d**o**rmir (d**ue**rmo) (**u**) ⟶	d**u**rmiendo

Using Pronouns with the Present Progressive

Reflexive pronouns can be attached to a present participle or precede the conjugated form of **estar**. Note the accent on the present participle when pronouns are attached.

Pablo **se está** bañando.
Pablo está **bañándose**.] *Pablo is taking a bath.*

¿Qué está haciendo?

---

*__Ir, poder,__ *and* __venir__ *have irregular present participles:* **yendo, pudiendo, viniendo.** *These three verbs, however, are seldom used in the progressive.*

Práctica

A. ¡Anticipemos! Un sábado típico

Paso 1. Imagina que es un sábado típico para ti. Indica lo que estás haciendo a las horas indicadas. En algunos (*some*) casos hay más de una respuesta posible.

Son las ocho de la mañana y...   **SÍ**   **NO**

1. estoy durmiendo.   ❏ ❏
2. estoy duchándome.   ❏ ❏
3. estoy haciendo ejercicio.   ❏ ❏
4. estoy trabajando.   ❏ ❏
5. estoy _____.   ❏ ❏

Es mediodía (*noon*) y...   **SÍ**   **NO**

1. estoy almorzando.   ❏ ❏
2. estoy estudiando.   ❏ ❏
3. estoy tomando un café.   ❏ ❏
4. estoy viendo una película.   ❏ ❏
5. estoy _____.   ❏ ❏

Son las diez de la noche y...   **SÍ**   **NO**

1. estoy preparándome para salir.   ❏ ❏
2. estoy bailando en una fiesta.   ❏ ❏
3. estoy trabajando.   ❏ ❏
4. estoy hablando por teléfono.   ❏ ❏
5. estoy _____.   ❏ ❏

Son las ocho de la mañana y estoy cantando en la ducha (*shower*).

Paso 2. Ahora, en parejas, túrnense para determinar si hacen las mismas (*same*) cosas a la misma hora.

> **MODELO: E1:** A las ocho de la mañana los sábados, ¿estás durmiendo?
>
> **E2:** No, a esa hora estoy trabajando.

B. La familia de Lola.
Hoy no es un día como todos los días para la familia de Lola, porque su tío de Costa Rica está de visita. Completa las siguientes oraciones para expresar lo que está pasando (*happening*).

> **MODELO:** Casi siempre, Lola almuerza con su hija. Hoy Lola...
> (almorzar con su tío en un restaurante) ⟶
> Hoy Lola *está almorzando* con su tío en un restaurante.

1. Generalmente, Lola pasa la mañana en la universidad. Hoy Lola...
   (pasar el día con su tío Ricardo)
2. Casi siempre, Lola va a casa después de sus clases. Hoy Lola y su tío...
   (tomar un café en casa)
3. De lunes a viernes, Marta, la hija de Lola, va a la escuela (*school*)
   por la tarde. Pero esta tarde ella... (jugar con Ricardo)
4. Generalmente, la familia cena (*has dinner*) a las nueve. Esta noche todos...
   (cenar a las diez)

C. En casa con la familia Duarte.

Empareja los dibujos con las acciones. Di quién está haciendo cada acción—el padre, la madre, la hija, los gemelos (*twins*)— y a qué hora.

MODELO: Está saliendo de la ducha (*shower*). →
El padre está saliendo de la ducha a las seis de la mañana.

1. Está levantándose.
2. Está haciendo la tarea.
3. Se está vistiendo.
4. Está haciendo la cena (*dinner*).
5. Está leyendo el periódico.

6. Están durmiendo.
7. Está trabajando.
8. Están jugando con el perro.
9. Están comiendo.
10. Está quitándose la blusa.

Por la mañana: A las seis de la mañana

a.

b.

c.

d.

Más tarde: A las ocho de la mañana

e.

f.

g.

h.

Por la tarde: A las seis y media de la tarde

i.

j.

k.

l.

Conversación

Entrevista

Paso 1. En parejas, túrnense para entrevistarse sobre los siguientes temas. Deben obtener detalles interesantes y personales de su compañero/a.

MODELOS: ¿Pasas mucho tiempo mirando la tele? ¿Cuántas horas al (*per*) día?
¿Qué programas te gusta mirar?
¿Cómo te diviertes más, bailando o tocando un instrumento musical?

continuar/seguir divertirse estar pasar más tiempo pasar mucho/poco tiempo	**+**	bailando estudiando hablando español después de la clase leyendo (¿ ?) mirando la tele oyendo música siendo amigo/a de tu mejor (*best*) amigo/a de la escuela primaria tocando un instrumento musical trabajando (en ¿ ?) ¿ ?

Paso 2. Digan a la clase lo que Uds. tienen en común.

You have been using forms of **ser** and **estar** since **Primeros pasos**, the preliminary chapter of *¡Apúntate!* The following section will help you consolidate everything you know so far about these two verbs, both of which express *to be* in Spanish. You will learn a bit more about them as well.

Before you begin **Gramática 15**, think in particular about the following questions: **¿Cómo está Ud.? ¿Cómo es Ud.?** What do these questions tell you about the difference between **ser** and **estar**?

15 *Ser* o *estar* • Summary of the Uses of *ser* and *estar*

Gramática en acción: Una conversación de larga distancia

Aquí hay un lado de la conversación entre una esposa que está en un viaje de negocios y su esposo, que está en casa. Habla el esposo. Primero, lee lo que él dice.

Aló. […¹] ¿Cómo estás, mi amor? […²] ¿Dónde estás ahora? […³] ¿Qué hora es allí? […⁴] ¡Huy!, es muy tarde. Y el hotel, ¿cómo es? […⁵] Oye, ¿qué estás haciendo ahora? […⁶] Ay, pobrecita, lo siento. Estás muy ocupada. ¿Con quién estás citada mañana? […⁷] ¿Quién es el dueño de la compañía? […⁸] Ah, él es de Cuba, ¿verdad? […⁹] Bueno, ¿qué tiempo hace allí? […¹⁰] Muy bien, mi vida. Hasta luego, ¿eh? […¹¹] Adiós.

Comprensión Aquí está el otro lado de la conversación: las respuestas de la esposa que está de viaje. Pero no están en orden. Léelas y luego emparéjalas (*match them*) con los comentarios y preguntas del esposo.

a. _____ Es muy moderno. Me gusta mucho.
b. _____ Sí, pero vive en Nueva York ahora.
c. _____ Son las once y media.
d. _____ Hola, querido (*dear*). ¿Qué tal?
e. _____ Es el Sr. Cortina.
f. _____ Pues, todavía (*still*) tengo que trabajar.
g. _____ Sí, hasta pronto.
h. _____ Estoy en Nueva York.
i. _____ Un poco cansada (*tired*), pero estoy bien.
j. _____ Pues, hace buen tiempo, pero está un poco nublado.
k. _____ Con un señor de Computec, una nueva compañía de computadoras.

A long-distance conversation *Here is one side of a conversation between a wife who is on a business trip and her husband, who is at home. The husband is speaking. First, read what he says. Hello . . . How are you, dear? . . . Where are you now? . . . What time is it there? . . . Boy, it's very late. And how's the hotel? . . . Hey, what are you doing now? . . . You poor thing, I'm sorry. You're very busy. Who(m) are you meeting with tomorrow? . . . Who's the owner of the company? . . . Ah, he's from Cuba, isn't he? . . . Well, what's the weather like there? . . . Very well, sweetheart. See you later, OK? . . . Good-bye.*

Summary of the Uses of ser

- To *identify* people and things

  Ella es doctora.
  Tikal **es una ciudad maya.**

- To express *nationality;* with **de** to express *origin*

  Son cubanos.
  Son de La Habana.

- With **de** to tell of what *material* something is made

  Este bolígrafo **es de plástico.**

- With **de** to express *possession*

  Es de Carlota.

- With **para** to tell *for whom* something is intended

  El regalo **es para** Sara.

- To tell *time*

  Son las once.
  Es la una y media.

- With *adjectives* that describe *basic, inherent characteristics*

  Ramona **es inteligente.**

- To form many *generalizations*

  Es necesario llegar temprano.
  Es importante estudiar.

Summary of the Uses of estar

- To tell *location*

  El libro **está en la mesa.**

- To describe *health*

  Estoy muy **bien,** gracias.

- With *adjectives* that describe *conditions*

  Estoy muy ocupada.

- In a number of *fixed expressions*

  (No) Estoy de acuerdo.
  Está bien.

- With *present participles* to form the *progreessive tense*

  Estoy estudiando ahora mismo.

Ser and *estar* with Adjectives

1. *Ser* = Fundamental Qualities *Ser* is used with adjectives that describe the fundamental qualities of a person, place, or thing.	Esa mesa **es** muy **baja.** *That table is very short/low.* Sus calcetines **son morados.** *His socks are purple.* Este sillón **es cómodo.** *This armchair is comfortable.* Sus padres **son cariñosos.** *Their parents are affectionate people.*

2. *Estar* = Conditions Estar is used with adjectives to express conditions or observations that are true at a given moment but that do not describe inherent qualities of the noun. The adjectives at right are generally used with **estar**.

abierto/a	open	**limpio/a**	clean
aburrido/a	bored	**loco/a**	crazy
alegre	happy	**molesto/a**	annoyed
cansado/a	tired	**nervioso/a**	nervous
cerrado/a	closed	**ocupado/a**	busy
congelado/a	frozen; very cold	**ordenado/a**	neat
contento/a	content, happy	**preocupado/a**	worried
desordenado/a	messy	**seguro/a**	sure, certain
enfermo/a	sick	**sucio/a**	dirty
furioso/a	furious, angry	**triste**	sad

3. *Ser* or *estar* Many adjectives can be used with either **ser** or **estar,** depending on what the speaker intends to communicate. In general, when *to be* implies *looks, feels,* or *appears,* **estar** is used. Compare the pairs of sample sentences.

Daniel **es guapo.**
Daniel is handsome. (He is a handsome person.)
Daniel **está** muy guapo esta noche.
Daniel looks very nice (handsome) tonight.

—¿Cómo **es** Amalia?
What is Amalia like (as a person)?
—**Es simpática.**
She's nice.

—¿Cómo **está** Amalia?
How is Amalia (feeling)?
—**Está enferma** todavía.
She's still sick.

Práctica

A. Un regalo. Completa las siguientes oraciones con **es** o **está.**

La computadora...

1. _____ en la mesa del comedor.
2. _____ un regalo de cumpleaños.
3. _____ para mi compañero de cuarto.
4. _____ de la tienda Computec.
5. _____ en una caja (*box*) verde.
6. _Son_ de los padres de mi compañero.
7. _es_ un regalo muy caro, pero estupendo.
8. _es_ de metal y plástico gris.
9. _es_ una Dell, el último (*latest*) modelo.
10. _es_ muy fácil (*easy*) de usar.

Amalia está enferma todavía.

B. Descripciones

Paso 1. Haz oraciones con **soy** o **estoy**. Corrige las ideas incorrectas.

Yo...

1. _Soy_ estadounidense.
2. _Soy_ de Nevada.
3. _Soy_ estudiante de primer año en la universidad. (*2ⁿᵈ* = segundo, *3ʳᵈ* = tercer, *4ᵗʰ* = cuarto)
4. _Estoy_ muy cansado/a hoy.
5. _estoy_ bien en este momento.
6. _estoy_ de acuerdo con las ideas del presidente / primer ministro.
7. _estoy_ estudiando química en este momento.
8. _Soy_ muy inteligente.

Paso 2. Ahora entrevista a un compañero o compañera sobre los temas del **Paso 1.**

MODELO: 1. estadounidense. ⟶ ¿Eres estadounidense?

C. Publicidad.
Complete the text of the following ad with the correct form of **ser** or **estar,** as suggested by context.

Costa Rica... bellezaª natural

¿(*Tú*) _eres_ ¹ de una gran ciudad? ¿(*Tú*) _eres_² una persona aventurera? ¿ _Es_ ³ la naturaleza una gran atracción en tu vidaᵇ? ¿ _Estás_ ⁴ preocupado/a por los cambiosᶜ en el clima global? Entonces,ᵈ Costa Rica _es_ ⁵ el país para ti. Imagina: _Estás_ ⁶ en un lugar cerca del marᵉ en donde hay increíbles especies de animales y plantas: caimanes, iguanas, tortugas, orquídeas, heliconias...

(*Nosotros*) _somos_⁷ los expertos en turismo natural en Costa Rica. Todos nuestros guíasᶠ _son_ ⁸ costarricenses de nacimiento,ᵍ pero (*ellos*) _son_ ⁹ contentos de conocerʰ a personas de todo el mundo y hacer nuevos amigos. Con sus conocimientos,ⁱ con su gran paciencia, con su español, (*ellos*) _son_ ¹⁰ como profesores... ¡pero sus clases _son_ ¹¹ mucho más interesantes que las clases académicas!

No _es_ ¹² necesario viajarʲ a Costa Rica en una estación específica. _Es_ ¹³ bueno viajar a Costa Rica en cualquierᵏ mes del año.

¡Ven!ˡ ¡Costa Rica _____¹⁴ esperándoteᵐ!

ᵃ*beauty* ᵇ*life* ᶜ*changes* ᵈ*Then* ᵉ*ocean* ᶠ*guides* ᵍ*de... by birth* ʰ*de... to meet* ⁱ*knowledge* ʲ*to travel* ᵏ*any* ˡ*Come (to visit)!* ᵐ*waiting for you*

Una heliconia

Comprensión: ¿Cierto o falso? Corrige las oraciones falsas.

	CIERTO	FALSO
1. El turismo tiene poca importancia en la economía de Costa Rica.	❑	❑
2. La flora y fauna de Costa Rica son muy interesantes.	❑	❑
3. Los costarricenses son poco hospitalarios (*welcoming*).	❑	❑
4. Es mejor viajar a Costa Rica en ciertas estaciones del año.	❑	❑

D. Una tarde terrible

Paso 1. Describe lo que pasa hoy por la tarde en esta casa, cambiando (*exchanging*) por antónimos las palabras azules.

1. No hace buen tiempo; hace _____.
2. El bebé no está bien; está _____.
3. El gato no está limpio; está _____.
4. El esposo no está tranquilo; está _____ por el bebé.
5. El garaje no está cerrado; está _____.
6. Los niños no están ocupados; están _____.
7. La esposa no está contenta; está _____ por el tiempo.
8. El baño no está ordenado; está _____.

Paso 2. Ahora imagina que son las seis y media de la tarde. Expresa lo que están haciendo los miembros de la familia en este momento. Usa tu imaginación y di también lo que generalmente hacen estas personas a esa hora.

MODELO: Ahora son las seis y media. La madre está conduciendo su coche. Quiere llegar a casa a preparar la comida. Generalmente llega a esa hora.

Vocabulario útil	
cenar	to have dinner
conducir (conduzco)	to drive
ladrar	to bark
llorar	to cry

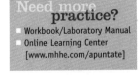

Need more **practice?**
■ Workbook/Laboratory Manual
■ Online Learning Center
[www.mhhe.com/apuntate]

Conversación

A. Ana y Estela. Contesta las preguntas para describir el siguiente dibujo de un cuarto típico de una residencia. **¡OJO!** Inventa otros detalles necesarios.

Ana

Estela

> **Vocabulario útil**
>
> **el cajón** drawer
> **el cartel** poster
> **la foto**
> **el piso** floor

1. ¿Quiénes son las dos compañeras de cuarto?
2. ¿De dónde son? ¿Cómo son?
3. ¿Dónde están en este momento?
4. ¿Qué hay en el cuarto?
5. ¿Cómo está el cuarto?
6. ¿Son ordenadas las dos o desordenadas?

B. Entrevista. ¿Cómo están Uds. en estas situaciones? En parejas, túrnense para entrevistarse, según el model.

> **Vocabulario útil**
>
> **agobiado/a** overwhelmed
> **desahogado/a** relieved
> **enérgico/a**
> **estresado/a**

> **MODELO:** cuando / tener mucha tarea ⟶
> **E1:** ¿Cómo estás cuando *tienes* mucha tarea?
> **E2:** Estoy cansado y estresado, como ahora. ¿Y tú?
> **E3:** Yo también.

1. cuando / tener mucha tarea / una tarea fácil/difícil
2. cuando / no tener trabajo académico
3. cuando / sacar (*to get*) A/D en un examen
4. en verano/invierno
5. cuando llueve/nieva
6. los lunes por la mañana / los domingos por la tarde / los…
7. después de una fiesta / después de un examen
8. durante la clase de _____
9. cuando una persona / hablar y hablar y hablar
10. cuando / estar con la familia
11. cuando / estar de vacaciones
12. cuando / no funcionar el coche
13. cuando / ir al consultorio del dentista
14. ¿ ?

Parte de un sendero[a] en el Parque Nacional Arenal

[a]*trail*

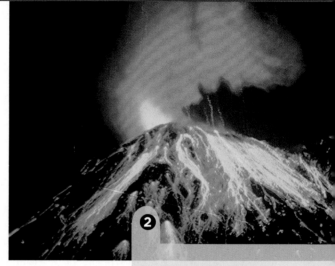

El Volcán Arenal El Parque Nacior
es una de las atracciones más pop
de Costa Rica. El centro del parqu
el Volcán Arenal, que tiene erupcic
espectaculares desde 1968. Los ec
pueden alojarse[a] en hoteles y cab
vistas[c] al volcán, hacer excursione
por los senderos del parque y bañ
aguas termales.[e]

[a]*stay* [b]*cabins* [c]*views* [d]*hacer... hike* [e]*springs*

Carreta[a] de Sarchí Sarchí es el pueblo principal de las artesanías[b] costarricenses y su producto más famoso son sus carretas pintadas.[c] En el siglo XIX,[d] las carretas eran[e] esenciales para transportar al mercado la cosecha de los granos de café,[f] y las familias pintaban y decoraban[g] sus carretas para llamar la atención.[h] Hoy día[i] las carretas de Sarchí representan una tradición nacional.

[a]*Oxcart* [b]*arts and crafts* [c]*painted* [d]*siglo... 19th century* [e]*were* [f]*cosecha... coffee bean harvest* [g]*pintaban... painted and decorated* [h]*llamar... attract attention* [i]*Hoy... Today*

Un cafetal[a] en Costa Rica La rica tierra volcánica de Costa Rica es ideal para el cultivo del café. Costa Rica fue el primer país en exportar café, primero a sus vecinos[b] latinoamericanos y luego a Inglaterra y a otros países. El café sigue siendo un producto importante de la economía costarricense.

[a]*coffee plantation* [b]*neighbors*

Una rana calzonuda[a] Costa Ric
como un puente migratorio[b] pa
muchas especies de animales c
pasan parte del año en los par
reservas nacionales del país. La
calzonuda se cuenta entre[c] los
especies de anfibios que viven
Costa Rica.

[a]*rana... red-eyed tree frog* [b]*puente... migratory bridge* [c]*se... is included ar*

16   Describing • Comparisons

Gramática en acción: México, D.F. y Sevilla, España

México, D.F. (Distrito Federal)

- La Ciudad de México es más grande que Sevilla.
- Tiene más edificios altos que Sevilla.
- En el D.F. no hace tanto calor como en Sevilla.

Pero...

- Sevilla es tan bonita como la Ciudad de México.
- No tiene tantos habitantes como el D.F.
- Sin embargo, los sevillanos son tan simpáticos como los mexicanos.

¡Me gusta Sevilla tanto como la Ciudad de México!

El barrio de Santa Cruz, en Sevilla, España

¿Y tú?

1. Mi ciudad/pueblo...

- es / no es tan grande como Chicago.
- es más/menos cosmopolita que Quebec.

2. Me gusta _____ (nombre de mi ciudad/pueblo)...

- más que _____ (nombre de otra ciudad).
- menos que _____ (nombre de otra ciudad).
- tanto como _____ (nombre de otra ciudad).

In English the *comparative* (**el comparativo**) is formed in a variety of ways. Equal comparisons are expressed with the word *as.* Unequal comparisons are expressed with the adverbs *more* or *less,* or by adding *-er* to the end of the adjective.

as *cold* **as**
as *many* **as**

more *intelligent,*
less *important,*
*tall**er**, smart**er***

comparative = a form of or structure with nouns, adjectives, and adverbs used to compare nouns, qualities, or actions

---

Mexico City and Seville, Spain • *Mexico City is bigger than Seville.* • *It has more tall buildings than Seville.*
• *It is not as hot in Mexico City as it is in Seville. But . . .* • *Seville is as beautiful as Mexico City.* • *It doesn't have as many inhabitants as Mexico City.* • *Nevertheless, the people from Seville are as nice as those from Mexico City. I like Seville as much as Mexico City!*

Comparisons of Inequality  ■ ≠ ■ . ■ ≠ ■

1. **más/menos** + *adjective/noun/adverb* + **que** =
more/less ("-er") . . . than

Finish

Juan es **más alto que** Elena.
Juan is taller than Elena.

Elena es **menos alta que** Juan.
Elena is shorter than Juan.

Juan tiene **más lápices que** Elena.
Juan has more pencils than Elena.

Elena tiene **menos lápices que** Juan.
Elena has fewer pencils than Juan.

Juan corre **más rápido que** Elena.
Juan runs faster (more quickly) than Elena.

Elena corre **menos rápido que** Juan.
Elena runs slower (more slowly) than Juan.

2. *verb* + **más/menos que** = . . . more/less than

Juan **estudia más que** Elena.
Juan studies more than Elena.

Elena **estudia menos que** Juan.
Elena studies less than Juan.

3. **más/menos de** + number + *noun* = more/less
than . . .

¿Quién es más alto,
el niño o la niña?

¡OJO!

The preposition **de** is used
instead of **que** when the
comparison is followed by
a number.

Juan tiene **más de dos** lápices.
Juan has more than two pencils.

Elena tiene **menos de tres** lápices.
Elena has less (fewer) than three pencils.

Comparisons of Equality ■ = ■

1. **tan** + *adjective/adverb* + **como** = as . . . as

Patricia es **tan alta como** Juan.
Patricia is as tall as Juan.

Patricia juega al tenis **tan bien como** Juan.
Patricia plays tennis as well as Juan.

2. **tant**o/a/os/as + *noun* + **como** = as much/many . . . as

Patricia tiene **tanto dinero como** Juan.
Patricia has as much money as Juan.

Patricia tiene **tantas hermanas como** Juan.
Patricia has as many sisters as Juan.

¡OJO!

Like all adjectives, **tanto** must agree in gender and number with the noun it modifies: **tant**o **dinero**, **tant**a **prisa**, **tant**os **abrigos**, **tant**as **hermanas**.

3. *verb* + **tanto como** = as much as

Patricia **estudia tanto como** Juan.
Patricia studies as much as Juan.

Juan **lee tanto como** Patricia.
Juan reads as much as Patricia.

Irregular Forms

1. **bueno/a/os/as** → **mejor, mejores** **bien** → **mejor**	Estos coches son **buenos**, pero esos son **mejores**. *These cars are good, but those are better.* Yo hablo español **mejor** que mi hermano. *I speak Spanish better than my brother (does).*
2. **malo/a/os/as** → **peor, peores** **mal** → **peor**	Aquí las cosas van de **mal** en **peor**. *Things here are going from bad to worse.* Yo juego al tenis **peor** que mi hermano. *I play tennis worse than my brother (does).*
3. **mayor, mayores**	Mi hermana es **mayor** que yo. *My sister is older than I (am).*
4. **menor, menores**	Mis primos son **menores** que yo. *My cousins are younger than I (am).*

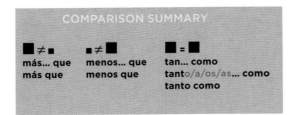

COMPARISON SUMMARY

■ ≠ ■
más... que
más que

■ ≠ ■
menos... que
menos que

■ = ■
tan... como
tanto/a/os/as**... como**
tanto como

Práctica

A. Alfredo y Gloria. Compara la casa y las posesiones de Alfredo con las de Gloria.

MODELOS: La casa de Alfredo tiene más cuartos que la casa de Gloria.
Gloria tiene tantas bicicletas como Alfredo.

		ALFREDO	GLORIA
1.	cuartos en total	8	6
2.	baños	2	1
3.	alcobas	3	3
4.	camas	3	5
5.	coches	3	1
6.	bicicletas	2	2
7.	dinero en el banco	$500.000	$5.000
8.	CDs	100	80
9.	libros de texto	15	30
10.	sudaderas	7	7

B. ¿De verdad (*Really*)**?** Contesta las siguientes preguntas lógicamente.

¿Eres....

1. tan guapo/a como Antonio Banderas / Jennifer López?
2. tan rico como Bill Gates?
3. tan fiel como tu mejor amigo/a?
4. tan inteligente como Einstein?
5. tan simpático/a como tu mejor amigo/a?

¿Tienes....

1. tantos libros como CDs?
2. tantos amigos como amigas?
3. tanto talento como Carlos Santana?
4. tanta sabiduría (*knowledge*) como tu profesor(a)?
5. tanto interés en la clase de español como en la clase de historia?

C. Opiniones. Modifica las siguientes declaraciones para expresar tu opinión personal. Si estás de acuerdo con la declaración, di: **«Estoy de acuerdo».**

MODELO: El invierno es tan divertido como el verano. ⟶
El invierno es *menos* divertido *que* el verano.

1. Para mí, el fútbol (*soccer*) es tan divertido como el fútbol americano.
2. En esta sociedad (universidad), las artes son tan importantes como las ciencias.
3. La comida (*food*) de la cafetería es tan buena como la de mi casa.
4. Los profesores trabajan más que los estudiantes.
5. Me divierto tanto con mis amigos como con mis padres.
6. Los jóvenes duermen tanto como los adultos.
7. Aquí llueve más en primavera que en invierno.
8. En este momento de mi vida (*life*), necesito más a mis amigos que a mis padres (mi esposo/a).
9. El español es tan difícil como el inglés.
10. Los exámenes de matemáticas son más fáciles que los exámenes de español.
11. El dinero es tan importante como la salud (*health*).
12. Los amigos son tan importantes como la familia.
13. En esta universidad, los estudios son menos importantes que los deportes.
14. En mi vida, los estudios son más importantes que los deportes.
15. Necesito más el dinero que la amistad (*friendship*).

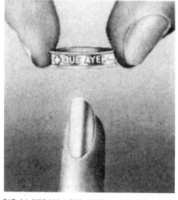

Lee el anuncio, expresando las comparaciones con palabras. ¿Qué significan las palabras **alianza** y **amor**?
[a]la... *you love her*

El verano es tan divertido como el invierno.

Need more **practice?**
■ Workbook/Laboratory Manual
■ Online Learning Center
[www.mhhe.com/apuntate]

Conversación

A. La familia de Lucía y Miguel

Paso 1. Mira el dibujo e identifica a los miembros de esta familia. Piensa en la edad de cada persona. **¡OJO!** Lucía y Miguel tienen tres hijos.

> **MODELO:** Amalia es la hija de Lucía y Miguel. Es la hermana de Ramón y Sancho.

Amalia (19)   Ramón (24)
Sancho (25)
Lucía (43)   Miguel (45)
Ramoncito (1)   Sarita (25)

Laurel (75)   Javier (

Paso 2. Compara a cada miembro de la familia con otra persona.

> **MODELO:** Amalia es menor que Sancho pero es más alta que él.

Paso 3. Ahora compara a los miembros de tu propia (*own*) familia. Haz por lo menos cinco declaraciones.

> **MODELOS:** Mi hermana Mary es mayor que yo, pero yo soy más alto que ella.
> Mi abuela es mayor que mi abuelo, pero ella es más activa que él.

Paso 4. Lee tus oraciones del **Paso 3** a un compañero o compañera. Luego hazle preguntas (*ask him/her*) sobre tu familia.

> **MODELO:** ¿Qué miembro de mi familia es mayor que yo?

B. La rutina diaria… en invierno y en verano

Paso 1. ¿Es diferente nuestra rutina diaria en cada estación? Completa las siguientes oraciones sobre tu rutina.

EN INVIERNO…	EN VERANO…
1. me levanto a _____ (hora)	me levanto a _____
2. almuerzo en _____	almuerzo en _____
3. me divierto con mis amigos / mi familia en _____	me divierto con mis amigos / mi familia en _____
4. estudio _____ horas todos los días	(no) estudio _____ horas todos los días
5. estoy / me quedo en _____ (lugar) por la noche	estoy / me quedo en _____ por la noche
6. me acuesto a _____	me acuesto a _____

Vocabulario útil

el gimnasio
el parque

afuera outside

Paso 2. En parejas, comparen sus actividades de invierno con las de verano.

> **MODELO:** E1: En invierno, ¿te levantas más temprano que en verano?
> E2: No, en invierno, me levanto tan temprano como en verano.
> (No, en invierno, me levanto a la misma hora que en verano.)

Paso 3. Ahora digan a la clase una o dos cosas que Uds. tienen en común.

> **MODELO:** Nosotros nos levantamos más tarde en verano que en invierno.
> En verano no hay clases y, por lo general, nos acostamos más tarde.

UN POCO DE TODO

Es diciembre en Buenos Aires. ¿Qué tiempo hace?

Lengua y cultura: Dos hemisferios. Complete the following paragraphs with the correct forms of the words in parentheses, as suggested by context. When two possibilities are given in parentheses, select the correct word.

¿**S**abes[a] algo de las diferencias entre los hemisferios del norte y del sur? Hay (mucho[1]) diferencias entre el clima del hemisferio norte y el del hemisferio sur. Cuando (ser/estar[2]) invierno en este país, por ejemplo, (ser/estar[3]) verano en la Argentina, en Bolivia, en Chile... Cuando yo (salir[4]) para la universidad en enero, con frecuencia tengo que (llevar[5]) abrigo y botas. En (los/las[6]) países del hemisferio sur, un estudiante (poder[7]) asistir (a/de[8]) un concierto en febrero llevando sólo pantalones (corto[9]), camiseta y sandalias. En muchas partes de este país, (antes de / durante[10]) las vacaciones de diciembre, casi siempre (hacer[11]) frío y a veces (nevar[12]). En (grande[13]) parte de Sudamérica, al otro lado del ecuador, hace calor y (muy/mucho[14]) sol durante (ese[15]) mes. A veces en los periódicos, hay fotos de personas que (tomar[16]) el sol y nadan[b] en las playas sudamericanas en enero.

Tengo un amigo que (ir[17]) a (hacer/tomar[18]) un viaje a Buenos Aires. Él me dice[c] que allí la Navidad[d] (ser/estar[19]) una fiesta de verano y que todos (llevar[20]) ropa como la que[e] llevamos nosotros en julio. Parece[f] increíble, ¿verdad?

[a]*Do you know*   [b]*are swimming*   [c]*Él... He tells me*   [d]*Christmas*   [e]*la... that which*   [f]*It seems*

Comprensión. ¿Probable o improbable?

1. Los estudiantes argentinos van a la playa en julio.
2. Muchas personas sudamericanas hacen viajes de vacaciones en enero.
3. En Santiago (Chile) hace frío en diciembre.
4. Los estudiantes chilenos llevan abrigo en enero.
5. Los argentinos se ponen guantes en julio.
6. Muchos sudamericanos toman el sol en la playa en agosto.

Resources for Review and Testing Preparation

- Workbook/Laboratory Manual
- Online Learning Center
  [www.mhhe.com/apuntate]

En resumen

Gramática en breve

14. Present Progressive: **Estar** + **-ndo**

Present Progressive Endings
-ar ⟶ -ando
-er / -ir ⟶ = iendo

Unaccented = **i-** ⟶ **-y-**

-ir Stem-Changing Verbs
e ⟶ **i, o** ⟶ **u**

15. Summary of the Uses of **ser** and **estar**

Ser	Estar
inherent qualities, characteristics	mental, physical, health conditions
nationality, origin	location
possession	present progressive
time, date	

16. Comparisons

Comparisons of Inequality	Comparisons of Equality
más/menos... que	**tan... como**
más/menos que	**tanto/a(s)... como**
más/menos... de	**tanto como**
mejor/peor que	

Vocabulario

Los verbos

celebrar	to celebrate
continuar (continúo)	to continue
pasar	to spend (*time*); to happen
quedarse	to stay, remain (*in a place*)
seguir (sigo) (i)	to continue

Repaso: divertirse (me divierto) (i)

¿Qué tiempo hace?

está (muy) nublado	it's (very) cloudy, overcast
hace...	it's ...
(muy) buen/mal tiempo	(very) good/bad weather
(mucho) calor	(very) hot
fresco	cool
(mucho) frío	(very) cold
(mucho) sol	(very) sunny
(mucho) viento	(very) windy
hay (mucha)	there's (lots of)
contaminación	pollution
llover (llueve)	to rain (it's raining)
nevar (nieva)	to snow (it's snowing)

Los meses del año

¿Cual es la fecha de hoy? ¿Qué fecha es hoy?	What's today's date?
el primero de	the first of (*month*)

Los meses (enero–diciembre)

enero	julio
febrero	agosto
marzo	septiembre
abril	octubre
mayo	noviembre
junio	diciembre

Las estaciones del año

la primavera	spring
el verano	summer
el otoño	fall, autumn
el invierno	winter

Los lugares

la capital	capital city
la isla	island
el mundo	world
la playa	beach

Otros sustantivos

el año	year
el clima	climate
el cumpleaños	birthday
la estación	season
la fecha	date (*calendar*)
el mes	month
el/la novio/a	boyfriend/girlfriend
la respuesta	answer
el tiempo	weather; time

Los adjetivos

abierto/a	open
aburrido/a	bored
alegre	happy
cansado/a	tired
cariñoso/a	affectioate
cerrado/a	closed
congelado/a	frozen; very cold
contento/a	content, happy
desordenado/a	messy
difícil	hard, difficult
enfermo/a	sick
fácil	easy
furioso/a	furious, angry
limpio/a	clean
loco/a	crazy
mismo/a	same
molesto/a	annoyed
nervioso/a	nervous
ocupado/a	busy
ordenado/a	neat
preocupado/a	worried
querido/a	dear
seguro/a	sure, certain
sucio/a	dirty
triste	sad

Las comparaciones

más/menos… que	more/less (-er) . . . than
más/menos que	more/less than
tan… como	as . . . as
tanto como	as much as
tanto/a(s)… como	as much/many . . . as
mayor	older
mejor	better; best
menor	younger
peor	worse

Las preposiciones

a la derecha de	to the right of
a la izquierda de	to the left of
al lado de	alongside of
cerca de	close to
debajo de	below
delante de	in front of
detrás de	behind
encima de	on top of
entre	between, among
lejos de	far from

Los puntos cardinales

el norte, el sur, el este, el oeste

Palabras adicionales

afuera	outdoors
ahora mismo	right now
conmigo	with me
contigo	with you (*fam.*)
esta noche	tonight
estar bien	to be comfortable (*temperature*)
mí (*obj. of prep.*)	me
por	about; because of
sin embargo	nevertheless
tener (mucho) calor	to be (very) warm, hot
tener (mucho) frío	to be (very) cold
ti (*obj. of prep.*)	you (*fam.*)
todavía	still

 VOCABULARIO PERSONAL

Un mercado en
la Ciudad de Panamá

1. ¿Qué colores ves en los productos de este mercado?

2. ¿Dónde compras las verduras (*vegetables*) y frutas?

3. ¿Hay mercados al aire libre (*open air*) donde vives?
   ¿Qué se vende en ellos?

¡A comer!

6

paso 1 Vocabulario

La comida y las comidas°

La... *Food and meals*

EL DESAYUNO°

BREAKFAST

la leche · el cereal · el café · el jugo (de fruta) · la mantequilla · el huevo · el pan tostado · el té

EL ALMUERZO°

LUNCH

la sopa · la ensalada · el queso · el agua mineral* · el tomate · la manzana · la hamburguesa · el sándwich · la cerveza

LA CENA°

DINNER, SUPPER

el pastel · el vino blanco · el vino tinto · el pescado · la patata/papa† · los espárragos · el bistec · el pan · el pollo (asado)

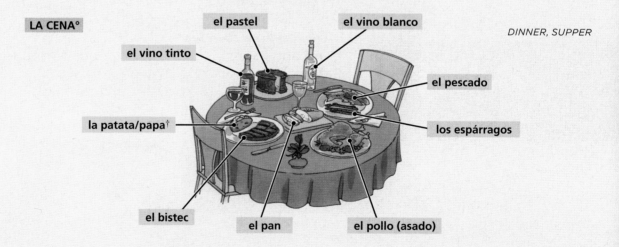

*The noun **agua** (water) is feminine, but the masculine articles are used with it in the singular: **el agua**. This occurs with all feminine nouns that begin with a stressed **a** sound, for example, **el (un) ama de casa** (homemaker).

†In Latin America, many speakers use **la papa,** not **la patata,** to refer to potatoes.

OTRA BEBIDA

el refresco	soft drink

OTRAS FRUTAS

la banana	banana
la naranja	orange

OTRAS VERDURAS

las arvejas	green peas
los champiñones	mushrooms
los frijoles	beans
la lechuga	lettuce
la zanahoria	carrot

OTRAS CARNES

la barbacoa	barbeque
la chuleta (de cerdo)	(pork) chop
el jamón	ham
el pavo	turkey
la salchicha	sausage; hot dog

OTROS PESCADOS Y MARISCOS

el atún	tuna
los camarones	shrimp
la langosta	lobster
el salmón	salmon

OTROS POSTRES

los dulces	sweets; candy
el flan	(baked) custard
la galleta	cookie
el helado	ice cream

OTRAS COMIDAS

el aceite	oil
el arroz	rice
el azúcar	sugar
la pimienta	pepper
la sal	salt
el yogur	yogurt

LOS VERBOS

desayunar	to have (eat) breakfast
almorzar (almuerzo)	to have (eat) lunch
cenar	to have (eat) dinner, supper
cocinar	to cook

¿Qué hay en la parrilla (*grill*)?

Conversación

⏩ NOTA COMUNICATIVA

More Food-Related Phrases

tener (mucha) hambre/sed	to be (very) hungry/thirsty
merendar (meriendo)	to snack
la merienda	snack
los comestibles	groceries, foodstuff
el plato	dish (*food prepared in a particular way*)
el plato principal	main course
caliente	hot (*in temperature, not taste*)
picante	hot, spicy
rico/a	tasty, savory; rich (*in the caloric sense*)

A. ¿Qué quieres tomar? Match the following descriptions of meals with a category.

1. ___ una sopa fría, langosta, espárragos, ensalada de lechuga y tomate, vino blanco y, para terminar, un pastel
2. ___ jugo de fruta, huevos con jamón, pan tostado y café
3. ___ un vaso (*glass*) de leche y unas galletas
4. ___ pollo asado, arroz, arvejas, agua mineral y, para terminar, una manzana
5. ___ una hamburguesa con patatas fritas, un refresco y un helado

a. un menú ligero (*light*) para una dieta
b. una comida rápida
c. una cena elegante
d. un desayuno estilo norteamericano
e. una merienda

B. Definiciones

Paso 1. Da las palabras definidas.

1. un plato de lechuga y tomate
2. una bebida alcohólica blanca o roja
3. una verdura anaranjada
4. la carne típica para la barbacoa en este país
5. la comida favorita de los ratones (*mice*)
6. una verdura que se come frita con las hamburguesas
7. una fruta roja o verde

Paso 2. Ahora, en parejas, túrnense para crear (*create*) definiciones de comidas y bebidas, según el modelo del **Paso 1.** Una persona da (*gives*) la definición y la otra da la palabra correspondiente.

⏺) NOTA CULTURAL

La comida del mundo hispánico

Often when we think of dishes from the Spanish-speaking world, what comes to mind are rice, beans, spicy chiles, corn or flour tortillas, and burritos. That, however, is a misconception. Corn and flour tortillas and burritos are unknown in many Spanish-speaking countries. Many Hispanic cuisines are not spicy at all, and if you are in Spain and order **una tortilla**, you will be served a wedge of potato omelette!

The cuisines of Spanish-speaking countries are as diverse as their inhabitants. With the arrival of the Spaniards in the Americas, indigenous cuisines were influenced by European foods that did not exist there before, such as beef and chicken. Likewise, European cuisines were influenced by the introduction of foods from the Americas, such as the tomato, the potato, and chocolate. Later, immigration from countries such as Ireland, Germany, Italy, China, and Japan further influenced American cuisines.*

Una tortilla española

_____
Remember that, in this context, American *refers to all the countries in North, Central, and South America.*

C. Consejos (*Advice*) a la hora de comer.

¿Qué debe comer o beber tu compañero o compañera en las siguientes situaciones? Dale consejos, según el modelo.

MODELO: Tengo mucha/poca hambre (sed). $\longrightarrow$
E1: Tengo mucha hambre.
E2: Debes comer un bistec con papas fritas.

1. Tengo mucha/poca hambre (sed).
2. Tengo hambre a las cuatro de la mañana, después de una fiesta.
3. Estoy a dieta.
4. Estoy de vacaciones en Maine (Texas, California, la Florida, la Colombia Británica, ¿ ?).
5. Es hora de merendar. Estoy en (casa, la universidad).
6. Soy un vegetariano estricto / una vegetariana estricta.

D. Las preferencias gastronómicas

Chuletas de Cerdo Maggi

Maggi
Tu Sabor Latino y

Rinde[a] de 6 a 8 porciones

Ingredientes

3 tazas[b] de hojas de cilantro o de perejil
1 taza de mermelada de uva[c]
1 tableta de MAGGI® Caldo[d] Sabor a Pollo y Tomate,
    disuelta en ¼ taza[e] de agua caliente
3 dientes de ajo picados[f]
1 a 2 chiles chipotle en salsa de adobo, sin semillas[g]
Jugo de 2 limones verdes[h]
2 cucharadas[i] de Jugo Sazonador MAGGI®
6 a 8 chuletas de cerdo de ½ pulgada de anchura[j]
    sin o con hueso
2 cucharadas de aceite canola
Cilantro fresco picado (opcional)

Paso 1. Haz una lista de los ingredientes principales de por lo menos dos de tus platos favoritos. La receta (*recipe*) de las Chuletas de Cerdo Maggi puede servir de modelo.

Paso 2. Haz una lista de tus tres lugares favoritos para comer en esta ciudad.

Paso 3. Haz una lista de los tres tipos de cocinas (*cuisines*) que prefieres. Consulta la lista de nacionalidades de la página 64 si es necesario.

Paso 4. Entre todos, comparen las listas. ¿Cuáles son los platos, lugares para comer y cocinas favoritos de la clase? ¿Cuáles son los ingredientes más necesarios para cocinar sus platos favoritos?

[a]*It (The recipe) yields* [b]*cups* [c]*grape* [d]*Broth* [e]¼... un cuarto de taza [f]dientes... *garlic cloves, chopped* [g]*seeds* [h]limones... *limes* [i]*tablespoons* [j]½... (media pulgada) *half an inch thick*

As you know, two Spanish verbs express *to be*: **ser** and **estar**. They are not interchangeable, and their use depends on the meaning the speaker wishes to express. Similarly, two Spanish verbs express *to know*: **saber** and **conocer**. **Conocer** is frequently used with the word **a** when referring to a person (as in the phrase **¿a quién conoces?** from the title of this section).

Saber and *conocer*

En un restaurante panameño
Julio y Estela están comiendo en un restaurante panameño… pero no comen juntos; no se **conocen**. Julio quiere **conocer a** Estela. También quiere **saber** su número de teléfono. ¿Y Estela? ¿Quiere **conocer a** Julio? ¡No! Quiere **conocer a** Felipe, el chef del restaurante, porque él **sabe** hacer sus platos panameños favoritos.

---

saber = to know (*facts or information*); to know how to (*do something*)

sé	**sabemos**
sabes	**sabéis**
sabe	**saben**

una dirección (*address*)
un número de teléfono
un nombre
la letra (*lyrics*) de una canción
hacer algo (tocar el piano…)

---

conocer = to know (*a person*); to meet (*a person*); to be acquainted, familiar with (*a place or thing*)

conozco	**conocemos**
conoces	**conocéis**
conoce	**conocen**

a una persona
un lugar
una cosa

Direct Objects (Part 1): The Personal *a*

Note the use of the word **a** in the preceding sample paragraph and chart. This **a** is called "the personal **a**." It is used in Spanish before a direct object that refers to a specific person or persons, and it has no equivalent in English. You will learn more about it in **Gramática 17** in this chapter. In this section, the activities will always show you when to use the personal **a**.

At a Panamanian restaurant *Julio and Estela are eating at a Panamanian restaurant . . . but they're not eating together; they don't know each other. Julio wants to meet Estela. He also wants to know her telephone number. And Estela? Does she want to meet Julio? No! She wants to meet Felipe, the chef at the restaurant, because he knows how to make her favorite Panamanian dishes.*

Conversación

A. ¡Anticipemos! ¿Cierto o falso?
Di si las siguientes declaraciones son ciertas o falsas para ti. Corrige las declaraciones falsas.

Sé...

		CIERTO	FALSO
1.	el número de teléfono de mi profesor(a) de español.	☐	☐
2.	la dirección de e-mail de mi profesor(a) de español.	☐	☐
3.	los nombres de las capitales de todos los estados de los Estados Unidos / de todas las provincias del Canadá.	☐	☐
4.	los nombres de las capitales de todos los países hispanohablantes.	☐	☐
5.	hacer varios platos hispanos.	☐	☐
6.	la letra del himno nacional de este país.	☐	☐
7.	tocar un instrumento musical.	☐	☐
8.	el nombre de todos mis compañeros de esta clase.	☐	☐

Conozco...

		CIERTO	FALSO
9.	al padre / a la madre de mi mejor amigo/a.	☐	☐
10.	a un actor / a una actriz personalmente.	☐	☐
11.	Panamá.	☐	☐
12.	un restaurante panameño.	☐	☐
13.	al rector / a la rectora (*president*) de esta universidad personalmente.	☐	☐
14.	la ciudad de Quebec.	☐	☐

B. Los usos de *saber* y *conocer*

Paso 1. Llena (*Fill in*) los espacios en blanco con la forma apropiada de **saber**. Luego da su equivalente en inglés.

—¿(*Tú*)_____[1] la dirección de un restaurante panameño?

—¡Cómo no![a] Hay uno en la calle[b] Park. El chef, Felipe, _____[2] hacer unos platos muy originales.

—¿(*Tú*)_____[3] a qué hora abren los sábados?

—No (*yo*)_____[4] exactamente. ¿Por qué no llamamos al restaurante?

[a]¡Cómo... *Of course!*   [b]*street*

Paso 2. Ahora llena los espacios en blanco con la forma apropiada de **conocer**. Luego da su equivalente en inglés.

—¿(*Tú*)_____[1] ese restaurante panameño que está en la calle Park?

—Sí, y también (*yo*)_____[2] al chef, Felipe.

—¿Ah sí? Yo quiero _____[3] a Felipe. Es muy famoso.

C. Personas famosas. ¿Qué saben hacer estas personas?

MODELO: Jennifer López y Shakira saben bailar.

Enrique Iglesias Jennifer López y Shakira Alex Rodríguez (A-Rod) Lance Armstrong J.K. Rowling Serena y Venus Williams Emeril Lagasse y Wolfgang Puck ¿ ?	**+** sabe(n) **+**	jugar al béisbol montar en (*to ride a*) bicicleta cantar (en español) cocinar jugar al tenis escribir novelas bailar ¿ ?

D. Otras personas famosas. ¿Quién conoce a quién?

Adán Napoleón Romeo Rhett Butler Marco Antonio George Washington	**+**	conoce a	**+**	Martha Cleopatra Eva Julieta Scarlett O'Hara Josefina

E. ¿Dónde cenamos? En este diálogo, Lola y Manolo quieren salir a cenar. Pero, ¿dónde? Completa el diálogo con la forma apropiada de **saber** o **conocer**.

LOLA: ¿(Sabes/Conoces¹) adónde quieres ir a cenar?

MANOLO: No (sé/conozco²). ¿Y tú?

LOLA: No. Pero hay un restaurante nuevo en la calle Betis. Creo que se llama Guadalquivir. ¿(Sabes/Conoces³) el restaurante?

MANOLO: No, pero (sé/conozco⁴) que tiene mucha fama. Es el restaurante favorito de Virginia. Ella (sabe/conoce⁵) al dueño.ᵃ

LOLA: ¿(Sabes/Conoces⁶) qué tipo de comida tienen?

MANOLO: No (sé/conozco⁷). Pero podemos llamar a Virginia. ¿(Sabes/Conoces⁸) su teléfono?

LOLA: Está en mi guía telefónica. Y pregúntaleᵇ a Virginia si ella (sabe/conoce⁹) si aceptan reservaciones con anticipaciónᶜ o no.

MANOLO: De acuerdo.

ᵃ*owner* ᵇ*ask* ᶜ*con... in advance*

F. ¡Qué talento!

Paso 1. Inventa oraciones sobre tres cosas que tú sabes hacer.

> **MODELO:** Sé tocar el acordeón.

Paso 2. Ahora, en grupos de tres estudiantes, pregúntales (*ask*) a tus compañeros si saben hacer esas actividades. Escribe sí o no, según sus respuestas.

> **MODELO:** ¿Sabes tocar el acordeón?

Paso 3. Ahora describe las habilidades de los estudiantes de tu grupo.

> **MODELO:** Marta y yo sabemos tocar el acordeón, pero Elena no.
> (En el grupo, sólo yo sé tocar el acordeón.)

G. Entrevista

1. ¿Qué restaurantes conoces en esta ciudad? ¿Cuál es tu restaurante favorito? ¿Por qué es tu favorito? ¿Es buena la comida allí? ¿Qué tipo de comida sirven? ¿Te gusta el ambiente (*atmosphere*)? ¿Comes allí con frecuencia? ¿Llamas para hacer reservaciones?
2. ¿Qué platos sabes hacer? ¿Tacos? ¿enchiladas? ¿pollo frito? ¿hamburguesas? ¿Te gusta cocinar? ¿Cocinas con frecuencia? ¿Qué ingredientes usas con más frecuencia?

Need more practice?
- Workbook/Laboratory Manual
- Online Learning Center
[www.mhhe.com/apuntate]

Panamá

DATOS ESENCIALES

NOMBRE OFICIAL: República de Panamá
CAPITAL: la Ciudad de Panamá
POBLACIÓN: más de 3 millones de habitantes

FÍJATE

- **Panamá** es una palabra indígena que significa «tierra de muchos peces[a]».
- La Carretera[b] Panamericana, el sistema de carreteras que va de Alaska a la Argentina, se interrumpe[c] en la densa e[d] impenetrable selva[e] panameña de Darién. Para llegar a Sudamérica es necesario tomar un barco[f] hasta Colombia, donde continúa la carretera.
- Mireya Moscoso ganó[g] las elecciones presidenciales de 1998. Doña Mireya, viuda[h] de otro presidente, es la primera mujer panameña en asumir la presidencia de Panamá. El Presidente actual[i] es Martín Torrijos.

[a]fish [b]Highway [c]se... is interrupted [d]y
[e]jungle [f]boat [g]won [h]widow [i]current

¡MÚSICA!

El calipso es la forma musical más popular y famosa de Panamá. El calipso llegó[a] a Panamá de la isla de Trinidad durante la construcción del Canal. Muchas de las canciones de calipso son improvisaciones, y son muy comunes los «duelos[b]» entre cantantes.[c]

[a]arrived [b]duels [c]singers

★ RUBÉN BLADES

Rubén Blades es unos de los cantautores[a] de salsa más conocidos[b] en todo el mundo. Como está claro en su canción «Prohibido olvidar[c]», la letra de sus canciones con frecuencia refleja[d] su gran compromiso[e] social y político. (Fue candidato a la presidencia de Panamá y recientemente[f] ha sido[g] ministro de turismo.) «Prohibido olvidar» es de su álbum *Caminando*.[h]

[a]singer-songwriters [b]más... best known [c]Prohibido... (It's) Forbidden to Forget [d]reflect [e]commitment [f]recently [g]ha... he has been [h]Walking

Rubén Blades durante «Una Noche de Paz», un concierto en California

17 Expressing *what* or *who(m)* • Direct Objects (Part 2): The Personal *a*; Direct Object Pronouns

Gramática en acción: De compras en el supermercado

Indica cuáles de estas declaraciones expresan lo que tú haces.

1. **la carne**
   - ❑ La como todos los días. Por eso tengo que comprarla con frecuencia.
   - ❑ La como de vez en cuando (*once in a while*). Por eso no la compro a menudo (*often*).
   - ❑ Nunca la como. No necesito comprarla.
2. **el café**
   - ❑ Lo bebo todos los días. Por eso tengo que comprarlo con frecuencia.
   - ❑ Lo bebo de vez en cuando. Por eso no lo compro a menudo.
   - ❑ Nunca lo bebo. No necesito comprarlo.
3. **los huevos**
   - ❑ Los como todos los días. Por eso tengo que comprarlos con frecuencia.
   - ❑ Los como de vez en cuando. Por eso no los compro a menudo.
   - ❑ Nunca los como. No necesito comprarlos.
4. **las bananas**
   - ❑ Las como todos los días. Por eso tengo que comprarlas con frecuencia.
   - ❑ Las como de vez en cuando. Por eso no las compro a menudo.
   - ❑ Nunca las como. No necesito comprarlas.

Direct Objects (Part 2): The Personal *a*

1. **Direct Objects** In English and in Spanish, the *direct object* (**el complemento directo**) of a sentence answers the question *what?* or *who(m)?* in relation to the subject and verb.

   > Ana is preparing dinner.
   > What is Ana preparing? ⟶ dinner

   > They can't hear the waiter.
   > Who(m) can't they hear? ⟶ the waiter

Indicate the direct objects in the following sentences.

1. I don't see Betty and Mary here.
2. Give the dog a bone.
3. No tenemos dinero.
4. ¿Por qué no pones la sopa en la mesa?

> **direct object** = a noun or pronoun that receives the action of the verb

2. **The Personal *a*.** In Spanish, the word **a** immediately precedes the direct object of a sentence when the direct object refers to a specific person or persons. This **a**, called the personal **a**, has no equivalent in English.*

Vamos a visitar **a nuestros abuelos**.
We're going to visit our grandparents.
But
Vamos a visitar **la casa de nuestros abuelos**.
We're going to visit our grandparents' house.

Necesitan **a** sus padres.
They need their parents.
But
Necesitan **el coche de sus padres**.
They need their parents' car.

¿**A** quién llamas? ¿**al** camarero?
Who(m) are you calling? The waiter?

¡OJO!

The personal **a** is used before the interrogative words **¿quién?** and **¿quiénes?** when they function as direct objects.

¡OJO!

The verbs **escuchar** (*to listen to*) and mirar (*to look at*) include the sense of the English preposition *at*. The verb **esperar** (*to wait* [*for*]; *to expect*) includes the meaning of English *for*. These verbs take direct objects in Spanish, not prepositional phrases, as in English, but you must still use the personal **a** before direct objects that are persons or personified animals (e.g., family pet) or things.

[Práctica A]

Miro el menú.
I'm looking at the menu.
Escucho los pájaros.
I'm listening to the birds.
Espero el autobús.
I'm waiting for the bus.
But
Miro a mi gato, Scout.
I'm looking at my cat, Scout.
Escucho a mi madre.
I listen to my mother.
Espero a mi amigo Jorge.
I'm waiting for my friend Jorge.

Miramos el menú mientras esperamos a nuestro amigo Adolfo.

---
*The personal **a** is not generally used with **tener: Tenemos cuatro hijos**.

Direct Object Pronouns

me	me	**nos**	us
te	you (*fam. sing.*)	**os**	you (*fam. pl.*)
lo*	you (*form. sing.*), him, it (*m.*)	**los**	you (*form. pl.*), them (*m., m. + f.*)
la	you (*form. sing.*), her, it (*f.*)	**las**	you (*form. pl.*), them (*f.*)

1. Direct Object Pronouns Like direct object nouns, *direct object pronouns* (**los pronombres del complemento directo**) are the first recipient of the action of the verb. Direct object pronouns are placed before a conjugated verb and after the word **no** when it appears. Third person direct object pronouns are used only when the direct object noun has already been mentioned.

[Práctica B]

¿El menú? Diego **no lo necesita.**
The menu? Diego doesn't need it.

¿Dónde están el pastel y el helado? **Los necesito** ahora.
Where are the cake and the ice cream? I need them now.

Ellos **me ayudan.**
They're helping me.

2. With Infinitives or Present Participles The direct object pronouns may be attached to an infinitive or a present participle.

[Práctica C–E]

Las tengo que leer.
Tengo que **leerlas.** ⎤ *I have to read them.*

Lo estoy comiendo.
Estoy **comiéndolo.** ⎤ *I am eating it.*

3. The Pronoun *lo* Note that the direct object pronoun **lo** can refer to actions, situations, or ideas in general. When used in this way, **lo** expresses English *it* or *that.*

Lo comprende muy bien.
He understands it (that) very well.

No **lo** creo.
I don't believe it (that).

Lo sé.
I know (it).

¿Quieres probarlos *(try them)?*

---

*In Spain and in some other parts of the Spanish-speaking world, **le** is frequently used instead of **lo** for the direct object pronoun him. This usage, called **el leísmo,** will not be followed in ¡Apúntate!*

Práctica

A. ¿A personal o no?

Completa las siguientes oraciones breves. **¡OJO!** Usa la **a** personal cuando sea (*whenever it is*) necesario.

Busco...

1. el presidente.
2. una clase de historia.
3. mi amiga.
4. la clase de matemáticas.
5. un trabajo (*job*).
6. mi perro Sultán.

Miro...

7. la televisión.
8. mis niños en el parque.
9. películas en español.
10. el profesor / la profesora en clase.

B. ¿Qué comen los vegetarianos?

Paso 1. Aquí hay una lista de diferentes comidas. ¿Crees que las come un vegetariano? Contesta según los modelos.

> **MODELO:** el bistec ⟶ No *lo* come.
> la banana ⟶ *La* come.

¿Lo come?

1. las patatas
2. el arroz
3. las chuletas de cerdo
4. los huevos
5. las zanahorias
6. las manzanas
7. los camarones
8. el pan
9. los champiñones
10. los frijoles
11. la ensalada
12. los dulces

Paso 2. Si hay estudiantes vegetarianos en la clase, pídeles que verifiquen (*ask them to verify*) tus respuestas.

C. La cena de Lola y Manolo.

La siguiente descripción de la cena de Lola y Manolo es muy repetitiva. Combina las oraciones, cambiando los sustantivos de complemento directo en azul por (*with*) pronombres.

> **MODELO:** El camarero (*waiter*) trae un menú. Lola lee el menú. ⟶
> El camarero trae un menú y Lola *lo* lee.

1. El camarero trae una botella de vino tinto. Pone la botella en la mesa.
2. El camarero trae las copas (*glasses*) de vino. Pone las copas delante de Lola y Manolo.
3. Lola quiere la especialidad de la casa. Va a pedir la especialidad de la casa.
4. Manolo prefiere el pescado fresco (*fresh*). Pide el pescado fresco.
5. Lola quiere una ensalada también. Por eso pide una ensalada.
6. El camarero trae la comida. Sirve la comida.
7. Manolo necesita otra servilleta (*napkin*). Pide otra servilleta.
8. «¿La cuenta (*bill*)? El dueño está preparando la cuenta para Uds.»
9. Manolo quiere pagar con tarjeta (*card*) de crédito. Pero no trae su tarjeta.
10. Por fin, Lola toma la cuenta. Paga la cuenta.

D. ¿Quién o qué lo hace? Empareja los sujetos con las siguientes declaraciones de una forma lógica. **¡OJO!** Hay más de una respuesta posible.

DECLARACIONES

1. Por la mañana, _____ me despierta.
2. En un restaurante, _____ nos sienta.
3. En una barbería (*barber shop*), _____ nos afeita.
4. En un hospital, _____ nos examina.
5. _____ nos escuchan cuando tenemos problemas.
6. _____ nos esperan cuando vamos a llegar tarde.
7. ¿Los niños? _____ los bañan, los acuestan y los visten.
8. En una clase, _____ hacen preguntas y _____ las contestan (*answer*).

SUJETOS

a. el barbero
b. los (buenos) amigos
c. la camarera
d. el despertador (*alarm clock*)
e. el médico
f. los estudiantes
g. los padres
h. los profesores

◆)) NOTA COMUNICATIVA

Talking About What You Have Just Done

To talk about what you have *just* done, use the phrase **acabar** + **de** + *infinitive*.

Acabo de almorzar con Beto.   *I just had lunch with Beto.*
Acabas de celebrar tu   *You just celebrated your birthday,*
  cumpleaños, ¿verdad?   *didn't you?*

Note that the infinitive follows **de**. Remember that the infinitive is the only verb form that can follow a preposition in Spanish.

E. ¡Acabo de hacerlo! Imagine that a friend is pressuring you to do the following things. With a classmate, tell him or her that you just did each one, using either of the forms in the model.

MODELO: E1: ¿Por qué no estudias la lección? ⟶
E2: Acabo de estudiar*la.* (*La* acabo de estudiar.)

1. ¿Por qué no escribes las composiciones para tus clases?
2. ¿Vas a comprar el periódico hoy?
3. ¿Por qué no pagas los cafés?
4. ¿Vas a cocinar la comida para la fiesta?
5. ¿Puedes pedir la cuenta?
6. ¿Quieres ayudarme?

¿Vas a comprarlo hoy?

Need more **practice?**
■ Workbook/Laboratory Manual
■ Online Learning Center [www.mhhe.com/apuntate]

Conversación

A. ¿Quién ayuda?
Todos necesitamos ayuda (*help*) en algún momento, ¿verdad? ¿Quién los ayuda a Uds. en los siguientes casos? **¡OJO!** Usen **nos** en sus respuestas.

MODELO: con las cuentas → Nuestros padres *nos* ayudan con las cuentas.

Vocabulario útil
ayudar + a + *inf.*   to help to (*do something*)
nuestros padres (compañeros, consejeros, amigos...)

1. con las cuentas
2. con la tarea
3. con la matrícula
4. con el horario de clases
5. resolver los problemas personales
6. pagar las deudas (*debts*)
7. estudiar para los exámenes
8. con el español

¡Mi padre me ayuda mucho!

B. Una encuesta sobre la comida.
Hazles (*Ask*) preguntas a tus compañeros de clase para saber si consumen las comidas o bebidas indicadas y con qué frecuencia. Deben explicar por qué toman o comen cierta cosa o no.

MODELO: la carne → **E1:** ¿Comes carne?
                E2: No, no *la* como casi nunca porque tiene mucho colesterol.

Vocabulario útil
la cafeína	**ser bueno/a para la salud** (*health*)
las calorías	
el colesterol	**lo/la/los/las detesto**
la grasa *fat*	**me pone(n) nervioso/a** *it / they* make me nervous
estar **a dieta**	**me sienta(n) mal** *it / they don't* agree with me
ser **alérgico/a a**	

1. la carne
2. los mariscos
3. el yogur
4. la pizza
5. las hamburguesas
6. el pollo
7. el café
8. los dulces
9. las bebidas alcohólicas
10. el atún
11. los espárragos
12. el hígado (*liver*)

C. Entrevista

1. ¿Conoces a una persona famosa? ¿Quién es? ¿Cómo es? ¿Qué detalles sabes de la vida (*life*) de esa persona? ¿A qué persona famosa te gustaría (*would you like*) conocer? ¿Por qué?
2. ¿Esperas a tus amigos para ir a la universidad? ¿Esperas a tus amigos después de la clase? ¿A quién buscas cuando necesitas ayuda con el español? ¿cuando necesitas hablar de un problema personal?
3. ¿Quién te invita a cenar con frecuencia? ¿Quién te invita a ir al cine? ¿a tomar un café? ¿a salir por la noche? ¿a bailar?

You have been using a few words that express indefinite and negative qualities since the first chapter of this text. Review what you already know about the content of **Gramática 18** by giving the English equivalent of the following words.

1. siempre **2.** algo **3.** nunca **4.** también

18 Expressing Negation • Indefinite and Negative Words

Gramática en acción: ¿Un refrigerador típico?

—En este refrigerador...

- ¿hay algo bueno de comer?
  —Sí, hay algo.
  —No, no hay nada.
- ¿hay fruta y pan?
  —Sí, hay fruta y pan.
  —No, no hay fruta. Tampoco hay pan.
- ¿hay algunas manzanas?
  —Sí, hay manzanas.
  —No, no hay ninguna manzana.

—En esta casa, ...

- ¿alguien compra comida con frecuencia?
  —Sí, alguien la compra.
  —No, nadie la compra.

¿Y tú?

Este refrigerador, ¿es un refrigerador típico de una casa de estudiantes? ¿de jóvenes profesionales? ¿de padres con hijos? ¿En qué se parece (*In what* [*way*] *does it resemble*) al refrigerador de tu casa o apartamento?

A typical refrigerator?   —*In this refrigerator... • is there anything good to eat? —Yes, there's something. / No, there isn't anything. (No, there's nothing.) • is there fruit and bread? —Yes, there's fruit and bread. / No, there isn't any fruit. There isn't any bread either. (Neither is there any bread.) • are there any (some) apples? —Yes, there are apples. / No, there aren't any apples. (Lit. No, there is no apple.) —In this house... • does anyone (someone) buy food frequently? —Yes, someone buys it. / No, no one (nobody) buys it.*

Here is a list of the most common indefinite and negative words in Spanish. You have been using many of them since the first chapters of *¡Apúntate!*

algo	something, anything	**nada**	nothing, not anything
alguien	someone, anyone	**nadie**	no one, nobody, not anybody
algún (alguna/os/as)	some, any	**ningún (ninguna)**	no, not any
siempre	always	**nunca, jamás**	never
también	also	**tampoco**	neither, not either

Pronunciation hint: Pronounce the **d** in **nada** and **nadie** as a fricative, that is, like the *th* sound in *the*: [**na-da**],[**na-die**].

The Double Negative

When a negative word comes after the main verb, Spanish requires that another negative word—usually **no**—be placed before the verb. When a negative word precedes the verb, **no** is not used.

¿**No** estudia **nadie**? ¿**Nadie** estudia?	*Isn't anyone studying?*
No estás en clase **nunca**. **Nunca** estás en clase.	*You're never in class.*
No quieren cenar aquí **tampoco**. **Tampoco** quieren cenar aquí.	*They don't want to have dinner here, either.*

The Adjectives *algún* and *ningún*

Algún (**Alguna/os/as**) and **ningún** (**ninguna**) are adjectives. Unlike **nadie** and **nada** (nouns) or **nunca, jamás,** and **tampoco** (adverbs), **algún** and **ningún** must agree with the noun they modify. Note the shortened masculine singular forms **algún** and **ningún** (no final **-o**, accented **ú**).

Ningún (**Ninguna**) has no plural form. Note the use of the singular (**ningún recado**) in the example.

—¿Hay **algunos recados** para mí hoy?
Are there any messages for me today?

— Lo siento, pero hoy no hay **ningún recado para** Ud.
I'm sorry, but there are no messages for you today. (There is not a single message for you today.)

AUTOPRUEBA

Give the corresponding negative word.

1. siempre   **4.** alguna
2. también   **5.** algo
3. alguien

Answers: **1.** nunca **2.** tampoco **3.** nadie **4.** ninguna **5.** nada

Práctica

A. ¡Anticipemos! ¿Qué pasa esta noche en casa? Tell whether the following statements about what is happening at this house are true (**cierto**) or false (**falso**). Then create as many additional sentences as you can about what is happening, following the model of the sentences.

	CIERTO	FALSO
1. No hay nadie en el baño.	❏	❏
2. En la cocina, alguien está haciendo la cena.	❏	❏
3. No hay ninguna persona en el patio.	❏	❏
4. Hay algo en la mesa del comedor.	❏	❏
5. Algunos amigos se están divirtiendo en la sala.	❏	❏
6. Hay algunos platos en la mesa del comedor.	❏	❏
7. No hay ningún niño en la casa.	❏	❏

B. ¡Por eso no come nadie allí! Expresa negativamente, usando la negativa doble.

> **MODELO:** Hay alguien en el restaurante. ⟶ *No* hay *nadie* en el restaurante.

1. Hay algo interesante en el menú.
2. Tienen algunos platos típicos.
3. El profesor cena allí también.
4. Mis amigos siempre almuerzan allí.
5. Preparan un menú especial para grupos grandes.
6. Siempre hacen platos nuevos.
7. Y también sirven paella, mi plato favorito.

C. Todo lo contrario

Paso 1. Cambia las siguientes declaraciones para que sean (*so that they are*) completamente negativas.

> **MODELO:** Hay algunas personas simpáticas en mi familia. ⟶
> No hay ninguna persona simpática en mi familia.

1. Esta semana hay muchas actividades interesantes en la universidad.
2. Me divierto tomando café con mis amigos todos los días.
3. Hay algunos políticos buenos hoy día.
4. Todos mis profesores de este año son simpáticos.
5. Me gusta la comida de la cafetería.

Paso 2. Ahora inventa preguntas para las siguientes respuestas. **¡OJO!** Hay más de una respuesta posible en algunos casos.

> **MODELO:** No, no hay nada interesante en la tele. ⟶
> ¿Hay algo interesante en la tele (esta noche)?

1. No, no hay ningún programa interesante esta noche.
2. No, no hay ningún estudiante de Nicaragua.
3. No, esta semana no pasan (*they're not showing*) ninguna buena película aquí.
4. No, nunca ceno en la universidad.
5. No, tampoco estudio en la biblioteca.

Need more practice?
- Workbook/Laboratory Manual
- Online Learning Center
  [www.mhhe.com/apuntate]

Conversación

Entrevista. En parejas, túrnense para entrevistarse sobre los siguientes temas. Deben obtener detalles interesantes y personales de su compañero/a.

> **MODELO:** **E1:** ¿Tienes alguna buena excusa para no hacer la tarea de física esta semana?
> **E2:** No, no tengo ninguna buena excusa esta semana. (Sí, tengo una buena excusa para no hacerla. ¡No entiendo nada en esa clase!)

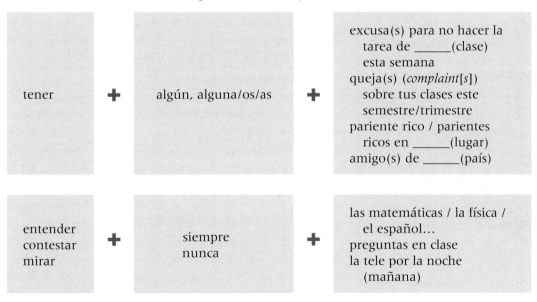

tener	**+** algún, alguna/os/as **+**	excusa(s) para no hacer la tarea de _____ (clase) esta semana queja(s) (*complaint[s]*) sobre tus clases este semestre/trimestre pariente rico / parientes ricos en _____ (lugar) amigo(s) de _____ (país)
entender contestar mirar	**+** siempre nunca **+**	las matemáticas / la física / el español… preguntas en clase la tele por la noche (mañana)

Lectura cultural 2 Panamá

1

Una esclusa[a] del Canal de Panamá La idea de abrir un canal por Panamá para conectar los dos oceános viene del siglo[b] XVI, pero la construcción no empezó[c] hasta finales[d] del siglo XIX. Cuarenta y ocho millas de canales y esclusas unen el Atlántico con el Pacífico. Los barcos[e] pasan por el Canal, dos lagos[f] artificiales y tres series de esclusas y canales.

[a]lock [b]century [c]no... didn't begin [d]the end [e]boats [f]lakes

2

El Casco Antiguo *(Old City Center)* **de la Ciudad de Panamá**

3

La parte moderna de la Ciudad de Panamá
La Ciudad de Panamá, capital del país, es una ciudad moderna y cosmopolita. La influencia de la cultura y el dólar estadounidenses en esta ciudad es notable. Dentro de[a] la capital hay tres áreas de marcadas diferencias: Panamá la Vieja (restos[b] de la ciudad original que datan[c] del siglo XVI), el Casco Antiguo (la parte colonial española que data del siglo XVII) y la Ciudad Moderna con sus rascacielos.[d]

[a]Dentro... Within [b]remains [c]date [d]skyscrapers

4

Una mujer kuna con sus molas Los kunas, una tribu indígena, viven en las islas de San Blas. Las mujeres kunas son famosas por sus molas, una artesanía textil de múltiples capas de telas,[a] cortadas y bordadas[b] en diseños coloridos y complejos.[c] Las artesanas también se decoran las piernas y los brazos[d] con los mismos diseños de sus molas.

[a]capas... *layers of material* [b]cortadas... *cut and embroidered* [c]diseños... *colorful and complex designs* [d]se... *decorate their legs and arms*

La cordillera[a] de Talamanca Panamá protege[b] el 22 por ciento de su territorio con parques y reservas nacionales. La cordillera de Talamanca queda[c] en la frontera[d] entre Panamá y Costa Rica. Las reservas de la cordillera de Talamanca y el Parque Internacional de La Amistad, junto con[e] otras propiedades, fueron[f] declarados Patrimonio Mundial[g] de la Humanidad por la UNESCO en 1990.

[a]mountain range [b]protects [c]is located [d]border [e]junto... *together with* [f]were [g]Patrimonio... *World Heritage Site*

5

¿Recuerdas?

In **Gramática 19,** you will learn to form one type of command. In Spanish, the formal commands are based on the first person singular of the present tense. Review what you already know about irregular first person present tense forms by giving the **yo** form of the following infinitives.

1. salir   **3.** conocer   **5.** hacer   **7.** perder
2. tener   **4.** pedir   **6.** dormir   **8.** traer

19 Influencing Others • Commands [Part 1]: Formal Commands

Gramática en acción: Receta para guacamole

En español, los mandatos se usan con frecuencia en las recetas. Estos verbos se usan en forma de mandato en esta receta. ¿Puedes encontrarlos?

El guacamole

Ingredientes:
1 aguacate[a]
1 diente de ajo,[b] prensado[c]
1 tomate
jugo de un limón
sal
un poco de cilantro fresco[d]

Cómo se prepara
Corte el aguacate y el tomate en trozos[e] pequeños. Añada el jugo del limón, el ajo, el cilantro y la sal a su gustó. Mezcle bien todos los ingredientes y sirvalo con tortillas de maíz[f] fritas.

añadir	to add
cortar	to cut
mezclar	to mix
servir (sirvo) (i)	to serve

[a]*avocado* [b]*diente... clove of garlic* [c]*crushed* [d]*fresh* [e]*pieces* [f]*corn*

Formal Command Forms

In *¡Apúntate!* you have seen plural formal commands in the direction lines of activities since the beginning of the text: **hagan, completen, contesten,** and so on.

Commands (imperatives) are verb forms used to tell someone to do something. In Spanish, *formal commands* (**los mandatos formales**) are used with people whom you address as **Ud.** or **Uds.*** Here are some of the basic forms.

> **command or imperative** = a verb form used to tell someone to do something

	hablar	comer	escribir	volver	poner
Ud.	**hable**	**coma**	**escriba**	**vuelva**	**ponga**
Uds.	**hablen**	**coman**	**escriban**	**vuelvan**	**pongan**
English	speak	eat	write	come back	put, place

You will learn how to form informal (tú**) commands in **Gramática 33** (Cap. 12).*

1. Regular Verbs Most formal command forms can be derived from the **yo** form of the present tense.	<table><tr><td colspan="2">**-ar: -o → -e, -en**</td><td colspan="2">**-er/-ir: -o → -a, -an**</td></tr><tr><td>hablo</td><td>→ hable hablen</td><td>como escribo</td><td>→ coma coman → escriba escriban</td></tr></table>
2. Stem-changing Verbs Formal commands of stem-changing verbs will show the stem change.	**pi**ense Ud. **v**uelva Ud. **pi**da Ud.
3. Verbs Ending in *-car, -gar, -zar* These verbs have a spelling change to preserve the **-c-, -g-,** and **-z-** sounds.	c → qu bus**car: busque** Ud. g → gu pa**gar: pague** Ud. z → c empe**zar: empiece** Ud.

¡OJO!

From this chapter on, these three spelling changes for verbs in formal commands will be indicated in parentheses in vocabulary lists. If these three verbs were active in this chapter, they would be listed in the end-of-chapter vocabulary list as follows: bus**car** (qu), pa**gar** (gu), empe**zar** (empie**zo**) (c).

4. Irregular *yo* **Forms** Verbs that have irregular **yo** forms in the present tense reflect the irregularity in the **Ud./Uds.** commands.	conocer: **conozco** → **conozca** Ud. decir* (*to say, tell*): **digo** → **diga** Ud. hacer: **hago** → **haga** Ud. oír: **oigo** → **oiga** Ud. salir: **salgo** → **salga** Ud. tener: **tengo** → **tenga** Ud. traer: **traigo** → **traiga** Ud. venir: **vengo** → **venga** Ud. ver: **veo** → **vea** Ud.
5. Irregular Formal Commands A few verbs have irregular **Ud./Uds.** command forms.	dar* (*to give*) → **dé** Ud. estar → **esté** Ud. ir → **vaya** Ud. saber → **sepa** Ud. ser → **sea** Ud.

No hablen en la biblioteca.

*__*Decir__ and **dar** are used primarily with indirect objects. Both of these verbs and indirect object pronouns will be formally introduced in **Gramática 20** [**Cap. 7**].*

Position of Pronouns with Formal Commands

1. Pronouns with Affirmative Commands Direct object pronouns and reflexive pronouns must follow affirmative commands and be attached to them. In order to maintain the original stress of the verb form, an accent mark is added to the stressed vowel if the original command has two or more syllables.	**Pídalo** Ud. *Order it.* **Siéntese**, por favor. *Sit down, please.*
2. Pronouns with Negative Commands Direct object and reflexive pronouns must precede the verb form in negative commands.	**No lo pida** Ud. *Don't order it.* **No se siente.** *Don't sit down.*

Práctica

A. ¡Anticipemos! Mandatos típicos en el salón de clase.
Indica los mandatos que oyes en la clase de español. Si hay algo que nunca oyes, di: «**Este nunca lo oigo**». Luego, en parejas, inventen tres mandatos que les gustaría darle (*you would like to give*) a su profesor(a) de español o a otro profesor.

1. Traigan los libros a clase.
2. Cierren los libros.
3. Siéntense en círculo.
4. Lleguen a tiempo.
5. No se duerman en clase.
6. Repitan más alto (*louder*).
7. Hagan esta actividad como tarea.
8. ¡No hablen en inglés!

B. Profesor(a) por un día.
Imagina que eres el profesor o profesora hoy. ¿Qué mandatos vas a darles (*will you give*) a tus estudiantes?

MODELOS: hablar español ⟶ Hablen Uds. español.
hablar inglés ⟶ No hablen Uds. inglés.

1. llegar a tiempo
2. leer la lección
3. escribir una composición
4. abrir los libros
5. volver a clase mañana
6. traer los libros a clase
7. estudiar los nuevos verbos
8. ¿ ?

C. ¡Pobre Sr. Casiano!

Paso 1. El Sr. Casiano no se siente (*feel*) bien. Lee la descripción que él da de las cosas que hace.

Trabajo[1] muchísimo[a]—¡me gusta trabajar! En la oficina, soy[2] impaciente y critico[3][b] bastante[c] a los otros. En mi vida personal, a veces soy[4] un poco impulsivo. Fumo[5][d] bastante y también bebo[6] cerveza y otras bebidas alcohólicas, a veces sin moderación... Almuerzo[7] y ceno[8] fuerte,[e] y casi nunca desayuno[9]. Por la noche, con frecuencia salgo[10] con los amigos—me gusta ir a las discotecas—y vuelvo[11] tarde a casa.

[a]*a great deal* [b]critico ⟶ criticar [c]*a good deal* [d]Fumo ⟶ fumar (*to smoke*) [e]*a lot*

Paso 2. ¿Qué *no* debe hacer el Sr. Casiano? Aconséjalo (*Advise him*) y dile (*tell him*) lo que no debe hacer. Usa los verbos indicados en azul o cualquier (*any*) otro, según los modelos.

MODELOS: Trabajo ⟶ Sr. Casiano, *no trabaje* tanto.
soy ⟶ Sr. Casiano, *no sea* tan impaciente.

D. Hablando con el médico. El Sr. Casiano debe adelgazar (*lose weight*). ¿Qué debe o no debe comer y beber? En parejas, imaginen una conversación entre el Sr. Casiano y su médico.

MODELOS: ensalada ⟶ **E1:** ¿Ensalada?   postres ⟶ **E1:** ¿Postres?
                                        E2: Cóma*la*.   **E2:** No *los* coma.

1. bebidas alcohólicas
2. verduras
3. pan
4. dulces
5. leche
6. hamburguesas con queso
7. frutas frescas
8. refrescos dietéticos
9. pollo
10. carne
11. pizza
12. jugo de fruta

E. ¡Qué desastre! Imagina los mandatos que un padre o madre les daría (*would give*) a sus hijos adolescentes. ¿Te resultan (*Do they sound*) familiares estos mandatos?

MODELO: no acostarse muy tarde ⟶
                    ¡*No se acuesten* muy tarde!

1. levantarse más temprano
2. bañarse todos los días
3. quitarse esa ropa sucia
4. ponerse ropa limpia
5. no divertirse todas las noches con los amigos
6. ir más a la biblioteca y estudiar más
7. ¿ ?

⟲)NOTA COMUNICATIVA

El subjuntivo

Except for the command form, all verb forms that you have learned thus far in *¡Apúntate!* have been part of the *indicative mood* (**el modo indicativo**). In both English and Spanish, the indicative is used to state facts and to ask questions. It objectively expresses most real-world actions or states of being.

   Both English and Spanish have another verb system called the *subjunctive mood* (**el modo subjuntivo**), which will be introduced in **Capítulo 12**. The **Ud./Uds.** command forms that you have just learned are part of the subjunctive system. From this point on in *¡Apúntate!* you will see the subjunctive used where it is natural to use it, without translation. What follows is a brief introduction to the subjunctive that will make it easy for you to recognize it when you see it.

   Here are some examples of the forms of the subjunctive. The **Ud./Uds.** forms (identical to the **Ud./Uds.** command forms) are highlighted.

hablar		comer		servir		salir	
hable	hablemos	coma	comamos	sirva	sirvamos	salga	salgamos
hables	habléis	comas	comáis	sirvas	sirváis	salgas	saláis
hable	hablen	coma	coman	sirva	sirvan	salga	salgan

The subjunctive is used to express more subjective or conceptual states, in contrast to the indicative, which reports facts, information that is objectively true. Here are just a few of the situations in which the subjunctive is used in Spanish.

1. to express what the speaker wants others to do (I want you to . . .)
2. to express emotional reactions (I'm glad that . . .)
3. to express probability or uncertainty (It's likely that . . .)

F. El cumpleaños de María.
Fíjate en (*Notice*) los verbos subrayados (*underlined*) en los siguientes diálogos. Di en inglés por qué razón están subrayados. (Usa la lista de la **Nota comunicativa** de la página 192.)

EN EL PARQUE

RAÚL: Como hoy es tu cumpleaños, quiero invitarte a cenar. ¿En qué restaurante quieres que <u>cenemos</u>[1]?

MARÍA: Prefiero que tú me[a] <u>hagas</u>[2] una de tus espléndidas cenas.

RAÚL: ¡Con mucho gusto!

EN CASA DE MARÍA

MADRE: (*Hablando por teléfono*) No, lo siento,[b] pero María no está en casa.

LUISA: ¿Es posible que <u>esté</u>[3] en la biblioteca?

MADRE: No. Sé que ella y Raúl están cenando en casa de él.

LUISA: Ah, sí. Bueno, ¿puede decirle[c] que <u>llame</u>[4] a Luisa cuando regrese?

MADRE: Sí, con mucho gusto,[d] Luisa. Adiós.

LUISA: Hasta luego.

[a]*for me*   [b]*lo… I'm sorry*   [c]*tell her*   [d]con… *with pleasure*

Conversación

A. ¡Esta es su oportunidad!
Hoy tienes la oportunidad de decirles (*tell*) a las siguientes personas lo que tienen que hacer. En parejas, inventen dos o tres mandatos para ellos.

1. al presidente / a la presidenta o al primer ministro / a la primera ministra
2. a algún candidato político o líder (nacional o mundial)
3. al rector / a la rectora (*president*) de la universidad
4. a algún profesor o alguna profesora
5. a alguna persona famosa
6. ¿ ?

B. ¿Chefs?
Demuéstrales (*Show*) a tus compañeros de clase tu talento culinario. Escribe una receta para un plato delicioso, usando las dos recetas de este capítulo (páginas 173 y 189) como modelo.

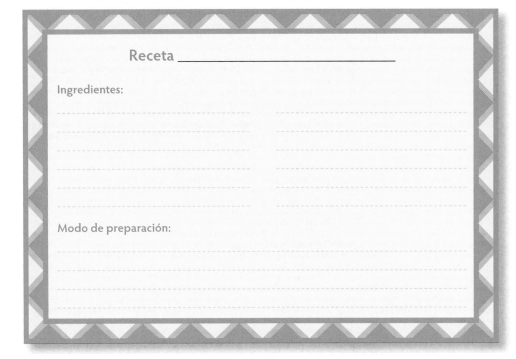

Receta _____

Ingredientes:

Modo de preparación:

Lengua y cultura: La cocina panameña. Complete the following paragraphs with the correct form of the words in parentheses, as suggested by context. When two possibilities are given in parentheses, select the correct word. **¡OJO!** As you conjugate the verbs in this activity, note that you will make formal commands with some infinitives.

¿**C**reen Uds. que la comida panameña es similar a la[a] de México? ¿(*Uds.*: Creer[1]) que los tacos y las tortillas (ser/estar[2]) parte de la comida típica de los panameños? Si creen que sí,[b] entonces[c] no (*Uds.*: saber/conocer[3]) (algo/nada[4]) de la comida de (este[5]) nación. (*Uds.*: Seguir[6]) (leer[7]), porque van a aprender mucho.

Hoy en día, Panamá tiene muy (bueno[8]) relaciones con los Estados Unidos y el Canadá, especialmente por la (grande[9]) importancia que tiene su canal para Norteamérica. En Panamá, se observa mucho la influencia de los Estados Unidos. Muchos panameños (saber/conocer[10]) inglés perfectamente y (lo/la[11]) hablan con frecuencia.

La influencia (extranjero[12]) en la comida de la cosmopolita Ciudad de Panamá es muy visible. Hay (mucho[13]) restaurantes que (servir[14]) comida italiana, china, (francés[15]),

El arroz con pollo, un típico plato panameño

estadounidense y comidas de otros países también.

Sin embargo, los panameños no (perder[16]) su identidad nacional, y frecuentemente (preferir[17]) servir la comida tradicional de ellos. En la comida tradicional panameña hay muchos platos de mariscos y pescados, entre ellos el ceviche. Las personas vegetarianas no (tener[18]) problema con la comida tradicional porque hay una variedad de platos (preparado[d19]) con arroz y verduras. El arroz es un ingrediente importante en la comida de Panamá. Si Uds. desean (saber/conocer[20]) cuál es el plato nacional de Panamá, los panameños (contestar[21]): (*Uds.*: Pedirlo[22]). Les va a gustar.

[a]*that* [b]Si... *If you think so* [c]*then* [d]*prepared*

Comprensión. Contesta las siguientes preguntas.

1. ¿Por qué tiene Panamá muy buenas relaciones con los Estados Unidos y el Canadá?
2. ¿Cómo se sabe que la Ciudad de Panamá es cosmopolita?
3. ¿Cuál es el plato que representa mejor la cocina panameña?
4. ¿Qué ingredientes son comunes en la comida de Panamá?

En resumen

Gramática en breve

17. Direct Objects (Part 2): The Personal **a;** Direct Object Pronouns

Direct Object Pronouns

me, te, lo/la, nos, os, los/las

18. Indefinite and Negative Words

Indefinite and Negative Words

algo	**nada**
alguien	**nadie**
algún (alguna/os/as)	**ningún (ninguna)**
siempre	**nunca, jamás**
también	**tampoco**

19. Commands (Part 1): Formal Commands

Formal Command Endings

-ar $\longrightarrow$ **-e, -en**

-er/-ir $\longrightarrow$ **-a, -an**

Vocabulario

Los verbos

acabar de + *inf.*	to have just (*done something*)
ayudar	to help
cenar	to have (eat) dinner, supper
cocinar	to cook
conocer (conozco)	to know, be acquainted, familiar with; to meet
contestar	to answer
desayunar	to have (eat) breakfast
esperar	to wait (for); to expect
invitar	to invite
llamar	to call
merendar (meriendo)	to have a snack
preguntar	to ask (*a question*)
preparar	to prepare
saber (sé)	to know
saber + *inf.*	to know how to (*do something*)

Repaso: almorzar (almuerzo) (c)

La comida

el aceite	oil
el arroz	rice
las arvejas	green peas
el atún	tuna
el azúcar	sugar
el bistec	steak
los camarones	shrimp
la carne	meat
los champiñones	mushrooms
la chuleta (de cerdo)	(pork) chop
la comida	food
los dulces	sweets; candy
los espárragos	asparagus
el flan	(baked) custard
los frijoles	beans
la galleta	cookie
el helado	ice cream
el huevo	egg
el jamón	ham
la langosta	lobster
la lechuga	lettuce
la mantequilla	butter
la manzana	apple
los mariscos	shellfish
la naranja	orange
el pan	bread
el pan tostado	toast
la papa (frita)	(French fried) potato
el pastel	cake; pie
la patata (frita)	(French fried) potato
el pavo	turkey
el pescado	fish
la pimienta	pepper
el pollo (asado)	(roast) chicken
el postre	dessert
el queso	cheese
la sal	salt
la salchicha	sausage; hot dog
la sopa	soup
las verduras	vegetables
la zanahoria	carrot

Cognados: la banana, la barbacoa, el cereal, la ensalada, la fruta, la hamburguesa, el salmón, el sándwich, el tomate, el yogur

Las bebidas

el agua (mineral)	(mineral) water
la cerveza	beer
el jugo (de fruta)	(fruit) juice
la leche	milk
el refresco	soft drink
el vino (blanco, tinto)	(white, red) wine

Cognado: el té

Repaso: el café

Las comidas

el almuerzo	lunch
la cena	dinner, supper
las comidas	meals
el desayuno	breakfast
la merienda	snack

En un restaurante

el/la camarero/a	waiter/waitress
la cuenta	check, bill
el plato	dish; course
el plato principal	main course

Cognados: el menú

Repaso: los platos (*dishes*)

Otros sustantivos

la ayuda	help
la cocina	cuisine
los comestibles	groceries, foodstuff
la comida	food; meal
el consejo	(piece of) advice
la dirección	address
el/la dueño/a	owner
la letra	(*song*) lyrics
el mandato	command

el nombre	name
la receta	recipe
la tarjeta de crédito	credit card

Repaso: la bebida

Los adjetivos

asado/a	roast(ed)
caliente	hot (*temperature*)
fresco/a	fresh
frito/a	fried
ligero/a	light, not heavy
picante	hot, spicy
rico/a	tasty, savory; rich
tostado/a	toasted

Las palabras indefinidas y negativas

alguien	someone, anyone
algún (alguna/os/as)	some, any
jamás	never
nada	nothing, not anything
nadie	no one, nobody, not anybody
ningún (ninguna)	no, not any
tampoco	neither, not either

Repaso: algo, nunca, siempre, también

Palabras adicionales

estar a dieta	to be on a diet
tener (mucha) hambre	to be (very) hungry
tener (mucha) sed	to be (very) thirsty

➤➤ VOCABULARIO PERSONAL

El Caribe

mogotes*, en el Valle de Viñales, Cuba

¿Cómo se caracteriza el Caribe como región? ¿Qué tienen en común los países caribeños? Primero, naturalmente, el mar Caribe. El mar ha influido mucho en[a] la historia y estilo de vida de los caribeños.[b] La región también se caracteriza por la diversidad étnica, que se debe al influjo[c] de razas[d] diferentes durante su historia, especialmente la raza de los esclavos[e] africanos. La música, el baile, la comida, los pasatiempos,[f] la literatura y las creencias[g] religiosas del Caribe muestran huellas claras[h] de esta rica diversidad étnica.

El Castillo de San Felipe del Morro, Puerto Rico

La música caribeña muestra[i] su tradición africana en su claro[j] sentido del ritmo. El ritmo está marcado por instrumentos de percusión. Hay diferentes tipos de tambores[k] que varían de un país a otro: la tumbadora, el bongo, las pailas, la conga, el cajón, etcétera. Además de[l] los instrumentos de percusión, se incorporan[m] muchos otros, como la guitarra, el contrabajo[n] y el tres y el cuatro (instrumentos de la familia de la guitarra y el laúd), la trompeta y el piano.

Son demasiados[ñ] los tipos de música caribeña para nombrarlos aquí, pero se pueden mencionar, entre otros, el son cubano, la bomba y plena puertorriqueña, el merengue dominicano, la cumbia colombiana y el

Unos niños que participan en el Festival de Barranquilla, Colombia

joropo venezolano. Además, estas formas musicales tienen muchos parientes, entre ellos la salsa, hija de ritmos y músicos cubanos y puertorriqueños aunque nacida[o] en los Estados Unidos.

En un restaurante de Puerto Rico

Jugando al dominó en la República Dominicana

[a]ha... *has influenced much of*   [b]habitantes del Caribe   [c]se... *is due to the influx*   [d]*races*   [e]*slaves*   [f]*pastimes*   [g]*beliefs*   [h]muestran... *show clear signs*   [i]*shows*   [j]*strong*   [k]*drums*   [l]Además... *In addition to*   [m]se... *are used*   [n]*double bass*   [ñ]*too many*   [o]aunque... *although born*

*Los mogotes, *tower-like hills found in Karst regions, are remnants of limestore layers that have eroded.*

Una playa de arena (*sand*) fina, en la República Dominicana

1. ¿Conoces alguna playa de arena fina? ¿Hay alguna cerca de donde vives? ¿Te gusta?

2. ¿Por qué son las playas caribeñas destinos (*destinations*) populares para las vacaciones?

3. ¿Qué crees que pensaron (*thought*) los españoles al llegar(*upon arriving*) a las playas de esta isla en 1492?

De vacaciones

7

De viaje°

De... *Traveling, On a trip*

En el aeropuerto

VUELO 33
SALIDA 10:35

el maletero

el asistente de vuelo

la asistente de vuelo

el equipaje — Jorge

la maleta

Javier

Anita

facturar el equipaje

Alejandro   Josefina   Juana

el pasajero   la pasajera

LOS MEDIOS DE TRANSPORTE

la cabina	cabin (*on a ship*)
el crucero	cruise (ship)
la estación	station
de autobuses	bus station
del tren	train station
el puerto	port
la sala de espera	waiting room
la sala de fumar/ fumadores	smoking area
el vuelo	flight
ir en...	to go/travel by . . .
autobús	bus
avión	plane
barco	boat, ship
tren	train

EL VIAJE

la agencia de viajes	travel agency
el/la agente de viajes	travel agent
el asiento	seat
el billete (*Sp.*) / el boleto (*L.A.*)*	ticket
de ida	one-way ticket
de ida y vuelta	round-trip ticket
la demora	delay
la llegada	arrival
el pasaje*	fare, price (*of a transportation ticket*)
la salida	departure
bajarse (de)	to get down (from); to get off (of) (*a vehicle*)
estar atrasado/a	to be late
facturar el equipaje	to check baggage
guardar (un puesto)	to save (a place [*in line*])

*****El boleto** *is generally understood to express* ticket *throughout the Spanish-speaking world. The word* **el tiquete** *is heard in Mexico and Central America, as well as in this country, and* **el billete** *is used in Spain. The words* **la entrada** *and* **la localidad** *are used to refer to tickets for movies, plays, or other events.*

hacer **cola**	to stand in line	**quejarse (de)**	to complain (about)
hacer **escalas/**	to make stops	**subir (a)**	to go up; to get on
paradas			(*a vehicle*)
hacer **la(s)**	to pack one's	**viajar**	to travel
maleta(s)	suitcase(s)	v**o**lar (v**ue**lo) **en avión**	to fly, go by plane
hacer **un viaje**	to take a trip		
pasar por el control	to go/pass through		
de la seguridad	security (check)		

Conversación

A. Un viaje en avión. Imagina que vas a hacer un viaje en avión. El vuelo sale a las siete de la mañana. Usando los números del 1 al 9, indica en qué orden van a pasar las siguientes cosas.

a. _____ Subo al avión.
b. _____ Voy a la sala de espera.
c. _____ Hago cola para facturar el equipaje.
d. _____ Llego al aeropuerto a tiempo (*on time*) y me bajo del taxi.
e. _____ Por fin se anuncia la salida del vuelo.
f. _____ Estoy atrasado/a. Salgo para el aeropuerto en taxi.
g. _____ La asistente me indica el asiento en clase turística.
h. _____ Pido un asiento de ventanilla (*window seat*), pero sólo hay asientos de pasillo (*aisle*).
i. _____ Hay demora. Todos tenemos que esperar el vuelo allí antes de subir al avión.

B. Usemos la lógica

Paso 1. ¿Qué vas a hacer en estas situaciones?

1. Tienes poco dinero. Si tienes que viajar, ¿qué clase de pasaje vas a comprar?
 a. clase turística **b.** primera clase **c.** clase de negocios (*business*)

2. Tienes miedo de volar en avión, pero necesitas ir desde Nueva York a Madrid. ¿Qué alternativa tienes?
 a. una cabina en un barco **b.** un vuelo sin escalas **c.** un autobús con baño

Paso 2. Ahora, en parejas, contesten las siguientes preguntas.

1. Uds. viajan en tren y tienen muchas maletas. Pesan (*They weigh*) mucho y Uds. no pueden cargarlas (*carry them*). ¿Qué hacen?
2. El vuelo de Uds. está atrasado. ¿Qué dicen Uds. (*will you say*)? ¿Con quién se quejan?
3. Uno de Uds. tiene claustrofobia, pero no tiene más remedio que (*has no other option than*) volar en avión. ¿Qué debe pedir?

C. Definiciones. Da las palabras definidas.

1. Es la persona que nos ayuda con el equipaje en la estación del tren.
2. Es la cosa que se compra antes de hacer un viaje.
3. Es el antónimo de **subir a**.
4. Se va allí cuando se hace un viaje en avión.
5. Se va allí cuando se hace un viaje en tren.
6. Es la persona que nos ayuda durante un vuelo.

D. En el aeropuerto. En parejas, nombren (*name*) o describan las cosas y acciones representadas en este dibujo.

⟶ NOTA CULTURAL

Los nuevos tipos de turismo en el mundo hispánico

El turista de hoy ya no es el turista tradicional y fácil de complacer.[a] Por eso hay nuevas industrias para satisfacer su interés en **la ecología, la agricultura** o **la aventura:** el ecoturismo, el agroturismo y el aventurismo. Los países hispanos ofrecen variadas oportunidades para disfrutar de[b] estas nuevas formas de hacer turismo.

El ecoturismo consiste en viajar a **lugares no explotados por el ser humano.**[c] Los lugares del mundo hispano que ofrecen amplias oportunidades para el ecoturismo son **las selvas tropicales** de Centroamérica y la Amazonia, especialmente en Costa Rica y el Ecuador. Las Islas Galápagos y la Patagonia (en el sur de la Argentina y Chile) también son **destinos**[d] populares entre los ecoturistas.

El agroturismo indica **viajes a lugares rurales** donde el turista se queda en casas rurales renovadas, a veces visitando más de una casa o zona durante su viaje. Algunas excursiones son informativas o educativas, con visitas a **granjas y campos de cultivo.**[e] Otras son simplemente parte de un programa para renovar casas y pueblos rurales. España ofrece varias oportunidades al agroturista por todo el país, especialmente en el País Vasco y en las Islas Baleares. La isla Chiloé de Chile también tiene una organización agroturística.

Un grupo de estudiantes que participa en un taller (*workshop*) ecoturístico en la Amazonia, en el Perú

El aventurista, o sea[f] el turista que busca viajes emocionantes, a veces peligrosos,[g] también tiene amplias oportunidades en los países hispánicos. En los Andes, la Patagonia y las montañas de España, puede practicar **alpinismo, ciclismo de montaña, navegación en rápidos, esquí** y **snowboard** extremos.

[a]*please*   [b]*disfrutar... enjoying*   [c]*por... by humans*   [d]*destinations*   [e]*granjas... farms and croplands*   [f]*o... or in other words*   [g]*dangerous*

las montañas

el camping

la camioneta

la tienda (de campaña)

la playa

nadar

hacer camping

el mar

Carlos

Ana María

Flor

Alejandra

Alberto

tomar el sol

sacar (qu) fotos

el *camping*	campground
el mar	sea
el océano	ocean
estar de vacaciones	to be on vacation
ir de vacaciones a...	to (go on) vacation to/in . . .
pasar las vacaciones en...	to spend one's vacation in . . .
salir de vacaciones	to leave on vacation
tomar unas vacaciones	to take a vacation

Conversación

A. ¿Qué haces? Di si las siguientes declaraciones son ciertas o falsas para ti. Corrige las declaraciones falsas.

	CIERTO	FALSO
1. Cuando estoy de vacaciones, tomo el sol.	❑	❑
2. Prefiero ir de vacaciones a las montañas.	❑	❑
3. Duermo muy bien en una tienda de campaña.	❑	❑
4. Saco muchas fotos cuando estoy de vacaciones.	❑	❑
5. Es fácil ir a playas bonitas desde (*from*) aquí.	❑	❑

B. Entrevista

1. Por lo general, ¿cuándo tomas tus vacaciones? ¿En invierno? ¿en verano? ¿Cuánto tiempo tienes de vacaciones, en general? ¿Dos semanas? ¿tres semanas? ¿más?
2. Durante tus vacaciones, ¿te gusta viajar o prefieres no salir del lugar donde vives? ¿Prefieres sólo viajar por (*through*) este país o quieres conocer otros países del mundo?
3. ¿Te gusta ir de vacaciones con tu familia a algún lugar en particular? ¿Prefieres ir solo/a, con uno de tus amigos o con un grupo de personas?
4. ¿Cuáles de los medios de transporte en **De viaje** (páginas 200–202) conoces por experiencia? ¿Cómo prefieres viajar? ¿Viajas en avión con frecuencia? ¿Prefieres un asiento de ventanilla o de pasillo? ¿la clase turística o primera clase?

⟷ NOTA COMUNICATIVA

Other Uses of *se* (For Recognition)

It is likely that you have often seen and heard the phrase shown in the photo that accompanies this box: **Se habla español.** (*Spanish is spoken* [*here*]). Here are some additional examples of this use of **se** with Spanish verbs. Note how the meaning of the verb changes slightly.

San Diego, California

Se venden billetes aquí.	*Tickets are sold here.*
Aquí no **se fuma.**	*You don't (One doesn't) smoke here. Smoking is forbidden here.*

Be alert to this use of **se** when you see it because it will occur with some frequency in readings and in direction lines in *¡Apúntate!* The activities in this text will not require you to use this grammar point on your own, however.

C. ¿Dónde se hace esto? Indica el lugar (o los lugares) donde se hacen las siguientes actividades.

1. Se factura el equipaje y se anuncian los vuelos.
2. Se hacen las maletas.
3. Se compran los boletos.
4. Se hace una reservación.
5. Se espera en la sala de espera.
6. Se pide una bebida.
7. Se mira una película.
8. Se nada y se toma el sol.
9. Se hacen las camas.
10. Se pide información sobre los viajes.
11. No se fuma.
12. Se hace cola.

D. La publicidad

Paso 1. Lee con cuidado (*carefully*) este anuncio de una aerolínea latinoamericana.

Paso 2. Ahora, en parejas, contesten las siguientes preguntas. ¡Piensen como expertos en *marketing*!

1. ¿Cómo se llama la aerolínea?
2. ¿A qué tipo de persona va dirigido (*directed*) el anuncio?
3. ¿Por qué se usa un plato con comida en el anuncio?
4. ¿Qué se ve en el plato? ¿Qué representa?
5. ¿En qué tipo de publicación creen Uds. que se encuentra (*is found*) este anuncio?

CUBA

HAITÍ

REPÚBLICA
DOMINICANA

Santo
Domingo

OCÉANO
ATLÁNTICO

PUERTO
RICO

MAR CARIBE

La República Dominicana

DATOS ESENCIALES

NOMBRE OFICIAL: República Dominicana
CAPITAL: Santo Domingo
POBLACIÓN: más de 9 millones de habitantes

FÍJATE

- La República Dominicana ocupa los dos tercios orientales[a] de la isla de La Española en el mar Caribe. Cuando Cristóbal Colón llegó[b] a la Isla por primera vez en 1492, declaró[c] que era[d] la isla más bella[e] del mundo.
- España le cedió[f] el tercio occidental[g] de La Española a Francia en 1697. Por eso, esa parte de la Isla, el actual país de Haití, tiene una cultura y un idioma diferentes de los de la República Dominicana.
- La ciudad de Santo Domingo fue fundada[h] por Bartolomé Colón, hermano de Cristóbal, en 1496, y es la ciudad más antigua del continente americano.

[a]dos... *eastern two thirds* [b]*arrived* [c]*he said* [d]*it was* [e]*beautiful* [f]*ceded* [g]*western* [h]*founded*

¡MÚSICA!

La música y baile nacional de la República Dominicana es el merengue. Los orígenes del merengue se desconocen,[a] pero casi todos concurren en[b] que el merengue es una fusión de tradiciones africanas y europeas con tendencias de la música cubana de los siglos[c] VII y XVIII.

[a]se... *are unknown* [b]casi... *almost everyone agrees* [c]*centuries*

★ KINITO MÉNDEZ

El merengue es ahora un ritmo que se baila por todo el mundo hispano, y hasta en los Estados Unidos. Kinito Méndez es uno de los merengueros más famosos. En el merengue «A caballo»,[a] del álbum *Caballo*, se puede escuchar una parte de «llamada y respuesta»,[b] donde los merengueros hacen una oración divertida[c] al «santo[d] Merengue». «Llamada y respuesta» es un diálogo musical, típico de la música afrocaribeña, en el que[e] los músicos establecen una especie de diálogo mientras[f] tocan.

[a]A... *On horseback* [b]llamada... *call and response* [c]oración... *entertaining prayer* [d]*Saint* [e]el... *which* [f]*while*

Kinito Méndez, merenguero dominicano

¿Recuerdas?

In **Gramática 17 (Cap. 6)**, you learned how to use direct object pronouns to avoid repetition. Can you identify the direct object pronouns in the following exchange? To what or to who(m) do these pronouns refer?

— Roberto, ¿tienes los boletos?

— No, no los tengo, pero mi agente de viajes ya los tiene listos (*ready*).

— Si quieres, te acompaño a la agencia.

— Encantado. Casi nunca te veo. También podemos pasar por la plaza a tomar un café.

— De acuerdo.

20 Expressing *to who(m)* or *for who(m)*
Indirect Object Pronouns; **Dar** and **decir**

Gramática en acción: En el aeropuerto

1. En el mostrador

   —_____.

   —Lo siento, pero ya no hay. Pero puedo asignarle un asiento de pasillo.

2. En el control de la seguridad

   —_____.

   —¿Le enseño también el pasaporte?

Comprensión. ¿Quién lo dice?

a. «¿Me puede dar un asiento de ventanilla?»
b. «¿Me enseña la tarjeta de embarque (*boarding pass*), por favor?»

---

*At the airport 1. At the counter — . . . —I'm sorry, but there aren't any more. But I can assign you an aisle seat. *2.* At the security check — . . . —Should I show you my passport too?

Indirect Object Pronouns

me	to/for me	**nos**	to/for us
te	to/for you (*fam. sing.*)	**os**	to/for you (*fam. pl.*)
le	to/for you (*form. sing.*), him, her, it	**les**	to/for you (*form. pl.*), them

Note that indirect object pronouns have the same form as direct object pronouns, except in the third person: **le, les.**

1. Indirect Objects Indirect object nouns and pronouns are the second recipient of the action of the verb. They usually answer the questions *to whom?* or *for whom?* in relation to the verb. The word *to* is frequently omitted in English.

> **indirect object** = a noun or pronoun that indicates *to who(m)* or *for who(m)* an action is performed

Indicate the direct and indirect objects in the following sentences.

1. I'm giving her the present tomorrow.
2. Could you tell me the answer now?
3. El profesor nos va a hacer algunas preguntas.
4. ¿No me compras una revista ahora?

2. Placement of Indirect Object Pronouns Like direct object pronouns, *indirect object pronouns* (**los pronombres del complemento indirecto**) are placed immediately before a conjugated verb. Alternatively, they may be attached to an infinitive or a present participle.

No, no **te presto** el coche.
No, I won't lend you the car.

Voy a **guardarte** el asiento.
Te voy a guardar el asiento.
I'll save your seat for you.

Le estoy escribiendo una carta a Marisol.
Estoy **escribiéndole** una carta a Marisol.
I'm writing Marisol a letter.

3. With Commands As with direct object pronouns, indirect object pronouns are attached to the affirmative command form and precede the negative command form.

Sírvanos un café, por favor.
Serve us some coffee, please.

No me dé su número de teléfono ahora.
Don't give me your phone number now.

4. Clarification of *le*(*s*) Since **le** and **les** have several different equivalents, their meaning is often clarified or emphasized with the preposition **a** followed by a pronoun (object of a preposition).

Voy a mandar**le** un telegrama **a Ud. (a él, a ella).**
I'm going to send you (him, her) a telegram.

Les hago una comida **a Uds. (a ellos, a ellas).**
I'm making you (them) a meal.

5. Third Person Indirect Objects With third person forms, it is common for a Spanish sentence to contain both the indirect object noun and the indirect object pronoun.

Vamos a contar**le** el secreto **a Juan.**
Let's tell Juan the secret.

¿**Les** guardo los asientos **a Jorge y Marta?**
Shall I save the seats for Jorge and Marta?

6. Verbs Often Used with Indirect Objects Here are some verbs frequently used with indirect objects. Be sure you know their meaning before starting the activities in the **Práctica** section.

con**t**ar (**cuen**to)	to tell, narrate	pe**d**ir (**pi**do) (**i**)	to ask for
entre**g**ar (**gu**)	to hand in	preguntar	to ask (*a question*)
escribir	to write	prestar	to lend
expli**c**ar (**qu**)	to explain	prometer	to promise
hablar	to speak	recomen**d**ar (recom**ien**do)	to recommend
mandar	to send	regalar	to give (*as a gift*)
mo**s**trar (m**ues**tro)	to show	se**r**vir (**sir**vo) (**i**)	to serve
ofre**c**er (ofre**zc**o)	to offer		

Dar and decir

dar (*to give*)		decir (*to say; to tell*)	
doy	damos	digo	decimos
das	dais	dices	decís
da	dan	dice	dicen

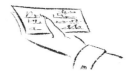

Juan les **dice** a sus padres
que necesita dinero.

Su padre le **da** un cheque.

1. ***Dar / Decir* + Indirect Objects** **Dar** and **decir** are almost always used with indirect object pronouns in Spanish.

> ### ¡OJO!
>
> In Spanish there are two verbs for *to give:* **dar** (*to give in general*) and **regalar** (*to give as a gift*). Also, do not confuse **decir** (*to say* or *to tell*) with **hablar** (*to speak*) or **contar** (*to tell, narrate*).

¿Cuándo **me das** el dinero?
When will you give me the money?

¿Por qué no **le dice** Ud. la verdad, señor?
Why don't you tell him/her the truth, sir?

2. Formal Commands of *dar / decir* **Dar** and **decir** also have irregular formal command forms. There is a written accent on **dé** to distinguish it from the preposition **de**.

Formal commands of **dar** and **decir**:

dar	⟶ **dé, den**
decir	⟶ **diga, digan**

«Le puedo dar un asiento de ventanilla (*window*).»

Práctica

A. Asociaciones. ¿Qué verbos asocias con los siguientes objetos y situaciones?

1. un coche, el dinero
2. la comida en un restaurante
3. las fotos
4. hacer algo por (*for*) alguien
5. la gramática, un profesor
6. la tarea, un informe (*report, paper*)
7. algo de comer o beber
8. algo para un cumpleaños o para un día festivo (*holiday*)
9. un restaurante, una película, un libro
10. flores (*flowers*), un e-mail
11. un secreto, un chiste (*joke*)

B. ¡Anticipemos!

Paso 1. Indica si las siguientes declaraciones son ciertas o falsas.

	CIERTO	FALSO
1. Todos los años le mando una tarjeta de cumpleaños a mi abuelo/a.	❏	❏
2. El Día de la Madre le regalo flores a mi madre.	❏	❏
3. Todos los días les escribo e-mails a mis padres (hijos).	❏	❏
4. Siempre les entrego la tarea a los profesores a tiempo.	❏	❏
5. Mis amigos me dan dinero para mi cumpleaños.	❏	❏
6. Un buen amigo me presta su coche cuando lo necesito.	❏	❏
7. Los profesores nos cuentan chistes en clase con frecuencia.	❏	❏
8. El profesor / La profesora de español nos da mucha tarea.	❏	❏

Paso 2. Ahora, en parejas, túrnense para entrevistarse, usando las declaraciones del **Paso 1** como modelo. Deben corregir los detalles incorrectos.

> MODELO: **E1:** ¿Tus amigos te dan dinero para tu cumpleaños?
> **E2:** ¡No! Mis abuelos me dan dinero. (Nadie me da dinero.)

C. De vuelta (*Returning*) a la República Dominicana.
Algunos amigos dominicanos necesitan ayuda para arreglar su vuelta a casa. Explícales cómo los puedes ayudar, usando las siguientes palabras.

> MODELO: confirmar el vuelo $\longrightarrow$ *Les* confirmo el vuelo.

1. llamar un taxi
2. bajar (*to carry down*) las maletas
3. guardar (*to keep an eye on*) el equipaje
4. facturar el equipaje
5. guardar un puesto en la cola
6. guardar el asiento en la sala de espera
7. comprar una revista
8. por fin dar un abrazo

Un avión que despega (*is taking off*), en el aeropuerto de Santo Domingo, República Dominicana

D. ¿Qué hacen estas personas? Completa las siguientes oraciones lógicamente con un verbo y un pronombre de complemento indirecto.

MODELO: El vicepresidente _le ofrece_ consejos al presidente.

1. Romeo _____ flores a Julieta.
2. Snoopy _____ besos (kisses) a Lucy… ¡Y a ella no le gusta!
3. Eva _____ una manzana a Adán.
4. El Doctor Phil _____ consejos a sus televidentes.
5. Los bancos _____ dinero a las personas que quieren comprar una casa.
6. Los asistentes de vuelo _____ bebidas a los pasajeros.
7. Yo siempre _____ la verdad a todos.

Vocabulario útil

dar
decir
ofrecer (ofrezco)
prestar
regalar
servir (sirvo) (i)

E. En un restaurante. Explícale al pequeño Benjamín, que sólo tiene 4 años, lo que se hace en un restaurante. Llena los espacios en blanco con pronombres de complemento indirecto.

Primero el camarero _____¹ ofrece una mesa desocupada.ª Luego tú _____² pides el menú al camarero. También _____³ haces preguntas sobre los platos y las especialidades de la casa y _____⁴ dices lo que quieres comer. El camarero _____⁵ trae la comida. Por fin tu papá _____⁶ pide la cuenta al camarero. Si tú quieres pagar, _____⁷ pides dinero a tu papá y _____⁸ das el dinero al camarero.

ªvacant

Need more practice?
- Workbook/Laboratory Manual
- Online Learning Center [www.mhhe.com/apuntate]

Conversación

Entrevista. En parejas, túrnense para entrevistarse sobre los siguientes temas. Traten de (Try to) continuar la conversación.

MODELO: E1: ¿Quién te hace buenos regalos?
E2: Mis padres siempre me hacen buenos regalos.
E1: ¿Qué te regalan, por ejemplo?
E2: Bueno, me regalan dinero, CDs, muebles para mi apartamento…

1. regalar: buenas cosas / cosas feas / dinero
2. decir: la verdad / mentiras (lies)
3. contar: secretos / los secretos de otras personas
4. hacer: favores / recomendaciones / la cena
5. escribir: e-mails / poemas de amor / tarjetas postales cuando están de vacaciones
6. mostrar: las fotos de sus vacaciones / las notas (grades) de sus exámenes
7. servir: la comida / bebidas
8. pedir / dar: ayuda / consejos
9. prestar: dinero / ropa / su coche
10. prometer: cosas que no haces
11. recomendar: películas / restaurantes / clases en la universidad
12. ¿ ?

¿Quién te cuenta secretos?

In **Primeros pasos** you started to use forms of **gustar** to express your likes and dislikes. Review what you know by answering the following questions. Then, changing their form as needed, interview your instructor.

1. ¿Te gusta el café (el vino, el té...)? .
2. ¿Te gusta jugar al béisbol (al golf, al voleibol, al...)?
3. ¿Te gusta viajar en avión (fumar, viajar en tren...)?
4. ¿Qué te gusta más, estudiar o ir a fiestas (trabajar o descansar, cocinar o comer)?

21 Expressing Likes and Dislikes • Gustar (Part 2)

Gramática en acción: Los chilenos viajeros

Según el anuncio, a muchos chilenos les gusta viajar a otros países. Lee el anuncio y luego indica si las oraciones son ciertas o falsas.

1. A los chilenos les gusta viajar sólo en este hemisferio.
2. A los chilenos les gustan mucho las playas.
3. Sólo les gusta viajar a los países de habla española.
4. No les gustaría el precio del viaje.

MEDIO MILLÓN DE CHILENOS
DE VACACIONES 2010 AL EXTRANJERO
Y USTED... NO SE QUEDE SIN VIAJAR
¡ RESERVE AHORA MISMO !

El próximo verano '10, con el bajo valor del dólar, muchas personas desearán viajar, los cupos disponibles se agotarán rapidamente. ¡Asegure sus vacaciones! Elija ahora cualquiera de nuestros fantásticos programas.

**MIAMI - ORLANDO - BAHAMAS - MÉXICO - CANCÚN
ACAPULCO - IXTAPA - COSTA RICA - RÍO - SALVADOR
PLAYA TAMBOR - PUNTA CANA - LA HABANA
VARADERO - GUATEMALA - SUDÁFRICA**

Infórmese sobre nuestro SÚPER CRÉDITO PREFERENCIAL
Economy Tour
Santa Magdalena 94, Providencia
☎2334429 - 2331774 - 2314252
2328294 - 2318608 - 2334862
Fax: 2334428

¿Y a ti? ¿Te gusta viajar? ¿Te gustan los viajes en avión? ¿Cuál de estos lugares te gustaría visitar?

Constructions with gustar

Spanish	Literal equivalent	English Phrasing
Me gusta la playa.	The beach is pleasing to me.	*I like the beach.*
No le gustan sus cursos.	His courses are not pleasing to him.	*He doesn't like his courses.*
Nos gusta leer.	Reading is pleasing to us.	*We like to read.*

You have been using the verb **gustar** since the beginning of *¡Apúntate!* to express likes and dislikes. However, **gustar** does not literally mean *to like*, but rather *to be pleasing*.

Me gusta viajar.
Traveling is pleasing to me. (I like to travel.)

Me gustan los viajes de aventura.
Adventurous trips are pleasing to me. (I like adventurous trips.)

1. **Gustar + Indirect Object Pronouns** Gustar is always used with an indirect object pronoun: Someone or something is pleasing *to* someone else. The verb must agree with the subject of the sentence — that is, the person or thing that is pleasing.

> An infinitive is viewed as a singular subject in Spanish.

Me gusta **este asiento** de pasillo.
This aisle seat is pleasing to me. (I like this aisle seat.)

No **me** gusta**n** **los asientos** de ventanilla.
Window seats are not pleasing to me. (I don't like window seats.)

Me gusta mucho **volar** en avión.
Flying is really pleasing to me. (I really like to fly.)

2. **Indirect Object Noun + Pronoun** When the person pleased is stated as a noun, the phrase **a** + *noun* must be used in addition to the indirect object pronoun. The prepositional phrase usually appears before the indirect object pronoun, but it can also appear after the verb.

¡OJO!

The indirect object pronoun *must* be used with **gustar** even when the prepositional phrase **a** + *noun* or *pronoun* is used.

A David no **le** gustan los aviones.
No **le** gustan los aviones **a David**.
David doesn't like airplanes.

A Raquel y **a Arturo les** gusta viajar en las vacaciones.
Les gusta viajar en las vacaciones **a Raquel** y **Arturo**.
Raquel and Arturo like to travel while on vacation.

3. **Clarification or Emphasis** A phrase with **a** + *pronoun* is often used for clarification or emphasis. The prepositional phrase can appear before the indirect object pronoun or after the verb.

¡OJO!

Mí (accent) and **ti** (no accent) are used as the object of most prepositions, except **conmigo** and **contigo**. Subject pronouns (**Ud., él, ella,...**) are used as the object of all prepositions for all other persons.

[Práctica A]

CLARIFICATION

¿**Le** gusta **a Ud.** viajar?
Do you like to travel?

¿**Le** gusta **a él** viajar?
Does he like to travel?

EMPHASIS

A mí me gusta viajar en avión, pero **a mi esposo le** gusta viajar en coche. Y **a ti,** ¿en qué **te** gusta viajar?

I like to travel by plane, but my husband likes to travel by car. How do you like to travel?

Would Like / Wouldn't Like

What one *would* or *would not* like to do is expressed with the form **gustaría*** + *infinitive* and the appropriate indirect objects.

[Práctica B]

A mí **me gustaría viajar** a Colombia.
I would like to travel to Colombia.

Nos **gustaría hacer** *camping* este verano.
We would like to go camping this summer.

AUTOPRUEBA

Complete each verb with **-a** or **-an**.

1. Me gust_____ las playas de México.
2. Les gust_____ esquiar en las montañas.
3. No nos gust_____ viajar con mi padre.
4. ¿Te gust_____ este restaurante?
5. A Julio le gust_____ mucho las fotos de mi viaje.

Answers: 1. gustan 2. gusta 3. gusta 4. gusta 5. gustan

---

*This is one of the forms of the conditional of **gustar**. You will study all of the forms of the conditional in **Gramática 45 (Cap. 18)**.

Práctica

A. Los gustos y preferencias

Paso 1. Expresa tus gustos con oraciones completas.

> **MODELO:** ¿el café? ⟶ (No) Me gusta el café.
> ¿los pasteles? ⟶ (No) Me gustan los pasteles.

1. ¿el vino?
2. ¿los niños pequeños?
3. ¿la música clásica?
4. ¿volar en avión?
5. ¿el invierno?
6. ¿hacer cola?
7. ¿el chocolate?
8. ¿las películas de terror?
9. ¿las clases que empiezan a las ocho de la mañana?
10. ¿cocinar?
11. ¿la gramática?
12. ¿tus clases este semestre/trimestre?
13. ¿los vuelos con muchas escalas?
14. ¿Jennifer López?

Paso 2. Ahora, en parejas, túrnense para entrevistarse sobre las ideas del **Paso 1.** Luego digan a la clase dos cosas que Uds. tienen en común.

> **MODELO:** **E1:** A mí no me gusta el café.
> **E2:** A mí tampoco. ⟶
> **E1:** (*a la clase*): A mí no me gusta el café y a Miguel tampoco (le gusta).

Vocabulario útil			
A mí también.	So do I.	**Pues a mí, sí.**	Well, I do.
A mí tampoco.	I don't either. / Neither do I.	**Pues a mí, no.**	Well, I don't.

B. Las vacaciones de los Soto.
Imagina que eres uno de los hijos de la familia Soto y haz oraciones completas para describir lo que prefieren hacer en sus vacaciones.

> **MODELO:** padre / nadar: ir a la playa ⟶
> A mi padre *le gusta* nadar. *Le gustaría* ir a la playa.

1. padre / el mar: ir a la playa
2. hermanos pequeños / nadar: también ir a la playa
3. hermano Ernesto / hacer *camping*: ir a las montañas
4. abuelos / descansar: quedarse en casa
5. madre / la tranquilidad: visitar un pueblecito (*small town*) en la costa
6. hermana Elena / discotecas: pasar las vacaciones en una ciudad grande
7. mí / ¿ ?

Comprensión. Contesta las siguientes preguntas.

1. ¿A quién le gustaría ir a Nueva York?
2. ¿A quién le gustaría viajar a Acapulco?
3. ¿Quién no quiere salir de casa?
4. ¿A quién le gustaría ir a la República Dominicana?
5. ¿Quién quiere ir a Colorado?

Need more practice?
- Workbook/Laboratory Manual
- Online Learning Center [www.mhhe.com/apuntate]

Conversación

A. ¿Conoces bien a... ?

Paso 1. Piensa en tu profesor(a) de español. En tu opinión, ¿le gustan a él/ella las siguientes cosas o no?

	SÍ, LE GUSTA(N).	NO, NO LE GUSTA(N).
1. la música clásica	❑	❑
2. el color negro	❑	❑
3. las canciones (*songs*) de los años 70	❑	❑
4. viajar en coche	❑	❑
5. la comida mexicana	❑	❑
6. dar clases por la mañana	❑	❑
7. estudiar otras lenguas	❑	❑
8. el arte surrealista	❑	❑
9. las películas trágicas	❑	❑
10. ¿ ?	❑	❑

Paso 2. Entrevista. Ahora entrevista a tu profesor(a) para saber si le gustan las cosas del **Paso 1** o no.

> **MODELOS:** ¿A Ud. le gusta la música clásica?
> A Ud. le gusta la música clásica, ¿verdad?

Paso 3. Entrevista. Ahora entrevista a un compañero o compañera sobre las mismas cosas.

> **MODELO: E1:** ¿Te gusta la música clásica?
> **E2:** Sí, a mí me gusta. ¿Y a ti?

B. Perfil personal.
En parejas, inventen con detalles las preferencias de las siguientes personas.

> ### Vocabulario útil
> **la música rap,** *hip hop*
> **jugar (juego) (gu) a los videojuegos**
> **patinar en monopatín** to skateboard

1. Toño

2. los Sres. Sánchez

3. Memo

◑ NOTA COMUNICATIVA

More About Expressing Likes and Dislikes

Here are some ways to express intense likes and dislikes.

- Use the phrases **mucho/muchísimo** or **no... (para) nada**.

Me gusta mucho/muchísimo.	*I like it a lot / a whole lot.*
No me gusta (para) nada.	*I don't like it at all.*

- To express *love* and *hate* in reference to likes and dislikes, you can use **encantar** and **odiar**.

Encantar is used just like **gustar**.

Me encanta el chocolate.	*I love chocolate.*
Les encanta viajar, ¿verdad?	*They love traveling, right?*

Odiar, on the other hand, functions like a transitive verb (one that can take a direct object).

Odio el apio.	*I hate celery.*
Mi madre **odia** viajar sola.	*My mother hates traveling alone.*

- To express interest in something, use **interesar**. This verb is also used like **gustar** and **encantar**.

Me interesan las películas extranjeras.	*I'm interested in foreign films.*

Use as many of the preceding verbs as you can in the following activity.

C. Entrevista. En parejas, túrnense para describir lo que les gusta y lo que odian cuando están en las siguientes situaciones. Inventen los detalles necesarios.

MODELO: en la playa ⟶ Cuando estoy en la playa, me gusta mucho nadar en el mar, pero no me gusta el sol ni me gusta la arena (*sand*). Por eso no me gusta pasar todo el día en la playa. Prefiero nadar en una piscina.

Situaciones	
en un almacén grande	en el coche
en un autobús	en una discoteca
en un avión	en una fiesta
en la biblioteca	en un parque
en una cafetería	en la playa
en casa con mis amigos	en el salón de clase
en casa con mis padres/hijos	en un tren

¿Te gusta ir a la playa con tus amigos?

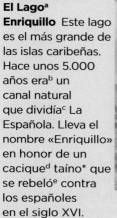

1 **La Avenida Hermanas Mirabal, en Santo Domingo** También llamada[a] «El Malecón» y «la discoteca más grande del mundo», la Avenida Hermanas Mirabal es un enorme bulevar donde hay discotecas, restaurantes y bares. Es el corazón[b] del Carnaval Dominicano en la primavera y del Festival del Merengue en el verano. Este festival representa diez días de música, bailes y espectáculos en las calles.

[a]called [b]heart

El Teatro Nacional, en Santo Domingo Inaugurado[a] en 1973, el Teatro Nacional cuenta con[b] 1.700 asientos en el auditorio principal. Es uno de los teatros más espléndidos de América. Varias estatuas[c] de dramaturgos,[d] compositores[e] y escritores rodean[f] la Plaza de la Cultura donde se encuentra[g] el teatro. A la entrada[h] del teatro se ve la estatua del dramaturgo español Pedro Calderón de la Barca (1600–1681).

[a]Inaugurated [b]cuenta... has [c]statues [d]playwrights [e]composers [f]surround [g]se... is found [h]entrance

2

4

3

El Lago[a] Enriquillo Este lago es el más grande de las islas caribeñas. Hace unos 5.000 años era[b] un canal natural que dividía[c] La Española. Lleva el nombre «Enriquillo» en honor de un cacique[d] taíno* que se rebeló[e] contra los españoles en el siglo XVI. Hoy día tiene la concentración más grande de cocodrilos americanos y una especie[f] de iguana endémica[g] de la Isla.

[a]Lake [b]Hace... About 5,000 years ago it was [c]divided [d]chief [e]se... rebelled [f]species [g]native

El Parque Colón, en Santo Domingo El Parque Colón está en el centro de la ciudad colonial de Santo Domingo. La estatua de Cristóbal Colón apunta hacia[a] España. A sus pies[b] está la imagen de Anacaona, una cacica[c] taína y la primera taína en aprender a leer y escribir en español. Los españoles consideraron[d] que era demasiado poderosa y peligrosa,[e] y por eso la asesinaron[f] en 1503.

[a]apunta... is pointing toward [b]feet [c]female chief [d]thought [e]era... she was too powerful and dangerous [f]they killed

5

Un partido de béisbol, en San Pedro, Macorís, la República Dominicana La República Dominicana también se conoce como «la República del Béisbol», ya que[a] produce más jugadores de las Ligas Mayores[b] que cualquier[c] otro país, excepto los Estados Unidos. Sin embargo, de cada cien aspirantes que asisten a las academias de béisbol dominicanas, sólo uno llega a las ligas menores, y muy pocos de esos llegan a las Ligas Mayores.

[a]ya... porque [b]Ligas... Major Leagues [c]any

---

*The Tainos were the Amerindian tribe that occupied what today are the islands of Hispaniola, Cuba, Puerto Rico, and Jamaica when the Spanish arrived.

paso 3 Gramática

¿Recuerdas?

You have already learned one of the irregular past tense verb forms that is presented in **Gramática 22**. Review it now by telling what day yesterday was: **Ayer...**

22 Talking About the Past (Part 1) • Preterite of Regular Verbs and of **dar, hacer, ir,** and **ser**

Gramática en acción: Un viaje a la República Dominicana

Elisa es reportera. Hace poco, fue a la República Dominicana para escribir un artículo sobre la isla de La Española. Habla Elisa.

- Yo hice el viaje en avión.
- El vuelo fue largo porque el avión hizo escala en Miami.
- Pasé una semana entera en la Isla.
- Visité muchos sitios de interés turístico e* histórico.
- Comí mucha comida típica del Caribe.
- Tomé el sol y nadé en el mar.
- ¡Lo pasé muy bien!

Comprensión. ¿Cierto o falso? Corrige las oraciones falsas.

	CIERTO	FALSO
1. Elisa fue a la República Dominicana para pasar sus vacaciones.	❑	❑
2. El avión hizo escala en los Estados Unidos.	❑	❑
3. Elisa no visitó ningún lugar importante de la Isla.	❑	❑
4. No lo pasó bien en la playa.	❑	❑

In previous chapters of ¡Apúntate! you have always talked in the present tense. In this section, you will begin to use forms of the preterite, one of the past tenses in Spanish. To talk about all aspects of the past in Spanish, there are two *simple tenses* (tenses formed without an auxiliary or "helping" verb): the *preterite* and the *imperfect*. In this chapter, you will learn the regular forms of the preterite and those of four irregular verbs: **dar, hacer, ir,** and **ser.** Then in **Capítulos 8, 9,** and **10,** you will learn more about preterite forms and their uses as well as about the imperfect and how it is used alone and with the preterite.

A trip to the Dominican Republic Elisa is a reporter. A little while ago, she went to the Dominican Republic to write an article about the island of Hispaniola. Here's Elisa. • I made the trip by plane. • The flight was long because the plane made a stop in Miami. • I spent a whole week on the Island. • I visited a lot of interesting tourist and historical sites. • I ate a lot of typical Caribbean food. • I sunbathed and swam in the ocean. • I had a really good time!

*The word y changes to e when used before a word begining with i- or hi-, to facilitate pronunciation.

218 doscientos dieciocho CAPÍTULO 7 ■ De vacaciones

Preterite of Regular Verbs

	hablar		comer		viver
hablé	I spoke (did speak)	comí	I ate (did eat)	viví	I lived (did live)
hablaste	you spoke	comiste	you ate	viviste	you lived
habló	you/he/she spoke	comió	you/he/she ate	vivió	you/he/she lived
hablamos	we spoke	comimos	we ate	vivimos	we lived
hablasteis	you spoke	comisteis	you ate	vivisteis	you lived
hablaron	you/they spoke	comieron	you/they ate	vivieron	you/they lived

1. **Equivalents of the Preterite** The *preterite* (**el pretérito**) has several equivalents in English. For example, **hablé** can mean *I spoke* or *I did speak*. The preterite is used to report finished, completed actions or states of being in the past. If the action or state of being is viewed as completed—no matter how long it lasted or took to complete—it will be expressed with the preterite.

Pasé dos meses en el Caribe.
I spent two months in the Caribbean.

El verano pasado **hicimos** *camping* en Puerto Rico.
Last summer we went camping in Puerto Rico.

Regular Preterite Endings

–ar	
–é	–amos
–aste	–asteis
–ó	–aron

–er / –ir	
–í	–imos
–iste	–isteis
–ió	–ieron

2. ***Nosotros* Forms** Note that the **nosotros** forms of regular preterites for **-ar** and **-ir** verbs are the same as the present tense forms. Context usually helps determine meaning.

Ayer **hablamos** del viaje con nuestros amigos. Hoy **hablamos** con el agente de viajes a las dos de la tarde.

Yesterday we spoke about the trip with our friends. Today we're speaking with the travel agent at 2:00 P.M.

3. **Accent Marks** Note the accent marks on the first and third person singular of the preterite tense. These accent marks are dropped in the conjugation of **ver: vi, vio.**

ver:	vi	vimos
	viste	visteis
	vio	vieron

4. **Verbs Ending in *-car, -gar,* and *-zar*** These verbs show a spelling change in the first person singular (**yo**) of the preterite. (This is the same change you have already learned to make in formal commands, **Gramática 19 [Cap. 6]**).

-car ⟶ qu	busqué	buscamos
buscar	buscaste	buscasteis
	buscó	buscaron

-gar ⟶ gu	pagué	pagamos
pagar	pagaste	pagasteis
	pagó	pagaron

-zar ⟶ c	empecé	empezamos
empezar	empezaste	empezasteis
	empezó	empezaron

5. **Stem-Changing Verbs** **-Ar** and **-er** stem-changing verbs show no stem change in the preterite.
-Ir stem-changing verbs do show a change.*

despertar (despierto): desperté, despertaste,...
volver (vuelvo): volví, volviste,...

---

*You will learn more about and practice the preterite of **-ir** stem-changing verbs in **Gramática 24 (Cap. 8).**

6. Unstressed *-i-* An unstressed **-i-** between two vowels becomes **-y-**. Also, note the accent on the **í** in the **tú, nosotros,** and **vosotros** forms.

creer		leer	
creí	creímos	leí	leímos
creíste	creísteis	leíste	leísteis
creyó	creyeron	leyó	leyeron

Irregular Preterite Forms

dar		hacer		ir/ser	
di	dimos	hice	hicimos	fui	fuimos
diste	disteis	hiciste	hicisteis	fuiste	fuisteis
dio	dieron	hizo	hicieron	fue	fueron

1. **Preterite Endings for *dar*** The preterite endings for **dar** are the same as those used for regular **-er/-ir** verbs, except that the accent marks are dropped.

2. **Special Change for *hacer* Hizo** is spelled with a **z** to keep the [s] sound of the infinitive.

   hic- + -o $\longrightarrow$ hizo

3. **Preterite Forms for *ir* and *ser* Ir** and **ser** have identical forms in the preterite. Context will make the meaning clear. In addition, forms of **ir** are often followed by **a** (as in the first example), so they are easy to spot in the preterite.

   Fui a la playa el verano pasado.
   I went to the beach last summer.

   Fui agente de viajes.
   I was a travel agent.

AUTOPRUEBA

Give the correct preterite forms.

1. (nosotros) buscar
2. (mi papá) volver
3. (yo) despertarme
4. (Ud.) ver
5. (ellas) leer
6. (tú) ser

Answers: 1. *buscamos* 2. *volvió* 3. *me desperté* 4. *vio* 5. *leyeron* 6. *fuiste*

Práctica

A. ¡Anticipemos! ¿Es esto lo que hiciste el verano pasado?

Paso 1. Lee las siguientes declaraciones y contesta **sí** o **no,** según tu experiencia.

El verano pasado...

	SÍ	NO
1. tomé clases en la universidad.	❑	❑
2. asistí a un concierto.	❑	❑
3. trabajé mucho.	❑	❑
4. hice *camping* con algunos amigos / mi familia.	❑	❑
5. pasé todo el tiempo con mis padres / mis hijos.	❑	❑
6. me quedé en este pueblo / esta ciudad.	❑	❑
7. fui a una playa.	❑	❑
8. hice un viaje a otro país.	❑	❑
9. fui a muchas fiestas.	❑	❑
10. no hice nada especial.	❑	❑

Paso 2. Ahora, en parejas, túrnense para entrevistarse sobre las ideas del **Paso 1.** Luego digan a la clase dos cosas que Uds. tienen en común.

> **MODELO:** tomé clases en la universidad. ⟶
> **E1:** El verano pasado, ¿tomaste alguna clase en la universidad?
> **E2:** No, ¿y tú?
> **E1:** Yo tampoco. ⟶
>
> Nosotros no tomamos ninguna clase el verano pasado.

B. El viernes por la tarde... Los siguientes dibujos representan lo que Julio hizo el viernes por la tarde. Empareja las acciones con los dibujos. Luego usa las frases para narrar la secuencia de acciones. **¡OJO!** Usa palabras como **primero, luego, después, finalmente, por fin,** etcétera.

1.   2.   3.   4.

5   6.   7.   8.

9.   10.   11.   12.

a. _____ hacer cola para comprar las entradas (*tickets*)
b. _____ regresar tarde a casa
c. _____ volver a casa después de trabajar
d. _____ ir a un café a tomar algo
e. _____ llegar al cine al mismo tiempo
f. _____ llamar a un amigo
g. _____ no gustarles la película
h. _____ comer rápidamente
i. _____ ducharse y afeitarse
j. _____ entrar en el cine
k. _____ ir al cine en autobús
l. _____ decidir encontrarse (*to meet up*) en el cine

C. El día de tres compañeras

Paso 1. Teresa, Evangelina y Liliana son compañeras de apartamento. Ayer, Teresa y Evangelina fueron a la universidad mientras que (*while*) Liliana se quedó en casa. Haz oraciones completas para describir lo que hicieron, según la perspectiva de cada una.

TERESA
1. yo / levantarse / a / siete y media
2. salir / de / apartamento / a / nueve
3. llegar / biblioteca / a / diez
4. estudiar / toda la mañana / para / examen
5. almorzar / con / amigos / en / cafetería
6. ir / a / laboratorio / a / una
7. hacer / experimentos / de / manual (*m.*)
8. regresar / casa / y / ayudar / a / hacer / cena

EVANGELINA
9. yo / también / ir / a / universidad / pero / salir / más tarde
10. estudiar / en casa / toda la mañana
11. tomar / examen / a / tres
12. ¡examen / ser / horrible!
13. volver / casa / después de / examen
14. hacer / postre / para / cena

LILIANA
15. yo / quedarse / en casa / todo el día
16. ver / tele / por / mañana
17. llamar / mi / padres / a / once
18. escribir / composición / para / clase de inglés
19. ir / a / supermercado / y / comprar / comestibles
20. empezar / a / hacer / cena / a / cinco

¿A qué hora te levantaste esta mañana?

LAS TRES COMPAÑERAS
21. (ellas) cenar / juntas (*together*) a / siete
22. tomar / café / y / comer / postre
23. ver / tele / en / sala
24. hacer / tarea / para / día siguiente
25. acostarse / a / once / más o menos

Comprensión. ¿Quién lo dijo, Teresa, Evangelina o Liliana?

1. Mis compañeras no pasaron mucho tiempo en casa hoy.
2. Hoy estudié mucho.
3. ¡El examen fue desastroso!
4. Me gustó mucho el programa *Today*.
5. ¿Saben? Hablé con mis padres hoy y…

Paso 2. Vuelve a contar cómo fue el día de una de las tres compañeras.

    MODELO: **TERESA:** 1. Teresa se levantó…

Paso 3. Ahora cuenta lo que hicieron las tres compañeras juntas, usando **nosotras** como sujeto.

    MODELO: 21. Nosotras cenamos…

D. Un semestre en la República Dominicana. Cuenta la siguiente historia desde el punto de vista de la persona indicada, usando el pretérito de los verbos.

> **MODELO:** (yo) viajar a la República Dominicana el año pasado ⟶
> *Viajé* a la República Dominicana el año pasado.

1. (yo) pasar todo el semestre en Santo Domingo
2. mis padres/pagarme el vuelo...
3. ...pero (yo) trabajar para ganar el dinero para la matrícula y los otros gastos (*expenses*)
4. vivir con una familia dominicana encantadora (*enchanting*)
5. aprender mucho sobre la vida y la cultura dominicanas
6. visitar muchos sitios de interés turístico e histórico
7. mis amigos/escribirme cartas
8. (yo) mandarles tarjetas postales
9. comprarles recuerdos (*souvenirs*) a todos
10. volver al Canadá a fines de agosto

Need more practice?
- Workbook/Laboratory Manual
- Online Learning Center
  [www.mhhe.com/apuntate]

Conversación

A. Humor viajero. Mira el dibujo y contesta las preguntas.

¿El piloto o Superhombre? ¿Quién...

1. no vio el avión?
2. no vio a Superhombre?
3. sufrió un accidente?
4. juró (*swore*) algo?
5. no llegó a su destino?
6. fue al hospital?
7. hizo un informe sobre el accidente?

B. Viajes famosos. En parejas, digan adónde llegaron o viajaron las siguientes personas y en qué medio de transporte viajaron. Luego traten de (*try to*) añadir por lo menos un detalle más: ropa especial, compañeros de viaje, etcétera.

1. Cristóbal Colón
2. Dorotea, en *El Mago de Oz*
3. los astronautas de Apollo 11 en 1969
4. E. T.
5. Robinson Crusoe

C. Preguntas: La última (*last*) vez. Contesta las siguientes preguntas. Añade más detalles si puedes.

> **MODELO:** La última vez que fuiste a una fiesta, ¿le llevaste un regalo al anfitrión / a la anfitriona (*host/hostess*)? —→
> Sí, le llevé flores / una botella de vino. (No, no le llevé nada.)

La última vez que....

1. hiciste un viaje, ¿le mandaste una tarjeta postal a algún amigo o amiga?
2. tomaste el autobús / el metro, ¿le ofreciste tu asiento a una persona mayor?
3. viste a tu profesor(a) de español en público, ¿le hablaste en español?
4. comiste en un restaurante, ¿le recomendaste algún plato a tu compañero/a?
5. entraste en un edificio, ¿le abriste la puerta a otra persona?
6. volaste en avión, ¿le pediste algo a uno de los asistentes de vuelo?
7. le regalaste algo a alguien, ¿le gustó el regalo a la persona?
8. le prometiste a alguien hacer algo, ¿lo hiciste?
9. te quejaste de algo, ¿con quién hablaste?

D. Entrevista

Paso 1. Escribe una lista de diez de las acciones que hiciste ayer. Usa los siguientes verbos y añade cuatro más de tu preferencia. Haz oraciones completas.

> **MODELO:** levantarse —→ Ayer me levanté a las seis de la mañana.

1. levantarse
2. empezar
3. leer
4. dar
5. hacer
6. ir
7. ¿ ?
8. ¿ ?
9. ¿ ?
10. ¿ ?

Paso 2. En parejas, túrnense para entrevistarse sobre las acciones de su lista del **Paso 1.**

> **MODELO:** E1: Ayer me levanté a las seis de la mañana. ¿A qué hora te
> levantaste tú?
> E2: Me levanté a las diez.

Paso 3. Ahora digan a la clase en qué acciones los dos coincidieron ayer.

UN POCO DE TODO

Lengua y cultura: Mi abuela dominicana. Complete the following paragraphs with the correct form of the words in parentheses, as suggested by context. When two possibilities are given in parentheses, select the correct word. **¡OJO!** The verbs in the paragraphs will be present tense or preterite; the context will indicate which tense to use.

Ayer llegó de visita mi abuela Manuela. Ella vive en Santo Domingo, la capital de la República Dominicana, con mi tía Zaira, la (hermana/ sobrina[1]) de mi mamá. (*Nosotros:* Ir[2]) a recibir (la/le[3]) al aeropuerto y nos (ella: dar[4]) un abrazo[a] muy fuerte. (Mi/Mí[5]) abuela va (a/de[6]) pasar dos meses con nosotros en Connecticut, y luego (ir[7]) a quedarse un mes con el tío Julián en Nueva Jersey. Así es la vida[b] de muchas abuelas con hijos en otro país.

A mi abuela le (gusta/gustaría[8]) tener a todos sus hijos y (nietos/sobrinos[9]) en Santo Domingo. Siempre (ser/estar[10]) muy triste cuando (volver[11]) a la República Dominicana (antes de/después de[12]) visitarnos. Pero también (le/la[13]) gusta mucho la vida en los Estados Unidos. (Ella: Decir[14]) que aquí se vive muy bien y que las casas (ser/estar[15]) muy buenas. (El/La[16]) problema es que no le (gustan/gustarían[17]) los inviernos de (este/ esto[18]) país. ¡Es lógico! A ella le (gusta/gustan[19]) las playas y las palmeras, porque es lo que (conoce/sabe[20]) bien.

Cuando mi abuela regresa a Santo Domingo, (les/los[21]) mandamos con ella muchos regalos a nuestros (padres/parientes[22]). Casi todos los años mi familia (viaje/viaja[23]) a la República Dominicana, porque mis padres (vivir[24]) allá hasta que (ir[25]) a estudiar a la Universidad de Massachusetts. ¡(A/—[26]) mí me encanta ir de vacaciones a la República Dominicana!

[1]*hug*   [b]Así... *Such is the life*

Comprensión. Contesta las siguientes preguntas.

1. ¿Quién habla en la narración? ¿Se sabe si es hombre o mujer?
2. ¿Dónde vive la tía Zaira?
3. ¿Qué le gusta de la vida en los Estados Unidos a la abuela?
4. ¿Qué no le gusta?
5. ¿Cuándo emigraron a los Estados Unidos los padres del narrador / de la narradora?

Una abuela con su hija y su nieta

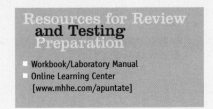

Resources for Review **and Testing** Preparation

■ Workbook/Laboratory Manual
■ Online Learning Center
   [www.mhhe.com/apuntate]

En resumen

See the Workbook/Laboratory Manual and Online Learning Center (www.mhhe.com/apuntate) for self-tests and practice with the grammar and vocabulary presented in this chapter.

Gramática en breve

20. Indirect Object Pronouns; **Dar** and **decir**

Indirect Object Pronouns
me, te, le, nos, os, les

dar: **doy, das, da, damos, dais, dan**
decir: **digo, dices, dice, decimos, decís, dicen**

21. Gustar (Part 2)

me, te, le, nos, os, les + gusta(n) / gustaría(n)

22. Preterite of Regular Verbs and of **dar, hacer, ir,** and **ser**

Regular Preterite *–ar* **Endings**
-é, -aste, -ó, -amos, -asteis, -aron

Regular Preterite *-er* **and** *-ir* **Endings**
-í, -iste, -ió, -imos, -isteis, -ieron

dar: **di, diste, dio, dimos, disteis, dieron**
hacer: **hice, hiciste, hizo, hicimos, hicisteis, hicieron**
ir/ser: **fui, fuiste, fue, fuimos, fuisteis, fueron**

Vocabulario

Los verbos

anunciar	to announce
bajarse (de)	to get down (from); to get off (of) (*a vehicle*)
contar (cuento)	to tell, narrate
dar (doy)	to give
decir (digo)	to say; to tell
encantar	to like very much, love
entregar (gu)	to hand in
explicar (qu)	to explain
fumar	to smoke
gustar	to be pleasing
interesar	to interest (*someone*)
mandar	to send
mostrar (muestro)	to show
odiar	to hate
ofrecer (ofrezco)	to offer
prestar	to lend
prometer	to promise
quejarse (de)	to complain (*about*)
recomendar (recomiendo)	to recommend
regalar	to give (*as a gift*)
subir (a)	to go up; to get on (*a vehicle*)

Repaso: escribir, hablar, pedir (pido) (i), preguntar, servir (sirvo) (i)

De viaje

el aeropuerto	airport
la agencia de viajes	travel agency
el/la agente de viajes	travel agent
el asiento	seat
el/la asistente de vuelo	flight attendant
el autobús	bus
el avión	airplane
el barco	boat, ship
el billete (*Sp.*) **/ el boleto** (*L.A.*)	ticket
de ida	one-way ticket
de ida y vuelta	round-trip ticket
la cabina	cabin (*on a ship*)
la clase turística	tourist class, coach
la cola	line (*of people*)
el crucero	cruise (ship)
la demora	delay
el equipaje	baggage, luggage
la estación	station
de autobuses	bus station
del tren	train station
la llegada	arrival
la maleta	suitcase
el maletero	porter

el medio de transporte	means of transportation
el pasaje	fare, price (*of a transportation ticket*)
el/la pasajero/a	passenger
el pasillo	aisle
la primera clase	first class
el puerto	port
la sala de espera	waiting room
la sala de fumar/ fumadores	smoking area
la salida	departure
la tarjeta (postal)	(post)card
el tren	train
la ventanilla	small window (*on a plane*)
el vuelo	flight

Repaso: el viaje

facturar el equipaje	to check baggage
guardar (un puesto)	to save (a place [*in line*])
hacer cola	to stand in line
hacer escalas /paradas	to make stops
hacer la(s) maleta(s)	to pack one's suitcase(s)
ir en...	to go/travel by . . .
autobús	bus
avión	plane
barco	boat, ship
tren	train
pasar por el control de la seguridad	to go/pass through security (check)
viajar	to travel
volar (vuelo) en avión	to fly, go by plane

Repaso: hacer un viaje

De vacaciones

la camioneta	station wagon; van; pickup truck
el *camping*	campground

la foto(grafía)	photo(graph)
el mar	sea
la montaña	mountain
el océano	ocean
la tienda (de campaña)	tent

Repaso: la playa

estar de vacaciones	to be on vacation
hacer *camping*	to go camping
ir de vacaciones a...	to go on vacation to/ in . . .
nadar	to swim
pasar las vacaciones en...	to spend one's vacation in . . .
sacar (qu) fotos	to take photos
salir de vacaciones	to leave on vacation
tomar el sol	to sunbathe
tomar unas vacaciones	to take a vacation

Otros sustantivos

el chiste	joke
la flor	flower

Los adjetivos

atrasado/a (*with* estar)	late
juntos/as	together

Palabras adicionales

a tiempo	on time
de vacaciones	on vacation
de viaje	traveling, on a trip
me gustaría (mucho)...	I would (really) like . . .
muchísimo	an awful lot
por	through; for

◆ VOCABULARIO PERSONAL

Una muchacha cubana que
reza (*prays*) en una iglesia
(*church*) de Santiago, Cuba,
durante las Navidades

1. ¿Crees que la Navidad es una fiesta importante
   en Cuba y en otros países hispanohablantes?
   ¿Por qué?

2. ¿Qué otros días festivos crees que son
   importantes en los países hispanohablantes?

3. ¿Celebras algún día festivo religioso? ¿Cuál?

8

Los días festivos°

°Los… *Holidays*

La fiesta de Javier

1. Es el cumpleaños de Javier. Rosa va a hacerle una fiesta de sorpresa.

2. Rosa va a la tienda para comprar refrescos y botanas.

3. La fiesta es en casa de Rosa.

4. Javier llega y es una gran sorpresa.

5. Todos se divierten.

6. Bailan hasta las cuatro de la mañana.

el anfitrión/la anfitriona	host/hostess
las botanas/tapas	appetizers
el cumpleaños	birthday
el día festivo	holiday
el pastel (de cumpleaños)	(birthday) cake
el regalo	present, gift
la tarjeta	card
celebrar	to celebrate
cumplir años	to have a birthday
dar/hacer una fiesta	to give/have a party
divertirse (me divierto) (i)	to enjoy oneself, have a good time
faltar (a)	to be absent (from), not attend
gastar	to spend (money)
invitar	to invite

pasarlo bien/mal	to have a good/bad time
regalar	to give (as a gift)
reunirse (me reúno) (con)	to get together (with)
ser + en + place	to take place in/at (a place)
— ¿Dónde es la fiesta?	Where is the party?
— (Es) En casa de Javier.	(It's) At Javier's house.
¡Felicitaciones!	Congratulations!
gracias por + noun Gracias por el regalo.	thanks for + noun Thanks for the present.
gracias por + inf. Gracias por invitarme.	thanks for + verb Thanks for inviting me.

Conversación

A. Asociaciones. ¿Qué palabras asocias con las siguientes ideas? Usa palabras de **La fiesta de Javier** u otras que sabes. Da por lo menos dos asociaciones para cada idea.

1. algo de comer o tomar
2. el cumpleaños de alguien
3. los regalos

4. una fiesta
5. divertirse
6. una persona

Vocabulario útil

el Día de Año Nuevo	New Year's Day
el Día de los Reyes Magos	Day of the Magi (Three Kings) (Jan. 6)
el Día de San Patricio	Saint Patrick's Day (Mar. 17)
la Pascua (judía)	Passover
la Pascua	Easter
la Semana Santa	Holy Week
las vacaciones de primavera	spring break
el Cinco de Mayo	Cinco de Mayo (*Mexican awareness celebration in some parts of the U.S.*)
el Día del Canadá	Canada Day (July 1)
el Cuatro de Julio (el Día de la Independencia [estadounidense])	Fourth of July ([U.S.] Independence Day)
el Día de la Raza	Columbus Day (*Indigenous/Hispanic awareness day in some parts of the U.S.*) (Oct. 12)
el Día de todos los Santos	All Saints' Day (Nov. 1)
el Día de los Muertos	Day of the Dead (Nov. 2)
el Día de Acción de Gracias	Thanksgiving
la Nochebuena	Christmas Eve
la Noche Vieja	New Year's Eve
el cumpleaños	birthday
el día del santo	saint's day (*the saint for whom one is named*)
la quinceañera	young woman's fifteenth birthday party

la Navidad

el Día de San Valentín

la Fiesta de las Luces

¡OJO!

Only the shaded items on this list are considered active vocabulary for this chapter. Feel free to learn any other holidays and celebrations that are relevant to you.

B. Definiciones. Primero da las palabras definidas. Luego crea (*create*) por lo menos dos definiciones más. La clase va a adivinar (*guess*) la palabra definida.

1. impresión que causa algo que no se espera o no se sabe
2. algo de comer o beber que se sirve en las fiestas
3. el día en que, por tradición, algunas personas visitan los cementerios
4. la fiesta de una muchacha que cumple 15 años
5. el día en que muchos, por tradición, llevan ropa verde
6. lo que se le dice a un amigo que celebra algo
7. una fiesta de los judíos (*Jewish people*) que dura 8 días

Vocabulario útil

el fin	end
el nacimiento	birth

C. Hablando de fiestas

Paso 1. ¿Cuáles de estas fiestas te gustan? ¿Cuáles te gustan mucho? ¿Cuáles no te gustan? Explica por qué. Compara tus respuestas con las (*those*) de tus compañeros de clase. ¿Tienen los mismos gustos?

MODELO: el Cuatro de Julio ⟶ Me gusta mucho el Cuatro de Julio porque vemos fuegos artificiales en el parque y...

1. el Cuatro de Julio
2. el Día de Acción de Gracias
3. el Día de San Patricio
4. la Noche Vieja
5. el Día de la Raza
6. el Día de los Enamorados

Vocabulario útil	
el árbol	tree
el corazón	heart
la corona	wreath
el desfile	parade
la fiesta del barrio	neighborhood (block) party
los fuegos artificiales	fireworks
el globo	balloon

Paso 2. Ahora piensa en tu fiesta favorita. Puede ser una de la lista del **Paso 1** o una del **Vocabulario útil** de la página 231. Piensa en cómo celebras esa fiesta, para explicárselo (*explain it*) luego a la clase. Debes pensar en lo siguiente.

- los preparativos que haces de antemano (*beforehand*)
- la ropa especial que llevas
- las comidas o bebidas especiales que compras o haces
- el lugar donde se celebra
- los adornos especiales que hay o que pones

⟫ NOTA CULTURAL

Los días festivos importantes del mundo hispánico

Aunque la mayoría de **los días festivos** varía de país a país y aun de ciudad a ciudad, algunas fiestas **se celebran** en casi todos los países hispánicos.

La Nochebuena   En esta fiesta los hispanos católicos siguen principalmente sus **tradiciones religiosas.** Celebran la víspera[a] de la Navidad con una gran cena. Esta **celebración familiar** puede incluir también a amigos y vecinos.[b] Muchas familias van a la Misa del Gallo,[c] un **servicio religioso** que se celebra a medianoche. Es posible que la fiesta de Nochebuena termine muy tarde con música y baile. En algunos lugares, los niños reciben la visita de Papá Noel, otro nombre que se le da a Santa Claus, quien les deja **regalos.**

Unos bailarines (*dancers*) durante celebraciones del Día de los Reyes Magos en La Habana, Cuba

La Noche Vieja   Como en este país, la Noche Vieja es una ocasión para **grandes celebraciones,** tanto entre familia como en lugares públicos. En España y otros países algunos siguen la tradición de comer una uva[d] por cada una de las doce campanadas[e] de medianoche.

El Día de los Reyes Magos   En España y otros países, se celebra el 6 de enero como el día de los Reyes Magos, una fiesta cristiana también conocida como **la Epifanía.** Los tres Reyes son los encargados[f] de traer regalos. Muchos niños ponen sus zapatos en la ventana o balcón antes de acostarse la noche del 5 de enero. Los Reyes llegan en camellos durante la noche y llenan los zapatos con **regalos** y **dulces.**

El Día de la Independencia   Todos los países latinoamericanos celebran el día de **la declaración de su independencia de España.** Por ejemplo, México celebra su independencia el 16 de septiembre, Bolivia el 6 de agosto, el Paraguay el 15 de mayo y El Salvador el 15 de septiembre.

La quinceañera   Las muchachas de muchos países celebran su **llegada a los 15 años** como la transición de niña a mujer. Ese día, se hace **una gran fiesta** que les dan su familia y sus amigos. La muchacha se viste de largo[g] y, con sus invitados, a veces asiste a una misa especial para ella. Luego se sirve **una cena** y hay una fiesta con música para bailar.

[a]eve   [b]neighbors   [c]Misa... *Midnight Mass*   [d]grape   [e]bell strokes   [f]los... *in charge*   [g]se... *dresses up (in a gown)*

1. reír(se)* ([me] río) (i) (de)

2. sonreír(se)* ([me] sonrío) (i)

3. llorar

4. enojarse (con)

5. enfermarse

discutir (con/sobre)	to argue (with/about)	**recordar (recuerdo)**	to remember
olvidar(se) (de)	to forget (about)	**reír(se)* ([me] río) (i) (de)**	to laugh (about)
ponerse + *adj.*	to become, get + *adj.*	**sentirse (me siento) (i)**	to feel (*an emotion*)
portarse bien/mal	to (mis)behave	**sonreír(se)* (*like* reír)**	to smile
quejarse (de)	to complain (about)		
		feliz (*pl.* felices)	happy

Conversación

A. ¿Cuándo... ? ¿En qué ocasiones sientes las siguientes emociones o haces las siguientes cosas? Completa las oraciones, según tu experiencia.

> **MODELOS:** Me porto muy bien en (+ lugar) / cuando (+ acción)… ⟶
> Me porto muy bien *en las fiestas.*
> Me porto muy bien *cuando alguien me está mirando.*

1. Me porto muy bien en / cuando…
2. Me quejo en / cuando…
3. Me río mucho en / cuando…
4. Sonrío en / cuando…
5. Lloro en / cuando…
6. Me enojo en / cuando…
7. Me enfermo en / cuando…

¿Cómo se siente?

---

*The verbs **reír** and **sonreír** are **e ⟶ i** stem-changing verbs. Due to the double vowels, accents are required on all present tense forms of these verbs, but not on their present participles: **(son)riendo, (son)río, (son)ríes, (son)ríe, (son)reímos, (son)reís, (son)ríen.** Usage of the reflexive **se** with both verbs varies regionally. In general, most Spanish speakers use **se** with **reír** but not with **sonreír.** ¡Apúntate! follows this pattern.*

⟫ NOTA COMUNICATIVA

Being Emphatic

To emphasize the quality described by an adjective or an adverb, speakers of Spanish often add **-ísimo/a/os/as** to an adjective and **-ísimo** to an adverb. This change adds the idea *extremely [exceptionally; very, very; super]* to the quality expressed. You have already used one emphatic adverb: **Me gusta muchísimo.**

Estas tapas son **difici-**   *These appetizers are very, very*
   lísimas de preparar.   *hard to prepare.*
Durante la época navideña,   *At Christmastime, kids are*
   los niños son **buenísimos.**   *extremely good.*

- If the word ends in a consonant, **-ísimo** is added to the singular form: **difícil** ⟶ **dificilísimo** (and any accents on the word stem are dropped).
- If the word ends in a vowel, the final vowel is dropped before adding **-ísimo: bueno** ⟶ **buenísimo** (and any accents on the word stem are dropped).
- Spelling changes occur when the final consonant of an adjective is **c, g,** or **z: riquísimo, larguísimo, felicísimo.**

Vocabulario útil

avergonzado/a
   embarrassed
contento/a
feliz/triste
furioso/a
nervioso/a
serio/a

B. Reacciones. ¿Cómo te pones en estas situaciones? Usa los adjetivos y verbos que sabes y también algunas formas enfáticas (**-ísimo**). ¿Cuántas emociones puedes describir?

1. Llueve todo el día.
2. Es Navidad. Alguien te hace un regalo carísimo.
3. Quieres bañarte. No hay agua caliente.
4. Estás solo/a en casa una noche y oyes un ruido.
5. Das una fiesta en tu casa o apartamento. Todos están muy serios.
6. Hoy hay un examen importante. No estudiaste nada anoche.
7. Cuentas un chiste pero nadie se ríe.
8. Acabas de terminar un examen difícil. Crees que lo hiciste muy bien/mal.

C. Opiniones

Paso 1. ¿Crees que son ciertas o falsas las siguientes declaraciones?

EN LAS FIESTAS DE FAMILIA	CIERTO	FALSO
1. Las fiestas de familia me gustan muchísimo.	❏	❏
2. Un pariente siempre se queja de algo.	❏	❏
3. Uno de mis parientes siempre me hace preguntas indiscretas.	❏	❏
4. Alguien siempre bebe / come demasiado (*too much*) y se enferma.	❏	❏
5. A todos les gustan las cosas que les regalamos.	❏	❏
LOS DÍAS FESTIVOS EN GENERAL		
6. La Navidad / La Fiesta de las Luces es solamente una excusa para gastar dinero.	❏	❏
7. Las vacaciones de primavera son las vacaciones más felices del año.	❏	❏
8. Sólo las personas que practican una religión deben tener vacaciones en los días festivos religiosos.	❏	❏

Need more practice?
- Workbook/Laboratory Manual
- Online Learning Center
   [www.mhhe.com/apuntate]

Paso 2. Hagan un resumen de las respuestas de toda la clase. Analicen las respuestas. ¿Están todos de acuerdo? Si todos —o casi todos— están de acuerdo en que una declaración es falsa, cámbienla para que sea cierta.

Cuba

ESTADOS UNIDOS (Florida)
OCÉANO ATLÁNTICO
Estrecho de Florida
ISLAS BAHAMAS
CUBA
• Camagüey
• Santiago
MAR CARIBE
HAITÍ
JAMAICA

DATOS ESENCIALES

NOMBRE OFICIAL: República de Cuba
CAPITAL: La Habana
POBLACIÓN: más de 11 millones de
   habitantes

FÍJATE

- Cuba obtuvo[a] su independencia de España en 1898, durante la Guerra Hispano-Norteamericana.[b] Después de esa guerra, los Estados Unidos gobernaron la Isla hasta 1909.
- En 1959 hubo una revolución socialista en Cuba para derrocar[c] al dictador Fulgencio Batista. Los líderes fueron Fidel Castro y «Che» Guevara. Esta revolución provocó un éxodo de cubanos a los Estados Unidos. Estos exiliados se establecieron principalmente en la Florida, con la esperanza[d] de volver muy pronto a su país. Sin embargo, a principios de[e] este siglo, Fidel Castro seguía gobernando[f] Cuba, aunque desde 2007 su hermano Raúl actúa como presidente.
- El régimen de Castro redujo el analfabetismo[g] a menos del 5 por ciento y reformó el sistema educativo con resultados admirables. Pero la situación económica de Cuba es difícil. Con la caída[h] de la Unión Soviética, Cuba perdió un apoyo[i] financiero indispensable para el país. El embargo económico estadounidense también sigue afectando las condiciones de vida[j] de los cubanos.

[a]obtained   [b]Guerra... Spanish-American War   [c]overthrow   [d]hope   [e]a... at the beginning of   [f]seguía... still governed   [g]redujo... reduced illiteracy   [h]fall   [i]support [j]condiciones... living conditions

¡MÚSICA!

La música y el baile de Cuba son una rica combinación de culturas, pero los ritmos predominantes son africanos. Algunos de los instrumentos musicales más comunes en la música popular cubana incluyen varios tipos de tambores, como el bongó, la conga, la paila y la tumbadora. También destacan[a] las maracas, los claves[b] y el güiro.[c] El estilo musical más conocido y popular se llama «el son». El son se originó en el este de Cuba y se considera el «abuelo» de toda la música cubana.

[a]of note are   [b]wooden sticks   [c]musical instrument made from a dried gourd

 ## REY RUIZ

Rey Ruiz empezó su exitosa[a] carrera musical en su ciudad natal,[b] La Habana. Después de una gira[c] por la República Dominicana se estableció en los Estados Unidos, en donde hoy reside. La canción «Mi tentación» es del álbum del mismo título. Otro famoso álbum suyo[d] es *Los soneros de hoy*, en el cual hace homenaje[f] a las estrellas[g] de la salsa de décadas anteriores.[h]

Rey Ruiz, durante un telemaratón contra el cáncer en Miami, Florida

[a]successful   [b]native   [c]tour   [d]of his   [e]players of **son** music   [f]en... in which he pays tribute [g]stars   [h]décadas... previous decades

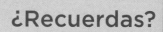

¿Recuerdas?

You have already learned the irregular preterite stem and endings for the verb **hacer.** All of the verbs presented in **Gramática 23** have irregular stems and they all use the same preterite endings as **hacer.** Review those endings by completing the following forms.

1. yo: hic___   **2.** nosotros: hic___   **3.** Ud.: hiz___   **4.** ellos: hic___

23 Talking About the Past (Part 2) • Irregular Preterites

Gramática en acción. La fiesta de la Noche Vieja

Contesta las siguientes preguntas sobre esta fiesta.

1. ¿Quién estuvo hablando por teléfono?
2. ¿Quiénes dieron la fiesta?
3. ¿Quién no pudo ir a la fiesta?
4. ¿Quién puso su copa de champán en la televisión?
5. ¿Quién hizo mucho ruido?
6. ¿Quiénes no quisieron beber más?
7. ¿Quiénes le trajeron regalo al anfitrión?

¿Y tú?

1. ¿Estuviste alguna vez en una fiesta como esta? (…estuve…)
2. ¿Tuviste que irte temprano de la fiesta? (…tuve…) ¿O te quedaste hasta medianoche (*midnight*)?
3. ¿Te pusiste ropa elegante para la fiesta? (…me puse…)

---

1. Additional Irregular Forms You have already learned the irregular preterite forms of **dar, hacer, ir,** and **ser.** The following verbs are also irregular in the preterite. Note that the first and third person singular endings, which are the only irregular ones, are unstressed, in contrast to the stressed endings of regular preterite forms.

Irregular Preterite Endings	
-e	-imos
-iste	-isteis
-o	-ieron

estar	
estuve	estuvimos
estuviste	estuvisteis
estuvo	estuvieron

estar:	estuv-	-e
poder:	pud-	-iste
poner:	pus-	-o
querer:	quis-	-imos
saber:	sup-	-isteis
tener:	tuv-	-ieron
venir:	vin-	

2. **Third Person Forms Ending in -j-** When the preterite verb stem ends in **-j-**, the **-i-** of the third person plural ending is omitted: **dijeron, trajeron.**	**decir: dij-** ⎤ -e, -iste, -o, -imos, -isteis, -eron **traer: traj-** ⎦
3. **Preterite of *hay*** The preterite of **hay (haber)** is **hubo** (*there was/were*).	**Hubo** un accidente ayer en el centro. *There was an accident yesterday downtown.*

Changes in Meaning

Several of the following Spanish verbs have an English equivalent in the preterite tense that is different from that of the infinitive.

	Infinitive Meaning	Preterite Meaning
saber	to know (*facts, information*) Ya lo **sé.** *I already know it.*	to find out, learn Lo **supe** ayer. *I found it out (learned it) yesterday.*
conocer	to know, be familiar with (*people, places*) Ya la **conozco.** *I already know her.*	to meet (*for the first time*) La **conocí** ayer. *I met her yesterday.*
querer	to want **Quiero** hacerlo hoy. *I want to do it today.*	to try **Quise** hacerlo ayer. *I tried to do it yesterday.*
no querer	not to want **No quiero** hacerlo hoy. *I don't want to do it today.*	to refuse **No quise** hacerlo anteayer. *I refused to do it the day before yesterday.*
poder	to be able to (*do something*) **Puedo** leerlo. *I can (am able to) read it.*	to succeed (*in doing something*) **Pude** leerlo ayer. *I could (and did) read it yesterday.*
no poder	not to be able, capable (*of doing something*) **No puedo** leerlo. *I can't (am not able to) read it.*	to fail (*to do something*) **No pude** leerlo anteayer. *I couldn't (did not) read it the day before yesterday.*

Práctica

A. ¡Anticipemos! La última Noche Vieja

Paso 1. Piensa en lo que hiciste la Noche Vieja del año pasado. ¿Es cierto o falso que hiciste las siguientes cosas?

	CIERTO	FALSO
1. Fui a una fiesta en casa de un amigo / una amiga.	❑	❑
2. Di una fiesta en mi casa.	❑	❑
3. No estuve con mis amigos, sino (*but rather*) con la familia.	❑	❑
4. Quise ir a una fiesta, pero no pude.	❑	❑
5. Les dije «¡Feliz Año Nuevo!» a muchas personas.	❑	❑
6. Conocí a algunas personas interesantes.	❑	❑
7. Tuve que hacer la comida de esa noche.	❑	❑
8. Me puse ropa elegante esa noche.	❑	❑
9. Pude quedarme despierto/a (*awake*) hasta medianoche.	❑	❑
10. No quise bailar. Me sentía (*I felt*) mal.	❑	❑

Paso 2. Ahora, en parejas, comparen sus respuestas. Si es posible, digan a la clase dos acciones en que coincidieron.

> **MODELO:** Douglas y yo fuimos a una fiesta en casa de un amigo.
> Conocimos a muchas personas.

B. En una fiesta. ¿Cómo se dice en inglés?

1. No pude abrir la botella de champán.
2. Supe que se murió (*died*) el abuelo de un amigo.
3. Conocí al primo cubano de una amiga.
4. No quise hablar con Jorge. Él es muy descortés con todos.

C. Una Nochebuena en casa de los Ramírez

Paso 1. Describe lo que pasó en casa de los Ramírez, haciendo el papel (*playing the role*) de uno de los hijos. Haz oraciones completas en el pretérito con las palabras indicadas, usando el sujeto pronominal cuando sea necesario.

1. todos / estar / en casa / abuelos / antes de / nueve
2. (nosotros) poner / mucho / regalos / debajo / árbol
3. (nosotros) invitar / vecinos (*neighbors*) / pero / no / poder / venir
4. tíos y primos / venir / con / comida y bebidas
5. yo / tener / que / ayudar / a / hacer / comida
6. haber / cena / especial / para / todos
7. más tarde / alguno / amigos / venir / a / cantar / villancicos (*carols*)
8. mi / hermana / menor / querer / beber / champán / pero / mi / padres / no / permitirlo
9. a medianoche / todos / decir / «¡Feliz Navidad!»
10. al día siguiente / todos / decir / que / fiesta / ser / estupendo

Paso 2. ¿Cierto, falso o no se sabe? Corrige las oraciones falsas.

	CIERTO	FALSO	NO SE SABE
1. Hubo muy poca gente (*people*) en la fiesta.	❑	❑	❑
2. Sólo estuvieron miembros de la familia.	❑	❑	❑
3. Todos comieron bien… ¡y mucho!	❑	❑	❑

D. Hechos (*Events*) históricos. Describe algunos hechos históricos, usando una palabra o frase de cada columna. Usa el pretérito de los verbos. Tu profesor(a) te puede ayudar con los datos (*information*) que no sabes.

en 1957 los rusos en 1969 los estadounidenses Adán y Eva George Washington los europeos los aztecas Stanley	traer saber conocer estar poner	en Valley Forge con sus soldados a un hombre en la luna un satélite en el espacio por primera vez el significado (*meaning*) de un árbol especial a Livingston en África el caballo (*horse*) al Nuevo Mundo a Hernán Cortés en Tenochtitlán

+ between columns one and two, and **+** between columns two and three.

Need more **practice?**
- Workbook/Laboratory Manual
- Online Learning Center
  [www.mhhe.com/apuntate]

Conversación

A. Entrevista

EL PRIMER DÍA DE CLASE DE ESTE SEMESTRE/TRIMESTRE

1. ¿En qué mes conocimos a nuestro profesor / a nuestra profesora de español? ¿A quiénes más conocimos ese mismo día?
2. ¿Tuvimos que hablar español el primer día de clase? ¿Tuvimos mucha tarea para el día siguiente?
3. ¿Les hablamos en español a nuestros compañeros de clase el primer día? ¿Qué les dijiste tú?

LOS DÍAS FESTIVOS DEL AÑO PASADO

4. ¿Qué días festivos celebraste?
5. ¿Celebraste la Nochebuena? ¿el Día de Acción de Gracias? ¿Dónde? ¿Con quiénes?
6. ¿Dónde estuviste durante las vacaciones de primavera?
7. ¿Ya hiciste planes para los días festivos de este año? ¿Dónde piensas estar en esas ocasiones?

B. La última fiesta que diste

Paso 1. Haz una lista de todos los detalles que recuerdas de la última fiesta que organizaste. Puede ser una fiesta que organizaste solo/a o con tu familia o con un grupo de amigos. Haz por lo menos ocho oraciones completas para describir la fiesta y usa por lo menos cinco de los siguientes verbos: **conocer, dar, estar, invitar, organizar, poder, saber, ser, venir.**

MODELO: Di una fiesta de sorpresa para el cumpleaños de mi mejor amigo. Mi amigo Clark y yo organizamos la fiesta…

Paso 2. Ahora, usando tus oraciones como base, entrevista a un compañero o compañera sobre la última fiesta que organizó él o ella. Luego digan a la clase dos detalles interesantes sobre las fiestas que Uds. organizaron.

¿Recuerdas?

You learned in **Gramática 14 (Cap. 5)** to make a change in the **-ndo** form of **-ir** stem-changing verbs. That same change occurs in some forms of the preterite of those verbs. Review the change by completing the following forms.

1. pedir: p__diendo   **2.** dormir: d__rmiendo

You will learn about this change in preterite in **Grámatica 24**.

24 Talking About the Past (Part 3) • Preterite of Stem-Changing Verbs

Gramática en acción: La quinceañera de Lupe Carrasco

Imagina los detalles de la fiesta de quince años de Lupe.

1. Lupe se vistió con
  - ❑ un vestido blanco muy elegante.
  - ❑ una camiseta y *jeans.*
  - ❑ el vestido de novia[a] de su abuela.

2. Mientras cortaba[b] el pastel de cumpleaños, Lupe
  - ❑ empezó a llorar.
  - ❑ se rio mucho.
  - ❑ sonrió para una foto.

3. Lupe pidió un deseo[c] al cortar el pastel. Ella
  - ❑ les dijo a todos qué fue lo que pidió.
  - ❑ prefirió guardarlo en secreto.

4. En la fiesta sirvieron
  - ❑ champán y otras bebidas alcohólicas.
  - ❑ refrescos.
  - ❑ sólo té y café.

5. Todos se divirtieron mucho en la fiesta. Los invitados se despidieron[d] a la(s) _____ (hora).

[a]vestido... *wedding gown*   [b]Mientras... *As she was cutting*   [c]*wish*   [d]se... *said good-bye*

¿Y tú?

1. ¿Recuerdas qué hiciste cuando cumpliste 15 años?
2. ¿Qué regalos pediste? (...pedí...)
3. ¿Qué sirvieron en la fiesta? (Sirvieron...)
4. ¿Te divertiste? (...me divertí...)
5. ¿Cómo te sentiste ese día? (...me sentí...)

1. Preterite of *-ar* and *-er* Stem-Changing Verbs In **Gramática 22 (Cap. 7)** you learned that **-ar** and **-er** stem-changing verbs have no stem change in the preterite (or in the present participle).

recordar (recuerdo)		perder (pierdo)	
recordé	recordamos	perdí	perdimos
recordaste	recordasteis	perdiste	perdisteis
recordó	recordaron	perdió	perdieron
recordando		perdiendo	

2. Preterite of -ir Stem-Changing Verbs

-Ir stem-changing verbs do have a stem change in the preterite, but only in the third person singular and plural, where the stem vowels **e** and **o** change to **i** and **u,** respectively. This is the same change that occurs in the present participle of **-ir** stem-changing verbs.

pedir (pido) (i)		dormir (duermo) (u)	
pedí	pedimos	dormí	dormimos
pediste	pedisteis	dormiste	dormisteis
pidió	pidieron	durmió	durmieron
pidiendo		durmiendo	

¡OJO!

Remember that this change is indicated in parentheses after the infinitive in vocabulary lists: **pedir (pido) (i), dormir (duermo) (u).**

3. Important -ir Stem-Changing Verbs

Here are some **-ir** stem-changing verbs. You already know or have seen many of them. The reflexive meaning, if different from the nonreflexive meaning, is in parentheses.

¡OJO!

Note the simplification:
**ri-ió → rio; ri-ieron → rieron
son-ri-ió → sonrió; son-ri-ieron → sonrieron**

despedirse (me despido) (i) (de)

conseguir (consigo) (i)	to get, obtain	**preferir (prefiero) (i)**	to prefer
conseguir + *inf.*	to succeed in (*doing something*)	**reír(se) ([me] río) (i) (de)**	to laugh (at)
		seguir (sigo) (i)	to continue
despedir(se) ([me] despido) (i) (de)	to say good-bye (to)	**sentirse (me siento) (i)**	to regret; to feel (*an emotion*)
divertir(se) ([me] divierto) (i)	to entertain (to have a good time)	**servir (sirvo) (i)**	to serve
dormir(se) ([me] duermo) (u)	to sleep (to fall asleep)	**sonreír(se) ([me] sonrío) (i)**	to smile
morirse (me muero) (u)	to die	**sugerir (sugiero) (i)**	to suggest
pedir (pido) (i)	to ask for; to order	**vestir(se) ([me] visto) (i)**	to dress (to get dressed)

Práctica

A. ¡Anticipemos! ¿Quién lo hizo? ¿Ocurrieron algunas de estas cosas en clase la semana pasada? Contesta con el nombre de las personas que lo hicieron. Si nadie lo hizo, contesta con **Nadie...** .

1. _____ se vistió con ropa muy elegante/extravagante.
2. _____ se durmió en clase.
3. _____ le pidió al profesor / a la profesora más tarea.
4. _____ se sintió muy contento/a.
5. _____ se divirtió muchísimo; se rio y sonrió mucho.
6. _____ no sonrió para nada.
7. _____ sugirió tener la clase afuera.
8. _____ prefirió no contestar ninguna pregunta.

AUTOPRUEBA

Complete the verbs with preterite stems.

1. nos div__rtimos
2. se d__rmieron
3. tú s__rviste
4. se v__stió
5. yo sug__rí
6. Uds. p__dieron

Answers: 1. divertimos 2. durmieron 3. serviste 4. vistió 5. sugerí 6. pidieron

B. Historias breves. Cuenta las siguientes historias breves en el pretérito. Luego continúalas, si puedes.

1. En un restaurante: Juan (sentarse) a la mesa. Cuando (llegar) el camarero, le (pedir) una cerveza. El camarero no (recordar) lo que Juan (pedir) y le (servir) una Coca-Cola. Juan no (querer) beber la Coca-Cola. Le (decir) al camarero: «Perdón, señor. Le (*yo*: pedir) una cerveza». El camarero le (contestar): «_____».

2. Dos noches diferentes: Yo (vestirse), (ir) a una fiesta, (divertirse) mucho y (volver) tarde a casa. Mi compañero de cuarto (decidir) quedarse en casa y (ver) la televisión toda la noche. No (divertirse), (perder) una fiesta excelente y después lo (sentir) mucho. Yo _____.

C. Las historias que todos conocemos. Cuenta detalles de algunas historias tradicionales, usando una palabra o frase de cada columna y el pretérito.

la Bella Durmiente (*Sleeping Beauty*) el lobo (*wolf*) Rip Van Winkle la Cenicienta (*Cinderella*) el Príncipe las hermanastras de la Cenicienta Romeo	**+**	conseguir perder divertirse preferir morirse sentir vestirse dormir	**+**	en un baile encontrar (*to find*) a la mujer misteriosa (por) muchos años por el amor de Julieta de (*as a*) abuela un zapato envidia (*envy*) de su hermanastra

Conversación

Una entrevista indiscreta

Paso 1. Un compañero o compañera va a usar las siguientes preguntas para entrevistarte en el **Paso 2** de esta actividad. Lee las preguntas ahora y piensa en las respuestas que vas a dar. Debes inventar también algunas respuestas falsas.

1. ¿A qué hora te dormiste anoche?
2. ¿Perdiste mucho dinero alguna vez?
3. ¿Con qué programa de televisión te divertiste mucho en los días o meses pasados... pero te avergüenzas de (*you're ashamed to*) admitirlo?
4. ¿Te vestiste de animal alguna vez? ¿En qué ocasión?
5. ¿Seguiste haciendo algo después de que tu padre/madre (compañero/a, esposo/a) te dijo que no lo hicieras (*not to do it*)?
6. ¿Pediste una bebida alcohólica antes de tener 21 años?
7. ¿Qué cosa o tarea no conseguiste terminar el mes pasado?

Paso 2. En parejas, usen las preguntas del **Paso 1** para entrevistarse. Luego digan a la clase las respuestas más interesantes de su compañero/a. La clase va a adivinar si la respuesta es cierta o falsa.

MODELO: E1: Julie, ¿a qué hora te dormiste anoche?
E2: Me dormí a las tres de la mañana.
E1: (*a la clase*): Julie se durmió a las tres de la mañana anoche.
CLASE: No es cierto.
E2: ¡Sí, es cierto! (Tienen razón. No es cierto.)

El Castillo[a] de los Tres Santos Reyes Magos del Morro Este castillo, también llamado[b] «El Morro», se construyó entre 1589 y 1630 para proteger la flotilla española,[c] que hacía paradas[d] dos veces al año en La Habana mientras transportaba[e] las riquezas[f] del Nuevo Mundo a España.

[a]Castle [b]called [c]proteger... protect the Spanish fleet [d]hacía... made stops [e]it transported [f]riches

Jugando al béisbol en Cuba Para los aficionados al[a] béisbol, Cuba es un paraíso donde el béisbol todavía es una pasión y se juega por amor al[b] juego. En Cuba, hasta ahora, las ligas no se ahogan[c] bajo el control de ningún negocio[d] ni de conflictos laborales. Los jugadores cubanos son regionales, es decir[e] que juegan en el equipo[f] regional, y no son agentes libres. Es de mencionar que Cuba ha ganado[g] más medallas[h] olímpicas en béisbol que ningún otro país desde que[i] el béisbol fue declarado[j] deporte olímpico en 1992. Los cubanos ganaron la medalla de oro en 1992, 1996 y 2004 y la medalla de plata en 2000. También fueron subcampeones[k] en el primer *World Baseball Classic* en 2006.

[a]aficionados... fans of [b]amor... love of the [c]se... choke [d]business [e]es... that is to say [f]team [g]ha... has won [h]medals [i]ningún... any other country since [j]declared [k]runners-up

El lechón[a] con frijoles y arroz La cocina cubana es una fusión de tradiciones e ingredientes europeos, africanos y americanos. El puerco y el pollo son las carnes principales de los platos cubanos. Los frijoles negros, el arroz y los plátanos[b] también son populares. El lechón asado servido con frijoles negros y arroz es uno de los platos típicos de Cuba.

[a]suckling pig [b]plantains

El Valle[a] de Viñales El turismo puede ser una manera de recuperar y suplementar la economía cubana, tradicionalmente agrícola. El ecoturista, por ejemplo, puede visitar plantaciones de tabaco y azúcar en lugares como el Valle de Viñales. Este valle carst[b] se caracteriza por sus mogotes[c] y cuevas[d] pintorescas.

[a]Valley [b]geographic formation often characterized by abundant caves and aquifers [c]limestone hillocks [d]caves

La Habana La Habana es la capital de Cuba y la ciudad más grande del Caribe. La arquitectura de la capital es muy variada. Los edificios y casas coloniales de La Habana Vieja son muy pinturescos.

25 Expressing Direct and Indirect Objects Together • Double Object Pronouns

Gramática en acción: Berta habla de la fiesta de Anita

1. Hice unas tapas y se las di a Anita para la fiesta.

2. Me encantó el CD que Anita puso en la fiesta. Por eso Anita me lo prestó para oírlo en casa.

3. Sergio sacó muchas fotos de la fiesta y nos las mostró en la computadora.

Comprensión. ¿Cierto o falso?

	CIERTO	FALSO
1. ¿Las tapas? Berta se las dio a Anita.	❏	❏
2. ¿El CD? Sergio se lo prestó a Berta.	❏	❏
3. ¿Las fotos? Anita se las mostró a todos.	❏	❏

Order of Pronouns

When both an indirect and a direct object pronoun are used in a sentence, the indirect object pronoun (**I**) precedes the direct (**D**): **ID**. Note that nothing comes between the two pronouns. The position of double object pronouns with respect to the verb is the same as that of single object pronouns.

—¿Tienes el trofeo?
Do you have the trophy?
—Sí, acaban de dármelo.
Yes, they just gave it to me.

—Mamá, ¿está listo el almuerzo?
Mom, is lunch ready?
—Te lo hago ahora mismo.
I'll make it for you right now.

Berta talks about Anita's party **1.** *I made some appetizers and gave them to Anita for the party.*
2. *I loved the CD that Anita played at the party. That's why Anita lent it to me to listen to at home.*
3. *Sergio took a lot of photos of the party and he showed them to us on the computer.*

Le(s) → se

1. **Use of *se*** When both the indirect and the direct object pronouns begin with the letter **l**, the indirect object pronoun always changes to **se**. The direct object pronoun does not change. Four combinations are possible: **se lo, se la, se los, se las.** In all cases, **se** represents the indirect object. The direct object is represented by **lo, la, los,** or **las.** In sentences of this kind, just use **se** automatically and focus only on the correct direct object form.

   Les dimos <u>el auto</u>. (les lo) — *We gave them the car.*
   Se lo dimos. — *We gave it to them.*

   Le escribí <u>la carta</u> ayer. (le la) — *I wrote him/her the letter yesterday.*
   Se la escribí ayer. — *I wrote it to him/her yesterday.*

   Le regaló <u>esos zapatos</u>. (le los) — *He gave him/her those shoes.*
   Se los regaló. — *He gave them to him/her.*

   Les mandamos <u>las invitaciones</u>. (le las) — *We sent them the invitations.*
   Se las mandamos. — *We sent them to them.*

2. **Clarifying *se*** Since **se** can stand for **le** (*to/for you* [sing.], *him, her*) or **les** (*to/for you* [pl.], *them*), it is often necessary to clarify its meaning by using **a** plus the pronoun objects of prepositions.

   Se lo escribo **a Uds.** (a ellos, a ellas...).
   I'll write it to you (*them . . .*).

   Se las doy **a Ud.** (a él, a ella...).
   I'll give them to you (*him, her . . .*).

AUTOPRUEBA

Match each sentence with the correct double object pronouns.

1. Le dieron el libro. → _____ _____ dieron.
2. Les sirvieron la paella → _____ _____ sirvieron.
3. Le di las direcciones. → _____ _____ di.
4. Les trajo los boletos. → _____ _____ trajo.

a. Se las
b. Se los
c. Se lo
d. Se la

Answers: 1. c 2. d 3. a 4. b

Práctica

A. **¡Anticipemos! Lo que se oye en casa.** ¿A qué se refieren las siguientes oraciones? Fíjate en (*Note*) los pronombres y en el sentido (*meaning*) de la oración.

1. _____ No **lo** prendan (*switch on*). Prefiero que los niños lean o que jueguen.
2. _____ ¿Me **la** pasas? Gracias.
3. _____ Tengo muchas ganas de comprárme**los** todos. Me encanta su música.
4. _____ ¿Por qué no se **las** mandas a los abuelos? Les van a gustar muchísimo.
5. _____ Tengo que reservárte**los** hoy mismo, porque se vence (*expires*) la oferta especial de Aeroméxico.
6. _____ Yo se **la** di a Lupe para su cumpleaños. Antonio y Diego le hicieron un pastel.

a. unas fotos
b. la ensalada
c. unos boletos de avión para Guadalajara
d. la fiesta
e. el radio
f. los CDs de Luis Miguel

B. En la mesa. Imagina que acabas de comer, pero todavía tienes hambre. Pide más comida, según el modelo. Fíjate en (*Note*) el uso del tiempo presente como sustituto para el mandato.

MODELO: ensalada⟶¿Hay más *ensalada*? ¿Me *la* pasas, por favor?

1. pan
2. tortillas
3. tomates
4. fruta
5. vino
6. jamón

C. En el aeropuerto. Cambia los sustantivos por pronombres para evitar (*avoid*) la repetición.

MODELO: ¿La maleta? Van a prestarme la maleta mañana. ⟶
¿La maleta? Van a prestár*mela* (*Me la* van a prestar) mañana.

1. ¿La hora de la salida? Acaban de decirnos la hora de la salida.
2. ¿El horario? Sí, léame el horario, por favor.
3. ¿Los boletos? No, no tiene que darle los boletos aquí.
4. ¿El equipaje? Claro que le guardo el equipaje.
5. ¿Los boletos? Ya te compré los boletos.
6. ¿El puesto? No te preocupes. Te puedo guardar el puesto.
7. ¿La clase turística? Sí, les recomiendo la clase turística, señores.
8. ¿La cena? La asistente de vuelo nos va a servir la cena en el avión.

Need more practice?
☐ Workbook/Laboratory Manual
☐ Online Learning Center
[www.mhhe.com/apuntate]

Conversación

Regalos especiales

Paso 1. The drawings in **Grupo A** show the presents that a number of people have just received. They were given by the people in **Grupo B.** Can you match the presents with the giver? Make as many logical guesses as you can.

GRUPO A

Ⓐ Estela
Ⓑ Maritere
Ⓒ Carlos y Juanita
Ⓓ Rigoberto

GRUPO B

① Pilar
② Jorge
③ Raúl
④ la Sra. Santana

Paso 2. Now compare your matches with those of a partner.

MODELO: **E1:** ¿Quién le regaló (dio) la computadora a Maritere?
E2: Se la regaló (dio) _____.

UN POCO DE TODO

Lengua y cultura: La Virgen de Guadalupe, quince siglos (*centuries*) de historia. Complete the following paragraphs with the correct form of the words in parentheses, as suggested by context. When two possibilities are given in parentheses, select the correct word. Use the present tense or the preterite of the infinitives, according to context.

En todos los países hispanohablantes, hay fiestas religiosas que son días festivos nacionales. Por ejemplo, el día de la Navidad se (celebrar[1]) en todo el mundo hispánico, como ocurre en (este/esta[2]) país.

Otro día religioso que también (es/está[3]) una fiesta nacional en muchos países es el día 12 (de/del[4]) diciembre, la fiesta de la Virgen de Guadalupe. La imagen de la Virgen es venerada[a] por los católicos de todo el mundo. En México, la Virgen de Guadalupe es la santa patrona[b] del país, y (para/por[5]) eso los mexicanos católicos celebran (eso/ese[6]) día con gran devoción. Pero lo que es más interesante (es/está[7]) que la fiesta del 12 de diciembre tiene una historia que (venir[8]) desde[c] los árabes* a través de[d] España y del México colonial hasta nuestros días.

«Guadalupe» es una palabra de origen árabe que significa «río oculto[e]». Ahora es el nombre de una pequeña ciudad (español[9]) en donde (haber[10]) un monasterio famoso.

La historia de la Virgen de Guadalupe (empezar[11]) en el siglo VI con una estatua de la Virgen que pertenecía[f] al Papa[g] Gregorio. Este[h] (se lo / se la[12]) (regalar[13]) al Obispo[i] Leandro de Sevilla. Pero la estatua (desaparecer[j][14]) durante los siglos en que los árabes ocuparon la Península. Curiosamente, después de la expulsión de los árabes por los cristianos en esa zona, un pastor[k] cristiano (le/la[15]) (encontrar[16]) en la ciudad de Guadalupe. Por eso la estatua (empezar[17]) a conocerse como «la Virgen de Guadalupe», por el lugar donde la estatua (volver[18]) a aparecer.

En el siglo XVI, en otro continente, en lo que hoy es México, un campesino[l] indígena, Juan Diego, (convertirse[m][19]) al cristianismo. Un día (*él:* ver[20]) a la Virgen en un lugar llamado «Tepeyac». Ese lugar (es/está[21]) un lugar sagrado[n] de los aztecas por su culto[ñ] a la diosa[o] madre Tonantzín. La Virgen (dejar[p][22]) su imagen en la tilma[q] de Juan Diego. Esta imagen (recibir[23]) el nombre de Virgen de Guadalupe porque Tepeyac estaba[r] cerca del pueblo mexicano de Guadalupe.

La Virgen de Guadalupe mexicana (es/está[24]) muy diferente de la Virgen española, pero las dos responden al gusto del arte de (su[25]) época respectiva. La tilma de Juan Diego, con la imagen de la Virgen, todavía se puede (ver[26]) en la Basílica[s] de la Virgen de Guadalupe, en la Ciudad de México.

La tilma (*shawl*) de Juan Diego en la Basílica de Guadalupe en la Ciudad de México

[a]*venerated, adored* [b]*santa... patron saint* [c]*from* [d]*a... through* [e]*río... hidden river* [f]*belonged* [g]*Pope* [h]*The latter (i.e., the Pope)* [i]*Bishop* [j]*to disappear* [k]*shepherd* [l]*peasant* [m]*convertirse (me convierto) (i)* [n]*sacred* [ñ]*worship* [o]*goddess* [p]*to leave* [q]*shawl* [r]*was* [s]*church*

Comprensión. ¿Cierto o falso? Corrige las oraciones falsas.

	CIERTO	FALSO
1. La Virgen de Guadalupe española es una estatua.	☐	☐
2. Guadalupe es un nombre de origen azteca.	☐	☐
3. Un campesino le regaló una estatua de la Virgen al Papa.	☐	☐
4. El campesino Juan Diego era (*was*) de origen español.	☐	☐
5. Tonantzín significa «río oculto».	☐	☐

Los árabes (musulmanes) conquistaron la Península Ibérica en el año 711. Inmediatamente los cristianos iniciaron una guerra de reconquista (war of reconquest) que terminó en 1492, el mismo año en que Cristóbal Colón llegó a América.

En resumen

Gramática en breve

23. Irregular Preterites

Irregular Preterite Endings

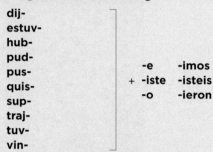

dij-
estuv-
hub-
pud-
pus-   -e   -imos
quis-   + -iste -isteis
sup-   -o   -ieron
traj-
tuv-
vin-

24. Preterite of Stem-Changing Verbs

Preterite Stem-Changing Patterns

e ⟶ i
-e-   -e-
-e-   -e-
-i-   -i-

o ⟶ u
-o-   -o-
-o-   -o-
-u-   -u-

25. Double Object Pronouns

Double Object Pronoun Order
IO + DO
le(s) lo/la/los/las ⟶ se lo/la/los/las

Vocabulario

Los verbos

conseguir (*like* **seguir**)	to get, obtain
conseguir + *inf.*	to succeed in (*doing something*)
despedir(se) (*like* **pedir**) **(de)**	to say good-bye (to)
encontrar (encuentro)	to find
morir(se) ([me] muero) (u)	to die
sugerir (sugiero) (i)	to suggest

Los días festivos y las fiestas

el anfitrión, la anfitriona	host, hostess
las botanas	appetizers
el deseo	dish
el día festivo	holiday
el/la invitado/a	guest
el pastel de cumpleaños	birthday cake
la sorpresa	surprise
las tapas	appetizers

Repaso: el cumpleaños, la fiesta, el pastel, el refresco, el regalo, la tarjeta

cumplir años	to have a birthday
dar una fiesta	to give a party
faltar (a)	to be absent (from), not attend
gastar	to spend (*money*)
hacer una fiesta	to have a party
pasarlo bien/mal	to have a good/bad time
reunirse (me reúno) (con)	to get together (with)

Repaso: bailar, celebrar, divertirse (me divierto) (i), invitar, regalar

Las emociones y los estados afectivos

el estado afectivo	emotional state
discutir (con/sobre)	to argue (with/about)
enfermarse	to become sick
enojarse (con)	to get angry (with)

llorar	to cry
olvidar(se) (de)	to forget (about)
ponerse + *adj.*	to become, get + *adj.*
portarse bien/mal	to (mis)behave
recordar (recuerdo)	to remember
reír(se) ([me] río) (i) (de)	to laugh (about)
sentirse (me siento) (i)	to feel (*an emotion*)
sonreír(se) (*like* **reír**)	to smile

Repaso: quejarse (de)

Otros sustantivos

el hecho	fact, event
(la) medianoche	midnight

Los adjetivos

avergonzado/a	embarrassed
feliz (*pl.* **felices**)	happy
-ísimo/a	very very

Algunos días festivos

la Navidad	Christmas
la Noche Vieja	New Year's Eve
la Nochebuena	Christmas Eve
la Pascua	Easter

Palabras adicionales

¡Felicitaciones!	Congratulations!
gracias por	thanks for
-ísimo (*adv.*)	very very
ser en + *place*	to take place (in/at) (*a place*)
ya	already

VOCABULARIO PERSONAL

Una pareja (*couple*) que pasea en canoa en el lago Calima, Colombia

1. ¿Qué otros deportes acuáticos (*water sports*) crees que son populares en este lago (*lake*) artificial?

2. ¿Qué tipo de lugares de recreo (*recreational areas*) hay donde tú vives?

3. ¿Qué te gusta hacer en tu tiempo libre? ¿Practicas algún deporte? ¿Cuál(es) ¿Tienes alguna afición (*hobby*)?

9

El tiempo libre

Los pasatiempos, diversiones y aficiones°

Los... *Pastimes, fun activities, and hobbies*

LOS PASATIEMPOS

los ratos libres	spare (free) time
caminar	to walk
dar/hacer una fiesta	to give a party
hacer *camping*	to go camping
hacer planes para + inf.	to make plans to (*do something*)
ir...	to go . . .
al cine	to the movies
a una discoteca / a un bar	to a disco / to a bar
al teatro / a un concierto	to the theater / to a concert
a ver una película	to see a movie
jugar (juego) (gu) al ajedrez / a las cartas	to play chess/ cards
sacar (qu) fotos	to take pictures
tomar el sol	to sunbathe
visitar un museo	to visit a museum
aburrirse	to get bored
ser...	to be . . .
aburrido/a	boring
divertido/a	fun

LOS DEPORTES

el ciclismo	bicycling
esquiar (esquío)	to ski
el fútbol	soccer
el fútbol americano	football
hacer *surfing*	to surf
nadar	to swim
la natación	swimming
patinar	to skate
patinar en línea	to rollerblade

Cognados: el basquetbol, el béisbol, el golf, el hockey, el tenis, el voleibol

el equipo	team
el/la jugador(a)	player
el partido	game, match
entrenar	to practice, train
ganar	to win
jugar (juego) (gu) al + *sport*	to play (*a sport*)
perder (pierdo)	to lose
practicar (qu)	to participate (*in a sport*)
ser aficionado/a (a)	to be a fan (of)

Conversación

A. ¿Cierto o falso?

Paso 1. Corrige las oraciones falsas, según tu opinión.

	CIERTO	FALSO
1. Ver un partido de fútbol en la televisión es más aburrido que ir al cine.	☐	☐
2. Lo paso mejor con mi familia que con mis amigos.	☐	☐
3. Las actividades educativas me gustan más que las deportivas (*sporting*).	☐	☐
4. Odio el béisbol tanto como el fútbol.	☐	☐
5. Los estudiantes universitarios tienen tanto tiempo libre como los de la escuela secundaria.	☐	☐

Paso 2. Ahora haz una lista de tus pasatiempos favoritos y de los que menos te gustan.

B. Definiciones

Paso 1. Da las palabras definidas.

MODELO: entrar en un lugar para ver una película ⟶ ir al cine

1. un grupo de jugadores
2. salir bien en una competencia y salir mal
3. practicar un deporte intensamente
4. asistir a todos los partidos de un equipo en particular
5. un deporte que se practica en una piscina o en el mar

Paso 2. Ahora define las siguientes palabras, según el modelo del **Paso 1.**

1. un jugador
2. un partido
3. aburrirse
4. hacer un *picnic*
5. dar un paseo

⟨⟩ NOTA CULTURAL

El fútbol, el béisbol y el basquetbol

Sin duda,[a] el deporte más popular en los países hispánicos es **el fútbol.*** La Copa **Mundial** de fútbol es el evento deportivo más popular del mundo. Este **torneo internacional** ocurre cada cuatro años y tiene más espectadores que cualquier[b] otro evento deportivo. Por ejemplo, en 2006, más de 284 millones de televidentes miraron el partido final de la Copa Mundial, en comparación con los 140 millones de espectadores del *Super Bowl* en los Estados Unidos. Como es un deporte tan popular, en todas las ciudades hispanas hay muchos **campos**[c] **de fútbol,** donde juegan niños y adultos.

El béisbol también es muy popular, sobre todo en el Caribe. Hay muchos hispanos en **las ligas profesionales de** los Estados Unidos. En 1973 el puertorriqueño Roberto Clemente fue el primer jugador hispano elegido al *Baseball Hall of Fame.*

Otro deporte muy popular es **el basquetbol** o **baloncesto.** En los Juegos Olímpicos de verano de 2004, la Argentina se llevó la medalla de oro[d] después de derrotar[e] a Italia. En la Asociación Nacional de Basquetbol (*NBA*) de los Estados Unidos hay varios jugadores hispanos, entre ellos Emanuel Ginobili (argentino), Eduardo Nájera (mexicano), Pau Gasol (español) y Carlos Arroyo (puertorriqueño).

Aficionados durante un partido de fútbol de las Eliminatorias (*Qualifying Rounds*) al Mundial (*World Cup*)

[a]*doubt* [b]*any* [c]*fields* [d]*se... took the gold medal* [e]*defeating*

---

*Remember that **fútbol** is soccer, not U.S.-style football.*

C. ¿Cómo pasan estas personas su tiempo libre?

Paso 1. ¿Qué crees que hacen las siguientes personas para divertirse los sábados? Usa tu imaginación pero sé (*be*) realista.

1. una persona rica que vive en Nueva York
2. unos amigos que trabajan en una fábrica (*factory*)
3. un matrimonio joven con poco dinero y dos niños pequeños

Paso 2. Este recorte (*clipping*) de una revista española indica el tiempo medio (*average*) que los jóvenes españoles dedican a sus aficiones. ¿Puedes explicar en español lo que significan los términos **tomar copas** y **prensa**? ¿A qué tipos de «**juegos**» se refiere el recorte?

Paso 3. En parejas, indiquen cuántos minutos les dedican Uds. a estas aficiones cada día. ¿Qué diferencia hay entre Uds. y los jóvenes españoles? Digan a la clase lo que supieron de su compañero/a.

TIEMPO QUE DEDICAN A SUS AFICIONES	
(Media de minutos diarios)	
Ver la televisión	120
Tomar copas	60
Pasear	22
Leer libros	15
Escuchar música	15
Oír la radio	8
Hacer deporte	9
Practicar *hobbies*	8
Leer la prensa	6
«Juegos»	4

Los quehaceres domésticos ° (Part 2) Los... *Household Chores*

planchar la ropa — Flor

pasar la aspiradora — Ignacio

lavar las ventanas — Pablo

hacer la cama — Nora

sacudir los muebles — Olga

barrer (el piso) — Sofía

sacar (qu) la basura — Mario

lavar los platos — Ana María

pintar (las paredes) — Sergio

ALGUNOS APARATOS DOMÉSTICOS

la aspiradora	vacuum cleaner
la cafetera	coffeemaker
el congelador	freezer
la estufa	stove
el horno de microondas	microwave oven
la lavadora	washing machine
el lavaplatos	dishwasher
el refrigerador	refrigerator
la secadora	clothes dryer
la tostadora	toaster

MÁS QUEHACERES DOMÉSTICOS

dejar (en)	to leave behind (in [*a place*])
lavar...	to wash . . .
los platos	the dishes
la ropa	the clothes
limpiar (la casa entera)	to clean (the whole house)
poner la mesa	to set the table
quitar la mesa	to clear the table

Conversación

A. Los quehaceres domésticos. ¿En qué cuarto o parte de la casa se hacen las siguientes actividades? Hay más de una respuesta en muchos casos.

1. Se hace la cama en _____.
2. Se saca la basura de _____ y se deja en _____.
3. Se sacuden los muebles de _____.
4. Uno se baña en _____. Pero es mejor que uno bañe al perro en _____.
5. Se barre el piso de _____.
6. Se pasa la aspiradora en _____.
7. Se lava y se seca la ropa en _____. La ropa se plancha en _____.
8. Se usa la cafetera en _____.

B. ¡Manos a la obra! (*Let's get to work!*)

Paso 1. De los siguientes quehaceres, ¿cuáles te gustan más? Ponlos en orden de preferencia (mayor = 1, menor = 10) para ti.

_____ barrer el suelo
_____ hacer la cama
_____ lavar los platos
_____ pasar la aspiradora
_____ lavar la ropa
_____ planchar la ropa
_____ limpiar el garaje
_____ sacar la basura
_____ sacudir los muebles
_____ pintar las paredes

Paso 2. ¿Hay un quehacer que prefieras entre todos? ¿Hay un quehacer que no le guste a la mayoría de los estudiantes? ¿Hay alguna diferencia entre lo que prefieren los hombres y lo que les gusta a las mujeres?

C. Las marcas (*Brand names*). ¿Para qué se usan los siguientes productos?

1. Windex
2. Mr. Coffee
3. Endust
4. Glad Bags
5. Joy
6. Cascade
7. Tide
8. Lysol

D. ¿En qué consiste un fin de semana? Lo que significa «el fin de semana» es diferente para cada individuo, según la vida (*life*) que lleva, su horario personal y también el lugar donde vive.

Paso 1. Lee las siguientes preguntas y piensa en tus respuestas.

1. Para ti, ¿cuándo comienza «oficialmente» el fin de semana (día y hora)?
2. ¿Qué haces para celebrar la llegada del fin de semana?
3. ¿Cuándo termina tu fin de semana (día y hora)?
4. ¿Qué haces, generalmente, los días de tu fin de semana?

Paso 2. Ahora, en parejas, túrnense para entrevistarse sobre el fin de semana. Deben obtener detalles interesantes y personales de tu compañero/a.

Talking About Obligation

You already know several ways to express the obligation to carry out particular activities.

Tengo que			I have to	
Necesito	barrer el suelo.		I need to	sweep the floor.
Debo			I should	

Of the three, **tener que** + *infinitive* expresses the strongest sense of obligation.

The concept *to be someone's turn or responsibility* (to do something) is expressed in Spanish with the verb **tocar** (**qu**) plus an indirect object.

—**¿A quién le toca** lavar los platos esta noche?

—**A mí me toca** solamente sacar la basura. Creo que **a papá le toca** lavar los platos.

Whose turn is it to wash the dishes tonight?

I only have to take out the garbage. I think it's Dad's turn to wash the dishes.

E. ¿A quién le toca?

Paso 1. ¿Mantienes tu casa en orden? Indica con qué frecuencia haces los siguientes quehaceres. Si vives en una residencia estudiantil, imagina que vives en una casa o en un apartamento.

Frecuencia

0 = nunca
1 = a veces
2 = frecuentemente
3 = todos los días

1. _____ lavar las ventanas
2. _____ hacer las camas
3. _____ poner la mesa
4. _____ preparar la comida
5. _____ sacudir los muebles
6. _____ lavar los platos
7. _____ limpiar la casa entera

8. _____ sacar la basura
9. _____ pasar la aspiradora
10. _____ limpiar la estufa
11. _____ planchar la ropa
12. _____ barrer el piso

_____ TOTAL

INTERPRETACIONES

0–8 puntos: ¡Cuidado! (*Careful!*) Eres descuidado/a (*careless*). ¿Eres perezoso/a o estudias demasiado (*too much*)? Por favor, ¡limpia tu casa! ¡No lo dejes para mañana!

9–17 puntos: Puedes vivir en tu casa, pero no debes invitar a nadie sin limpiarla bien primero.

18–27 puntos: Tu casa, aunque (*although*) no está limpísima, está limpia. Es un modelo para todos.

28–36 puntos: ¡Eres una maravilla y tienes una casa muy, muy limpia! Pero, ¿pasas demasiado tiempo limpiando? ¡Sal al aire libre (*Go outside*) de vez en cuando!

Paso 2. Ahora, en parejas, túrnense para entrevistarse sobre sus hábitos domésticos. Básense en el formulario del **Paso 1.** Luego hablen de los quehaceres domésticos que tienen para hoy, mañana o esta semana.

MODELO: lavar las ventanas →
E1: ¿Con qué frecuencia lavas las ventanas? (¿A quién le toca lavar las ventanas?)
E2: Nunca las lavo. (Las lavo frecuentemente.)
E1: ¿Y esta semana / hoy / mañana? ¿A quién le toca lavarlas?

Need more practice?
- Workbook/Laboratory Manual
- Online Learning Center
  [www.mhhe.com/apuntate]

Lectura cultural 1

Colombia

DATOS ESENCIALES

NOMBRE OFICIAL: República de Colombia

CAPITAL: Santafé de Bogotá (o Bogotá)

POBLACIÓN: más de 43 millones de habitantes

FÍJATE

- Colombia obtuvo su independencia de España en 1819. Simón Bolívar, líder de la independencia, fue declarado el primer presidente.
- Colombia es el único[a] país sudamericano con costas al Caribe y al Pacífico.
- Colombia tiene una gran riqueza[b] de recursos[c] naturales como petróleo, oro, platino[d] y esmeraldas. De hecho,[e] tiene los yacimientos[f] de platino más grandes del mundo.
- La economía colombiana depende de la exportación del petróleo, además de[g] otros recursos mineros[h] y productos agrícolas como el café y las flores.

[a]only [b]wealth [c]resources [d]platinum [e]De... In fact [f]deposits [g]además... in addition to [h]mining

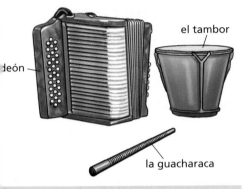

¡MÚSICA!

La música y el baile nacionales de Colombia son la cumbia y el vallenato, tradiciones folclóricas que combinan elementos africanos, indígenas y europeos. Los tambores[a] son importantes en ambos[b] estilos, además de que,[b] en el vallenato también se usa el acordeón alemán.

el tambor

deón

la guacharaca

rdeón, el tambor y la guacharaca, mentos básicos del vallenato

[a]drums [b]both [b]además... besides which

TOTÓ LA MOMPOSINA

Totó la Momposina es una cantante cuya[a] música mezcla[b] la tradición afrocaribeña con la indígena. Colombia también es el país de origen de cantantes tan internacionales como Shakira y Juanes.

[a]whose [b]mixes

Totó la Momposina, durante el Festival WOMAD* en Inglaterra

*World of Music, Art, and Dance

¿Recuerdas?

In **Capítulos 7** and **8,** you learned the forms and some uses of the preterite. Before you learn the other simple past tense (in **Gramática 26**), you might want to review the forms of the preterite in those chapters. The verbs in the following sentences are in the preterite. Can you identify any words in the sentences that emphasize the completed nature of the actions expressed by the verbs?

1. Esta mañana me levanté a las seis.
2. Ayer fui al cine con un amigo.
3. La semana pasada pinté las paredes de la cocina.

26 Talking About the Past (Part 4) • Descriptions and Habitual Actions in the Past: Imperfect of Regular and Irregular Verbs

Gramática en acción: Los indígenas colombianos

Cuando los españoles llegaron al territorio que hoy es Colombia, había allí diversos pueblos indígenas que pertenecían a tres grandes familias.

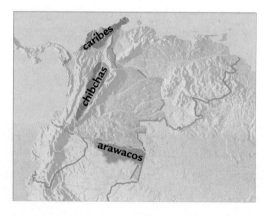

LOS CHIBCHAS: Vivían en los altiplanos y en las zonas frías de los Andes en el interior. Su organización social se basaba en el matriarcado.

LOS CARIBES: Habitaban la zona costera caribeña. Eran un pueblo guerrero y comerciante.

LOS ARAWACOS: Ocupaban el interior oriental, cerca de los ríos Amazonas, Putumayo y Caquetá. Tenían la arquitectura más avanzada de todas las tribus.

¿Y tú?

1. ¿Qué pueblos indígenas vivían en la zona donde vives ahora?
2. ¿Qué otros pueblos indígenas vivían en este país antes de la llegada de los europeos?
3. ¿Cómo era su civilización? Usa frases del diálogo sobre los indígenas colombianos.

Indigenous Colombians When the Spanish arrived in the territory that today is Colombia, there were diverse indigenous peoples there who belonged to three great families. THE CHIBCHAS: They lived in the highlands and in the cold areas of the Andes in the interior. Their social organization was based on matriarchy. THE CARIBS: They lived in the Caribbean coastal zone. They were a warrior and commercial people. THE ARAWACS: They occupied the Eastern interior, close to the Amazon, Putumayo, and Caquetá Rivers. They had the most advanced architecture of all the tribes.

You have already used the *preterite* (**el pretérito**) to express events in the past. The *imperfect* (**el imperfecto**) is the second simple past tense in Spanish. In contrast to the preterite, which is used when you view actions or states of being as begun or completed in the past, the imperfect is used when you view past actions or states of being as habitual or as "in progress." The imperfect is also used for describing the past.

Forms of the Imperfect

hablar		comer		vivir	
hablaba	hablábamos	comía	comíamos	vivía	vivíamos
hablabas	hablabais	comías	comíais	vivías	vivíais
hablaba	hablaban	comía	comían	vivía	vivían

1. **English Equivalents of the Imperfect** As you can see, the imperfect has several English equivalents. Most of these English equivalents indicate that the action was still in progress (*was/were -ing*) or that it was habitual (*used to, would*). The simple English equivalent (*I spoke, we ate, he lived*) can correspond to either the preterite or the imperfect.

yo hablaba = *I spoke, I was speaking, I used to speak, I would speak*

comíamos = *we ate, we were eating, we used to eat, we would eat*

él vivía = *he lived, he was living, he used to live, he would live*

¡OJO!

when *would* = repeated action ⟶ imperfect

Pronunciation Hint: The **b** between vowels, such as in the imperfect ending **-aba**, is pronounced as a fricative [ƀ] sound.

In **-er/-ir** imperfect forms, it is important not to pronounce the ending **-ía** as a diphthong, but to pronounce the **i** and the **a** in separate syllables. (The accent mark over the **í** helps remind you of this.)

Comíamos allí todos los domingos. *We would eat there every Sunday.*

Regular Imperfect Endings

-ar		-er/-ir	
-aba	-ábamos	-ía	-íamos
-abas	-abaís	-ías	-íais
-aba	-aban	-ía	-ían

2. **Imperfect Stem-Changing Verbs and *hay*** Stem-changing verbs do not show a change in the imperfect. The imperfect of **hay** (**haber**) is **había** (*there was, there were, there used to be*).

almorzar (almuerzo) ⟶ almorzaba
perder (pierdo) ⟶ perdía
pedir (pido) (i) ⟶ pedía

3. **Irregular Imperfects** Only three verbs are irregular in the imperfect: **ir, ser,** and **ver.**

ir		ser		ver	
iba	íbamos	era	éramos	veía	veíamos
ibas	íbais	eras	erais	veías	veíais
iba	íban	era	eran	veía	veían

4. **First and Third Person Forms** Note that the first and third person singular forms are identical for **-ar, -er,** and **-ir** verbs. When context does not make meaning clear, subject pronouns are used.

Los sábados **yo** jugaba al tenis y **él** paseaba en bicicleta.
On Saturdays I used to play tennis and he used to ride his bike.

Uses of the Imperfect

If you know when and where to use the imperfect, understanding where the preterite is used will be easier. When talking about the past, the preterite is used when the imperfect isn't. That is an oversimplification, but at the same time it is a general rule of thumb that will help you out at first.

The imperfect has the following uses.

■ To describe *repeated habitual actions* in the past	**Siempre nos quedábamos** en aquel hotel. *We always stayed (used to stay, would stay) at that hotel.* **Todos los veranos iban** a la costa. *Every summer they went (used to go, would go) to the coast.*
■ To describe an *action that was in progress* (when something else happened)	Ramón **pedía** la cena (cuando Cristina **llamó**). *Ramón was ordering dinner (when Cristina called).*
■ To describe two *simultaneous past actions in progress*, with **mientras**	Tú **leías mientras** Juan **escribía** la carta. *You were reading while Juan was writing the letter.*
■ To describe ongoing *physical*, *mental*, or *emotional states* in the past	**Estaban** muy **distraídos**. *They were very distracted.* La **quería** muchísimo. *He loved her a lot.*
■ To tell *time* in the past and to *express age* with **tener**	**Era la una. / Eran las dos.** *It was one o'clock. / It was two o'clock.* **Tenía 18 años.** *She was 18 years old.*

¡OJO!

Just as in the present, the singular form of the verb **ser** is used with one o'clock, the plural form from two o'clock on.

De niña, jugaba mucho con mi madre.

Práctica

A. ¡Anticipemos! Mi niñez (*childhood*)

Paso 1. ¿Es esto lo que hacías cuando tenías 10 años? Di si las siguientes declaraciones son ciertas o falsas, según tu experiencia de niño/a (*as a child*).

		CIERTO	FALSO
1.	Estaba en cuarto grado (*fourth grade*).	❑	❑
2.	Todas las noches me acostaba a las nueve.	❑	❑
3.	Los sábados me levantaba temprano para mirar los dibujos animados (*cartoons*).	❑	❑
4.	Mis padres me pagaban por los quehaceres que hacía: cortar el césped (*cutting the grass*), lavar los platos…	❑	❑
5.	Me gustaba ir con mi madre/padre al supermercado.	❑	❑
6.	Le pegaba (*I hit*) a mi hermano/a.	❑	❑
7.	Tocaba un instrumento musical en la orquesta de la escuela.	❑	❑
8.	Mis héroes eran personajes de los dibujos animados.	❑	❑

Paso 2. Ahora corrige las declaraciones que son falsas, según tu experiencia.

> **MODELO:** 2. Es falso. Me acostaba a las diez, no a las nueve.

B. Cuando Tina era niña…

Describe la vida de Tina cuando era niña, haciendo oraciones completas con las palabras indicadas.

La vida de Tina era muy diferente cuando tenía 6 años.

1. todos los días / asistir / a / escuela primaria
2. por / mañana / aprender / a / leer / y / escribir / en / pizarra
3. a / diez / beber / leche / y / dormir / un poco
4. ir / a / casa / para / almorzar / y / regresar / a / escuela
5. estudiar / geografía / y / dibujar (*to draw*)
6. jugar / con / compañeros / en / patio / de / escuela
7. camino de (*on the way*) casa / comprar / dulces / y / se los / comer
8. frecuentemente / pasar / por / casa / de / abuelos
9. cenar / con / padres / y / ayudar / a / lavar / platos
10. mirar / tele / un rato / y / acostarse / a / ocho

◆》NOTA COMUNICATIVA

The Past Progressive

Sometimes you want to emphasize that an action was in progress in the past. To do so, you can use the past progressive. It is formed with the imperfect of **estar** plus the present participle (**-ndo**) of another verb.*

Estábamos cenando a las diez.
We were having dinner at ten.

¿No **estabas estudiando?**
Weren't you studying?

You will use the past progressive in this way in **Práctica C.**

---

*A progressive tense can also be formed with the preterite of **estar**: **Estuvimos cenando** hasta las doce. *The use of the progressive with the preterite of **estar**, however, is relatively infrequent, and it will not be practiced in ¡Apúntate!*

C. El trabajo de niñera (baby-sitter)

Paso 1. El trabajo de niñera puede ser muy pesado (*difficult*), pero cuando los niños son traviesos (*mischievous*) también puede ser peligroso (*dangerous*). ¿Qué estaba pasando cuando la niñera perdió por fin la paciencia? Describe todas las acciones que puedas, usando **estaba(n)** + *past participle* (**-ndo**).

> **MODELO:** La niñera perdió la paciencia cuando... ⟶
> el bebé estaba llorando.

La niñera perdió la paciencia cuando...

Vocabulario útil

el timbre	doorbell
discutir	to argue
ladrar	to bark
pelear	to fight
sonar	to ring;
(**suena**)*	to sound

Paso 2. Ahora, en parejas, túrnense para hablar de sus experiencias cuidando a niños. ¿Trabajaban Uds. de niñero/a de joven? ¿Tenían que cuidar a (*take care of*) sus hermanos menores? ¿a los niños de sus parientes? ¿Qué acción o accidente ocurrió una vez? Cuéntense (*Tell each other*) su peor experiencia... o la más divertida. Deben completar la frase que empieza con **cuando** (**cuando yo estaba...**) con el imperfecto. Luego usen el pretérito para contar la acción.

> **MODELO:** Una vez, cuando yo estaba (leyendo, mirando la tele, hablando con un amigo / una amiga...), la niña que yo cuidaba (se cayó, salió de la casa sin permiso, sacó ___ de ___ y...).

Vocabulario útil

caerse (**me caigo**)	to fall down
cuidar	to take care of
sacar (qu)	to take (*something*) out

Need more practice?
- Workbook/Laboratory Manual
- Online Learning Center [www.mhhe.com/apuntate]

---

*Although **sonar** is a stem-changing verb, remember that the stem of present participles does not change with **-ar** verbs (**sonando**).*

Conversación

A. Los tiempos cambian. Las siguientes oraciones describen aspectos de la vida de hoy. En parejas, túrnense para describir cómo son las cosas ahora y cómo eran en otra época (*in another era*).

> **MODELO:** **E1:** Ahora casi todos los bebés nacen (*are born*) en un hospital, pero antes...
>
> **E2:** Antes casi todos los bebés nacían en casa.

1. Ahora muchas personas viven en una casa muy grande con un jardín pequeño.
2. Se come con frecuencia en los restaurantes.
3. Muchísimas mujeres trabajan fuera de casa.
4. Muchas personas van al cine y miran la televisión.
5. Ahora las mujeres —no sólo los hombres— llevan pantalones.
6. Ahora hay enfermeros (*male nurses*) y maestros (*male teachers*) —no sólo enfermeras y maestras.
7. Ahora tenemos coches pequeños que gastan (*use*) poca gasolina.
8. Ahora usamos más máquinas y por eso hacemos menos trabajo físico.
9. Ahora las familias son más pequeñas.
10. Muchas parejas viven juntas sin casarse (*getting married*).

B. Entrevista

Paso 1. En parejas, túrnense para entrevistarse sobre su adolescencia y los años de la escuela secundaria. Usen las siguientes categorías para organizar su conversación. Deben obtener detalles interesantes y personales de su compañero/a.

> **MODELO:** gustar: molestar (*to annoy*) a alguien ⟶
>
> **E1:** Cuando tenías 15 años, ¿a quién te gustaba molestar?
>
> **E2:** Me gustaba molestar a mi hermano menor. Él a veces tomaba mis cosas sin mi permiso.
>
> **E1:** ¿Y ahora todavía te gusta molestarlo?
>
> **E2:** La verdad es que sí. (*Actually, yes.*)

1. gustar: molestar a alguien, oír un tipo de música, vestirse con un estilo de ropa
2. preferir: programas de tele, películas, materias, comidas y bebidas
3. comer: a qué hora, dónde, con quién
4. leer: revistas, novelas
5. hacer: los fines de semana, después de las clases
6. discutir: con quién, sobre qué

Paso 2. Ahora digan a la clase dos cosas que Uds. tenían en común.

> **MODELO:** A Frank y a mí nos gustaba oír música rock. Preferíamos ver películas de acción.

Before beginning **Gramática 27**, review comparisons, which were introduced in **Gramática 16** (**Cap. 5**). How would you say the following in Spanish?

1. I work as much as you do.
2. I work more/less than you do.
3. Bill Gates has more money than I have.
4. My housemate has fewer things than I do.
5. I have as many friends as you do.
6. My computer is worse/better than this one.

27 Expressing Extremes • Superlatives

Gramática en acción: ¡El número uno!

Jennifer López

Alex Rodríguez

Juanes

¿Estás de acuerdo? Corrige las declaraciones falsas.

	CIERTO	FALSO
1. Jennifer López es la mujer más bella del mundo.	❏	❏
2. Alex Rodríguez es el mejor beisbolista hispano de la actualidad.	❏	❏
3. Juanes es el cantante colombiano más conocido del mundo	❏	❏

¿Y tú? Completa las siguientes declaraciones para expresar tu opinión.

1. El cantante hispano o hispana más popular del momento es _____.
2. La mejor actriz (*actress*) del momento es _____.
3. En la actualidad la música popular más interesante es _____ (la música de _____, la música de estilo _____).

Superlative Construction

el / la / los / las + *noun* + **más/menos** + *adjective* + **de**

> **superlative** = an adjective or adverb phrase used to express an extreme

1. **Forming the Superlative** The *superlative* (**el superlativo**) is expressed with comparatives but is always accompanied by the definite article. *In* or *at* is expressed with **de**.

El basquetbol es **el deporte** más **competitivo** del mundo.
Basketball is the most competitive sport in the world.

El hockey es **el deporte** más **peligroso de** todos.
Hockey is the most dangerous sport of all.

Number one! *Do you agree? Correct the false statements.* **1.** *Jennifer López is the most beautiful woman in the world.* **2.** *Alex Rodríguez is the best Hispanic baseball player right now (currently).* **3.** *Juanes is the best-known Colombian singer in the world.*

el / la / los / las + mejor(es) / peor(es) + *noun* + de

2. The Best and Worst   Mejor and **peor** tend to precede the noun in this construction.

Son **los mejores refrigeradores de** la tienda.
They're the best refrigerators in the store.

La verdad es que es **el peor jugador de**l equipo.
The truth is that he's the worst player on the team.

Práctica

A. ¡Anticipemos! ¿Estás de acuerdo o no?

Paso 1. Indica si estás de acuerdo o no con las siguientes declaraciones.

	SÍ	NO
1. El peor mes del año es enero.	❑	❑
2. La persona más influyente (*influential*) del mundo es el presidente de los Estados Unidos.	❑	❑
3. El problema más serio del mundo es la deforestación de la región del Amazonas.	❑	❑
4. El día festivo más divertido del año es la Noche Vieja.	❑	❑
5. La mejor novela del mundo es *Don Quijote de la Mancha*.	❑	❑
6. El animal menos inteligente de todos es el avestruz (*ostrich*).	❑	❑
7. El descubrimiento (*discovery*) científico más importante del siglo XX fue la vacuna (*vaccine*) contra la poliomielitis.	❑	❑
8. La ciudad más contaminada de los Estados Unidos es Los Ángeles.		

Paso 2. En parejas, comparen sus respuestas del **Paso 1.** Si están de acuerdo en que una declaración es falsa, inventen otra.

> **MODELO:** 4. No estamos de acuerdo. Creemos que el día festivo más divertido del año es el Cuatro de Julio.

B. Superlativos. Modifica las siguientes oraciones según el modelo. Luego repite cada oración con información verdadera si puedes.

MODELO: Es una estudiante muy trabajadora. (la clase) ⟶
Es *la* estudiante *más trabajadora de la clase.* ⟶
Carlota es la estudiante más trabajadora de la clase.

1. Es un día festivo muy divertido. (el año)
2. Es una clase muy interesante. (todas mis clases)
3. Es una persona muy inteligente. (todos mis amigos)
4. Es una ciudad muy grande. (los Estados Unidos / el Canadá)
5. Es un estado muy pequeño/una provincia muy pequeña. (los Estados Unidos / el Canadá)
6. Es un metro muy rápido. (el mundo)
7. Es una residencia muy ruidosa (*noisy*). (la universidad)
8. Es una montaña muy alta. (el mundo)
9. El Presidente Reagan fue un presidente viejo. (el país)
10. El Presidente Kennedy fue un presidente joven. (el país)
11. Rip Van Winkle fue un hombre perezoso. (el pueblo)
12. El chihuahua es un perro pequeño. (el mundo)

El chihuaua, el perro más pequeño del mundo, ya existía en el México azteca.

Need more pratice?
☐ Workbook/Laboratory Manual
☐ Online Learning Center [www.mhhe.com/apuntate]

Conversación

Entrevista. En parejas, túrnense para hacer declaraciones sobre las siguientes frases. Luego digan sus declaraciones a la clase y comenten los desacuerdos también. **¡OJO!** Los adjetivos que terminan en **-ísimo/a** no se pueden usar en la construcción superlativa. Vean el modelo.

MODELO: E1: Salma Hayek es guapísima, pero Shakira es la mujer más guapa del mundo.
E2: Estoy de acuerdo. / No estoy de acuerdo. Para mí Salma Hayek es la más guapa.

1. el hombre más guapo o la mujer más guapa del mundo
2. la noticia (*news item*) más seria de esta semana
3. un libro interesantísimo y otro aburridísimo
4. el mejor restaurante de la ciudad y el peor
5. el cuarto más importante de la casa y el menos importante
6. un plato riquísimo y otro malísimo
7. un programa de televisión interesantísimo y otro pesadísimo (*very boring*)
8. un lugar tranquilísimo, otro animadísimo y otro peligrosísimo
9. la canción (*song*) más bonita del año y la más fea
10. la mejor película del año y la peor

① El centro de Bogotá Bogotá, sede del gobierno[a] y capital de Colombia, está en los altiplanos.[b] Antes de la llegada de los españoles, la civilización indígena de los chibchas estableció allí una ciudad llamada[c] «Bacatá». Con el paso del tiempo, el nombre «Bacatá» se convirtió en «Bogotá» y en los años 90[d] el nombre oficial llegó a ser[e] «Santafé de Bogotá». Sin embargo, muchos siguen llamándola «Bogotá» por ser más fácil.

[a]sede... *government seat* [b]*highlands* [c]*called* [d]los... *the 1990s* [e]llegó... *became*

② El Castillo[a] de San Felipe Barajas, Cartagena Cartagena de Indias (su nombre oficial) es un puerto importante en la costa caribeña de Colombia. Durante el período colonial, los piratas buscaban los tesoros[b] de la ciudad y de los barcos que salían del puerto. Para proteger[c] Cartagena, los españoles construyeron un sistema extenso de fortificaciones y murallas.[d] Una de estas fortificaciones es el Castillo de San Felipe Barajas.

[a]*Castle* [b]*treasure* [c]*protect* [d]*fortified walls*

③ Un silletero durante el Desfile[a] de los Silleteros, en Medellín Los silleteros son los que cultivan[b] flores en las montañas alrededor de[c] Medellín y que bajan a la ciudad para vender sus arreglos[d] florales conocidos[e] como «silletas». Anualmente, se celebra el Desfile de los Silleteros durante la Feria de las Flores, en agosto. En este desfile se pueden ver enormes silletas que llegan a pesar hasta 60 kilogramos.[f]

[a]*Parade* [b]*grow* [c]alrededor... *around* [d]*arrangements* [e]*known* [f]llegan... *can weigh up to 132 pounds*

④ Algunas de las misteriosas esculturas[a] del Parque Arqueológico de San Agustín Se calcula que estas misteriosas figuras de piedra[b] volcánica fueron esculpidas[c] entre 100 y 1200 D.C.[d] Estas esculturas representan animales, guerreros[e] y caras[f] humanas a veces de manera realista y otras de manera fantástica. Las estatuas pueden medir[g] más de 7 metros de altura[h] y pesar varias toneladas.[i]

[a]*sculptures* [b]*rock* [c]*carved* [d]después de Cristo *(A.D.)* [e]*warriors* [f]*faces* [g]*measure* [h]7... *23 feet high* [i]*tons*

⑤ Un cafetal[a] colombiano El café es una de las exportaciones principales de Colombia. Sólo el Brasil exporta más. Después de sufrir problemas económicos con la caída[b] de los precios mundiales del café, los agricultores colombianos empezaron a diversificar sus cultivos. Ahora la exportación de productos como flores y frutas es cada vez más[c] importante, aunque[d] el petróleo es la exportación principal del país.

[a]*coffee plantation* [b]*fall* [c]cada... *more and more* [d]*although*

¿Recuerdas?

You have been using interrogative words since the beginning of *¡Apúntate!* so not much will be new for you in **Gramática 28**. Review what you already know by telling which interrogative word or phrase you associate with the following phrases.

1. un lugar
2. la hora
3. una persona
4. la manera de hacer algo
5. una selección
6. la razón (*reason*) por algo
7. el lugar de origen de una persona
8. el destino (*destination*)
9. una cantidad
10. ser el dueño de algo

28 Getting Information (Part 2) • Summary of Interrogative Words

Gramática en acción: Un restaurante de Connecticut

1. ¿Cómo se llama el restaurante?
2. ¿En qué ciudad de Connecticut está?
3. ¿En qué tipo de cocina se especializa el restaurante?
4. ¿Cuál es la especialidad de este restaurante?

¿Y tú? ¿Cuántas preguntas más puedes hacer sobre este restaurante, por lo que dice el anuncio?

¿Cómo?	How?	**¿Dónde?**	Where?
¿Cuándo?	When?	**¿De dónde?**	From where?
¿A qué hora?	At what time?	**¿Adónde?**	Where (to)?
¿Qué?	What? Which?	**¿Cuánto/a?**	How much?
¿Cuál(es)?	What? Which one(s)?	**¿Cuántos/as?**	How many?
¿Por qué?	Why?	**¿Quién(es)?**	Who?
		¿De quién(es)?	Whose?

The chart above shows all of the interrogatives you have learned so far. Be sure that you know what they mean and how they are used. If you are not certain, the index and end-of-book vocabularies will help you find where they are first introduced. Only the details about using **¿qué?** and **¿cuál?** are new information.

Using ¿qué? and ¿cuál?

1. ***¿Qué?* = Definition or Explanation** ¿Qué? asks for a definition or an explanation.	**¿Qué** es **esto**? *What is this?* **¿Qué** quieres? *What do you want?* **¿Qué** tocas? *What (instrument) do you play?*
2. ***¿Qué?* + Noun** ¿Qué? can be directly followed by a noun.	**¿Qué deporte** prefieres? *What (Which) sport do you prefer?* **¿Qué playa** te gusta más? *What (Which) beach do you like most?* **¿Qué instrumento musical** tocas? *What (Which) musical instrument do you play?*
3. **Use of *¿cuál(es)?*** ¿Cuál(es)? expresses *what?* or *which?* in all other cases. **¡OJO!** The **¿cuál(es)?** + *noun* structure is not used by most speakers of Spanish: **¿Cuál de los dos libros quieres?** (*Which of the two books do you want?*) BUT **¿Qué libro quieres?** (*Which [What] book do you want?*)	**¿Cuál** es la clase más grande? *What (Which) is the biggest class?* **¿Cuáles** son tus jugadores favoritos? *What (Which) are your favorite players?* **¿Cuál** es la capital del Uruguay? *What is the capital of Uruguay?* **¿Cuál** es tu (número de) teléfono? *What is your phone number?*

AUTOPRUEBA

Match each word to the kind of information it asks for.

1. ¿Cuándo?   **a.** un lugar
2. ¿Dónde?   **b.** un número o una cantidad
3. ¿Qué?   **c.** una definición
4. ¿Cuánto?   **d.** la hora

Answers: 1. d 2. a 3. c 4. b

Práctica

¿Qué o cuál(es)?

1. ¿_____ es esto? —Un lavaplatos.
2. ¿_____ son los Juegos Olímpicos? —Son un conjunto (*group*) de competiciones deportivas.
3. ¿_____ es el quehacer que más odias? —Lavar los platos.
4. ¿_____ bicicleta vas a usar? — La de mi hermana.
5. ¿_____ son los cines más modernos? —Los del centro.
6. ¿_____ DVD debo sacar? —El nuevo de Salma Hayek.
7. ¿_____ es una cafetera? —Es un aparato que se usa para hacer café.
8. ¿_____ es tu padre? —En la foto, es el hombre a la izquierda del coche.

Need more **practice?**
- Workbook/Laboratory Manual
- Online Learning Center
  [www.mhhe.com/apuntate]

Conversación

A. Entrevista: Datos (*Information*) personales

Paso 1. Haz preguntas para averiguar (*find out*) la siguiente información de un compañero o compañera. Es posible usar varias palabras interrogativas.

MODELO: su dirección (*address*) ⟶ ¿Cuál es tu dirección? (¿Dónde vives?)

1. su (número de) teléfono
2. su dirección
3. su cumpleaños
4. la ciudad en que nació (*he/she was born*)
5. su número de seguro (*security*) social
6. la persona en que más confía (*he/she trusts*)
7. su tienda favorita
8. la fecha de su próximo examen

Paso 2. Ahora, en parejas, usen sus preguntas del **Paso 1** para entrevistarse.

B. Las preferencias

Paso 1. En parejas, túrnense para entrevistarse sobre los siguientes temas. Empiecen las preguntas con **¿Qué... ?**

MODELO: estaciones del año ⟶
¿Qué estación del año prefieres (entre todas)?

1. estilo de música
2. pasatiempos o deportes
3. programas de televisión
4. materias este semestre/trimestre
5. colores
6. tipos de comida

¿Qué deporte practicabas de niño/a?

Paso 2. Ahora túrnense para entrevistarse sobre los mismos temas del **Paso 1** pero hablando de sus preferencias de niño/a. Deben obtener detalles interesantes y personales de su compañero/a.

MODELO: estaciones del año ⟶
E1: ¿Qué estación preferías (entre todas) de niño/a?
E2: Prefería el invierno.
E1: ¿Por qué?
E2: Porque me gustaba jugar en la nieve.

UN POCO DE TODO

Lengua y cultura: Diversiones familiares en Colombia. Complete the following passage with the correct forms of the words in parentheses, as suggested by context. When two possibilities are given, select the correct word. **¡OJO!** As you conjugate the verbs in this activity, put the infinitives preceded by *I:* in the imperfect.

Mayra y Joaquín son dos colombianos que llegaron recientemente a este país. Los dos (ser/estar[1]) de Cartagena, una gran ciudad colombiana con puerto[a] que (ser/estar[2]) en el mar Caribe. De niña, Mayra (*I:* vivir[3]) en la parte más antigua (en al / de la[4]) ciudad, el Centro Amurallado[b] colonial. En cambio,[c] la familia de Joaquín (*I:* tener[5]) un apartamento en Bocagrande, la zona (más/mejor[6]) moderna de Cartagena. La manera de (divertirse[7]) de cada uno[d] en su país los fines de semana era diferente.

En Cartagena, Mayra y su familia (*I:* ir[8]) con mucha frecuencia a la playa de La Boquilla* los fines de semana y (*I:* pasar[9]) allí todo el día (*pres. part:* nadar[10]). Por la noche iban a un restaurante a (comer[11]) mariscos y (*I:* bailar[12]) cumbia. Por su parte, a Joaquín (se/le[13]) (*I:* gustar[14]) pasear por las fortalezas y las viejas y enormes murallas[e] de la ciudad. ¿(Saber/Conocer[15]) Uds. que (alguno[16]) de (ese[17]) murallas miden veinte metros de ancho[f] por veinte metros de alto? ¡(Ser/Estar[18]) realmente impresionantes!

Joaquín y Mayra (ser/estar[19]) de acuerdo en que, al visitar[g] Cartagena, es necesario ir también al centro comercial Las Bóvedas[†] y a la isla Barú.[‡] Allí, en las aguas del Parque Natural Corales del Rosario, (son/hay[20]) unos bancos de coral[h] muy bonitos. ¡Qué chévere![i]

El centro histórico de Cartagena

[a]*port* [b]*Centro... Walled Center* [c]*En... On the other hand* [d]*cada... each of them* [e]*fortified walls*
[f]*veinte... 65 feet wide* [g]*al... when one visits* [h]*bancos... coral reefs* [i]*¡Qué... How cool!*

Comprensión. Contesta las siguientes preguntas.

1. ¿De qué ciudad son Mayra y Joaquín?
2. ¿De qué partes de esa ciudad son?
3. ¿Cómo pasaba Mayra los fines de semana en Cartagena?
4. ¿Qué hacía Joaquín los fines de semana?

Resources for Review **and Testing** Preparation

■ Workbook/Laboratory Manual
■ Online Learning Center
[www.mhhe.com/apuntate]

---

*La Boquilla, a fishing village outside Cartagena, has a long secluded beach with restaurants and bars.
[†]Las Bóvedas (The Vaults) were barracks and storerooms built by the Spanish into the outer walls of the old city. Twenty-two of the dungeon-like rooms have been turned into small, upscale shops.
[‡]Barú Island, approximately ten minutes by motorboat from Cartagena, offers white sand beaches, crystal clear water, and big coral reefs.

En resumen

Gramática en breve

26. Descriptions and Habitual Actions in the Past: Imperfect of Regular and Irregular Verbs

Imperfect –*ar* Endings

-aba, -abas, -aba, -ábamos, -abais, -aban

Imperfect –*er* and –*ir* Endings

-ía, -ías, -ía, -íamos, -íais, -ían

Irregular Imperfect Verbs

ir: iba, ibas, iba, íbamos, ibais, iban

ser: era, eras, era, éramos, erais, eran

ver: veía, veías, veía, veíamos, veíais, veían

27. Superlatives

Superlative Construction

el/la/los/las + *noun* + **más/menos** + *adjective* + **de**

el/la/los/las + **mejor(es)/peor(es)** + *noun* + **de**

28. Summary of Interrogative Words

¿qué? = definition, explanation

¿qué? + *noun* = what / which . . .?

¿cuál(es)? = what / which (one) . . . ?

Vocabulario

Los verbos

aburrirse	to get bored
dejar (en)	to leave behind (in [*a place*])
pegar (gu)	to hit
pelear	to fight
sonar (suena)	to ring; to sound

Repaso: deber, necesitar, tener que

Los pasatiempos, diversiones y aficiones

los ratos libres	spare (free) time
caminar	to walk
dar un paseo	to take a walk
hacer planes para + *inf.*	to make plans to (*do something*)
hacer un *picnic*	to have a picnic
ir...	to go . . .
a una discoteca / a un bar	to a disco / to a bar
al teatro / a un concierto	to the theater / to a concert
jugar (juego) (gu)	to play
al ajedrez	chess
a las cartas	cards

ser...	to be . . .
aburrido/a	boring
divertido/a	fun
visitar un museo	to visit a museum

Repaso: dar/hacer una fiesta, hacer *camping*, ir al cine / a ver una película, sacar (qu) fotos, tomar el sol

Los deportes

el ciclismo	bicycling
correr	to run
esquiar (esquío)	to ski
el fútbol	soccer
el fútbol americano	football
hacer *surfing*	to surf
montar a caballo	to ride a horse
la natación	swimming
pasear en bicicleta	to ride a bicycle
patinar	to skate
patinar en línea	to rollerblade

Cognados: el basquetbol, el béisbol, el golf, el hockey, el tenis, el voleibol

Repaso: nadar

el equipo	team	poner la mesa	to set the table
el/la jugador(a)	player	quitar la mesa	to clear the table
el partido	game, match	sacar (qu) la basura	to take out the trash
		sacudir los muebles	to dust the furniture
entrenar	to practice, train		
ganar	to win		
ser aficionado/a (a)	to be a fan (of)		

Otros sustantivos

Repaso: jugar (juego) (gu) al + *sport*, perder (pierdo), practicar (qu)

la afición	hobby
el aparato doméstico	home appliance
la dirección	address
la época	era, time (*period*)
la escuela	school
el grado	grade, year (*in school*)
el/la niñero/a	baby-sitter
la niñez	childhood
el quehacer doméstico	household chore

Algunos aparatos domésticos

la aspiradora	vacuum cleaner
la cafetera	coffeemaker
el congelador	freezer
la estufa	stove
el horno de microondas	microwave oven
la lavadora	washing machine
el lavaplatos	dishwasher
el refrigerador	refrigerator
la secadora	clothes dryer
la tostadora	toaster

Los adjetivos

deportivo/a	sporting, sports (*adj.*); sports-loving
pesado/a	boring; difficult

Palabras adicionales

de joven	as a youth
de niño/a	as a child
demasiado (*adv.*)	too much
en la actualidad	currently, right now
mientras	while
tocarle (qu) a uno	to be someone's turn

Los quehaceres domésticos

barrer (el piso)	to sweep (the floor)
hacer la cama	to make the bed
lavar...	to wash . . .
los platos	the dishes
la ropa	the clothes
las ventanas	the windows
limpiar (la casa entera)	to clean (the whole) house
pasar la aspiradora	to vacuum
pintar (las paredes)	to paint (the walls)
planchar la ropa	to iron clothing

Repaso: ¿a qué hora?, ¿adónde?, ¿cómo?, ¿cuál(es)?, ¿cuándo?, ¿cuánto/a?, ¿cuántos/as?, ¿de dónde?, ¿de quién(es)?, ¿dónde?, ¿por qué?, ¿qué?, ¿quién(es)?

VOCABULARIO PERSONAL

Una mujer que medita en un balcón en Caracas

1. ¿Qué rutinas son buenas para llevar una vida tranquila (*lead a calm life*)?

2. ¿Haces yoga? ¿Qué tipo de ejercicio prefieres?

3. ¿Qué efectos dañinos (*harmful*) pueden tener las ciudades grandes como Caracas en la salud (*health*) de sus residentes?

10

La salud°

°La... *Health*

La salud y el bienestar°

La... *Health and well-being*

la boca
el cerebro
la garganta
los pulmones
el estómago
Josefa
correr
caminar
Enrique
la cabeza
hacer yoga
el corazón
la rueda de molino
Laura

EL CUERPO HUMANO

el diente	(front) tooth
la muela	molar, back tooth
la nariz	nose
el oído	inner ear
el ojo	eye
la oreja	(outer) ear

PARA CUIDAR DE LA SALUD

comer comidas sanas	to eat healthy food
cuidarse	to take care of oneself
dejar de + *inf.*	to stop (*doing something*)
dormir (duermo) (u) lo suficiente	to get enough sleep
hacer ejercicio	to exercise; to get exercise
hacer...	to do . . .
ejercicios aeróbicos	aerobics
(el método) Pilates	Pilates
(el) yoga	yoga
llevar gafas / lentes de contacto	to wear glasses / contact lenses
llevar una vida sana/tranquila	to lead a healthy/calm life
practicar (qu) deportes	to practice, play sports

Conversación

A. Asociaciones

Paso 1. ¿Qué partes del cuerpo humano asocias con las siguientes palabras?
¡OJO! A veces hay más de una respuesta posible.

1.	un ataque	**5.**	pensar	**9.**	la música
2.	comer	**6.**	la digestión	**10.**	el perfume
3.	cantar	**7.**	el amor	**11.**	un beso (*kiss*)
4.	las gafas	**8.**	fumar	**12.**	una flor

Paso 2. ¿Qué palabras asocias con las siguientes partes del cuerpo?

1.	los ojos	**3.**	la boca	**5.**	el estómago
2.	los dientes	**4.**	el oído	**6.**	los pulmones

B. Hablando de la salud. ¿Qué significan, para ti, las siguientes oraciones?

> **MODELO:** Se debe comer comidas sanas. ⟶
> Eso quiere decir (*means*) que es necesario comer muchas verduras, que…
> También significa que no debemos comer muchos dulces o…

1. Se debe dormir lo suficiente todas las noches.
2. Hay que hacer ejercicio.
3. Es necesario llevar una vida tranquila.
4. En general, uno debe cuidarse mucho.
5. Es importante llevar una vida sana.

> **Vocabulario útil**
>
> **Eso quiere decir…**
> **Esto significa que…**
> **También…**

C. ¿Cómo vives? ¿Cómo vivías?

Paso 1. Di (*Say*) si haces las siguientes cosas para mantener la salud y el bienestar.

		SÍ	NO
1.	comer comidas sanas	❏	❏
2.	no comer muchos dulces	❏	❏
3.	caminar por lo menos dos millas por día	❏	❏
4.	correr	❏	❏
5.	hacer ejercicios aeróbicos	❏	❏
6.	dormir por lo menos ocho horas por día	❏	❏
7.	tomar bebidas alcohólicas en moderación	❏	❏
8.	no tomar bebidas alcohólicas en absoluto (*at all*)	❏	❏
9.	no fumar ni cigarrillos ni puros (*cigars*)	❏	❏
10.	llevar ropa adecuada (abrigo, suéter, etcétera) cuando hace frío	❏	❏

Paso 2. ¿Llevas una vida sana? Dile (*Tell*) a un compañero o compañera cómo vives, usando frases del **Paso 1** de esta actividad y de **Paso 1: Vocabulario.**

> **MODELO:** Creo que llevo una vida sana porque como comidas sanas. No como muchos dulces, excepto en ciertas ocasiones, como la Navidad…

Paso 3. Ahora modifica tu narración para describir lo que hacías de niño/a. ¿Qué hacías y qué *no* hacías? Organiza las ideas lógicamente.

> **MODELO:** De niño, no llevaba una vida muy sana. Comía muchos dulces. También odiaba comer frutas y verduras…

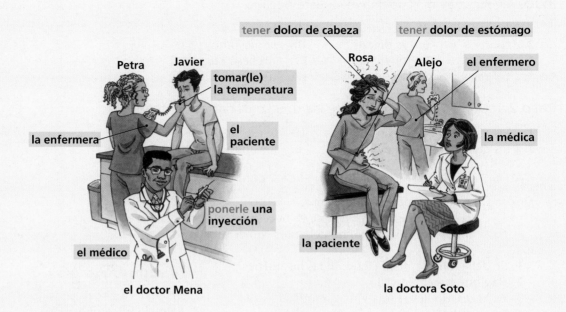

Petra · Javier

tener **dolor de cabeza** · tener **dolor de estómago**

Rosa · Alejo · **el enfermero**

tomar(le) la temperatura

la enfermera

el **paciente**

la médica

ponerle **una inyección**

el **médico**

la **paciente**

el doctor Mena · la doctora Soto

el antibiótico	antibiotic	**guardar cama**	to stay in bed
el dolor	pain, ache	**molestar***	to bother
el/la farmacéutico/a	pharmacist	**resfriarse (me resfrío)**	to get/catch a cold
la fiebre	fever	**respirar**	to breathe
la gripe	flu	**sacar (qu)**	to extract
el jarabe	(cough) syrup	**sacar la lengua**	to stick out one's tongue
la medicina	medicine		
la pastilla	pill	**sacarle un diente / una muela**	to extract (*someone's*) tooth/molar
la receta	prescription		
el resfriado	cold		
la tos	cough	**sentirse (me siento) (i)**	to feel
		tener dolor (de muela)	to have a (tooth) ache
cansarse	to get tired	**tener fiebre**	to have a fever
doler (duele)*	to hurt, ache	**toser**	to cough
enfermarse	to get sick		
estar sano/a	to be healthy	**mareado/a**	dizzy; nauseated
		resfriado/a	congested, stuffed-up

¿Tienes fiebre?

*Doler *and* molestar *are used like* gustar: Me duele la cabeza. Me molestan los ojos.

Conversación

A. Estudio de palabras. Completa las siguientes oraciones con una palabra de la misma familia que la palabra en letra azul.

1. Si me resfrío, es cierto que tengo _____.
2. La respiración ocurre cuando alguien _____.
3. Si me _____, estoy enfermo/a. Un(a) _____ me toma la temperatura.
4. Cuando alguien tose, es porque tiene _____.
5. Si me duele el estómago, tengo _____ de estómago.

B. Situaciones. Describe la situación de estas personas. ¿Dónde y con quiénes están? ¿Qué síntomas tienen? ¿Qué van a hacer?

1. Rosa está muy sana. Nunca le duele(n) _____. Nunca tiene _____. Siempre _____. Más tarde, ella va a _____.
2. Martín tiene _____. Debe _____. El dentista va a _____. Después, Martín va a _____.
3. A Inés le duele(n) _____. Tiene _____. El médico y la enfermera van a _____. Luego, Inés tiene que _____.

1.   2.   3.

⏴⏵ NOTA COMUNICATIVA

The Good News . . . The Bad News . . .

To describe general qualities or characteristics of something, use **lo** with the masculine singular form of an adjective.

lo bueno / lo malo   lo más importante   lo mejor / lo peor   lo mismo

This structure has a number of English equivalents, especially in colloquial speech.

lo bueno = the good thing/part/news, what's good

C. En esta universidad. En parejas, usen los siguientes adjetivos para describir esta universidad, según el modelo.

MODELO: malo ⟶ Lo malo de esta universidad es la matrícula.

1. malo / bueno
2. peor / mejor
3. interesante / aburrido
4. curioso (*strange*) / especial
5. insoportable (*unbearable*)

La medicina en los países hispánicos

Los hispanos pueden **consultar** a otros profesionales en el campo de la salud, además de los médicos, especialmente en relación con enfermedades que no son graves. La gente consulta a los **farmacéuticos** con frecuencia, pues estos son profesionales con un riguroso entrenamiento universitario en **farmacología**. Además, hay **farmacias** en cada barrio, lo cual hace que haya[a] una relación bien establecida entre los farmacéuticos y sus clientes.

En las ciudades y pueblos hispánicos siempre hay algunas farmacias abiertas las 24 horas del día. Se establecen **horarios de turnos,** y la farmacia que está abierta a horas en que las otras están cerradas se llama **farmacia de guardia.** Se puede saber cuáles son las farmacias de guardia a través del periódico o simplemente yendo a la farmacia más cercana, donde siempre hay una lista de todas las farmacias.

Otros profesionales al cuidado de la salud muy solicitados son los **practicantes,** que son **enfermeros** o estudiantes de medicina con varios años de estudio, que están capacitados[b] para poner inyecciones o **hacer visitas a domicilio** para tratamientos sencillos.

La cruz (*cross*) verde de una farmacia de guardia, en Alicante, España.

Finalmente, se debe mencionar la popularidad de **remedios tradicionales,** como la homeopatía. Aunque[c] hay expertos homeópatas con años de entrenamiento, también existe un repertorio popular de **remedios naturales** para enfermedades o molestias[d] cotidianas, conocimientos[e] que se transmiten de generación a generación.

[a]lo... which creates   [b]trained   [c]Although   [d]nuisances   [e]knowledge

D. Refranes sobre la salud. Empareja una frase de la columna A con otra de la columna B para formar algunos refranes muy comunes en el mundo hispano. En algunos casos te puede ayudar la rima. Luego explica lo que significan los refranes. ¿Cuál es el equivalente en inglés?

COLUMNA A
1. La salud no se compra:
2. Músculos de Sansón,
3. Si quieres vivir sano,
4. De médico, poeta y loco,
5. Para enfermedad de años,
6. Ojos que no ven,
7. Lo que no mata (*doesn't kill*),

COLUMNA B
a. engorda (*fattens*).
b. todos tenemos un poco.
c. no tiene precio.
d. y cerebro de mosquito.
e. no hay medicina.
f. acuéstate y levántate temprano.
g. corazón que no siente.

Need more practice?
- Workbook/Laboratory Manual
- Online Learning Center [www.mhhe.com/apuntate]

Lectura cultural **1**

Venezuela

DATOS ESENCIALES

Nombre oficial: República de Venezuela

Capital: Caracas

Población: más de 25 millones de habitantes

FÍJATE

- Venezuela es miembro de los Países Megadiversos Afines,[a] y es uno de los países con mayor biodiversidad del mundo.
- El clima venezolano varía entre el clima templado de la región andina y el clima tropical de los llanos[b] y de la costa. El clima es agradable la mayor parte del año.
- Por la variedad de climas, Venezuela le ofrece al turista atracciones diversas, entre ellas: (1) las hermosas[c] playas tropicales de la Isla Margarita y de la costa caribeña; (2) la famosa catarata[d] del Salto Ángel[e] que, siendo dieciséis veces más alta que las cataratas del Niágara, se considera la más alta del mundo; (3) la belleza[f] colonial de la Ciudad Bolívar y Coro; y (4) la moderna y cosmopolita ciudad de Caracas.
- Venezuela tiene uno de los depósitos petroleros más importantes del mundo, lo que constituye la principal riqueza[g] de su economía.

[a]Países... *Like-Minded Megadiverse Countries* [b]*plains* [c]*beautiful* [d]*waterfall* [e]Salto... *Angel Falls* [f]*beauty* [g]*wealth*

¡MÚSICA!

La música folclórica típicamente venezolana es el joropo, la música del llanero, el *cowboy* venezolano. El instrumento musical representativo del joropo es el arpa llanera.[a] Como baile, el joropo es semejante a un vals,[b] pero con influencias africanas.

[a]arpa... *type of harp* [b]*waltz*

 ## FRANCO DE VITA

Franco de Vita, hijo de emigrantes italianos, se crió[a] y se formó musicalmente entre Venezuela e Italia. Es un artista con proyección[b]

internacional, como lo demuestran[c] sus múltiples colaboraciones con músicos de otros países. «Tú de qué vas[d]», uno de sus éxitos[e] más recientes, apareció en su álbum *Stop*.

[a]se... *was raised* [b]*reach, influence* [c]como... *as is demonstrated by* [d]Tú ... *What do you mean?* [e]*hits*

Franco de Vita durante un concierto en la Ciudad de Guatemala

¿Recuerdas?

Since **Capítulo 7** you have been using first the preterite and then the imperfect in appropriate contexts. Do you remember which tense you used to do each of the following?

1. to tell what you did yesterday
2. to tell what you used to do when you were in grade school
3. to explain the situation or condition that caused you to do something
4. to tell what someone did as the result of a situation
5. to talk about the way things used to be
6. to describe an action that was in progress

If you understand these uses of the preterite and the imperfect, the following summary of their uses in **Gramática 29** will be very easy for you.

29 Narrating in the Past (Part 5) • Using the Preterite and the Imperfect

Gramática en acción: En el consultorio de la Dra. Méndez

DRA. MÉNDEZ: ¿Cuándo empezó a sentirse mal su hija?

MADRE: Ayer por la tarde. Estaba resfriada, tosía mucho y se quejaba de que le dolían el cuerpo y la cabeza.

DRA. MÉNDEZ: ¿Y le notó algo de fiebre?

MADRE: Sí. Por la noche le tomé la temperatura y tenía treinta y nueve grados.*

DRA. MÉNDEZ: A ver… Tal vez necesite ponerle una inyección…

98,6 grados Fahrenheit

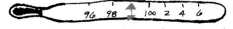

37,0 grados centígrados

Comprensión. Locate all of the past tense verbs in the preceding dialogue that do the following.

1. indicate actions
2. indicate conditions or descriptions

In Dr. Méndez's office DR. MÉNDEZ: *When did your daughter begin to feel ill?* MOTHER: *Yesterday afternoon. She was stuffed up, she was coughing a lot, and she was complaining that her body and head were hurting.* DR. MÉNDEZ: *And did you note any fever?* MOTHER: *Yes. At night I took her temperature and it was thirty-nine degrees.* DR. MÉNDEZ: *Let's see . . . Perhaps I'll need to give her a shot . . .*

Normal body temperature is 37 ˚C (98.6 ˚F).

When speaking about the past in English, you use different past tense forms, depending on the context: *I wrote letters, I was writing letters, I used to write letters,* and so on. Similarly, you can use either the preterite or the imperfect in many Spanish sentences, depending on the meaning you wish to convey. Often the question is: How do you view the action or state of being?

Preterite	Imperfect
■ beginning/end of past action ■ completed action ■ series of completed actions ■ interrupt**ing** action ■ the action on the "stage"	■ habitual/repeated action ■ progress of a past action ■ background details ■ interrupt**ed** action ■ the backdrop (setup) or the "stage"

Beginning/End vs. Habitual

Use the preterite to . . . ■ tell about the beginning or the end of a past action	El sábado pasado, el partido de fútbol empezó a la una. Terminó a las cuatro. El entrenador habló a las cinco. *Last Saturday, the soccer game began at one. It ended at four. The coach spoke (began to speak) at five.*
Use the imperfect to . . . ■ talk about the habitual nature of an action (something you always did)	Había un partido **todos los sábados**. Muchas personas jugaban **todas las semanas**. *There was a game every Saturday. Many people played every week.*

Completed vs. Ongoing

Use the preterite to . . . ■ express an action that is viewed as completed	El partido duró tres horas. Ganaron Los Lobos de Villalegre. *The game lasted three hours. The Lobos of Villalegre won.*
Use the imperfect to . . . ■ tell what was happening when another action took place and to tell about simultaneous events (with **mientras** = *while*)	Yo no vi el final del partido. Estaba en la cocina cuando **terminó**. *I didn't see the end of the game. I was in the kitchen when it ended.* **Mientras** mi amigo veía el partido, hablaba con su novia. *While my friend was watching the game, he was talking with his girlfriend.*

Series of Completed Actions vs. Background

Use the preterite to . . . ■ express a series of completed actions	Durante el partido, los jugadores corrieron, saltaron y gritaron. *During the game, the players ran, jumped, and shouted.*
Use the imperfect to . . . ■ give background details of many kinds: time, location, weather, mood, age, physical and mental characteristics	Todos los jugadores eran jóvenes; tenían 17 ó 18 años. ¡Y todos esperaban ganar! *All the players were young; they were 17 or 18 years old. And all of them hoped to win!*

Interrupting vs. Interrupted

The preterite and the imperfect frequently occur in the same sentence. In the first example, the imperfect tells what was happening when another action—conveyed by the preterite—broke the continuity of the ongoing activity. In the second example, the preterite reports the action that took place because of a condition—described by the imperfect—that was in progress or in existence at that time.	Miguel **estudiaba** cuando sonó el teléfono. *Miguel was studying when the phone rang.* Olivia comió tanto porque **tenía** mucha hambre. *Olivia ate so much because she was very hungry.*

Action vs. the Stage (Background)/Conditions/Ongoing

The preterite and imperfect are also used together in the presentation of an event. The preterite narrates the action while the imperfect sets the stage, describes the conditions that caused the action, or emphasizes the continuing nature of a particular action.	Era un día hermoso. Hacía mucho sol pero no hacía mucho calor. Como no tenía que ir a la oficina, **me puse** una camiseta vieja y unos pantalones cortos y **decidí** trabajar en el jardín. *It was a beautiful day. It was very sunny, but it wasn't very hot. Since I didn't have to go to the office, I put on an old T-shirt and some shorts and decided to work in the garden.*

Changes in Meaning

Remember that, when used in the preterite, **saber, conocer, querer,** and **poder** have English equivalents different from that of the infinitives. (See page 237.) In the imperfect, the English equivalents of these verbs do not differ from the infinitive meanings.

—Anoche conocí a Roberto.
Last night **I met** *Roberto.*

—¿Anoche? Yo pensaba que ya lo conocías.
Last night? I thought **you** *already* **knew** *him.*

Práctica

A. **En el consultorio.** ¿Qué pasó la última vez que tuviste cita (*an appointment*) con el médico / la médica? Empareja las condiciones con las acciones.

CONDICIONES
(Yo / A mí...)

1. _____ Tenía mucho frío y tiritaba (*I was shaking*).
2. _____ Me dolía la garganta.
3. _____ Me dolía el pecho (*chest*).
4. _____ Creía que estaba anémico/a.
5. _____ No sabía lo que tenía.
6. _____ Necesitaba medicinas.
7. _____ Sólo necesitaba un chequeo (*check-up*) rutinario.

ACCIONES
(El médico / La médica...)

a. Me hizo muchas preguntas.
b. Me dio una receta.
c. Me tomó la temperatura.
d. Me auscultó (*listened to*) los pulmones y el corazón.
e. Me analizó la sangre (*blood*).
f. Me hizo sacar la lengua.
g. Me hizo toser.

AUTOPRUEBA

Indicate preterite (*P*) or imperfect (*I*).

1. background details
2. repeated actions
3. completed action
4. habits
5. beginning of an action

Answers: 1. I / 2. I / 3. P / 4. I / 5. P

◆NOTA COMUNICATIVA

Words and Expressions That Indicate the Use of Preterite and Imperfect

Certain words and expressions are frequently associated with the preterite, others with the imperfect.

Some words often associated with the preterite are:

ayer, anteayer (*the day before yesterday*), **anoche** (*last night*) **una vez, dos veces** (*twice*)...

el año pasado, el lunes pasado...
de repente (*suddenly*)

Some words often associated with the imperfect are:

todos los días, todos los lunes...
siempre, frecuentemente

mientras
de niño/a, de joven

Some English equivalents also associated with the imperfect are:

was _____ *-ing, were* _____ *-ing* (in English)
used to, would (when *would* implies *used to* in English)

As you continue to practice preterite and imperfect, these expressions can help you determine which tense to use. These words do not *automatically* cue either tense, however. The most important consideration is the meaning that the speaker wishes to convey.

Ayer cenamos temprano.
Ayer cenábamos cuando Juan llamó.

Yesterday we had dinner early.
Yesterday we were having dinner when Juan called.

Jugaba al fútbol **de niño.**
Empezó a jugar al fútbol **de niño.**

He played soccer as a child.
He began to play soccer as a child.

B. Pequeñas historias. Completa los siguientes párrafos con una de las palabras o frases de cada lista. Antes de empezar, mira el dibujo que acompaña cada párrafo para tener una idea general del tema de la historia.

1. nos quedamos
   nos quedábamos
   íbamos
   nos gustó
   nuestra familia decidió
   vivíamos

Cuando éramos niños, Jorge y yo _____¹ en la Argentina. Siempre _____² a la playa, a Mar del Plata, para pasar la Navidad. Allí casi siempre _____³ en el Hotel Fénix. Un año, _____⁴ quedarse en otro hotel, el Continental. No _____⁵ tanto como el Fénix y por eso, al año siguiente, _____⁶ en el Fénix otra vez.

2. estaba leyendo
   había
   estaban apagadasª
   pasaba
   comprendí
   tenía
   salí
   se apagaronᵇ
   me levanté

Eran las once de la noche cuando ¡de repente _____¹ todas las lucesᶜ de la casa! Puse el libro que _____² en la mesa y _____³ para averiguarᵈ qué _____⁴. La verdad es que _____⁵ mucho miedo. _____⁶ a la calle y vi que _____⁷ las luces de todo el barrio.ᵉ En ese momento _____⁸ que _____⁹ un apagónᶠ por toda la ciudad.

ªout ᵇse... went out ᶜlights ᵈfind out ᵉneighborhood
ᶠpower outage

3. examinó
   intentabaª tomarle
   estaba
   esperaba
   puso
   llegó
   dio
   se sintió

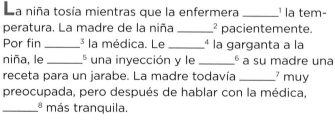
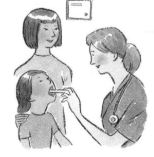

La niña tosía mientras que la enfermera _____¹ la temperatura. La madre de la niña _____² pacientemente. Por fin _____³ la médica. Le _____⁴ la garganta a la niña, le _____⁵ una inyección y le _____⁶ a su madre una receta para un jarabe. La madre todavía _____⁷ muy preocupada, pero después de hablar con la médica, _____⁸ más tranquila.

ªtried to

C. Rubén y Soledad. Primero lee el siguiente párrafo (sin conjugar los infinitivos) para tener una idea general de la historia y mira el dibujo. Luego completa el párrafo con la forma apropiada de los infinitivos, en el pretérito o en el imperfecto.

Rubén estaba estudiando cuando Soledad entró en el cuarto. Le (preguntar[1]) a Rubén si (querer[2]) ir al cine con ella. Rubén le (decir[3]) que sí porque se (sentir[4]) un poco aburrido de estudiar. Los dos (salir[5]) en seguida[a] para el cine. (Ver[6]) una película cómica y (reírse[7]) mucho. Luego, como (hacer[8]) frío, (entrar[9]) en su café favorito, El Gato Negro, y (tomar[10]) chocolate. (Ser[11]) las dos de la mañana cuando por fin (regresar[12]) a casa. Soledad (acostarse[13]) en seguida porque (estar[14]) cansada, pero Rubén (empezar[15]) a estudiar otra vez.

[a]en… *right away*

Comprensión. Ahora contesta las siguientes preguntas, según el párrafo. **¡OJO!** Una pregunta *no* se contesta siempre con el mismo tiempo verbal de la pregunta. Por ejemplo, si es necesario explicar por qué ocurrió algo, se usa el imperfecto.

1. ¿Qué hacía Rubén cuando Soledad entró?
2. ¿Qué le preguntó Soledad a Rubén?
3. ¿Por qué le dijo Rubén que sí?
4. ¿Les gustó la película? ¿Cómo se sabe?
5. ¿Por qué tomaron chocolate?
6. ¿Qué hora era cuando regresaron a casa?
7. ¿Qué hicieron cuando llegaron a casa?

D. La fiesta de Roberto. Primero lee el siguiente párrafo (sin conjugar los infinitivos) para tener una idea general de la historia y mire el dibujo. Luego completa el párrafo con la forma apropiada de los infinitivos, en el pretérito, en el imperfecto o en el presente.

Durante mi segundo año en la universidad, conocí a Roberto en una clase. Pronto nos (hacer[1]) muy buenos amigos. Roberto (ser[2]) una persona muy generosa que (dar[3]) una fiesta en su apartamento todos los viernes. Todos nuestros amigos (ir[4]). (Haber[5]) muchas bebidas y comida abundante, y todos (hablar[6]) y (bailar[7]) hasta muy tarde.

Una noche algunos de los vecinos[a] de Roberto (llamar[8]) a la policía porque les (parecer[b 9]) que nosotros (hacer[10]) demasiado ruido. (Llegar[11]) dos policías al apartamento y le (decir[12]) a Roberto que la fiesta (ser[13]) demasiado ruidosa. Nosotros no (querer[14]) aguar[c] la fiesta, pero ¿qué (poder[15]) hacer? Todos nos (despedir[16]) aunque[d] (ser[17]) solamente las once de la noche.

Aquella noche Roberto (aprender[18]) algo importantísimo. Ahora cuando (hacer[19]) una fiesta, siempre (invitar[20]) a sus vecinos.

[a]*neighbors*   [b]*to seem*   [c]*to spoil*   [d]*although*

E. Lo mejor de estar enfermo

Paso 1. Haz oraciones completas con las palabras indicadas, usando el pretérito o el imperfecto de los verbos. Añade palabras si es necesario.

1. cuando / yo / ser / niño, / pensar / que / lo mejor / de / estar enfermo / ser / guardar cama
2. lo peor / ser / que / con frecuencia / (yo) resfriarse / durante / vacaciones
3. una vez / (yo) ponerme / muy / enfermo / durante / Navidad
4. mi / madre / llamar / a / médico / con / quien / tener / confianza
5. Dr. Matamoros / venir / casa / y / darme / antibiótico / porque / tener / fiebre / altísimo
6. ser / cuatro / mañana / cuando / por fin / (yo) empezar / respirar / sin dificultad
7. desgraciadamente (*unfortunately*) / día / de / Navidad / (yo) tener / tomar / jarabe / y / no / gustar / nada / sabor (*taste, m.*)
8. lo bueno / de / este / enfermedad / ser / que / mi / padre / tener / dejar / fumar / mientras / yo / estar / enfermo

Paso 2. Ahora vuelve a contar la historia desde el punto de vista (*point of view*) de la madre. Sigue el modelo.

> **MODELO:** 1. cuando / yo / ser / niño, / pensar / que / lo mejor / de / estar enfermo / ser / guardar cama $\longrightarrow$
> Cuando mi hijo era niño, (él) pensaba que lo mejor de estar enfermo era guardar cama.

F. Caperucita Roja

Vocabulario útil

abalanzarse (c) sobre	to pounce on
avisar	to warn
dispararle	to shoot at (*someone/something*)
enterarse de	to find out about
esconderse	to hide
huir (*like* **construir**)	to flee
querer	to love
saltar	to jump

Paso 1. Retell this familiar story, based on the drawings, sentences, and cues that accompany each drawing, using the imperfect or preterite of the verbs in parentheses. Add as many details as you can. Using context, try to guess the meaning of words that are glossed with ¿ ?.

1.   **2.**   **3.**

1. Érase una vez[a] una niña hermosa que (llamarse[1]) Caperucita Roja. Todos los animales del bosque[b] (ser[2]) sus amigos y Caperucita Roja los (querer[3]) mucho.
2. Un día su mamá le (decir[4]): —Lleva en seguida esta jarrita de miel[c] a casa de tu abuelita. Ten cuidado[d] con el lobo[e] feroz.
3. En el bosque, el lobo (salir[5]) a hablar con la niña. Le (preguntar[6]): —¿Adónde vas, Caperucita? Esta le (contestar[7]) dulcemente:[f] —Voy a casa de mi abuelita.

[a]Érase... ¿ ?   [b]¿ ?   [c]jarrita... *jar of honey*   [d]Ten... *Be careful*   [e]¿ ?   [f]*sweetly*

4.   **5.**   **6.**   **7.**

4. —Pues, si vas por este sendero,[g] vas a llegar antes, le (decir[8]) el malvado[h] lobo. Él (irse[9]) por otro camino más corto.

5. El lobo (llegar[10]) primero a la casa de la abuelita y (entrar[11]) silenciosamente. La abuelita (tener[12]) mucho miedo. (*Ella:* Saltar[13]) de la cama y (correr[14]) a esconderse.

6. Caperucita Roja (llegar[15]) por fin a la casa de la abuelita. (*Ella:* Encontrar[16]) a su «abuelita», que (estar[17]) en la cama. Le (decir[18]): —¡Qué dientes tan largos tienes! —¡Son para comerte mejor!— le (decir[19]) su «abuelita».

7. Una ardilla[i] del bosque (enterarse[20]) del peligro. Por eso le (avisar[21]) a un cazador.[j]

8.   **9.**   **10.**

8. El lobo (saltar[22]) de la cama y (abalanzarse[23]) sobre Caperucita. Ella (salir[24]) de la casa corriendo y pidiendo socorro[k] desesperadamente.

9. El cazador (ver[25]) lo que (ocurrir[26]). (*Él:* Dispararle[27]) al lobo y le (hacer[28]) huir.

10. Caperucita (regresar[29]) a la casa de su abuelita. La (*ella:* abrazar[30]) y le (prometer[31]) escuchar siempre los consejos de su mamá.

[g]*path* [h]*¿?* [i]*¿?* [j]*¿?* [k]*help*

Paso 2. Hay varias versiones del cuento de Caperucita Roja. La que acabas de leer termina felizmente, pero otras no. Con otros dos compañeros, vuelve a contar la historia, empezando por el dibujo número 7. Inventen un diálogo más largo entre Caperucita y el lobo y cambien por completo el final del cuento.

Vocabulario útil

atacar (qu)	to attack
comérselo/la	to eat something up
matar	to kill

Need more **practice?**
- Workbook/Laboratory Manual
- Online Learning Center [www.mhhe.com/apuntate]

Paso 2: Gramática   **doscientos ochenta y nueve** ▪ **289**

Conversación

A. Una historia famosa

Paso 1. La siguiente historia está narrada en el presente. Ponla en (*Change it to*) el pasado, usando los verbos en el pretérito.

La niña abre[1] la puerta y entra[2] en la casa. Ve[3] tres sillas. Se sienta[4] en la primera silla, luego en la segunda, pero no le gusta[5] ninguna. Por eso se sienta[6] en la tercera. Ve[7] tres platos de comida en la mesa y decide[8] comer el más pequeño. Luego, va[9] a la alcoba para descansar un poco. Después de probar[a] las camas grandes, se acuesta[10] en la cama más pequeña y se queda[11] dormida.

[a]*trying*

Paso 2. ¿Reconoces la historia? Es el cuento de Ricitos de Oro y los tres osos (*bears*). Pero el cuento es un poco aburrido tal como está escrito (*as it is written*) en el **Paso 1.** Mejóralo (*Improve it*) con palabras de **Vocabulario útil** y dando detalles y descripciones (usando el imperfecto). También debes terminar el cuento: ¿Qué pasó al final?

Vocabulario útil	
Había una vez ... + *noun*	Once upon a time there was . . .
Un día ... + *pret.*	
el bosque	forest
la casita	little house
huir (*like* **construir**)	to flee*

MODELO: Había una vez una niña que *se llamaba* Ricitos de Oro. Un día la niña *fue…*

B. Entrevista. Mi primer día de clases en la universidad

Paso 1. En parejas, hagan y contesten las siguientes preguntas.

1. ¿Cuál fue la primera clase que tuviste? ¿A qué hora era la clase y dónde era?
2. ¿Llegaste a clase con alguien? ¿Ya tenías tu libro de texto o lo compraste después?
3. ¿Qué hiciste después de entrar en la sala de clase? ¿Qué hacía el profesor o profesora?
4. ¿A quién conociste aquel día? ¿Ya conocías a algunos estudiantes de la clase? ¿A quiénes conocías?
5. ¿Aprendiste mucho durante la clase? ¿Ya sabías algo de esa materia?
6. Te gustó el profesor o profesora? Explica tu respuesta. ¿Cómo era?
7. ¿Cómo te sentías durante la clase? ¿Nervioso/a? ¿aburrido/a? ¿cómodo/a?
8. ¿Les dio tarea el profesor o profesora? ¿Pudiste hacerla fácilmente?
9. ¿Cambió con el tiempo tu primera impresión de la clase y del profesor o profesora o aún (*still*) tienes esa impresión? Explica tu respuesta.

Paso 2. Ahora digan a la clase por lo menos tres detalles interesantes que obtuvieron en la entrevista del **Paso 1.**

---

* *Remember, the full conjugations of verbs set in all color can be found in the Verb Charts on the Online Learning Centers.*

C. Entrevista: Unas preguntas sobre el pasado

Paso 1. En parejas, hagan y contesten las siguientes preguntas.

¿Cuántos años tenías cuando... ?

1. aprendiste a pasear en bicicleta
2. hiciste tu primer viaje en avión
3. tuviste tu primera cita (*date*)
4. empezaste a afeitarte
5. conseguiste tu licencia de manejar (*driver's license*)
6. abriste una cuenta corriente (*checking account*)
7. dejaste de crecer (*grow*)

Paso 2. Ahora, en parejas, hagan y contesten estas preguntas. **¡OJO!** No deben hablar con la misma persona del **Paso 1.**

¿Cuántos años tenías cuando tus padres... ?

1. te dejaron cruzar la calle (*street*) solo/a
2. te permitieron ir de compras solo/a
3. te dejaron acostarte después de las nueve
4. te dejaron estar en casa sin niñero/a
5. te permitieron usar la estufa
6. te dejaron ver una película para mayores de 17 años («*R*»)
7. te dejaron buscar tu primer trabajo

Paso 3. Ahora, en grupos de cuatro, comparen sus respuestas. ¿Son muy diferentes las respuestas que dieron? Entre todos, ¿quién tiene los padres más estrictos? ¿los menos estrictos?

D. Experiencias en el pasado

Paso 1. Escribe preguntas sobre una de las siguientes experiencias. En el **Paso 2,** vas a usar esas preguntas para entrevistar a uno de tus compañeros de clase. Haz por lo menos cinco preguntas, usando el pretérito o el imperfecto, según el contexto.

EXPERIENCIAS
aprender a pasear en bicicleta
el primer trabajo
la primera cita
la elección (*choice*) de universidad
la última (*last*) enfermedad
estar en la sala de emergencias/urgencias
el primer día de clases en la universidad

Paso 2. Ahora, en parejas, túrnense para hacerse preguntas sobre la experiencia del **Paso 1** que Uds. eligieron. No tiene que ser la misma experiencia.

¿Cuántos años tenías cuando aprendiste a pasear en bicicleta?

1 **Una refinería de petróleo en la isla de Curaçao** Se descubrieron los primeros yacimientos[a] de petróleo en Venezuela en los años 20.[b] Hoy día Venezuela ocupa el quinto lugar en la lista de países exportadores de petróleo.[c] El petróleo que se extrae frente a[d] las costas del país se refina en las islas de Curaçao y Aruba bajo la supervisión de PDVSA (Petróleos de Venezuela, S.A.[e]).

[a]deposits [b]años... 1920s [c]ocupa... is the fifth largest oil-exporting country [d]se... is extracted off [e]Sociedad Anónima (Incorporated)

2

El Lago de Maracaibo El Lago de Maracaibo es el lago más grande de Sudamérica y el único del mundo que se comunica con[a] el mar, a través del[b] Golfo de Venezuela. Se encuentra en el estado occidental[c] de Zulia.

[a]se... is connected to [b]a... through the [c]western

El Salto Ángel El Parque Nacional Canaima es un bello[a] ejemplo de la biodiversidad de Venezuela. En los 7,4[b] millones de acres del parque hay tepuyes,[c] grandes ríos y la joya[d] del parque, el Salto Ángel. Este[e] es el salto de caída libre[f] más alto del mundo.

[a]beautiful [b]siete coma cuatro [c]table-top formations [d]jewel [e]The latter [f]de... free-fall

3

Cametro, el metro[a] de Caracas Cametro es uno de los mejores ejemplos de transporte público de Latinoamérica. Hay cuatro líneas con unas cuarenta estaciones que llegan a casi todas las zonas de la ciudad. Gracias a la integración de los sistemas, los pasajeros pueden usar los mismos billetes tanto para el metro como para los autobuses.

[a]subway

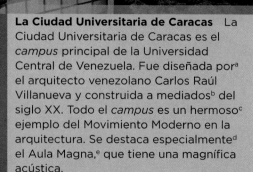

4

La Ciudad Universitaria de Caracas La Ciudad Universitaria de Caracas es el *campus* principal de la Universidad Central de Venezuela. Fue diseñada por[a] el arquitecto venezolano Carlos Raúl Villanueva y construida a mediados[b] del siglo XX. Todo el *campus* es un hermoso[c] ejemplo del Movimiento Moderno en la arquitectura. Se destaca especialmente[d] el Aula Magna,[e] que tiene una magnífica acústica.

[a]diseñada... designed by [b]construida... built around the middle [c]beautiful [d]Se... Especially noteworthy is [e]Aula... Main Amphitheater

5

¿Recuerdas?

Before learning how to express reciprocal actions in **Gramática 30,** review the reflexive pronouns in **Gramática 13 (Cap. 4),** then provide the correct reflexive pronouns for the following sentences.

1. _____ levanté a las ocho y media.

2. Laura _____ puso el vestido.

3. Mis amigos y yo _____ sentamos en un café.

4. ¿Prefieres duchar_____ o bañar_____?

30 Expressing _each other_ (Part 2) • Reciprocal Actions with Reflexive Pronouns

Gramática en acción: La amistad

Los buenos amigos...

- se conocen bien.
- se respetan.
- se quieren.
- se recuerdan siempre.

En las culturas hispánicas, cuando las buenas amigas se encuentran, se besan en la mejilla.*

¿Y tú? Cuando tú y tus amigos se encuentran, ¿cómo se saludan (_do you greet each other_)? ¿Se dan la mano (_hand_)? ¿Se besan?

1. Reciprocal Actions The plural reflexive pronouns, **nos, os,** and **se,** can be used to express _reciprocal actions_ (**las acciones recíprocas**). Reciprocal actions are usually expressed in English with _each other_ or _one another._	**Nos** queremos. _We love each other._ ¿**Os** ayudáis? _Do you help one another?_ **Se** miran. _They're looking at each other._
2. Important Reciprocal Action Verbs Verbs frequently used in this way include those at right, but any verb to whose meaning the phrase _each other_ can be added can be used to express a reciprocal action: **hablarse, mirarse,** and so on.	**abrazarse (c)** to embrace **besarse** to kiss each other **darse la mano** to shake hands **encontrarse** to meet **(se encuentran)** **quererse** to love; to be fond of **pelearse** to fight with each other **saludarse** to greet each other

**Friendship**   Good friends . . . • know each other well. • respect each other. • are fond of each other. • always remember each other. In Hispanic cultures, when close women friends meet, they kiss each other on the cheek.

*As in many cultures, in Spain and Latin America kissing on the cheek (**la mejilla**) is a common form of greeting and leave-taking. In Hispanic cultures, women kiss each other on the cheek, and men and women kiss each other on the cheek, but men and men do not. The number of kisses varies from country to country. In Spain, two kisses (one on each cheek) is common. In much of Latin America, only one kiss, usually on the right cheek, is the norm.

Práctica

A. ¡Anticipemos! Los buenos amigos. Indica las oraciones que describen lo que hacen tú y uno de tus mejores amigos para mantener su amistad (*friendship*).

1. ❏ Nos vemos con frecuencia.
2. ❏ Nos conocemos muy bien. No hay secretos entre nosotros.
3. ❏ Nos respetamos mucho.
4. ❏ Nos ayudamos cuando necesitamos ayuda.
5. ❏ Nos escribimos cuando estamos en lugares distantes.
6. ❏ Nos hablamos por teléfono con frecuencia.
7. ❏ Nos decimos la verdad siempre, lo bueno y lo malo.
8. ❏ Cuando no nos hablamos por mucho tiempo, comprendemos que es porque estamos muy ocupados.

B. ¿Qué pasa entre ellos? Describe las siguientes relaciones familiares o sociales, haciendo oraciones completas con una palabra o frase de cada columna.

> **MODELO:** Los buenos amigos se conocen bien.

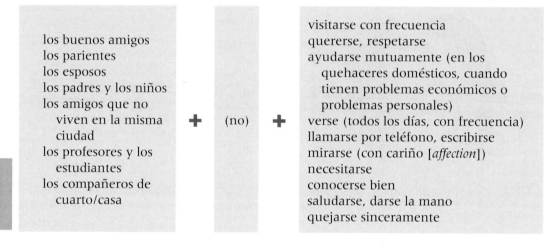

los buenos amigos
los parientes
los esposos
los padres y los niños
los amigos que no viven en la misma ciudad
los profesores y los estudiantes
los compañeros de cuarto/casa

+ (no) **+**

visitarse con frecuencia
quererse, respetarse
ayudarse mutuamente (en los quehaceres domésticos, cuando tienen problemas económicos o problemas personales)
verse (todos los días, con frecuencia)
llamarse por teléfono, escribirse
mirarse (con cariño [*affection*])
necesitarse
conocerse bien
saludarse, darse la mano
quejarse sinceramente

Conversación

Entrevista: Preguntas sobre tus relaciones

Paso 1. Haz por lo menos una pregunta con cada uno de los siguientes verbos. En el **Paso 2,** vas a usar esas preguntas para entrevistar a uno de tus compañeros de clase sobre las relaciones personales de él/ella con su pareja (esposo/a o novio/a), sus amigos, sus padres y sus parientes.

> **MODELOS:** ¿Tus parientes y tú se saludan dándose la mano?
> ¿Tu pareja y tú se besan en público?

1. verse
2. escribirse
3. mantenerse en contacto
4. llamarse por teléfono

5. abrazarse
6. besarse
7. saludarse dándose la mano
8. pelearse

Paso 2. Ahora, en parejas, túrnense para hacerse las preguntas del **Paso 1.** Luego digan a la clase lo que tienen en común.

Lengua y cultura: La leyenda del Lago de Maracaibo. Complete the following legend with the correct form of the word in parentheses, as suggested by context. The verbs will be in the preterite or imperfect. When two possibilities are given in parentheses, select the correct word.

En una tribu indígena de Venezuela, había una vez[a] un cacique[b] que se llamaba Zapara. Este[c] tenía una hija, Maruma, que (ser[1]) muy bonita. Al padre y a la hija (se / les[2]) (gustar[3]) pasar tiempo juntos y siempre caminaban por el bosque.[d]

Un día Zapara (comprender[4]) que su hija ya (ser[5]) una mujer y (se / le[6]) (decir[7]): «Debes escoger[e] esposo, pues ya tienes edad[f] para formar una familia. Pero (su / tu[8]) esposo debe ser guerrero,[g] como todos los hombres de nuestra familia». Maruma (ponerse[9]) triste porque debía separarse de su padre para casarse.[h]

Un residente del Lago de Maracaibo en su lancha (*boat*)

Un día, mientras su padre (estar[10]) ausente visitando otras tribus, Maruma (salir[11]) sola a cazar[i] en el bosque. Estaba a punto de dispararle a un ciervo[j] cuando (un / —[12]) otro cazador[k] (matar[13])[l] al animal. El otro cazador era un joven guapo y simpático. Maruma (ponerse[14]) muy enojada[m] y le gritó:[n] «¿Quién te (dar[15]) permiso para cazar en este bosque?» El joven le contestó: «El ciervo es para (tú / ti[16]). Sólo quiero conocerte. Me llamo Tamaré». A partir de ese día[ñ] los (joven[17]) (hacerse[18])[o] amigos. Pronto se enamoraron.[p]

Pero el joven no era guerrero y por eso el padre de Maruma (enojarse[19]) mucho cuando (saber[20]) que ella (querer[21]) casarse con él. Se enfadó tanto[q] que la naturaleza reaccionó y (haber[22]) grandes terremotos[r] e inundaciones:[s] las aguas cubrieron[t] las tierras del cacique Zapara y también a su hija con su amado,[u] formando así el Lago de Maracaibo. Zapara se convirtió en una de sus pequeñas islas.

[a]había... *once upon a time there was* [b]*chief* [c]*He* [d]*forest* [e]*choose* [f]ya... *you're old enough* [g]*warrior* [h]*get married* [i]*hunt* [j]Estaba... *She was about to shoot a deer* [k]*hunter* [l]*to kill* [m]ponerse... *to become very angry* [n]le... *she shouted at him* [ñ]A... *From that day on* [o]*to become* [p]se... *they fell in love* [q]Se... *He was so angry* [r]*earthquakes* [s]*floods* [t]*covered* [u]*beloved*

Comprensión. Contesta las siguientes preguntas.

1. ¿Quién era Zapara?
2. ¿Qué debía hacer su hija?
3. ¿De quién estaba enamorada (*in love*) Maruma?
4. ¿Por qué se enfadó Zapara?
5. ¿Cómo se formó el Lago de Maracaibo?

En resumen

Gramática en breve

29. Using the Preterite and the Imperfect

Do you know which tense to use to express habitual or repeated actions?
Which tense should be used to express the beginnings or end of an action?

Preterite Uses	Imperfect Uses
beginning/end of an action	habitual/repeated action
completed action	ongoing action
series of completed actions	background information
interrupting action	interrupted action

30. Reciprocal Actions with Reflexive Pronouns

Reciprocal Pronouns

nos, os, se

Vocabulario

Los verbos

abrazarse (c)	to embrace
besarse	to kiss each other
darse la mano	to shake hands
encontrarse	to meet (someone
(me encuentro) (con)	somewhere)
quererse	to love each other; to be
	fond of each other
saludarse	to greet each other

respirar	to breathe
sacar (qu)	to extract
sacar la lengua	to stick out one's tongue
sacarle un diente/	to extract (someone's)
una muela	tooth/molar
tener dolor de	to have a pain/ache in
tomarle la temperatura	to take someone's
	temperature
toser	to cough

Repaso: caminar, comer, correr, dormir (duermo) (u), enfermarse, hacer ejercicio, llevar (to wear), practicar (qu) deportes, sentirse (me siento) (i)

La salud y el bienestar

la rueda de molino	treadmill

Repaso: la comida

cansarse	to get tired
cuidarse	to take care of oneself
dejar de + inf.	to stop (doing something)
doler (duele)	to hurt, ache
examinar	to examine
guardar cama	to stay in bed
hacer...	to do . . .
ejercicios aeróbicos	aerobics
(el método) Pilates	Pilates
(el) yoga	yoga
llevar una vida	to lead a healthy/calm
sana/tranquila	life
molestar	to bother
ponerle una	to give (someone) a shot,
inyección	injection
resfriarse (me resfrío)	to get/catch a cold

Algunas partes del cuerpo humano

la boca	mouth
la cabeza	head
el cerebro	brain
el corazón	heart
el cuerpo	body
el diente	(front) tooth
el estómago	stomach
la garganta	throat
la muela	molar, back tooth
la nariz	nose
el oído	inner ear
el ojo	eye
la oreja	(outer) ear
los pulmones	lungs
la sangre	blood

Las enfermedades y los tratamientos

el bienestar	well-being
el chequeo	check-up
el consultorio	(medical) office
el dolor (de)	pain, ache (in)
la enfermedad	illness, sickness
la fiebre	fever
las gafas	glasses
la gripe	flu
el jarabe	(cough) syrup
los lentes de contacto	contact lenses
la pastilla	pill
la receta	prescription
el resfriado	cold
la sala de emergencias/ urgencia	emergency room
la salud	health
el síntoma	symptom
la tos	cough
el tratamiento	treatment

Cognados: el antibiótico, la medicina, la temperatura

El personal médico

el/la enfermero/a	nurse
el/la farmacéutico/a	pharmacist

Cognado: el/la dentista, el/la paciente

Repaso: el/la médico/a

Otro sustantivo

la cita	date; appointment

Los adjetivos

mareado/a	dizzy; nauseated
pasado/a	past, last
resfriado/a	congested, stuffed up
sano/a	healthy

Palabras adicionales

anoche	last night
anteayer	the day before yesterday
de repente	suddenly
desgraciadamente	unfortunately
dos veces	twice
en seguida	right away
eso quiere decir...	that means . . .
lo bueno	the good thing/news
lo malo	the bad thing/news
lo suficiente	enough

Repaso: ayer, de joven, de niño/a, mientras, siempre, una vez

 VOCABULARIO PERSONAL

Vocabularies

This **Spanish-English Vocabulary** contains all the words that appear in the text, with the following exceptions: (1) most close or identical cognates that do not appear in the chapter vocabulary lists; (2) most conjugated verb forms; (3) diminutives ending in **-ito/a;** (4) absolute superlatives in **-ísimo/a;** and (5) most adverbs ending in **-mente.** Active vocabulary is indicated by the number of the chapter in which a word or given meaning is first listed (**PP = Primeros pasos**); vocabulary that is glossed in the text is not considered to be active vocabulary and is not numbered. Only meanings that are used in the text are given. The **English-Spanish Vocabulary** is based on the chapter lists of active vocabulary.

The gender of nouns is indicated, except for masculine nouns ending in **-o** and feminine nouns ending in **-a.** Because **ch** and **ll** are no longer considered separate letters, words beginning with **ch** and **ll** are found as they would be found in English. The letter **ñ** follows the letter **n: añadir** follows **anuncio,** for example.

Irregular verbs found in the verb charts of Appendix 4 on the Online Learning Center are set all in color: andar. Verbs with stem changes or spelling changes in the *present tense* show the **yo** form of the present tense in parentheses with the stem-vowel or spelling changes indicated in color: **sentarse (me siento); conocer (conozco); escoger (escojo); actuar (actúo).** Verbs with stem changes in the third person *preterite* and the *present participle* show the stem vowel (**i** or **u**) in parentheses after the present tense **yo** form: **preferir (prefiero) (i); morirse (me muero) (u).** Verbs with any other spelling changes in the *preterite* show the change in parentheses: **buscar (qu); pagar (gu); empezar (empiezo) (c); averiguar (ü).**

The following abbreviations are used:

adj.	adjective	*form.*	formal	*obj.*	object
adv.	adverb	*gram.*	grammatical term	*(of prep.)*	(of a preposition)
Arg.	Argentina	*Guat.*	Guatemala	*pl.*	plural
Bol.	Bolivia	*ind. art.*	indefinite article	*poss.*	possessive
C.A.	Central America	*inf.*	infinitive	*p.p.*	past participle
Carib.	Caribbean	*i.o.*	indirect object	*prep.*	preposition
Ch.	Chile	*interj.*	interjection	*pron.*	pronoun
coll.	colloquial	*inv.*	invariable form	*refl. pron.*	reflexive pronoun
conj.	conjunction	*L.A.*	Latin America	*s.*	singular
def. art.	definite article	*m.*	masculine	*sl.*	slang
d.o.	direct object	*Mex.*	Mexico	*Sp.*	Spain
f.	feminine	*n.*	noun	*sub. pron.*	subject pronoun
fam.	familiar			*Uru.*	Uruguay

Spanish–English Vocabulary

A

a to (PP); at (*with time*) (PP); to the (3); **a base de** based on; **a casa** (with **regresar**) home (1); **a causa de** because of; **a continuación** following, below; **a dieta** (with **estar**) on a diet (6); **a la derecha de** to the right of (5); **a la izquierda de** to the left of (5); **a la(s)...** at . . . (*time of day*) (PP); **a la vez** at the same time; **a lo largo de** along; throughout; **a menos que** *conj.* unless (15); **a menudo** *adv.* often; **a partir de** as of; from (*this moment, date*) on; **a plazos** in installments (16); **a primera vista** at first sight (15); **¿a qué hora?** at what time? (PP); **a tiempo** on time (7); **a toda velocidad** at full speed; **a través de** across; through; throughout; **a veces** sometimes, at times (2)

abajo below, underneath
abalanzarse (c) (sobre) to pounce (on)
abandonar to abandon; to leave
abierto/a (*p.p. of* **abrir**) open(ed) (5)
abogado/a lawyer (16)
abolicionista *n. m., f.* abolitionist
abolir to abolish
abrazarse (c) to embrace, hug (10)
abrazo embrace, hug; **dar(se) un abrazo** to give (each other) a hug

abrigo coat (3)
abril *m.* April (5)
abrir (*p.p.* **abierto**) to open (2)
absoluto/a absolute; **en absoluto** at all
abstracto/a abstract
absurdo/a absurd (13); **es absurdo que...** it's absurd that . . . (13)
abuelo/a grandfather/grandmother (2); *m. pl.* grandparents (2)
abundante abundant
aburrido/a bored (5); **ser aburrido/a** to be boring (9)
aburrir to bore (13); **aburrirse** to get bored (9)
abuso abuse

acabar to finish; to run out of; to use up completely (11); **acabar de +** *inf.* to have just (*done something*) (6); **acabar por +** *inf.* to end up (*doing something*)

academia academy

académico/a *adj.* academic

acaso: por si acaso just in case

acceso access

acción *f.* action; **Día** (*m.*) **de Acción de Gracias** Thanksgiving

aceite *m.* oil (6); **aceite de oliva/canola** olive/canola oil; **revisar el aceite** to check the oil (14)

acelerado/a fast, accelerated (14)

acelerar to accelerate, speed up

acento accent

acentuado/a accentuated

aceptar to accept

acera sidewalk (14)

acerca de *prep.* about, concerning

acercarse (qu) (a) to come near (to); to become more familiar (with)

acertar (acierto) to ascertain

aclarar to clarify

acomodarse (a) to adapt oneself (to)

acompañar to accompany; to go with

acondicionado/a: aire (*m.*) **acondicionado** air conditioning

aconsejable advisable

aconsejar to advise

acontecimiento event, happening (17)

acorazado/a armored, steel-plated

acordarse (me acuerdo) (de) to remember (11)

acordeón *m.* accordion

acostarse (me acuesto) to go to bed (4)

acostumbrarse (a) to become accustomed (to), get used (to)

acre *m.* acre

acreditado/a accredited

acrílico acrylic

acrópolis *f.* acropolis

actitud *f.* attitude

actividad *f.* activity

activo/a active

actor *m.* actor (13)

actriz *f.* (*pl.* **actrices**) actress (13)

actual *adj.* current, present-day

actualidad *f.* present time

acuario aquarium; **Acuario** Aquarius

acuático/a: deportes (*m. pl.*) **acuáticos** water sports

acueducto aqueduct

acuerdo agreement; **de acuerdo** agreed; **de acuerdo con** in accordance with; **(no) estoy de acuerdo** I (don't) agree (2)

adaptar to adapt; **adaptarse (a)** to adapt oneself (to)

adecuado/a appropriate

adelante forward; **de ahora en adelante** from now on

adelgazar (c) to lose weight

además *adv.* moreover; **además de** *prep.* besides

adicional additional (PP)

adiós good-bye (PP)

adivinar to guess

administración *f.* administration (1); **administración de empresas** business administration (1)

admirar to admire

admitir to admit

adoctrinamiento indoctrination

adolescencia adolescence (15)

adolescente *n. m., f.* adolescent

¿adónde? where (to)? (3)

adoptar to adopt

adoquinado/a cobblestone

adornar to decorate

adorno decoration

adosado/a: casa adosada townhouse

aduana customs (18); **inspector(a) de aduana** customs agent (18)

adulto/a adult

adverbio adverb

aeróbico/a: hacer ejercicios aeróbicos to do aerobics (10)

aerolínea airline

aeropuerto airport (7)

afectar to affect

afectivo/a emotional (8); **estado afectivo** emotional state (8)

afectuoso/a affectionate

afeitarse to shave oneself (4)

afición *f.* pastime, fun activity, hobby (9)

aficionado/a fan (9); **ser aficionado/a (a)** to be a fan (of) (9)

afirmación *f.* statement

afirmar to affirm, state

afirmativo/a affirmative

afortunadamente fortunately

africano/a *n., adj.* African

afuera *adv.* outside, outdoors (5)

afueras *n. pl.* outskirts (12); suburbs (12)

agencia agency (7); **agencia de compra-ventas (de coches)** used car dealership; **agencia de viajes** travel agency (7)

agenda agenda; date book; **agenda digital/electrónica** electronic agenda, PDA

agente *m., f.* agent (7); **agente de viajes** travel agent (7)

ágil agile

agobiado/a overwhelmed

agosto August (5)

agotador(a) exhausting

agotar to use up

agradecer (agradezco) to thank; to be grateful

agradecido/a grateful

agresivo/a aggressive

agrícola *adj. m., f.* agricultural

agricultor(a) farmer (14)

agricultura agriculture

agroturismo agrotourism

agua *f.* (*but* **el agua**) water (6); **agua dulce** fresh water; **agua mineral** mineral water (6); **agua salada** salt water; **huevo pasado por agua** poached egg; **se le hace agua la boca** it makes your mouth water

aguacate *m.* avocado

aguar (ü) to spoil (*a party*)

agujero small hole; piercing

ahí there

ahogar(se) (gu) to drown

ahora now (1); **ahora mismo** right now (5); at once; **de ahora en adelante** from now on

ahorrar to save (*money*) (16)

ahorros: cuenta de ahorros savings account (16)

aire *m.* air (14); **aire acondicionado** air conditioning; **aire puro** clean air; **al aire libre** outdoors; **contaminación** (*f.*) **del aire** air pollution

aislamiento isolation

ajedrez *m.* chess (9); **jugar (juego) (gu) al ajedrez** to play chess (9)

al (*contraction of* **a + el**) to the (3); **al + inf.** upon, while, when (*doing something*); **al aire libre** outdoors; **al alcance** within reach; **al contrario** on the contrary; **al día siguiente** the next day; **al fondo** in the background; **al lado de** *prep.* alongside of (5); beside; next to; **al principio de** at the beginning of (16); **al revés** backward

alcanzar (c) to reach; to achieve

alce *m.* elk; moose

alcoba bedroom (4)

alcohol *m.* alcohol

alcohólico/a *adj.* alcoholic

alegrarse (de) to be happy (about) (12)

alegre happy (5)

alemán *m.* German (*language*) (1)

alemán, alemana *n., adj.* German (2)

Alemania Germany

alergeno allergen

alergia allergy; **tener alergia a** to be allergic to

alérgico/a: ser alérgico/a a to be allergic to

alertar to alert

alerto/a: ojo alerta eagle eye

alfombra rug (4)

alfombrado/a carpeted

algo something, anything (3)

algodón *m.* cotton (3); **es de algodón** it's made of cotton (3)

alguien someone, anyone (6); **caerle bien/mal a alguien** to make a good/bad impression on someone

algún, alguno/a some, any (6); **algún día** some day; **algún lugar** some place; **alguna vez** once; ever

alianza alliance

aliviar to alleviate

allá over there (3); **más allá** further, farther; **más allá de** beyond

allí there (3)

almacén *m.* department store (3)

almacenar to store, save (12)

almohada pillow (18)

almorzar (almuerzo) (c) to have lunch (4)

almuerzo lunch (6)

alojamiento lodging (18)

alojarse to stay (*in a place*) (18)

Alpes *m. pl.* Alps

alpinismo mountain climbing; **practicar (qu) el alpinismo** to mountain climb

alpinista *m., f.* mountain climber

alquilar to rent (12)

alquiler *m.* rent (12)

altar *m.* altar

alternado/a alternate, alternating

alternativa alternative

alto/a tall (2); high; **alto colesterol** high cholesterol; **en voz alta** aloud; **más alto** louder

altura altitude

amable kind (2); nice (2)

amado/a *adj.* beloved

amar to love (15)

amarillo/a yellow (3)

Amazonas *m. s.* Amazon (River); **Selva Amazonas** Amazon Jungle

ambiental environmental

ambiente *m.* atmosphere, environment; **medio ambiente** environment (*nature*) (14)

ambos/as both

América Central Central America

americano/a American; **fútbol** (*m.*) **americano** football; **jugar (juego) (gu) al fútbol americano** to play football

amigo/a friend (1); **encontrarse (me encuentro) con amigos** to get together with friends

amistad *f.* friendship (15)

amistoso/a friendly (15)

amo/a (ama *f. but* **el ama**) **de casa** (16)

amoblar (amueblo) to furnish

amor *m.* love (15)

amplio/a wide, broad

amueblado/a furnished

amurallado/a walled

análisis *m. inv.* analysis

analista *m., f.* analyst (16); **analista de sistemas** systems analyst (16)

analizar (c) to analyze

anaranjado/a orange (3)

ancho/a wide; **de ancho** in width

anciano/a *n.* old person; *adj.* old; ancient

andar to walk; **andar en bicicleta** to ride a bicycle

andino/a *adj.* Andean

anémico/a anemic

anfibio amphibian

anfiteatro amphitheater

anfitrión, anfitriona host(ess) (8)

anglohablante *m., f.* English-speaker

anglosajón, anglosajona *adj.* Anglo Saxon

anillo ring

animado/a lively; animated; **dibujos animados** cartoons

animal *m.* animal (14); **animal doméstico** pet (14); domesticated animal (14); **animal salvaje** wild animal (14)

animarse to cheer, brighten up; **anímate** cheer up

ánimo: dar ánimo to cheer up; **estado de ánimo** state of mind

aniversario anniversary

anoche *adv.* last night (10)

ansiedad *f.* anxiety, worry, nervousness

ante *prep.* before; in front of; **ante todo** above all; first of all

anteayer *adv.* the day before yesterday (10)

antecedente *m.* antecedent

antemano: de antemano beforehand

anterior previous, preceding

antes *adv.* before; **antes de** *prep.* before (4); **antes (de) que** *conj.* before (15)

antibiótico antibiotic (10)

anticipación: con anticipación in advance; ahead of time (18); **de anticipación** ahead

anticipar to anticipate

anticuado/a antiquated, old-fashioned

antiguo/a old; ancient; former

antillano/a: Islas Antillanas Antilles Islands

antipático/a unpleasant (2)

antónimo antonym

antropología anthropology

antropólogo/a anthropologist

anudado/a knotted

anunciar to announce (7)

anuncio announcement; advertisement; **anuncios clasificados** classified ads

añadir to add

año year (5); **al año** yearly, per year; **cada año** every year; **cumplir años** to have a birthday; **de los últimos años** in recent years; **el año entrante** next year; **el año pasado** last year; **el año que viene** next year; **el próximo año** next year; **Feliz Año Nuevo** Happy New Year; **por año** yearly, per year; **tener... años** to be . . . years old (2); **los años sesenta (ochenta...)** the sixties . . . (eighties...); **todo el año** all year

apagar (gu) to turn off (*lights, appliance*) (11); **apagar las luces** to turn out the lights; **apagarse** to go out (*lights*)

Apalaches: Montes (*m. pl.*) **Apalaches** Appalachian Mountains

aparato appliance (9); **aparato doméstico** home appliance (9); **aparato electrónico** electronic device

aparcar (qu) to park

apartamento apartment (1); **edificio de apartamentos** apartment building (12)

apartar to set aside; to separate

apellido surname

apio celery

apoyo support; help

apreciado/a appreciated

aprender to learn (2); **aprender a +** *inf.* to learn how to (*do something*) (2)

aprendizaje *m.* learning

apropiación *f.* appropriation

apropiado/a appropriate

aproximadamente approximately

apuntar to write down

apuntes *m. pl.* notes (*academic*) (11)

aquel, aquella *adj.* that (*over there*) (3); *pron.* that one (*over there*)

aquello that, that thing (*over there*) (3)

aquellos/as *adj.* those (*over there*) (3); *pron.* those ones (*over there*)

aquí here (1)

árabe *m.* Arabic (*language*); *n. m., f.* Arab

árbol *m.* tree (14); **árbol de Navidad** Christmas tree

archipiélago archipelago

archivo (computer) file (12)

arco arch

ardilla squirrel

área *f.* (*but* **el área**) area

arena sand

arete *m.* earring (3)

argentino/a *n., adj.* Argentine

argumento argument

árido/a arid, dry

aristocrático/a aristocratic

arma *f.* (*but* **el arma**) weapon

armario closet (4)

arpa *f.* (*but* **el arpa**) harp

arpista *m., f.* harpist

arqueológico/a archeological

arqueólogo/a archeologist

arquitecto/a architect (13)

arquitectura architecture (13)
arrancar (qu) to start up (*a car*) (14)
arreglar to fix (14); to repair
arroba @ ["at" sign]
arrogante arrogant
arroz *m.* rice (6)
arte *f.* (*but* **el arte**) art (1); **bellas artes** fine arts; **las artes** the arts (13); **obra de arte** work of art (13)
artesanía arts and crafts (13)
artesano/a artisan
artículo article; **artículo definido** *gram.* definite article
artificial: fuegos artificiales fireworks
artista *m., f.* artist (13)
artístico/a artistic
arvejas peas (6)
asado/a roast(ed) (6); **lechón** (*m.*) **asado** roast suckling pig; **pollo asado** roast chicken (6)
ascendencia ancestry, descent
ascensor *m.* elevator
asegurado/a insured
asegurar to assure
asesinar murder
asesinato murder; assassination (17)
así thus, so; **así como** as well as; **así que** therefore, consequently, so
asiático/a *adj.* Asian
asiento seat (7); **asiento de ventanilla** window seat
asignar(se) to assign (oneself)
asistencia assistance; care
asistente *m., f.* assistant (7); **asistente de vuelo** flight attendant (7); **asistente social** social worker
asistir (a) to attend, go to (*a class, function*) (2)
asociación *f.* association
asociado/a: estado libre asociado commonwealth
asociar to associate
aspecto aspect; appearance
aspiradora vacuum cleaner (9); **pasar la aspiradora** to vacuum (9)
aspirante *m., f.* candidate, applicant (16)
aspirina aspirin
astronauta *m., f.* astronaut (16)
astronomía astronomy
asumir to assume
asunto question, matter
atacar (qu) to attack
atado/a tied up
ataque *m.* **(terrorista)** (terrorist) attack (17)
atención *f.* attention
atender (atiendo) to attend to; to serve
atento/a attentive
Atlántico: (océano) Atlántico Atlantic (Ocean)
atleta *m., f.* athlete

atlético/a athletic
atmósfera atmosphere
atono/a *gram.* unstressed
atracción *f.* attraction
atractivo/a attractive
atraer (*like* **traer**) to attract (13)
atrás *adv.* back, backward; behind; **de atrás** backwards
atrasado/a: estar atrasado/a to be late (7)
atrevido/a daring
atún *m.* tuna (6)
audiencia audience
auditorio auditorium
aula *f.* (*but* **el aula**) classroom
aumentar to increase
aumento increase; raise (12); **aumento de sueldo** raise (*in salary*)
aun *adv.* even
aún *adv.* still, yet
aunque although
auscultar to listen (*with a stethoscope*)
ausente absent
auténtico/a authentic
autobús *m.* bus (7); **estación** (*f.*) **de autobuses** bus station (7) **ir en autobús** to go/travel by bus (7); **parada del autobús** bus stop (18)
automático/a automatic; **cajero automático** ATM (16); **contestador** (*m.*) **automático** answering machine; **tarjeta de cobro automático** debit card
automóvil *m.* automobile
automovilístico/a *adj.* automobile
autonomía autonomy
autónomo/a autonomous
autopista freeway (14)
autoprueba self-test
autor(a) author
autorretrato self-portrait
autostop: hacer autostop to hitchhike
avanzar (c) to advance
avenida avenue (12)
aventura adventure
aventurado/a adventurous
aventurero/a adventurous
aventurismo adventure tourism
aventurista *m., f.* adventure tourist
avergonzado/a embarrassed (8)
averiguar (ü) to find out
avestruz *m.* (*pl.* **avestruces**) ostrich
avión *m.* airplane (7); **billete** (*m.*) **de avión** plane ticket; **ir en avión** to go/travel by plane (7); **volar (vuelo) en avión** to fly, go by plane (7)
avisar to warn
¡ay! *interj.* ah!; ouch!
ayer yesterday (4); **ayer fue (miércoles)** yesterday was (Wednesday) (4)
ayuda *n.* help (6)

ayudar to help (6)
azteca *n., adj. m., f.* Aztec
azúcar *m.* sugar (6)
azul blue (3)

B

baba saliva; **se le cae la baba** he/she is drooling
bachiller *m.* Bachelor's degree
bahía bay
bailar to dance (1)
bailarín, bailarina dancer (13)
baile *m.* dance (13); **baile de salón** ballroom dance; **salón** (*m.*) **de baile** ballroom
bajado/a lowered
bajar to lower; **bajarse de** to get down, from, off (7)
bajo *prep.* under
bajo/a *adj.* low; short (*in height*) (2); **clase** (*f.*) **baja** lower class; **hablar en voz baja** to speak softly; **planta baja** ground floor (12)
balcón *m.* balcony
baldío/a uncultivated; waste (*land*)
Baleares: Islas Baleares Balearic Islands
ballena whale (14)
ballet *m.* ballet (13)
balneario thermal spa
baloncesto basketball (*Sp.*)
bamba *folkloric dance of Veracruz, Mexico*
banana banana (6)
bancario/a *adj.* bank; **tarjeta bancaria** debit card
banco bank (16)
bandoneón *m.* large concertina
bantú *n., adj. m., f.* Bantu
bañar to bathe; **bañarse** to take a bath (4)
bañera bathtub (4)
baño bathroom (4); **habitación** (*f.*) **con/sin baño** room with(out) bath (18); **traje** (*m.*) **de baño** bathing suit (3)
bar *m.* bar (9); **ir a un bar** to go to a bar (9)
barato/a inexpensive (3)
barbacoa barbecue (6)
barbaridad *f.*: **¡qué barbaridad!** how awful!
barbería barber's shop
barbero/a barber
barco boat, ship (7); **ir en barco** to go/travel by boat, ship (7)
barra bar; railing
barrer (el piso) to sweep (the floor) (9)
barrera barrier
barrio neighborhood (12)
barroco/a Baroque

basar to base; to support (*an opinion*); **basarse en** to base one's ideas, opinions on

base *f.* base, foundation; basis; **a base de** based on

básico/a basic

basílica basilica

basquetbol *m.* basketball (9); **jugar (juego) (gu) al basquetbol** to play basketball

bastante rather, sufficiently (15); enough (15)

basura trash, garbage (9); **sacar (qu) la basura** to take out the garbage (9)

basurero trashcan

bata robe

batería battery (14); drum set

batido milkshake (18)

bautizo baptism

beber to drink (2)

bebida drink (4); beverage

beca scholarship

béisbol *m.* baseball (9); **jugar (juego) (gu) al béisbol** to play baseball

beisbolista *m., f.* baseball player

Bélgica Belgium

bello/a beautiful (14); **Bella Durmiente** Sleeping Beauty; **bellas artes** *f. pl.* fine arts

beneficiarse (de) to benefit (from)

beneficio benefit

besar(se) to kiss (each other) (10)

beso kiss

biblioteca library (1)

bibliotecario/a librarian (1)

bicicleta (de montaña) (mountain) bike (12); **andar/montar en bicicleta** to ride a bicycle; **pasear en bicicleta** to ride a bicycle (9)

bien *adv.* well (PP); **bien pagado** well-paid (16); **caerle bien a alguien** to make a good impression on someone; **estar bien** to be comfortable (*temperature*) (5); **llevarse bien (con)** to get along well (with) (15); **(muy) bien** fine, (very) well (PP); **pasarlo bien** to have a good time (8); **salir bien** to turn, come out well (4)

bienestar *m.* well-being (10)

bilingüe bilingual

billete *m.* bill (*money*) (16); ticket (*Sp.*) (7); **billete de ida/vuelta** one-way/round-trip ticket (7)

billón *m.* billion

biodiversidad *f.* biodiversity

biología biology

biosfera biosphere

bisonte *m.* bison

bistec *m.* steak (6)

blanco/a white (3); **espacio en blanco** blank space; **vino blanco** white wine (6)

blindado/a armor-plated

blog *m.* blog (17)

blusa blouse (3)

boca mouth (10); **se le hace agua la boca** it makes your mouth water

bocina horn (14); **tocar (qu) la bocina** to honk (14)

boda wedding (15)

bolero love song

boleto ticket (*L.A.*) (7); **boleto de ida/vuelta** one-way/round-trip ticket (7)

bolígrafo pen (1)

boliviano/a *n., adj. m., f.* Bolivian

bolsa purse (3)

bolsillo pocket

bomba bomb (17)

bombardear to bomb

bombardeo bombing

bonito/a pretty (2)

bono voucher

bordado/a embroidered

boricua *n. adj. inv.* Puerto Rican

bosque *m.* forest (14); **bosque lluvioso** rain forest; **bosque primario** old-growth forest

bota boot (3)

botana appetizer (8)

botella bottle

botones *m. inv.* bellhop (18)

boutique *f.* boutique

Brasil *m.* Brazil

brasileño/a *n., adj.* Brazilian

bravo/a fierce; brave

bravura ferocity; bravery

brazo arm (11)

breve brief

brillante brilliant, bright

británico/a *adj.* British

bromear to joke

bronce *m.* bronze

bruja witch

brujo warlock; magician

bucear to scuba dive; to snorkel

buen, bueno/a *adj.* good (2); **buenas noches** good evening, night (PP); **buenas tardes** good afternoon (PP); **bueno...** well . . . (2); **buenos días** good morning (PP); **es bueno que...** it's good that . . . ; **hace (muy) buen tiempo** it's (very) good weather (5); **lo bueno** the good thing (10); **sacar (qu) buenas notas** to get good grades (11); **tener buena suerte** to have good luck (11)

bulevar *m.* boulevard

bullicioso/a boisterous

busca: en busca de in search of

buscar (qu) to look for (1)

búsqueda search

C

caballero knight; gentleman

caballo horse; **montar a caballo** to ride a horse (9)

cabaña cabin

caber to fit

cabeza head (10); **dolerle (me duele) la cabeza** to have a headache (10); **dolor (m.) de cabeza** headache

cabina cabin (*on a ship*) (7)

cacique, cacica chief

cada *inv.* each, every (4); **cada vez más** increasingly

cadena channel (*television*); chain

caer to fall; **caerse** to fall down (11); **caerle bien/mal a alguien** to make a good/bad impression on someone; **se le cae la baba** he/she is drooling

café *m.* café (18); coffee (1); **(de) color café** brown (3); **granos de café** coffee beans

cafeína caffeine

cafetera coffeemaker (9)

cafetería cafeteria (1)

caída fall; **caída libre** free fall

caimán *m.* alligator

caja box; register; cashier window (16)

cajero/a cashier (16); **cajero automático** ATM (16)

cajón *m.* drawer

calabaza gourd

calcetines *m. pl.* socks (3)

calculadora calculator (1)

calcular to calculate; **máquina de calcular** calculator

cálculo calculus

caldera crater

calefacción *f.* heating (12)

calendario calendar (11)

calentar (caliento) to heat

calidad *f.* quality

calidez *f.* warmth

caliente hot (*temperature*) (6)

calipso *Caribbean music of African origin*

calle *f.* street (12)

callejero/a *adj.* street

calor *m.* heat; **hace (mucho) calor** it's (very) hot (5); **tener (mucho) calor** to be (very) warm, hot (5)

caloría calorie

caluroso/a warm

calzonudo/a timid

cama bed (4); **guardar cama** to stay in bed (10); **hacer la cama** to make the bed (9)

cámara (de vídeo/digital) (video/digital) camera (12)

camarero/a waiter, waitress (6)

camarones *m. pl.* shrimp (6)

cambiar (de) to change (12); **cambiar de canal** to change channels (12)

cambio change; **en cambio** on the other hand, on the contrary
camello camel
caminar to walk (9)
caminata walk; **dar/hacer una caminata** to take a walk
camino way; road, street
camioneta station wagon (7); van
camisa shirt (3)
camiseta T-shirt (3)
campamento campground
campanario bell tower
campaña: tienda de campaña tent (7)
campeonato championship
campesino/a farm worker, peasant (14)
camping m. campground (7); **hacer** *camping* to go camping (7)
campo field (14); countryside (12); **campo de fútbol** soccer field
campus m. inv. (university) campus (12)
Canadá m. Canada; **Día** (m.) **del Canadá** Canada Day
canadiense n., adj. m., f. Canadian
canal m. canal; channel (12); **cambiar de canal** to change channels (12)
cancelar to cancel
cáncer m. cancer
canción f. song (13)
candidato/a candidate (17); **postularse a un cargo como candidato** to run for office as a candidate (17)
candombe m. *Uruguayan drum music of African origins*
canola: aceite (m.) **de canola** canola oil
cansado/a tired (5)
cansarse to get tired (10)
cantante m., f. singer (13)
cantar to sing (1)
cántaro pitcher, jug
cantidad f. quantity
cantinero/a bartender
cañón m. cannon
capa layer (14); cape; **capa de ozono** ozone layer (14)
capacidad f. ability
capacitado/a trained
capaz (pl. **capaces**) capable, able
Caperucita Roja Little Red Ridinghood
capital f. capital (city) (5)
caprichoso/a capricious
Capricornio Capricorn
cara face
caracola large shell
característica n. characteristic
caracterizar (**c**) to characterize
cardar to comb, card (*wool*)
cardinal: punto cardinal cardinal direction (5)
cargar (**gu**) to carry
cargo position; post (17); **estar a cargo (de)** to be in control (of) (17);

postularse a un cargo como candidato to run for office as a candidate (17)
Caribe m. Caribbean; **mar** (m.) **Caribe** Caribbean Sea
caribeño/a n., adj. Caribbean
cariño affection
cariñoso/a affectionate (5)
Carnaval m. Carnival
carne f. meat (6)
caro/a expensive (3)
carpintero/a carpenter
carrera career; major (*academic*)
carreta cart
carretera highway (14)
carro (descapotable) (convertible) car (12)
carta letter (2); pl. cards (9); **carta de recomendación** letter of recommendation; **jugar (juego) (gu) a las cartas** to play cards; **papel** (m.) **para cartas** stationery (18)
cartel m. poster
cartera wallet (3); handbag (3)
cartón m. cardboard
casa house (2); **casa particular** private home; **en casa** at home (1); **limpiar la casa (entera)** to clean the (entire) house (9); **regresar a casa** to go home (1)
casado/a married (2); **recién casado/a (con)** newlywed (to) (15)
casamiento wedding
casarse (con) to get married (to) (15)
cascanueces m. inv. nutcracker
casi almost (2); **casi nunca** almost never (2)
caso case; **en caso de que** conj. in case (15)
castaño/a brown
castellano Spanish (language) (*Sp.*)
castigar (**gu**) to punish
castillo castle
catálogo catalog
catarata waterfall
catastrófico/a catastrophic
catedral f. cathedral
categoría category
católico/a n., adj. Catholic
catorce fourteen (PP)
causa cause; **a causa de** because of
causar to cause
cazador(a) hunter
cazar (**c**) to hunt
CD m. CD (12)
CD-ROM m. CD-ROM (12)
cebolla onion
celebración f. celebration
celebrar to celebrate (5)
celular: teléfono celular cell phone (12)
cementerio cemetery

cena dinner, supper (6)
cenar to have (eat) dinner, supper (6)
Cenicienta Cinderella
ceniza ash
centígrado Celsius
central central; **América Central** Central America
céntrico/a central
centro center; downtown (3); **centro comercial** shopping mall (3)
Centroamérica Central America
centroamericano/a n., adj. Central American
cepillarse los dientes to brush one's teeth (4)
cerámica pottery (13)
cerca adv. near, nearby, close; **cerca de** prep. close to (5); **de cerca** up close
cercano/a adj. close, near
cerdo pork (6); **chuleta de cerdo** pork chop (6)
cereal m. cereal (6)
cerebro brain (10)
cero zero (PP)
cerrado/a closed (5)
cerradura lock
cerrajería locksmith's shop
cerrar (cierro) to close (4)
cerro hill
certeza certainty
certificado/a certified
cervantino/a pertaining to (Miguel de) Cervantes
cerveza beer
césped m. lawn, grass
ceviche m. *raw fish dish*
champán m. champagne
champiñones m. pl. mushrooms
champú m. shampoo (18)
chanclas flip-flops (3)
chaqueta jacket (3)
charango *stringed instrument*
charlar to chat
checa Czech; **República Checa** Czech Republic
chele blond (*C.A.*)
cheque m. check (16); **cheque de viajero** traveler's check; **cobrar un cheque** (16) to cash a check; **talonario de cheques** checkbook (*Sp.*)
chequeo checkup (10)
chequera checkbook
chévere cool; **¡qué chévere!** cool!
chico/a boy, girl
chileno/a n., adj. Chilean
chimpancé m. chimpanzee
chino Chinese (*language*)
chino/a n., adj. Chinese
chirimía oboe
chirriar to screech
chirrido squawk, screech
chisme m. gossip

chiste *m.* joke (7)
chistoso/a funny
chocar (qu) con/contra to run into, bump against (11)
chocolate *m.* chocolate; hot chocolate
chofer *m., f.* driver
chola *indigenous woman of Bolivia*
choque *m.* collision (17); **choque de trenes** train wreck
chubasco rain shower
chuleta (de cerdo) (pork) chop (6)
ciclismo bicycling (9)
ciclo cycle
ciclón *m.* cyclone
ciego/a blind
cielo sky; heaven
cien, ciento one hundred (2); **por ciento** percent
ciencia science (1); **ciencia ficción** science fiction; **ciencias naturales** natural sciences (1); **ciencias políticas** political science (1); **ciencias sociales** social sciences (1)
cierto/a true; certain (13); **en cierta medida** in some measure, to some degree; **es cierto que...** it's true that . . . (13)
ciervo deer; stag
cigarrillo cigarette
cilantro cilantro, fresh coriander
cima peak
cinco five (PP)
cincuenta fifty (2)
cine *m.* movies (4); movie theater (4)
cineasta *m., f.* film director
cinta tape (12)
cinturón *m.* belt (3)
circulación *f.* traffic (14)
circular to circulate
círculo circle
circunstancia circumstance
cisne *m.* swan
cita date (6); appointment (10)
citado/a quoted; summoned; **estar citado/a con** to have an appointment with
ciudad *f.* city (2)
ciudadano/a citizen (17)
cívico/a civic (17)
civil civil
civilización *f.* civilization
claro/a clear
clase *f.* class (*of students*) (1); class, course (*academic*) (1); **clase baja** lower class; **clase particular** private class; **clase turística** tourist class (7); **compañero/a de clase** classmate (1); **primera clase** first class (7); **sala de clase** classroom; **salón** (*m.*) **de clase** classroom (1)
clásico/a classic(al) (13)

clasificado/a classified; **anuncios clasificados** classified ads
clasificar (qu) to classify
claustrofobia claustrophobia
cláusula *gram.* clause
clavadista *m., f.* diver
cliente/a client (1)
clima *m.* climate (5)
climático/a climatic
climatología climatology
clínica clinic
clínico/a clinical
club *m.* club
cobrar to charge; to cash (*a check*) (16); to charge (*someone for an item or service*) (16); **cobrar un cheque** to cash a check (16)
cobro: tarjeta de cobro automático debit card
coche *m.* car (2); **agencia de compraventas de coches** used car dealership; **coche de lujo** luxury car; **coche deportivo** sports car; **coche descapotable** convertible car
cocina kitchen (4); cuisine (6)
cocinar to cook (6)
cocinero/a cook (16); chef (16)
coco coconut
cocodrilo crocodile
cocotero coconut palm
código code
cognado cognate
coincidencia coincidence
coincidir to coincide
cola line (*of people*) (7); **hacer cola** to stand in line (7)
colección *f.* collection
coleccionar to collect
colega *m., f.* colleague
colesterol *m.* cholesterol
colgar (cuelgo) (gu) to hang
collar *m.* necklace
colombiano/a *n., adj.* Colombian
colonia colony
colonizador(a) colonizer
colono/a settler
color *m.* color (3); **color kaki** khaki; **(de) color café** brown (3); **de color violeta** violet; **¿de qué color es?** what color is it?
colorear to color
colorido/a colorful
columna column
combatir to fight, combat
combinación *f.* combination
combinar to combine
comedia comedy (13)
comediante *m., f.* comedian
comedor *m.* dining room (4)
comentar to comment on; to discuss
comentario comment

comenzar (comienzo) (c) to begin; **comenzar a** + *inf.* to begin (*to do, doing something*)
comer to eat (2); **comer comidas sanas** to eat healthy food
comercial: centro comercial shopping mall (3)
comercio business, commerce
comestibles *m. pl.* foodstuff, groceries (6)
cómico/a *n.* comedian; *adj.* funny
comida food (6); meal (6); **comer comidas sanas** to eat healthy food; **comida rápida** fast food
como like, as; **así como** as well as; **tal como** just as; **tan... como** as . . . as (5); **tan pronto como** as soon as; **tanto como** as much as (5); **tanto/a(s)... como** as much/ many . . . as (5)
¿cómo? how?; what? (PP); **¿cómo es usted?** what are you (*form. s.*) like? (PP); **¿cómo está(s)?** how are you? (PP); **¿cómo se llama usted?** what is your (*form. s.*) name? (PP); **¿cómo se llega a... ?** how do you get to . . . ? (14); **¿cómo te llamas?** what is your (*fam. s.*) name? (PP)
cómoda bureau (4); dresser (4)
cómodo/a comfortable (3)
compacto: disco compacto compact disc (CD) (12)
compañero/a companion; friend; **compañero/a de clase** classmate (1); **compañero/a de cuarto** roommate (1); **compañero de trabajo** co-worker; **compañero/a de viaje** traveling companion
compañía company
comparación *f.* comparison; **en comparación con** compared to
comparar to compare
compartir to share (16)
competencia competition
competición *f.* competition
complacer (complazco) to please
complejo/a complex
complemento directo *gram.* direct object; **complemento indirecto** *gram.* indirect object
completar to complete, finish
completo/a complete; full, no vacancy (18); **de tiempo completo** full-time (16); **pensión** (*f.*) **completa** room and full board (18); **por completo** completely; **trabajo de tiempo completo** full-time work (11)
complicado/a complicated
componer (*like* **poner**) (*p.p.* **compuesto**) to compose
composición *f.* composition
compositor(a) composer (13)

compra: hacer la compra to go shopping

comprar to buy (1)

compras: de compras shopping (3); **ir de compras** to go shopping (3)

compra-ventas: agencia de compra-ventas de coches used car dealership

comprender to understand (2)

comprensión *f.* understanding; comprehension

comprensivo/a understanding

comprimido/a compressed

compromiso commitment

compuesto/a (*p.p. of* **componer**) composed

computación *f.* computer science (1)

computadora computer (1); **computadora portátil** laptop; **disco de computadora** computer disc (12); **escribir a computadora** to key in (type) (16)

común common, usual, ordinary; **tener en común** to have in common

comunicación *f.* communication; *pl.* **medios de comunicación** mass media (17)

comunicarse (qu) (con) to communicate (with) (17)

comunicativo/a communicative; **nota comunicativa** note about communication

comunidad *f.* community (12)

comunión *f.* communion; **primera comunión** first communion

con with (1); **con anticipación** in advance; ahead of time (18); **con cheque** with a / by check (16) **con cuidado** carefully; **con frecuencia** frequently (1); **con permiso** excuse me (PP); **¿con qué frecuencia?** how often, frequently? (2); **con relación a** regarding; **con respecto a** with regard to, with respect to; **con (tal) de que** provided (that) (15)

concedido/a conceded; granted

concentración *f.* concentration

concentrarse to concentrate

concepto concept

concertar (concierto) to arrange; to agree upon

concierto concert (9); **ir a un concierto** to go to a concert (9)

conclusión *f.* conclusion

concordar (concuerdo) (con) to agree (with); to reconcile

concurrir to concur

concurso contest

condición *f.* condition

condicional *m. gram.* conditional

conducir to drive (14); **licencia de conducir** driver's license (14)

conductor(a) driver (14)

conectarse (a) to connect (to)

conexión *f.* connection

conferencia lecture

confiabilidad *f.* reliability

confianza trust

confiar (confío) to trust

confirmación *f.* confirmation

confirmar to confirm (18)

confitería sweetshop

conflicto conflict

confundido/a confused

congelado/a frozen (5); very cold (5)

congelador *m.* freezer (9)

conjugar (gu) *gram.* to conjugate

conjunción *f. gram.* conjunction

conjunto group

conmigo with me (5)

conocer (conozco) to know, be acquainted with (6); **conocerse** to meet (15)

conocido/a known, famous

conocimiento knowledge

conquistador(a) conqueror

conquistar to conquer

consciente conscious, aware

conscripto draftee

consecuencia consequence

conseguir (*like* **seguir**) to get, obtain (8); **conseguir** + *inf.* to succeed in (*doing something*) (8)

consejero/a advisor (1)

consejo (piece of) advice (6); **dar consejos** to give advice

conservación *f.* conservation

conservar to save, conserve (14); **conservar energía** to conserve energy

considerar to consider

consigo with themselves

consistir en to consist of

constante *adj.* constant

constitución *f.* constitution

constitucional constitutional

constituir (*like* **construir**) to constitute

construcción *f.* construction

construir to build, construct (14)

consulta consultation

consultar to consult

consultorio (medical) office (10)

consumidor(a) consumer

consumir to consume

contable *m., f.* accountant

contacto contact; **lentes** (*m. pl.*) **de contacto** contact lenses (10); **mantenerse** (*like* **tener**) **en contacto** to stay in touch; **ponerse en contacto con** to get in touch with

contado: pagar (gu) al contado to pay in cash

contador(a) accountant (16)

contaminación *f.* **(de aire)** (air) pollution; **hay (mucha) contaminación** there's (a lot of) pollution (5)

contaminante *m.* pollutant

contaminar to pollute (14)

contar (cuento) to tell, narrate (7)

contemplar to contemplate

contener (*like* **tener**) to contain

contento/a content, happy (5)

contestador (*m.*) **automático** answering machine (12)

contestar to answer (6)

contexto context

contigo with you (*fam., s.*) (5)

continente *m.* continent

continuación *f.* continuation; **a continuación** following, below

continuamente continually

continuar (continúo) to continue (5)

contorno perimeter

contra against; **chocar (qu) con/ contra** to run into, bump against (11); **darse contra** to run into, bump against

contrabando contraband

contraer (*like* **traer**) **matrimonio** to get married

contrario/a opposite; **al contrario** on the contrary; **lo contrario** the opposite

contraste *m.* contrast

contratar to hire

contrato contract

contribución *f.* contribution

contribuir (*like* **construir**) to contribute

control *m.* control; **control remoto** remote control (12); **pasar por el control de la seguridad** to go through security (check) (7)

controlar to control

convencer (convenzo) to convince

conveniente convenient

conversación *f.* conversation

conversar to converse

convertir (convierto) (i) to change, convert; **convertirse en** to turn into

cooperativo/a cooperative

copa glass; drink (*alcoholic*) (18); **Copa Mundial** World Cup; **tomar una copa** to have a drink

copia copy; **hacer copia** to copy (12)

copiar to copy (12); to cheat

coraje *m.* courage

corazón *m.* heart (10)

corbata necktie (3)

cordillera mountain range

Corea Korea

coro choir

corona wreath

correcto/a correct

correo mail (18); **correo electrónico** e-mail (12); **oficina de correos** post office (18)

correr to run; to jog (9)

corresponder to correspond

correspondiente *m., f.* correspondent

corrida de toros bullfight

corriente: cuenta corriente checking account (16); **estar al corriente** to be up to date

cortar to cut

corte *m.* cut; **corte de pelo** haircut; *f.* court (*of law*)

cortés *m., f.* courteous, polite

cortesía courtesy

cortina curtain

corto/a short (*in length*) (2); **pantalones** (*m. pl.*) **cortos** shorts

cosa thing (4)

cosecha harvest

cosechar to harvest

cosmopolita *adj. m., f.* cosmopolitan

costa coast

costar (cuesto) to cost; **¿cuánto cuesta(n)?** how much does it (do they) cost? (3)

costarricense *n., adj. m., f.* Costa Rican

costero/a coastal

costo cost

costumbre *f.* custom

cotidiano/a everyday, daily

cráter *m.* crater

creación *f.* creation

creador(a) creator

crear to create (13)

creativo/a creative

crecer (crezco) to grow (15)

creciente growing

crédito credit; **tarjeta de crédito** credit card (6)

creencia belief

creer (en) to think; to believe (in) (2)

crema cream

Creta Crete

criada maid (18)

crimen *m.* crime

cristianismo Christianity

cristiano/a Christian

crítico/a *n.* critic; *adj.* critical

crucero cruise (ship) (7)

crudo crude (oil)

cruz *f.* (*pl.* **cruces**) cross; **Día** (*m.*) **de la Cruz** Day of the Cross

cruzar (c) to cross (18); **cruzar la frontera** to cross the border (18)

cuaderno notebook (1)

cuadrado/a squared

cuadro painting (13); **de cuadros** plaid (3)

¿cuál(es)? what? (1); which? (1); **¿cuál es la fecha de hoy?** what is today's date? (5)

cualidad *f.* quality

cualquier *adj.* any

cualquiera *pron.* anyone; either

cuán *adv.* however much

cuando when; **de vez en cuando** once in a while

¿cuándo? when? (1)

cuanto: en cuanto *conj.* as soon as (16); **en cuanto a** regarding

¿cuánto/a? how much? (1); **¿cuánto cuesta(n)?** how much does it (do they) cost? (3); **¿cuánto es?** how much is it? (3); **¿cuánto tiempo hace que… ?** how long has it been since . . . ?

¿cuántos/as? how many? (1); **¿a cuántos estamos?** what's today's date?

cuarenta forty (2)

cuarto *n.* room (1); one-fourth; quarter (of an hour); **compañero/a de cuarto** roommate (1); **menos cuarto** a quarter to (*hour*) (PP); **servicio de cuartos** room service (18); **y cuarto** a quarter after (*hour*) (PP)

cuarto/a *adj.* fourth (13)

cuatro four (PP)

cuatrocientos/as four hundred (3)

cubano/a *n., adj.* Cuban

cubanoamericano/a *n., adj.* Cuban American

cubierto/a (*p.p. of* **cubrir**) covered

cubo cube

cubrir (*p.p.* **cubierto**) to cover (14)

cuchara spoon

cuenta account; check, bill (6); **cuenta corriente** checking account (16); **cuenta de ahorros** savings account (16); **estado de cuentas** bank statement; **tomar en cuenta** to take into account

cuento story

cuerda cord; string

cuero leather (3); **es de cuero** it's (made of) leather (3)

cuerpo body (10)

cuervo crow

cuestión *f.* question, issue (16)

cueva cave

cuidado care; *interj.* careful!; **con cuidado** carefully; **tener cuidado** to be careful

cuidarse to take care of oneself (10)

cultivación *f.* cultivation, raising (*of crops*)

cultivo cultivation, raising (*of crops*)

culto cult

cultura culture

cumbia *Colombian folk dance now popular throughout Latin America*

cumpleaños *m. inv.* birthday (5); **feliz cumpleaños** happy birthday;

tarjeta de cumpleaños birthday card; **pastel** (*m.*) **de cumpleaños** birthday cake (8); **tarta de cumpleaños** birthday cake

cumplir años to have a birthday (8)

cuñado/a brother-in-law, sister-in-law

cupo quota, share

cura priest

curandero/a healer

curar to cure

curioso/a curious

currículum *m.* résumé (16)

cursivo/a: letra cursiva italics

curso course

curva curve

cuyo/a whose

D

dama lady

danza dance (13); **danza güegüense** *traditional dance of Nicaragua*

daño harm; **hacerse daño en** to hurt one's (*body part*) (11)

dar to give (7); **dar ánimo** to cheer up; **dar consejos** to give advice; **dar(se) un abrazo** to give (each other) a hug; **dar un paseo** to take a walk (9); **dar una caminata** to take a walk; **dar una fiesta** to give a party (8); **darse con/contra** to run into, bump against; **darse la mano** to shake hands (10); **darse la vuelta** to turn (oneself) around

datos *pl.* data

de *prep.* of (PP); from (PP); **de acuerdo** agreed; **de acuerdo con** in accordance with; **de ahora en adelante** from now on; **de antemano** beforehand; **de anticipación** ahead; **de atrás** backwards; **de cerca** up close; **(de) color café** brown (3); **de color violeta** violet; **de compras** shopping (3); **de cuadros** plaid (3); **de doble vía** two-way; **de guardia** on-call; **de habla española** Spanish-speaking; **de ida** one-way (7); **de ida y vuelta** round-trip (7); **de joven** as a youth (9); **de la mañana** in the morning, A.M. (PP); **de la noche** in the evening, P.M. (PP); **de la tarde** in the afternoon, P.M. (PP); **de largo** in length; **de los últimos años** in recent years; **de lunares** polka-dot (3); **de manera que** *conj.* so that, in such a way that; **de moda** in style; **de modo que** in such a way that; **de nada** you're welcome (PP); **de niño/a** as a child (9); **de primera** first-class; **de rayas** striped (3); **de repente** suddenly (10); **¿de qué color**

es? what color is it?; **¿de quién?** whose? (2); **de tiempo completo/ parcial** full-/part-time (16); **de todo** everything (3); **de todas formas** anyway; **de última moda** trendy (hot) (3); **de vacaciones** on vacation (7); **de vez en cuando** once in a while; **de viaje** on a trip (7)

debajo (de) *prep.* below (5)

deber *n.* responsibility (17); obligation (17)

deber *v. + inf.* should, must, ought to (*do something*) (2)

debido a due to; because of

década decade

decidir to decide

décimo/a tenth (13)

decir to say (7); to tell (7); **eso quiere decir...** that means . . . (10)

decisión *f.* decision

declaración *f.* statement

declarar(se) to declare

decoración *f.* decoration

decorar to decorate

decorativo/a decorative

dedicar (qu) to dedicate

dedo (de la mano) finger (11); **dedo del pie** toe (11)

definición *f.* definition

definido/a defined; **artículo definido** *gram.* definite article

definir to define

deforestación *f.* deforestation

dejar to leave; to let, allow; to quit (16); **dejar de + inf.** to stop (*doing something*) (10); **dejar (en)** to leave behind (in [*a place*]) (9)

del (*contraction of* **de** + **el**) of the, from the (2)

delante de in front of (5); in the presence of

deleitarse to enjoy oneself, delight in

delgado/a thin (2)

deliberado/a deliberate

delicado/a delicate

delicioso/a delicious

delito crime (14)

demanda demand

demás: los/las demás the rest, others (12)

demasiado *adv.* too (9)

demasiado/a *adj.* too many; too much

democracia democracy

demócrata *m., f.* Democrat

democrático/a democratic

demonio devil, demon

demora delay (7)

demostración *f.* march, demonstration

demostrar (demuestro) to demonstrate, show

demostrativo *gram.* demonstrative

denso/a dense (14)

dental: pasta dental toothpaste (18)

dentista *m., f.* dentist (16)

dentro inside; **dentro de** inside; within, in (*time*)

departamento department; apartment

depender (de) to depend (on)

dependiente/a clerk (1)

deporte *m.* sport (9); **deportes acuáticos** water sports; **hacer un deporte** to play, do a sport; **practicar (qu) un deporte** to play, practice a sport

deportivo/a *adj.* sporting, sport-related (9); **club** (*m.*) **deportivo** sports club; **coche** (*m.*) **deportivo** sports car; **evento deportivo** sporting event; **reportero/a deportivo/a** sports reporter

depositar to deposit (16)

depósito deposit

derecha *n.* right-hand side; **a la derecha** to the right (5)

derecho right (17); **tener derecho a** to have the right to; **(todo) derecho** straight ahead (14)

derivarse (de) to derive (from)

derrotar to defeat

desafío challenge

desafortunadamente unfortunately

desahogado/a relieved

desaparecer (desaparezco) to disappear

desarrollar to develop (14)

desarrollo development

desastre *m.* disaster (17)

desastroso/a disastrous

desayunar to have (eat) breakfast (6)

desayuno breakfast (6)

descansar to rest (4)

descapotable: carro/coche (*m.*) **descapotable** convertible (car) (12)

descendiente *m., f.* descendent

descifrar to decipher, figure out

descompuesto/a (*p.p. of* **descomponer**) broken

desconocido/a unknown

descortés impolite

describir (*p.p.* **descrito**) to describe

descripción *f.* description

descriptivo/a descriptive

descubierto/a (*p.p. of* **descubrir**) discovered (14)

descubrimiento discovery (14)

descubrir (*p.p.* **descubierto**) to discover (14)

descuidado/a careless

desde *prep.* from; since; **desde entonces** since then; **desde que** *conj.* since

desear to want (1)

desecho waste (*product*)

deseo wish (8)

desequilibrio imbalance

desértico/a *adj.* desert

desesperadamente desperately

desfile *m.* parade

desgracia disgrace

desgraciadamente unfortunately (10)

desierto desert

desierto/a deserted

designado/a designated

desigualdad *f.* inequality (17)

desinflado/a: llanta desinflada flat tire (14)

desocupado/a vacant, unoccupied (18)

desordenado/a messy (5)

despedirse (de) (*like* **pedir**) to say good-bye (to) (8)

despensa pantry

desperdiciar to waste

despertador *m.* alarm clock (11)

despertar(se) (me despierto) (*p.p.* **despierto**) to wake up (4)

despierto/a (*p.p. of* **despertar**) awake

desprivilegiado/a without privilege

después *adv.* after; later, then; **después de** *prep.* after (4); **después de que** *conj.* after (16)

destacar (qu) to emphasize; to stand out; **destacarse** to distinguish oneself

destino destiny; destination

destreza skill

destrucción *f.* destruction

destruido/a destroyed

destruir (*like* **construir**) to destroy (14)

desventaja disadvantage

detalle *m.* detail

detective *m., f.* detective

detener (*like* **tener**) to detain

detenido/a detained

determinado/a determined

determinar to determine

detestar to detest

detrás de *prep.* behind (5)

deuda debt

devoción *f.* devotion

devolver (*like* **volver**) to return (*something*) (16)

día *m.* day (1); **al día siguiente** the next day; **algún día** some day; **buenos días** good morning (PP) **Día de Acción de Gracias** Thanksgiving; **Día de la Cruz** Day of the Cross; **Día de la Independencia** Independence Day; **Día de la Madre** Mother's Day; **Día de la Raza** Columbus Day (Hispanic Awareness Day); **Día de los Enamorados** Valentine's Day; **Día de los Inocentes** April Fool's Day; **Día de los Muertos**

Day of the Dead; **Día de los Reyes Magos** Day of the Magi (Three Kings); **Día de San Patricio** St. Patrick's Day; **Día de San Valentín** St. Valentine's Day; **Día de Todos los Santos** All Saints Day; **Día del Año Nuevo** New Year's Day; **Día del Canadá** Canada Day; **día feriado** holiday; **día festivo** holiday (8); **estar al día** to be up to date; **hoy (en) día** nowadays (17); **¿qué día es hoy?** what day is today? (4); **todo el día** all day; **todos los días** everyday (1)

diablo devil
diagrama *m.* diagram
dialecto dialect
diálogo dialogue
diamante *m.* diamond
diámetro diameter
diario/a daily (4); **rutina diaria** daily routine (4)
dibujante *m., f.* sketch artist
dibujar to draw (13)
dibujo drawing; **dibujos animados** cartoons
diccionario dictionary (1)
diciembre *m.* December (5)
dictador(a) dictator (17)
dictadura dictatorship (17)
dictar to dictate
diecinueve nineteen (PP)
dieciocho eighteen (PP)
dieciséis sixteen (PP)
diecisiete seventeen (PP)
diente *m.* tooth (10); **cepillarse los dientes** to brush one's teeth (4); **pasta de dientes** toothpaste; **sacarle (qu) un diente** to pull a tooth (10)
dieta diet (6); **estar a dieta** to be on a diet (6)
dietético/a *adj.* diet
diez ten (PP)
diferencia difference
diferente different
difícil hard, difficult (5)
dificultad *f.* difficulty
digital digital; **agenda digital** electronic agenda, PDA; **cámara digital** digital camera (12); **edición** (*f.*) **digital** digital edition; **impresión** (*f.*) **digital** digital printing
dilema *m.* dilemma
Dinamarca Denmark
dinero money (1); **sacar (qu) (dinero)** to withdraw (money)
dios *m.* god; **Dios** God; **por Dios** for heaven's sake (11)
diosa goddess
diptongo *gram.* diphthong
dique *m.* dike

dirección *f.* address (6); direction
directo/a direct; **complemento directo** *gram.* direct object
director(a) director (13); conductor (13)
disciplina discipline
disco: disco compacto compact disc (CD) (12); **disco de computadora** computer disc (12); **disco duro** hard drive (12)
discoteca disco (9); **ir a una discoteca** to go to a disco (9)
discriminación *f.* discrimination (17)
disculpa apology, excuse; **pedir disculpas** to apologize (11)
disculpar to excuse, pardon; **discúlpeme** pardon me (11); I'm sorry (11)
discutir (sobre) (con) to argue (about) (with) (8)
diseñador(a) designer
diseñar to design
diseño design
disfraz *m.* (*pl.* disfraces) disguise
disfrutar to enjoy
disminuir (*like* construir) to diminish
disolver (disuelvo) (*p.p.* disuelto) to dissolve
disparar shoot at (*someone/something*)
disponible available
disputar to dispute
distancia distance; **llamada a larga distancia** long-distance call
distante distant
distinguir (distingo) to distinguish
distinto/a distinct, different
distracción *f.* distraction
distraer (*like* traer) to distract
distraído/a absent-minded, distracted (11)
distrito district
disuelto/a (*p.p. of* disolver) dissolved
diversidad *f.* diversity
diversificar (qu) to diversify
diversión *f.* diversion (9)
diverso/a diverse
divertido/a fun (9); **ser divertido/a** to be fun (9)
divertir (divierto) (i) to entertain; **divertirse** to have a good time, enjoy oneself (4)
dividir to divide
división *f.* division
divorciado/a divorced (15)
divorciarse (de) to get divorced from (15)
divorcio divorce (15)
divulgar (gu) to make known
doblar to turn (14)
doble double; **de doble vía** two-way (14); **habitación** (*f.*) **doble** double room (18)

doce twelve (PP)
dócil docile
doctor(a) doctor
documento document
dólar *m.* dollar
doler (duele) to hurt, ache (10); **doler(le) la cabeza / el estómago** to have a headache/stomachache
dolor *m.* **(de)** pain, ache (in) (10); **dolor de cabeza** headache; **tener dolor de** to have a pain in (10); **tener dolor de cabeza/muela** to have a headache/toothache
doméstico/a domestic; **animal** (*m.*) **doméstico** pet (14); domesticated animal (14); **aparato doméstico** home appliance (9); **quehacer** (*m.*) **doméstico** household chore (9)
domicilio home, residence
domingo Sunday (4)
dominicano/a Dominican
don *m. title of respect used with a man's first name*
donde where
¿dónde? where? (PP)
dondequiera wherever
doña *title of respect used with a woman's first name*
dormir (duermo) (u) to sleep (4); **dormir la siesta** to take a nap (4); **dormir lo suficiente** to sleep enough (10); **dormirse** to fall asleep (4)
dormitorio bedroom
dos two (PP); **dos veces** twice (10)
doscientos/as two hundred (3)
drama *m.* drama (13)
dramático/a dramatic
dramaturgo/a playwright (13)
droga drug
dromedario dromedary (camel)
ducha shower
ducharse to shower (4)
duda doubt; **no hay duda** there is no doubt; **sin duda** without a doubt
dudar to doubt (12)
dudoso/a doubtful
dueño/a owner (6); landlord/lady (12)
dulces *m.* candy, sweets (6); *adj.* sweet; **agua** (*f. but* el agua) **dulce** fresh water
dúo duo
durante during (4)
durar to last (17)
durmiente: Bella Durmiente Sleeping Beauty
duro/a hard, firm; **disco duro** hard drive (12); **huevo duro** hard-boiled egg
DVD *m.* DVD; **lector** (*m.*) **de DVD** DVD player (12)
DVD-ROM *m.* DVD-ROM (12)

E

e and (*used instead of* **y** *before words beginning with stressed* **i** *or* **hi**, *except* **hie-**)

echarse una siesta to take a nap

ecología ecology

ecológico/a ecological

economía economy; *s.* economics (1)

económico/a economic

economizar (c) to economize (16)

ecoturismo ecotourism

ecoturista *m., f.* ecotourist

ecuatoriano/a Ecuadorian

edad *f.* age

edición *f.* edition; **edición digital** online edition

edificio building (1); **edificio de apartamentos** apartment building (12)

educación *f.* education

educador(a) educator

educativo/a educational

efectivo cash (16); **en efectivo** in cash (16); **pagar (gu) en efectivo** to pay with cash (16)

efecto effect

eficiente efficient

Egipto Egypt

egoísta *m., f.* selfish

ejecutivo/a executive

ejemplificar (qu) to exemplify

ejemplo example; **por ejemplo** for example (11)

ejercicio exercise (4); **hacer ejercicio** to exercise (4); **hacer ejercicios aeróbicos** to do aerobics (10)

ejército army (17)

el *def. art. m. s.* the; **el primero de** the first of (*month*) (5)

él *sub. pron.* he (1)

elección *f.* election

electricidad *f.* electricity

electricista *m., f.* electrician (16)

electrónica *n.* electronic equipment (12)

electrónico/a electronic; **agenda electrónica** electronic agenda, PDA; **aparato electrónico** electronic device; **correo electrónico** e-mail (12)

elefante *m.* elephant (14)

elegante elegant

elegir (elijo) (i) to elect

elemento element

eliminar to eliminate

ella *sub. pron.* she (1); *obj. (of prep.)* her

ellos/as *sub. pron.* they (1); *obj. (of prep.)* them

e-mail *m.* e-mail (12)

embargo: sin embargo nevertheless (5)

embarque: tarjeta de embarque boarding pass

embotellamiento de tráfico traffic jam

emergencia emergency; **sala de emergencias** emergency room (10)

emigrante *m., f.* emigrant

emigrar to emigrate

emisario (radio, television) station

emisión *f.* emission; programming

emoción *f.* emotion (8)

emocional emotional

emocionante exciting

empanada *turnover pie or pastry*

empapelado/a (wall) papered

emparejar to pair

empezar (empiezo) (c) to begin (4); **empezar a** + *inf.* to begin to (*do something*) (4)

empleado/a employee

emplear to employ

empleo (bien/mal pagado) (well/poorly paying) job (16)

empresa business, corporation (16); company; **administración** (*f.*) **de empresas** business administration (1)

en in (PP); on (PP); at (PP); **en absoluto** at all; **en cambio** on the other hand, on the contrary; **en casa** at home (1); **en caso de que** *conj.* in case (15); **en cierta medida** in some measure, to some degree; **en comparación con** in comparison with; **en cuanto** as soon as (16); **en efectivo** in cash (16); **en este momento** right now; **en exceso** excessively; **en fin** in short; **en general** in general; **en la actualidad** currently, right now (9); **en lugar de** in place of; **en onda** in style; **en punto** on the dot (PP); **en resumen** in summary; **en seguida** right away (10); **en torno a** around; **en vez de** instead of; **en voz alta** aloud

enamorado/a (de) in love (with) (15); **Día** (*m.*) **de los Enamorados** Valentine's Day

enamorarse (de) to fall in love (with) (15)

encantado/a pleased to meet you (PP)

encantador(a) enchanting, delightful

encantar to like very much, love (7)

encargado/a in charge

encender (enciendo) to turn on (*appliance*); to light; **encender la luz** to turn on the light

enchufar to plug in

encima de *prep.* on top of (5); in addition to

encontrar (encuentro) to find (8); **encontrarse (con)** to meet (*someone somewhere*) (10);

encontrarse con amigos to get together with friends

encuesta survey

encuestar to survey

endémico/a endemic

energético/a energetic

energía energy (14); **conservar energía** to conserve energy; **energía eléctrica/ nuclear/solar** electric/nuclear/solar energy (14)

enérgico/a energetic

enero January (5)

enfadar to anger; **enfadarse** to get, become mad

enfático/a emphatic

enfermarse to get sick (8)

enfermedad *f.* illness (10)

enfermero/a nurse (10)

enfermo/a sick (5); **estar enfermo/a** to be sick

enfoque *m.* focus

enfrente de *prep.* in front of

engordar to gain weight

enmascarado/a masked

enojado/a angry, mad

enojarse (con) to get angry (8)

enorme enormous

ensalada salad (6)

ensayar to rehearse

ensayo essay

enseñanza teaching

enseñar to teach (1); **enseñar a** + *inf.* to teach to (*do something*)

entender (entiendo) to understand (4)

enterarse (de) to find out (about) (17)

entero/a entire (9); **limpiar la casa entera** to clean the entire house (9)

entonces then, next; **desde entonces** since then

entrada entrance; ticket

entrante: el año entrante next year

entrar (en/a) to enter

entre *prep.* between (5); among

entregar (gu) to hand in (7)

entremeses *m. pl.* hors d'œuvres

entrenador(a) trainer, coach

entrenamiento training, practice

entrenar to practice, train (9)

entrevista interview (16)

entrevistador(a) interviewer (16)

entrevistar to interview (16)

entusiasmar to enthuse

enviar (envío) to send

epifanía epiphany

época era, time (*period*) (9)

equilibradamente in a balanced way

equilibrar to balance

equipaje *m.* luggage, baggage (7); **facturar el equipaje** to check baggage (7)

equipo team (9); equipment; **equipo fotográfico** photography equipment

equivalente *m.* equivalent

equivocarse (qu) (de) to be wrong, make a mistake (about) (11)

érase una vez once upon a time

eres you (*fam. s.*) are (PP)

es he/she is, you (*form. s.*) are (PP)

error *m.* error

erupción *f.* eruption (17)

escala stop (7); **hacer escalas** to make stops (7)

escalado/a climbed

escalador(a) climber

escalón *m.* step

escándalo scandal

escaparate *m.* store (display) window

escaparse to escape

escasez (*pl.* **escaseces**) lack; shortage

escena scene

escenario setting (13)

esclavitud *f.* slavery

esclavo/a slave

esclusa lock, sluice

escoger (escojo) to choose

esconder(se) to hide

escribir (*p.p.* **escrito**) to write (2); **escribir a computadora** to key in (type) (16)

escrito/a (*p.p. of* **escribir**) written (11); **informe** (*m.*) **escrito** written report (11)

escritor(a) writer (13)

escritorio desk (to) (1)

escritura writing

escuchar to listen (to) (1)

escuela school (9); **escuela primaria** elementary school; **escuela secundaria** high school; **escuela superior** high school; **maestro/a de escuela** schoolteacher (16)

esculpir to sculpt (13)

escultor(a) sculptor (13)

escultura sculpture (13)

ese, esa *pron.* that one; *adj.* that (3)

esencial essential

eso that (3); **eso quiere decir...** that means . . . (10)

esos/as *pron.* those ones; *adj.* those (3)

espacial space; **nave** (*f.*) **espacial** space ship; **transbordador** (*m.*) **espacial** space shuttle

espacio space; **espacio en blanco** blank space

espalda back

espantoso/a frightening

español *m.* Spanish (*language*) (1)

español(a) *n.* Spaniard; *adj.* Spanish (2); **de habla española** Spanish-speaking

espárragos *m. pl.* asparagus (6)

especial special

especialidad *f.* specialty

especialista *m., f.* specialist

especialización *f.* specialization; major (*academic*)

especializarse (c) (en) to major (in)

especialmente especially

especie *f.* species (14); **especie en peligro de extinción** endangered species (14)

específico/a specific

espectacular spectacular

espectáculo show (13)

espectador(a) spectator (13)

especular to speculate

espejo mirror

espera wait; **llamada en espera** call-waiting; **sala de espera** waiting room (7)

esperanza hope (17)

esperar to wait (for) (6); to expect (6); to hope (12)

espíritu *m.* spirit

espiritual spiritual

espléndido/a splendid

espontáneo/a spontaneous

esposo/a husband/wife (2); spouse

esqueleto skeleton

esquí *m.* skiing; **estación** (*f.*) **de esquí** ski resort

esquiar (esquío) to ski (9)

esquina corner (14)

esta noche tonight (5)

establecer (establezco) to establish

estación *f.* season (5); station (7); **estación de autobuses / del tren** bus/train station (7); **estación de esquí** ski resort; **estación de gasolina** gas station (14); **estación de metro** subway station (18); **estación de radio** radio station

estacionamiento parking lot; parking spot

estacionar to park (11)

estadía stay (*in a place*)

estadio stadium

estadística statistic

estado state (2); **estado afectivo** emotional state (8); **estado de ánimo** state of mind; **estado de cuentas** bank statement; **estado libre asociado** commonwealth

estadounidense *n., adj.* of the United States of America (2)

estampilla stamp (18)

estancia stay (*in a hotel*) (18)

estanco tobacco stand/shop (18)

estanque *m.* pond

estante *m.* bookshelf (4)

estar to be (1); **¿a cuántos estamos? / ¿en qué fecha estamos?** what's today's date?; **estar a cargo (de)** to be in control (of); **estar a dieta** to be on a diet (6); **estar al corriente** to be up to date; **estar al día** to be up to date; **estar al tanto** to be up to date; **estar atrasado/a** to be late; **estar bien** to be well (5); **estar de vacaciones** to be on vacation (7); **estar en rebaja** to be on sale; **estar en un lío** to be in trouble, a problem; **estar enfermo/a** to be sick; **está** he/she/it is; you (*form. s.*) are; **está (muy) nublado** it's (very) cloudy (5); **(no) estar seguro/a (de)** to be (un)sure (of); **(no) estoy de acuerdo** I (don't) agree (2)

estatal *adj.* state

estatua statue

estatus *m.* status

este *m.* east (5)

este, esta *pron.* this one; *adj.* this (2); **esta noche** tonight (5); **en este momento** right now

estéreo stereo (12)

estereofónico/a *adj.* stereo

estereotipo stereotype

estilo style

estimado/a esteemed

esto this (2)

estómago stomach (10); **dolerle (me duele) el estómago** to have a stomachache

estos/as *pron.* these ones; *adj.* these (2)

estoy de acuerdo I agree (2)

estratégico/a strategic

estrecho strait; **Estrecho de Magallanes** Strait of Magellan

estrecho/a narrow

estrella star; **hotel de 2 (3, 4, 5) estrellas** two- (three-, four-, five-) star hotel (18)

estrés *m.* stress (11)

estresado/a stressed (11)

estructura structure

estudiante *m., f.* student (1)

estudiantil *adj.* student (11)

estudiar to study (1)

estudio study

estudioso/a studious

estufa stove (9)

estupendo/a stupendous

etapa stage, phase (15)

etcétera etcetera

étnico/a ethnic

Europa Europe

europeo/a European

evento event (17); **evento deportivo** sporting event

evidencia evidence

evitar to avoid (14)

evocar (qu) to evoke

evolución *f.* evolution

exacto/a exact
exagerado/a exaggerated
examen *m.* exam, test (3)
examinar to examine (10)
exceder to exceed
excelencia excellence
excelente excellent
excepto except
exceso excess; **en exceso** excessively
exclamación *f.* exclamation
exclusivo/a exclusive
excursión *f.* excursion
excusa excuse
exhibición *f.* exhibition
exigente demanding
exigir (exijo) to demand
exilio exile
existir to exist
éxito success; **tener éxito** to be successful
exitoso/a successful
exótico/a exotic
expansión *f.* expansion
expansivo/a expansive
experiencia experience
experimentar to experiment
experimento experiment
experto/a expert
explicación *f.* explanation
explicar (qu) to explain (7)
exploración *f.* exploration
explorador(a) explorer
explorar to explore
explotado/a exploited
explotar to exploit
exportar to export
exposición *f.* exposition
expresar to express
expresión *f.* **(de cortesía)** expression (of courtesy) (PP)
expulsar to expulse
expulsión *f.* expulsion
exquisito/a exquisite
extender (extiendo) to extend
extensión *f.* extension
extenso/a extensive
extinción *f.* extinction; **especie** (*f.*) **en peligro de extinción** endangered species (14)
extranjero abroad (18)
extranjero/a *n.* foreigner (1); *adj.* foreign; **lenguas extranjeras** foreign languages (1)
extraño/a strange (13); **es extraño que...** it's strange that . . . (13); **¡qué extraño que... !** how strange that . . . ! (13)
extraordinario/a extraordinary
extravagante extravagant
extremo/a extreme
extrovertido/a extroverted
exuberancia exuberance
exuberante exuberant

F

fábrica factory (14)
fabricar (qu) to manufacture
fabuloso/a fabulous
fachada facade
fácil easy (5)
facilidad *f.* ease
facilitar to facilitate
factor *m.* factor
factoría factory
factura bill (16)
facturar to check (*baggage*) (7); **facturar el equipaje** to check baggage (7)
Fahrenheit: grados Fahrenheit degrees Fahrenheit
falda skirt (3)
fallar to "crash" (*computer*) (12)
falsificado/a falsified
falso/a false
falta lack (14); absence (14)
faltar (a) to be absent (from), not attend (8)
fama fame
familia family (2)
familiar *n. m.* relation, member of the family; *adj.* pertaining to a family
famoso/a famous
fantasía fantasy
fantástico/a fantastic
farmacéutico/a pharmacist (10)
farmacia pharmacy (18)
farmacología pharmacology
farmacológico/a pharmacological
fascinante fascinating
fascinar to fascinate (13)
fatal *sl.* bad, awful
favor *m.* favor; **favor de** + *inf.* please (*do something*); **por favor** please (PP); **me hace el favor de...** if you would do me the favor of . . .
favorito/a favorite
fax *m.* fax (12)
fe *f.* faith
febrero February (5)
fecha date (5); **¿cuál es la fecha de hoy?** what's today's date? (5); **¿en qué fecha estamos?** what's today's date? **fecha tope** deadline; **¿qué fecha es hoy?** what's today's date? (5)
¡felicitaciones! *interj.* congratulations! (8)
feliz (*pl.* **felices**) happy (8); **felicísimo/a** very happy; **Feliz Año Nuevo** Happy New Year; **feliz cumpleaños** happy birthday; **Feliz Navidad** Merry Christmas
femenino/a feminine
fénix *m.* phoenix
fenomenal phenomenal
feo/a ugly (2)
feria fair (*event*)

feriado: día (*m.*) **feriado** holiday
feroz (*pl.* **feroces**) ferocious
festival *m.* festival
festividad *f.* festivity
festivo: día (*m.*) **festivo** holiday (8)
ficción *f.* fiction; **ciencia ficción** science fiction
fiebre *f.* fever (10); **tener fiebre** to have a fever
fiel faithful (2)
fiesta party (1); **fiesta de sorpresa** surprise party; **hacer/dar una fiesta** to have, give a party (8)
figura figure
fijar to set; **fijarse (en)** to take note (of), pay attention (to)
fijo/a fixed, set (3); **precio fijo** fixed, set price (3)
fila line, row; **en fila** in single file
Filipinas: Islas Filipinas Philippines
filipino/a Philippine
filme *m.* movie; film
filosofía philosophy (1)
fin *m.* end; **en fin** in short; **fin de semana** weekend (1); **por fin** at last (4)
final *n. m.* end; *adj.* final
finalmente finally
financiación *f.* financing
financiamiento financing
financiero/a financial
finanza finance
finca farm (14)
Finlandia Finland
física physics (1)
físico/a physical
flabiol *m. traditional flute-like instrument of Catalonia*
flaco/a thin
flamenco *music of Andalusia and southern Spain*
flan *m.* (baked) custard (6)
flauta flute
flexibilidad *f.* flexibility (11)
flexible flexible (11)
flor *f.* flower (7)
florecer (florezco) to flourish; to bloom
flota fleet
folclórico/a folkloric (13)
folklórico/a folkloric
fondo fund; bottom; **al fondo** in the background
fontanero/a plumber
forma form; shape; **de todas formas** anyway
formar to form
formulario form (*to fill out*) (18)
fortaleza fort
fortificación *f.* fortification
fósforo match (18)
foto(grafía) photo(graph) (7); photography (13); **sacar (qu) fotos** to take pictures (7)

fotográfico/a photographic; **equipo fotográfico** photography equipment

fotógrafo/a photographer (16)

francés *m.* French (*language*) (1)

francés, francesa *n.* French person; *adj.* French

Francia France

frase *f.* sentence; phrase

frecuencia frequency (1); **con frecuencia** frequently (1); **¿con qué frecuencia?** how often, frequently?

frecuente frequently

freír (*like* **reír**) (*p.p.* **frito**) to fry

frenos brakes (14)

fresa strawberry

fresco/a fresh (6); cool (*weather*); **hace fresco** it's cool (*weather*) (5)

frijoles *m.* beans (6)

frío cold(ness); *adj.* cold; **hace (mucho) frío** it's (very) cold (*weather*) (5); **tener (mucho) frío** to be (very) cold (5)

frisbee: jugar (juego) (gu) al frisbee to play Frisbee

frito/a (*p.p. of* **freír**) fried (6); **papas/ patatas fritas** French fries (6); **pollo frito** fried chicken

frontera border (18); **cruzar (c) la frontera** to cross the border (18)

fructuoso/a fructiferous

fruta fruit (6); **jugo de fruta** fruit juice (6)

frutal *adj.* fruit

fue sin querer I didn't mean it (11)

fuego fire; **fuegos artificiales** fireworks

fuente *f.* source; fountain

fuera *adv.* outside

fuerte strong

fuerza strength

fumador(a) smoker; **sala de fumadores** smoking area (7)

fumar to smoke (7); **sala de fumar** smoking area (7)

función *f.* function

funcionar to work, function (12); to run (*machines*) (12)

fundado/a founded

furioso/a furious (5)

fusión *f.* fusion

fútbol *m.* soccer (9); **fútbol americano** football (9); **campo de fútbol** soccer field; **partido de fútbol** soccer game; **jugar (juego) (gu) al fútbol** to play soccer; **jugar (juego) (gu) al fútbol americano** to play football

futbolista *m., f.* soccer player

futuro *n.* future

futuro/a *adj.* future

G

gafas glasses (10)

gaita bagpipe

Galápagos: Islas Galápagos Galapagos Islands

galla gal (*sl. Ch.*)

galleta cookie (6)

gallina hen

gallinero chicken house

gallo rooster; guy (*sl. Ch.*); **misa del gallo** midnight mass

gamba shrimp

gana desire; wish; **tener ganas de** + *inf.* to feel like (*doing something*) (3)

ganado cattle

ganador(a) winner

ganar to win (9); to earn (16)

ganga bargains (3); **¡qué ganga!** what a bargain!

garaje *m.* garage (4); **limpiar el garaje** to clean the garage

garantía guarantee

garantizar (c) to guarantee

garganta throat (10)

garífunas Black Caribs (*descendents of Carib indigenous people and African slaves in Honduras*)

gas *m.* gas (*not for cars*) (12)

gasolina gasoline (14); **estación** (*f.*) **de gasolina** gas station (14)

gasolinera gas station (14)

gastar (dinero) to spend (*money*) (8); to use (*gasoline*) (14)

gasto expense (12)

gastronómico/a gastronomic

gato/a cat (2)

gaucho Argentine cowboy

gemelo/a twin

general general; **en general** in general; **por lo general** in general (4)

género genre

generoso/a generous

génesis *f.* genesis

genio genius

gente *f. s.* people (12)

geografía geography

geográfico/a geographic

geología geology

geoturismo geotourism

gerente *m., f.* manager (16)

gerundio *gram.* gerund

gigantesco/a gigantic

gimnasio gym(nasium)

glaciar glacial

globo balloon

gobernar (gobierno) to govern

gobierno government (14)

golf *m.* golf (9); **jugar (juego) (gu) al golf** to play golf

gordo/a fat (2)

gorila *m.* gorilla (14)

gorra hat; cap (3)

gorro hat

GPS: sistema (*m.*) **GPS** GPS

grabadora (tape) recorder/player (12)

grabar to record; to tape (12)

gracia grace

gracias thank you (PP); **gracias por** thank you for (8); **muchas gracias** thank you very much (PP); **Día** (*m.*) **de Acción de Gracias** Thanksgiving

grado grade level (*in school*) (9)

graduarse (me gradúo) (en) to graduate (from) (16)

gráfico/a *adj.* graphic

gramática grammar

gramaticalmente grammatically

gran, grande big, large (2); great (2); **pantalla grande** big screen (monitor) (12)

granito granite

granja farm

grano grain; **granos de café** coffee beans

grasa fat

gratis *inv.* free (of charge)

gratuito/a free (of charge)

grave serious

Grecia Greece

gripe *f.* flu (10)

gris gray (3)

gritar to shout

grúa crane; tow truck

grupo group

guagua bus (*Carib.*)

guancasco *dance of the Lenca indigenous group of Honduras*

guante *m.* glove

guaraní *m. indigenous language of South America*

guardar to save (*a place*) (7); to keep (12); to save (*documents*) (12); **guardar cama** to stay in bed (10); **guardar en secreto** to keep as a secret; **guardar un puesto** to save a place (in line) (7)

guardia: de guardia on-call

guatemalteco/a *n., adj.* Guatemalan

gubernamental governmental

güegüense: danza güegüense *traditional dance of Nicaragua*

guerra war (17)

guerrero/a warrior

guía guide book; **guía telefónica** telephone book; *m., f.* guide (*person*) (13)

guión *f.* script (13)

guitarra guitar

guitarrista *m., f.* guitarist

gustar to be pleasing (7); **me gustaría… muchísimo** I would (really) like . . . an awful lot (7); **¿le gusta… ?** do you (*form. s.*) like . . . ?

(PP); **¿te gusta… ?** do you (*fam. s.*) like . . . ? (PP); **no, no me gusta…** no, I don't like . . . (PP); **sí, me gusta…** yes, I like . . . (PP)
gusto like, preference, taste (PP); **mucho gusto** pleased to meet you (PP)

H

haber *infinitive form of* **hay** (12); **hay** there is/are (PP); **hay (mucha) contaminación** there's (a lot of) pollution (5); **no hay** there is/ are not (PP); **hay que** + *inf.* it's necessary to (*do something*) (13); **no hay de qué** you're welcome (PP); **no hay duda** there is no doubt
habilidad *f.* ability, skill
habitación *f.* room (18); **habitación con/sin baño** room with(out) bath (18); **habitación individual/ doble** single/double room (18)
habitado/a inhabited
habitante *m., f.* inhabitant
habitar to inhabit
hábito habit
habla *f.* (*but* **el habla**) speech; **de habla española** Spanish-speaking
hablar to speak (1); to talk (1); **hablar en voz baja** to speak softly; **hablar por teléfono** to talk on the phone (1)
hacer (*p.p.* **hecho**) to do; to make; **hacerse** to become; **hace** + *period of time* + **que** + *present tense* to have been (*doing something*) for (*a period of time*); **hace** + *time* ago; **hace (muy) buen/mal tiempo** it's (very) good/bad weather (5); **hace fresco** it's cool (*weather*) (5); **hace (mucho) frío/calor** it's (very) cold/ hot (*weather*) (5); **hace (mucho) sol** it's (very) sunny (5); **hace (mucho) viento** it's (very) windy (5); **hacer autostop** to hitchhike; **hacer** *camping* to go camping (7); **hacer cola** to stand in line (7); **hacer copia** to copy (12); **hacer deporte** to play, do a sport; **hacer ejercicio** to exercise (4); **hacer ejercicios aeróbicos** to do aerobics (10); **hacer escalas** to make stops (7); **hacer la cama** to make the bed (9); **hacer la compra** to go shopping; **hacer la(s) maleta(s)** to pack one's suitcase(s) (7); **hacer (el método) Pilates** to do Pilates (10); **hacer planes para** to make plans to (9); **hacer un** *picnic* to go on a picnic (9); **hacer un viaje** to take a trip (4); **hacer**

una caminata to take a walk; **hacer una fiesta** to have a party (8); **hacer una pregunta** to ask a question; **hacer una reservación** to make a reservation; **hacer surfing** to surf; **hacer (el) yoga** to do yoga; **hacerse daño** to hurt oneself (11); **hacerse daño en** to hurt one's (*body part*) (11); **me hace el favor de…** if you would do me the favor of . . . ; **¿qué tiempo hace hoy?** what's the weather like today? (5); **se le hace agua la boca** it makes your mouth water
hacia toward
Haití Haiti
hambre *f.* (*but* **el hambre**) hunger; **tener (mucha) hambre** to be (very) hungry (6)
hamburguesa hamburger (6)
hasta *adv.* until; even; *prep.* until (4); **hasta luego** see you later (PP); **hasta mañana** see you tomorrow (PP); **hasta pronto** see you soon; **hasta que** *conj.* until (16)
hay there is/are (PP); **no hay** there isn't/aren't (PP); **¿hay… ?** is/ are there . . . ?; **hay que** + *inf.* it's necessary to (*do something*) (13)
hecho *n.* fact, event (8)
hecho/a (*p.p. of* **hacer**) made; done
hectárea *land measure equal to 2.5 acres*
heladera freezer
helado ice cream (6)
heliconia *flowering tropical plant*
hemisferio hemisphere
heredar to inherit
herencia inheritance
hermanastro/a stepbrother/stepsister
hermano/a brother/sister (2); **medio/a hermano/a** half-brother/ half-sister
hermoso/a beautiful
héroe *m.* hero
herramienta tool
híbrido/a hybrid (14)
hidroeléctrico/a hydroelectric
hidrógeno hydrogen
hielo ice
hijastro/a stepson/stepdaughter
hijo/a son/daughter (2); *m. pl.* children (2)
himno hymn, anthem
hipopótamo hippopotamus
hipoteca mortgage
hispánico/a Hispanic
hispano/a Hispanic
hispanocanadiense *n., adj. m., f.* Hispanic-Canadian
hispanohablante *adj. m., f.* Spanish-speaking
historia history (1); story
histórico/a historic

hockey *m.* hockey (9)
hogar *m.* home; hearth
¡hola! hi! (PP)
Holanda Holland
hombre *m.* man (1); **hombre de negocios** businessman (16)
homenaje *m.* homage
homeópata *inv.* homeopathic
homeopatía homeopathy
homogéneo/a homogeneous
hondureño/a *n., adj.* Honduran
hongo mushroom; toadstool; fungus; **sombrero hongo** bowler hat, derby
honor *m.* honor
honrado/a honest; honorable
hora hour; time; **¿a qué hora?** at what time? (PP); **es hora de** + *inf.* it's time to (*do something*); **¿qué hora es?** what time is it? (PP)
horario schedule (11)
horno oven (9); **horno de microondas** microwave oven (9)
horóscopo horoscope
horror *m.* horror
hospital *m.* hospital
hospitalario/a hospitable
hotel *m.* **(de lujo)** (luxury) hotel (18); **hotel de 2 (3, 4, 5) estrellas** two- (three-, four-, five-) star hotel (18)
hotelero/a *adj.* hotel
hoy today (PP); **hoy (en) día** nowadays (17); **¿cuál es la fecha de hoy?** what's today's date? (5); **¿qué día es hoy?** what day is today?; **¿qué fecha es hoy?** what's today's date? (5)
huayno *traditional folk tune, ballad (Arg., Bol., Ch., Peru)*
huelga strike (17)
huésped(a) (hotel) guest (18)
huevo egg (6); **huevo duro** hard-boiled egg; **huevo tibio / pasado por agua** poached egg
huir (*like* **construir**) to flee
humanidad *f.* humanity; *pl.* humanities (2)
humano/a human (10); **ser** (*m.*) **humano** human being
humilde humble
humor *m.* humor

I

ibérico/a *adj.* Iberian
icono icon
ida: de ida one-way (7); **de ida y vuelta** round-trip (7)
idealista *m., f.* idealistic
idéntico/a identical
identidad *f.* identity

identificación *f.* identification; **tarjeta de identificación** identification card (11)

identificado/a identified; **objeto volante no identificado (OVNI)** unidentified flying object (UFO)

identificar (qu) to identify

idioma *m.* language

iglesia church

igual equal, same

igualdad *f.* equality (17)

igualmente likewise, same here (PP)

ilegal illegal

imagen *f.* image

imaginación *f.* imagination

imaginar(se) to imagine

imitar to imitate

impaciente impatient

impedir (*like* **pedir**) to impede

imperfecto *gram.* imperfect

imperio empire

impermeable *m.* raincoat (3)

impertinente impertinent

imponente imposing; majestic

importado/a imported

importancia importance

importante important

importar to matter, be important

imposible impossible (13); **es imposible que...** it's impossible that . . . (13)

imposición *f.* imposition

impresión *f.* impression; **impresión digital** digital printing

impresionante impressive

impresora printer (12)

imprimir to print (12)

improbable unlikely (13); **es improbable que...** it's unlikely that . . . (13)

improvisación *f.* improvisation

impuesto tax

impulsivo/a impulsive

inaugurado/a inaugurated

inca *n. m., f.* Inca; *adj. m., f.* Incan

incendio fire

incidente *m.* incident

incluir (*like* **construir**) to include

incómodo/a uncomfortable

incompleto/a incomplete

inconcebible inconceivable

incorrecto/a incorrect

increíble incredible (13); **es increíble que...** it's incredible that . . . (13)

indefinido/a: artículo indefinido *gram.* indefinite article

independencia independence; **Día (m.) de la Independencia** Independence Day

independiente independent

independizarse (c) to become independent

indicación *f.* instruction; direction

indicar (qu) to indicate

indicativo *gram.* indicative

índice *m.* index

indígena *n. m., f.* indigenous person; *adj. m., f.* indigenous

indio/a *n., adj.* Indian

indirecto/a indirect; **complemento indirecto** *gram.* indirect object

individual: habitación (*f.*) **individual** single room (18)

individuo *n.* individual

individuo/a *adj.* individual

indoctrinar to indoctrinate

industria industry

industrializado/a industrialized

infancia infancy (15)

infantil *adj.* child, children's

infinitivo *gram.* infinitive

inflexibilidad *f.* inflexibility (11)

inflexible unyielding (11)

influencia influence

influir (*like* **construir**) **(en)** to influence

influjo influx

influyente influential

información *f.* information

informar to inform (17)

informativo/a informative

informe *m.* **(oral/escrito)** (oral/written) report (11)

ingeniería engineering

ingeniero/a engineer (16)

Inglaterra England

inglés *m.* English (*language*) (1)

inglés, inglesa *n.* English person; *adj.* English (2)

ingrediente *m.* ingredient

ingresar to deposit (*money*); to pay money into

iniciar to begin, initiate

inmediato/a immediate

inmenso/a immense

inmigración *f.* immigration

inmigrante *m., f.* immigrant

inmigrar to immigrate

innecesario/a unnecessary

inocente innocent; **Día** (*m.*) **de los Inocentes** April Fool's Day

inquilino/a tenant (12)

inscribir(se) (*p.p.* **inscrito**) **(en)** to sign up, register (for)

inscrito/a (*p.p. of* **inscribir**) registered

insistir (en) + *inf.* to insist (on) (*doing something*) (12)

insoportable unbearable

inspección *f.* inspection

inspector(a) inspector (18); **inspector(a) de aduana** customs agent (18)

instalar to install (12)

instituto institute

instrumento instrument

integración *f.* integration

intelectual intellectual

inteligencia intelligence

inteligente intelligent (2)

intención *f.* intention

intencionadamente intentionally

intenso/a intense

intercambiar to exchange

interés *m.* interest (16)

interesante interesting

interesar to interest (*someone*) (7)

internacional international

Internet *m.* Internet (17); **tarjeta Internet móvil** wireless Internet card

interno/a internal

interpretación *f.* interpretation

interpretado/a interpreted

interpretar to interpret

interrogativo/a *gram.* interrogative (PP)

intranquilidad *f.* uneasiness, restlessness

introducción *f.* introduction

introducir (*like* **producir**) to introduce

introvertido/a introverted

inundación *f.* flood

inusual unusual

inventar to invent

inventario inventory

invertir (invierto) (i) to invest

investigación *f.* investigation

investigar (gu) to investigate

invierno winter (5)

invitación *f.* invitation

invitado/a guest (8)

invitar to invite (6)

inyección *f.* injection (10); **ponerle una inyección** to give (*someone*) a shot, injection (10)

iPod *m.* iPod (12)

ir to go; **ir a** + *inf.* to be going to (*do something*) (3); **ir a un bar** to go to a bar (9); **ir a un concierto** to go to a concert (9); **ir a una discoteca** to go to a disco (9); **ir al cine** to go to the movies; **ir al mar** to go to the sea(side); **ir al teatro** to go to the theater (9); **ir de compras** to go shopping (3); **ir de mal en peor** to go from bad to worse; **ir de safari** to go on a safari; **ir de vacaciones a...** to go on vacation to . . . (7); **ir en autobús/avión/barco/tren** to go/travel by bus/plane/boat/train (7); **irse** to leave

Irlanda Ireland

irresponsable irresponsible

-ísimo *adv.* very very (8)

-ísimo/a *adj.* very very (8)

isla island (5); **isla desértica** deserted island; **Islas Antillanas** Antilles Islands; **Islas Baleares** Balearic Islands; **Isla de Pascua** Easter Island; **Islas Filipinas** Philippine Islands; **Islas Galápagos** Galapagos Islands

Italia Italy

italiano Italian (*language*) (1)

italiano/a *n., adj.* Italian

itinerario itinerary

izquierda *n.* left-hand side; **a la izquierda (de)** to the left (of) (5); **levantarse con el pie izquierdo** to get up on the wrong side of the bed (11)

J

jabón *m.* soap (18)

jaguar *m.* jaguar

jamás never (6); not ever

jamón *m.* ham (6)

Japón Japan

japonés *m.* Japanese (*language*)

jarabe *m.* (cough) syrup (10)

jardín *m.* garden; yard (4)

jarrita small jar

jeans *m. pl.* jeans (3)

jefe/a boss (12)

jeroglífico/a hieroglyphic

jersey *m.* sweater

jesuita *m., f.* Jesuit

jirafa giraffe

joropo *folkloric music of Venezuela*

joven *n. m., f.* youth; *adj.* young (2); **de joven** as a youth (9)

joya jewel

joyería jewelry store

jubilarse to retire (16)

judío/a *n.* Jewish person; *adj.* Jewish; **Pascua Judía** Passover

juego game; **Juegos Olímpicos** Olympic Games

jueves *m. inv.* Thursday (4)

jugador(a) player (9)

jugar (juego) (gu) a/al to play (*a game, sport*) (4); **jugar a la lotería** to play the lottery; **jugar a las cartas** to play cards; **jugar a los videojuegos** to play video games; **jugar al ajedrez** to play chess (9); **jugar al basquetbol** to play basketball; **jugar al béisbol** to play baseball; **jugar al frisbee** to play Frisbee; **jugar al fútbol** to play soccer; **jugar al fútbol americano** to play football; **jugar al golf** to play golf; **jugar al voleibol** to play volleyball

jugo (de fruta) (fruit) juice (6)

juguete *m.* toy

julio July (5)

jungla jungle

junio June (5)

junto a near, next to

juntos/as together (7)

jurar to swear (*promise, oath*)

justificar (qu) to justify

justo/a fair

juventud *f.* youth (15)

juzgar (gu) to judge

K

kaki: color (*m.*) **kaki** khaki

kallawaya *Bolivian healer*

kilo(gramo) kilo(gram)

kilómetro kilometer

kiosco kiosk

L

la *def. art. f. s.* the; *d.o. f. s.* you (*form.*); her, it

laboral *adj.* labor; **jornada laboral** work day

laboratorio laboratory

lado side; **al lado de** *prep.* alongside of (5); beside; next to; **por otro lado** on the other hand; **por un lado** on the one hand

ladrar to bark

ladrón, ladrona thief

lago lake (14)

lamentar to regret (13); to feel sorry (13)

lámpara lamp (4)

lana wool (3); **es de lana** it's (made of) wool (3)

langosta lobster (6)

lápiz *m.* (*pl.* **lápices**) pencil (1)

largo *n.: de largo* in length

largo/a long (2); **a lo largo de** along; throughout; **llamada a larga distancia** long-distance call

las *def. art. f. pl.* the; *d.o. f. pl.* you

lástima shame (13); **es una lástima** it's a shame (13); **¡qué lástima que... !** what a shame that . . . ! (13)

latín *m.* Latin (*language*)

latino/a *adj.* Latin

Latinoamérica Latin America

latinoamericano/a Latin American

lavabo (bathroom) sink (4)

lavadora washing machine (9)

lavanda lavender

lavaplatos *m. inv.* dishwasher (9)

lavar to wash (9); **lavar los platos** to wash dishes (9); **lavar la ropa** to wash clothes, do laundry (9); **lavar las ventanas** to wash windows (9); **lavarse** to wash (oneself); **lavarse las manos** to wash one's hands

le *i.o. pron.* to him/her/you (*form. s.*); **¿le gusta...?** do you (*form. s.*) like . . . ? (PP)

leal loyal

lección *f.* lesson

leche *f.* milk (6)

lechón (*m.*) **asado** roast suckling pig

lechuga lettuce (6)

lector(a) reader; **lector** (*m.*) **de DVD** DVD player (12)

lectura reading

leer (*like* **creer**) to read (2)

lejos de *prep.* far from (5)

lempira *currency of Honduras*

lenca *indigenous people of Honduras and El Salvador*

lengua language (1); tongue (10); **lenguas extranjeras** foreign languages (1); **sacar (qu) la lengua** to stick out one's tongue (10)

lente *m.* lens (10); **lentes de contacto** contact lenses (10); **llevar lentes de contacto** to wear contacts

leña firewood

león *m.* lion

letra lyrics (*song*) (6); letter (*alphabet*); **letra cursiva** *s.* italics

letrero sign

levantar to raise, lift; **levantar la mano** to raise one's hand; **levantarse** to get up (4); to stand up (4); **levantarse con el pie izquierdo** to get up on the wrong side of bed (11)

ley *f.* law (17)

leyenda legend

libertad *f.* liberty, freedom

libra pound

libre free; **al aire libre** outdoors; **caída libre** free fall; **estado libre asociado** commonwealth; **ratos libres** spare (free) time (9); **tiempo libre** free time

librería bookstore (1)

libro (de texto) (text)book (1)

licencia license (14); **licencia de conducir/manejar** driver's license (14)

licenciatura Bachelor's degree

líder *m., f.* leader

liga league

ligero/a light (*not heavy*) (6)

limitado/a limited

limitar(se) to limit (oneself)

límite *m.* limit (14); **límite de velocidad** speed limit (14)

limón *m.* lemon

limonada lemonade

limpiar to clean (9); **limpiar la casa (entera)** to clean the (entire) house (9); **limpiar el garaje** to clean the garage; **limpiar en seco** to dry clean

limpio/a clean (5)

lindo/a pretty, lovely

línea line; **patinar en línea** to inline skate (9); **línea de teléfono** telephone line

lío problem; trouble; **lío de tráfico** traffic jam; **estar en un lío** to be in trouble, a problem

líquido liquid

Lisboa Lisbon

lista list

listo/a smart, clever (2); ready

literario/a literary

literatura literature

llamada (telephone) call; **llamada a larga distancia** long-distance call; **llamada en espera** call-waiting

llamar to call (6); **¿cómo se llama usted?** what is your (*form. s.*) name? (PP); **¿cómo te llamas?** what is your (*fam. s.*) name? (PP); **llamarse** to be called (4); **me llamo…** my name is . . . (PP)

llanero/a person of the plains

llanta (desinflada) (flat) tire (14)

llanto weeping, crying

llave *f.* key (4)

llegada arrival (7)

llegar (gu) to arrive (2); **llegar a ser** to become; **llegar a tiempo** to arrive on time; **¿cómo se llega a… ?** how do you get to . . . ? (14)

llenar to fill (up) (14); to fill out (*a form*) (16); **llenar una solicitud** to fill out an application (16)

lleno/a full

llevar to wear (3); to carry (3); to take (3); to lead; **llevar gafas** to wear glasses; **llevar lentes de contacto** to wear contacts; **llevar una vida saludable** to lead a healthy life; **llevar una vida sana/tranquila** to lead a healthy/calm life (10); **llevarse bien/mal (con)** to get along well/poorly (with) (15)

llorar to cry (8)

llover (llueve) to rain (5); **llueve** it's raining (5)

lluvia rain

lluvioso/a *adj.* rainy; rain; **bosque** (*m.*) **lluvioso** rain forest

lo *d.o. m.s.* you (*form.*); him, it; **a lo largo de** along; **lo bueno / lo malo** the good/bad thing (10); **lo contrario** the opposite; **lo mismo** the same thing; **lo que** what, that which (4); **¡lo siento (mucho)!** I'm (very) sorry! (11); **lo suficiente** enough (10)

lobo/a wolf

localidad *f.* ticket (*to a movie, play*)

localización *f.* location

localizar (c) to locate

loco/a crazy (5)

lógica logic

lógico/a logical

lograr to achieve

loma hill

Londres London

longaniza sausage

loro parrot

los *def. art. m. pl.* the; *d.o. m. pl.* you (*form. pl.*); them; **los años sesenta (ochenta…)** the sixties (eighties . . .); **los/las demás** the others, the rest (12); **los lunes (martes…)** on Mondays (Tuesdays . . .) (4)

lotería lottery; **billete** (*m.*) **de lotería** lottery ticket; **ganar la lotería** to win the lottery; **jugar (juego) (gu) a la lotería** to play the lottery

lubricar (qu) to lubricate

lucha fight, struggle (17)

luchar to fight (17)

luego then, afterward, next (4); **hasta luego** see you later (PP)

lugar *m.* place (1); **algún lugar** some place; **en lugar de** in place of; **ningún lugar** nowhere; **tener lugar** to take place

lujo luxury (12); **coche** (*m.*) **de lujo** luxury car; **hotel** (*m.*) **de lujo** luxury hotel (18)

lujoso/a luxurious

luna moon; **luna de miel** honeymoon (15)

lunar: de lunares polka-dot (3)

lunes *m. inv.* Monday (4); **el lunes…** Monday . . . (4); **los lunes** on Mondays (4)

Luxemburgo Luxembourg

luz *f.* (*pl.* **luces**) light (11); electricity (11); **apagar (gu) las luces** to turn out the lights; **encender (enciendo) la luz** to turn on the lights

M

macho male

madera wood

madrastra stepmother

madre *f.* mother (2); **Día** (*m.*) **de la Madre** Mother's Day

madurez *f.* maturity (15)

maestro/a schoolteacher (16); **maestro/a de escuela** schoolteacher (16); **obra maestra** masterpiece (13)

Magallanes: Estrecho de Magallanes Strait of Magellan

magia magic

magnífico/a magnificent

magno/a great

mago wizard; **Mago de Oz** Wizard of Oz; **Día** (*m.*) **de los Reyes Magos** Day of the Magi (Three Kings)

maíz *m.* (*pl.* **maíces**) corn

mal *adv.* poorly (1); badly

mal *n.* evil; illness, sickness; **mal pagado** poorly paid (16); **caerle mal a alguien** to make a bad impression on someone; **ir de mal en peor** to go from bad to worse; **llevarse mal (con)** to get along poorly (with) (15); **pasarlo mal** to have a bad time (8); **portarse mal** to misbehave (4); **salir mal** to turn out badly (4); **sentirse (me siento) (i) mal** to feel badly; to feel ill

mal, malo/a *adj.* bad (2); **hace (muy) mal tiempo** it's (very) bad weather (5); **lo malo** the bad thing, news (10); **¡qué mala suerte!** what bad luck!; **sacar (qu) malas notas** to get bad grades (11); **tener mala suerte** to have bad luck (11)

maleta suitcase (7); **hacer la(s) maleta(s)** to pack one's suitcase(s) (7)

maletero porter (7)

maletín *m.* briefcase; small suitcase

maleza bramble, weed

malvado/a evil

mamá mother, mom (2)

mami mom, mommy

mamífero/a mammal

mancha stain

mandar to send (7); to order (*someone to do something*) (12)

mandato command (6)

manejar to drive (12); to operate (*machines*) (12); to manage; **licencia de manejar** driver's license (14)

manera way, manner; **de manera que** *conj.* so that, in such a way that

manicura manicure

manifestación *f.* demonstration, march (17)

manifestar (manifiesto) to manifest; to demonstrate

mano *f.* hand (10); **darse la mano** to shake hands (10); **dedo de la mano** finger (11); **hecho/a a mano** handmade; **lavarse las manos** to wash one's hands; **levantar la mano** to raise one's hand

manso/a peaceful; gentle

manta blanket (18)

mantener (*like* **tener**) to maintain, keep (17); **mantener la paz** to maintain peace; **mantenerse en contacto** to stay in touch

mantequilla butter (6)

manzana apple (6)

mapa *m.* map

mañana *n.* morning; *adv.* tomorrow (PP); **de la mañana** in the morning, A.M. (PP); **hasta mañana** see you tomorrow (PP); **pasado mañana** the day after tomorrow (4)

máquina machine; **máquina de calcular** calculator

mar *m.* sea (7); **mar Caribe** Caribbean Sea; **mar Mediterráneo** Mediterranean Sea; **ir al mar** to go to the sea(side)

maratón *m.* marathon

maravilla wonder, marvel

maravilloso/a wonderful, marvelous

marca brand

marcar (qu) to mark

mareado/a dizzy (10)

marido husband (15)

marihuana marijuana

marimba *musical percussive instrument*

marino/a *adj.* marine

mariscos *pl.* shellfish

marítimo/a maritime; sea, marine

marroquí *m., f.* Moroccan

Marruecos Morocco

martes *m. inv.* Tuesday (4)

Martinica Martinique

marzo March (5)

más more (1); **más allá** further, farther; **más allá de** beyond; **más alto** louder; **más... que** more . . . than (5); **cada vez más** increasingly

máscara mask

mascota pet (2)

masculino/a masculine

masoquista *m., f.* masochist

matar to kill (17)

matemáticas mathematics (1)

materia (school) subject (1)

material *m.* material (*of which something is made*) (3)

materialista *m., f.* materialist

matriarcado matriarchy

matrícula tuition (1)

matricularse to enroll, register

matrimonio marriage (15); married couple (15); **contraer** (*like* **traer**) **matrimonio** to get married

máximo/a maximum

maya *n., adj. m., f.* Mayan

mayo May (5)

mayor older (5); oldest; greater; greatest

mayoría majority

me *d.o.* me; *i.o.* to/for me; *refl. pron.* myself; **me llamo...** my name is . . . (PP); **me gustaría... muchísimo** I would (really) like . . . an awful lot (7); **me molesta que...** it bothers me that (13); **me sorprende que...** it surprises me that (13); **no, no me gusta...** no, I don't like . . . (PP); **sí, me gusta...** yes, I like . . . (PP)

mecánico/a *n.* mechanic (14); *adj.* mechanical

medalla metal

medianoche *f.* midnight (8)

mediante *adv.* by means of; through

medias stockings (3)

medicina medicine (10)

médico/a doctor (2)

medida: en cierta medida in some measure; to some degree

medio *n.* medium; means; **medio ambiente** environment (*nature*) (14); **medios de comunicación** mass media (17); **medio de transporte** means of transportation (7); **por medio de** by means of

medio/a *adj.* half; middle; average; **media hermana** half-sister; **media pensión** room with breakfast and one other meal (18); **medio hermano** half-brother; **Oriente** (*m.*) **Medio** Middle East

medioambiental environmental

mediodía *m.* noon

mediterráneo/a Mediterranean; **mar** (*m.*) **Mediterráneo** Mediterranean Sea

mejilla cheek

mejor better (5); best (5)

mejorar to improve

memoria memory (12)

mencionar to mention

menor *m.* minor; *adj.* younger (5); youngest; less; least

menos less; least; minus; **a menos que** *conj.* unless (15); **menos cuarto (quince)** a quarter (fifteen minutes) to (*hour*) (PP); **menos... que** less . . . than (5); **por lo menos** at least (11)

mensaje *m.* message (12); **mensaje telefónico** phone message

mensual monthly

mensualidad *f.* monthly installment

mente *f.* mind

-mente -ly (*adverbial suffix*) (11)

mentira lie (12)

menú *m.* menu (6)

menudo: a menudo *adv.* often

mercadillo flea market

mercado market(place) (3)

merced *f.* mercy

merecer (merezco) to deserve

merendar (meriendo) to have a snack (6)

merengue *m. dance from the Dominican Republic*

merienda snack (6)

mermelada jam

mes *m.* month (5)

mesa table (1); **poner la mesa** to set the table (9); **quitar la mesa** to clear the table (9)

meseta plateau

mesita end table (4)

mesoamericano/a Meso-American

meteorológico/a meteorological

método method (10); **método Pilates** Pilates (10)

metro subway; **estación** (*f.*) **del metro** subway station (18)

metrópoli *f.* metropolis

metropolitano/a metropolitan

mexicano/a *n., adj.* Mexican (2)

mexicoamericano *n., adj.* Mexican American

mexica *pre-Columbian culture of Mexico (original name of the Aztecs)*

mezcla mix

mí *obj. of prep.* me (5)

mi(s) *poss. adj.* my (2)

microondas: horno de microondas microwave oven (9)

miedo fear; **tener miedo (de)** to be afraid (of) (3)

miel *f.* honey; **luna de miel** honeymoon (15)

miembro member

mientras while (9); *conj.* **mientras que** while

miércoles *m. inv.* Wednesday (4)

migratorio/a migratory

mil *m.* thousand, one thousand (3)

militar: servicio militar military service (17)

milla mile

millón *m.* million (3); **un millón de** one million (*of something*) (3)

mineral mineral; **agua** (*f. but* **el agua**) **mineral** mineral water

minifalda mini-skirt

mínimo/a minimum

ministerio ministry

ministro/a: primer ministro / primera ministra prime minister

minuto minute

mío/a(s) *poss. adj.* my

mirar to look at, watch (2); **mirar la televisión** to watch television (2)

misa mass; **misa del gallo** midnight mass

misión *f.* mission

misionero/a missionary

mismo *adv.* same; **ahora mismo** right now (5); at once

mismo/a *adj.* same (5); self; **lo mismo** the same thing

misterio mystery

misterioso/a mysterious

mitología mythology

mochila backpack (1)

moda fashion; style; **de moda** in style; **de última moda** trendy (hot) (3)

modelo model

módem *m.* modem (12)

moderación *f.* moderation
moderno/a modern (13)
modificar (qu) to modify
modo way, matter; mode; *gram.* mood;
de modo que in such a way that
mogote *m.* knoll; mound
molestar to bother (10); to annoy; **me
(te, le...) molesta que** it bothers
me (you, him . . .) that (13)
molesto/a annoyed (5)
molino: rueda de molino treadmill
(10)
momento moment; **en este momento**
right now
monarquía monarchy
monasterio monastery
moneda coin; currency (16)
monitor *m.* monitor
monolítico/a monolithic
monopatín *m.* skateboard (12)
monstruo monster
montaña mountain (7); **bicicleta de
montaña** mountain bike (12)
montañoso/a mountainous
montar to ride (9); **montar a caballo**
to ride a horse (9); **montar en
bicicleta** to ride a bicycle
monte *m.* mountain; **montes
Apalaches** Appalachian Mountains
montón *m.*: **un montón** a lot
monumento monument
morado/a purple (3)
moreno/a brunet(te) (2)
morir(se) (muero) (u) (*p.p.* **muerto**)
to die (8)
morro knoll; hill
mosaico mosaic
mostaza mustard
mostrar (muestro) to show (7)
motivo motive
moto(cicleta) motorcycle (12); moped
(12)
motor *m.* motor
móvil mobile; **tarjeta Internet móvil**
wireless Internet card; **teléfono
móvil** cell phone
mozo bellhop (18)
muchacho/a boy, girl
muchísimo an awful lot (7); **me
gustaría... muchísimo** I would
(really) like . . . an awful lot (7)
mucho *adv.* a lot, much (1); **¡lo
siento mucho!** I'm very sorry!
(11)
mucho/a *adj.* a lot (of) (2); *pl.* many (2);
muchas gracias thank you very
much (PP); **mucho gusto** pleased
to meet you (PP)
mudanza *n.* move
mudarse to move
mueble *m.* piece of furniture; *pl.*
furniture (4); **sacudir los muebles**
to dust the furniture (9)

muela molar, back tooth (10); **sacarle
(qu) una muela** to pull a tooth
(10); **tener dolor de muela** to
have a toothache
muerte *f.* death (15)
muerto/a (*p.p. of* **morir**) *n., adj.* dead;
Día (*m.*) **de los Muertos** Day of
the Dead
muestra sample; sign
muisca *pre-Columbian culture of central
Colombia*
mujer *f.* woman (1); wife (15); **mujer
de negocios** businesswoman (16);
mujer policía policewoman;
mujer soldado female soldier (16)
mundial *adj.* world; **Copa Mundial**
World Cup
mundo world (5)
municipalidad *f.* municipality
muñeca doll
mural *m.* mural
muralla city wall
murciélago bat
muro wall
musa muse
músculo muscle
museo museum (9); **visitar un museo**
to visit a museum (9)
música music (13); **música ranchera**
*traditional music of Mexico sung by
mariachis*
músico/a musician (13)
musulmán, musulmana *adj.* Moslem
mutuamente mutually
muy very (1); **muy bien** fine, very well
(PP); **muy buenas** good afternoon/
evening (PP)

N

nacer (nazco) to be born (15)
nacimiento birth
nación *f.* nation; **Naciones Unidas**
United Nations
nacional national
nacionalidad *f.* nationality (2)
nacionalismo nationalism
nada nothing, not anything (6); **de
nada** you're welcome (PP); **para
nada** at all
nadar to swim (7)
nadie no one, nobody, not anybody (6)
nana *term of endearment for a grandmother*
naranja orange (6)
nariz *f.* nose (10)
narración *f.* narration
narrado/a narrated
natación *f.* swimming (9)
natal *adj.* native
nativo/a native
natural natural (1); **ciencias naturales**
natural sciences (1); **recurso
natural** natural resource (14)

naturaleza nature (14)
naturismo naturism
nave *f.* ship; **nave espacial** spaceship
navegable navigable
navegar (gu) to sail; to navigate;
navegar la Red to surf the Internet
(12)
Navidad *f.* Christmas (8); **árbol** (*m.*)
de Navidad Christmas tree; **Feliz
Navidad** Merry Christmas
necesario/a necessary (2)
necesidad *f.* necessity
necesitar to need (1)
negación *f.* negation
negar (niego) (gu) to deny (13);
negarse to refuse
negativo/a negative
negocio business; **hombre** (*m.*) / **mujer**
(*f.*) **de negocios** businessman/
woman (16)
negro/a black (3)
neoclásico/a Neoclassical
neoyorquino/a *adj.* pertaining to New
York
nervioso/a nervous (5)
nevar (nieva) to snow (5); **nieva** it's
snowing (5)
ni neither; nor; not even; **ni... ni...** neither . . . nor . . .
nicaragüense *n., adj.* Nicaraguan
nieto/a grandson/granddaughter (2); *m.
pl.* grandchildren
ningún, ninguna no, none, not any
(6); **ningún lugar** nowhere
niñero/a baby-sitter (9)
niñez *f.* childhood (9)
niño/a small child (2); boy/girl (2); **de
niño/a** as a child (9)
nitrógeno nitrogen
no no (PP); not; **¿no?** right? (3); **no
hay** there isn't/aren't (PP); **no hay
de qué** you're welcome (PP); **no
hay duda** there is no doubt; **no,
no me gusta...** no, I don't like . . .
(PP)
noche *f.* night (PP); **buenas noches**
good evening, night (PP); **de la
noche** P.M. (PP); **esta noche**
tonight (5); **Noche Vieja** New
Year's Eve (8); **por la noche** in the
evening, at night (1)
Nochebuena Christmas Eve (8)
nocturno/a nocturnal
nombrar to name
nombre *m.* name (6)
normalidad *f.* normality
noroeste *m.* northwest
norte *m.* north (5)
Norteamérica North America
norteamericano/a *n., adj.* North
American
norteño/a northern
Noruega Norway

nos *d.o. pron.* us; *i.o. pron.* to/for us; *refl. pron.* ourselves; **nos vemos** see you around (PP)

nosotros/as *sub. pron.* we; *obj. (of prep.)* us

nota grade (in a course) (11); note; **nota comunicativa** note about communication; **sacar (qu) buenas/malas notas** to get good/bad grades (11)

notar to note, notice

noticia piece of news; *pl.* news (17)

noticiero newscast (17)

novecientos/as nine hundred (3)

novela novel

noveno/a ninth (13)

noventa ninety (2)

noviazgo engagement (15)

noviembre *m.* November (5)

novio/a boyfriend/girlfriend (5); fiancé(e) (15); groom, bride (15); **vestido de novia** wedding gown

nublado/a cloudy (5); **está (muy) nublado** it's (very) cloudy (5)

nuclear: energía nuclear nuclear energy

nuera daughter-in-law

nuestro/a(s) *poss. adj.* our (2); *poss. pron.* ours, of ours (17)

nueve nine (PP)

nuevo/a new (2); **Día** (*m.*) **del Año Nuevo** New Year's Day; **Feliz Año Nuevo** Happy New Year

número number (PP); **número de teléfono** phone number; **número ordinal** *gram.* ordinal number (13)

numeroso/a numerous

nunca never, not ever (2); **casi nunca** almost never (2)

O

o or (PP)

ó or (*between two numbers* [*digits*])

obedecer (obedezco) to obey (14)

obelisco obelisk

obertura overture

obispo bishop

objetivo *n.* objective

objeto object (1); **objeto volante no identificado (OVNI)** unidentified flying object (UFO)

obligación *f.* obligation

obligatorio/a obligatory, compulsory

obra work (13); **obra de arte** work of art (13); **obra de teatro** play (*theatrical*) (13); **obra maestra** masterpiece (13)

obrero/a worker, laborer (16)

observar to observe

observatorio observatory

obtener (*like* **tener**) to get, obtain (12)

obvio/a obvious

ocarina *ancient flute-like instrument*

ocasión *f.* occasion

occidental western

occidentalizar (c) to westernize

océano ocean (7); **océano Pacífico** Pacific Ocean

ochenta eighty (2)

ocho eight (PP)

ochocientos/as eight hundred (3)

octavo/a eighth (13)

octubre *m.* October (5)

oculto/a hidden

ocupación *f.* occupation

ocupado/a busy (5)

ocupar to occupy

ocurrir to occur

odiar to hate (7)

odio *n.* hate

oeste *m.* west (5)

oferta offer

oficial official

oficina office (1); **oficina de correos** post office (18)

oficio trade (*profession*) (16)

ofrecer (ofrezco) to offer (7)

oído inner ear (10)

oír to hear (4)

ojalá (que) I hope, wish (that) (13)

ojo eye (10); **ojo alerta** eagle eye; *interj.* **¡ojo!** watch out!

ola wave

olímpico/a: Juegos Olímpicos Olympic Games

oliva olive; **aceite** (*m.*) **de oliva** olive oil

olmeca *n., adj. m., f.* Olmec

olvidadizo/a forgetful

olvidar(se) (de) to forget (about) (8)

olvido forgetfulness; oblivion

ombligo navel

once eleven (PP)

onda wave; **¿qué onda?** what's new/happening?; **en onda** in style

ONU *f.* **(Organización** [*f.*] **de Naciones Unidas)** U.N. (United Nations)

opción *f.* option

opcional optional

ópera opera (13)

operación *f.* operation

operar to operate

opinar to think; to have, express an opinion

opinión *f.* opinion

oponerse (a) (*like* **poner**) to oppose

oportunidad *f.* opportunity

oposición *f.* opposition

optimista *m., f.* optimistic

opuesto/a opposite

oración *f.* sentence

oral oral (11); **informe** (*m.*) **oral** oral report (11); **patrimonio oral** oral history

orden *f.* order; **poner en orden** to put in order

ordenado/a neat (5)

ordenador *m.* computer (*Sp.*) (12)

ordinal: número ordinal *gram.* ordinal number (13)

oreja (outer) ear (10)

orgánico/a organic

organización *f.* organization; **Organización de Naciones Unidas (ONU)** United Nations (U.N.)

organizar (c) to organize

oriental eastern

oriente *m.* east; **Oriente Medio** Middle East

origen *m.* origin

orinar to urinate

orisha *m., f. spiritual being in Yoruba mythology*

oro gold (3); **es de oro** it's (made of) gold (3); **Ricitos de Oro** Goldilocks

orquesta orchestra (13)

os *d.o. pron.* you (*fam. pl.*); *i.o. pron.* to/for you (*fam. pl.*)

oso bear

ostra oyster

otavaleño/a of or pertaining to Otavalo (Ecuador)

otoño autumn (5)

otorgar (gu) to grant

otro/a other, another (2); **otra vez** again; **por otra parte / otro lado** on the other hand

OVNI (objeto volante no identificado) UFO (unidentified flying object)

Oz: Mago de Oz Wizard of Oz

ozono: capa de ozono ozone layer

P

paciencia patience

paciente *n. m., f.* patient (10); *adj.* patient

Pacífico: (océano) Pacífico Pacific (Ocean)

padrastro godfather

padre *m.* father (2); *pl.* parents (2)

paella *Spanish dish made with rice, shellfish, and often chicken, and flavored with saffron*

pagado: bien/mal pagado well-/poorly paid (15)

pagar (gu) to pay (1); **pagar a plazos** to pay in installments (16); **pagar al contado** to pay in cash; **pagar en efectivo** to pay in cash (16)

página page

país *m.* country (2)

paisaje *m.* landscape

pájaro bird (2)

Pakistán Pakistan

pakistaní *m., f.* Pakistani
palabra word (PP)
palacio palace
palmera palm tree
pampa plain (*geography, Arg.*)
pan (*m.*) bread (6); **pan tostado** toast (6)
panameño/a *n., adj.* Panamanian
pandereta tambourine
pandilla gang
panorámico/a panoramic
pantalla screen (12); **pantalla grande** big screen (12); **pantalla plana** flat screen (12)
pantalones *m., pl.* pants (3); **pantalones cortos** shorts
papá *m.* dad (2)
papa potato (6); **papas fritas** French fries (6)
papel *m.* paper (1); role (*in a play*) (13); **papel para cartas** stationery (18)
papelería stationery store (18)
paquete *m.* package (18)
par *m.* pair; **un par de veces** a couple of times
para *prep.* (intended) for (2); in order to (2); **para + inf.** in order to (*do something*); **para nada** at all; **para que** *conj.* so that (15)
parabrisas *m. inv.* windshield (14)
paracaidismo skydiving
parada stop (18); **hacer paradas** to make stops (7); **parada del autobús** bus stop (18)
paraguayo/a *n., adj.* Paraguayan
paraíso paradise
parar to stop (14)
parcial: de tiempo parcial part-time (11)
pardo brown
parecer (parezco) to seem
pared *f.* wall (4); **pintar las paredes** to paint the walls (9)
pareja (married) couple (15); partner (15)
paréntesis *m. inv.* parentheses
pariente *m., f.* relative (2)
parlamentario/a parliamentary
paro strike
párpado eyelid
parque *m.* park
párrafo paragraph
parranda party
parroquial parochial
parte *f.* part (4); **por otra parte** on the other hand; **por parte de** on behalf of; **por todas partes** everywhere
participación *f.* participation
participante *m., f.* participant
participio pasado *gram.* past participle
particular particular, private; **casa particular** private home; **clase** (*f.*) **particular** private class

partida: punto de partida starting point
partido game, match (*sports*) (9)
partir: a partir de... as of . . . ; from (*point in time*) on
pasado/a *adj.* last (10); past (10); **el año pasado** last year; **huevo pasado por agua** poached egg; **pasado mañana** the day after tomorrow (4)
pasado *n.* past
pasado mañana the day after tomorrow (4)
pasaje *m.* passage; ticket; fare, price (*of a transportation ticket*) (7)
pasajero/a passenger (7)
pasaporte *m.* passport (18)
pasar to happen (5); to pass; to spend (*time*) (5); **pasar la aspiradora** to vacuum (9); **pasar las vacaciones en...** to spend one's vacation in . . . (7); **pasar por el control de la seguridad** to go through security (7); **pasarlo bien/mal** to have a good/bad time (8)
pasatiempo pastime (9)
Pascua Easter (8); **Pascua Judía** Passover; **Isla de Pascua** Easter Island
pasear to take a walk, stroll; to go for a ride; **pasear en bicicleta** to ride a bicycle (9)
paseo walk, stroll (9); **dar un paseo** to take a walk (9)
pasillo hallway (7)
pasión *f.* passion
paso step
pasta pasta; paste; **pasta dental** toothpaste (18)
pastar to pasture
pastel *m.* cake (6); pie (6); **pastel de cumpleaños** birthday cake (8)
pastelería pastry shop (18)
pastel(ito) (small) pastry (18)
pastilla pill (10)
pastor(a) pastor
patata potato (6); **patatas fritas** French fries (6)
patín *m.* skate (12)
patinar to skate (9); **patinar en línea** to inline skate (9)
patio patio; yard (4)
patojo/a guy/gal (*sl. Guat.*)
Patricio: Día (*m.*) **de San Patricio** St. Patrick's Day
patrimonio patrimony; **patrimonio oral** oral history
patrón, patrona *adj.* patron; boss
pavimentado/a paved
pavo turkey (6)
pavo real peacock
paz *f.* (*pl.* **paces**) peace (17); **mantener** (*like* **tener**) **la paz** to maintain peace (17); **vivir en paz** to live in peace

PDA *m.* PDA (12)
pedir (pido) (i) to ask for (4); to order (*in a restaurant*) (4); **pedir disculpas** to apologize (11); **pedir prestado/a** to borrow (16)
pegar (gu) to hit (9); **pegarse con/contra/en** to run, bump into (11)
peinarse to comb one's hair (4)
pelado/a peeled
pelear to fight (9)
película movie (4); film; **ir a ver una película** to go to the movies; **rollo de película** roll of film
peligro danger; **especie** (*f.*) **en peligro de extinción** endangered species (14)
peligroso/a dangerous
pelo hair; **corte** (*m.*) **de pelo** haircut; **tomarle el pelo** to pull someone's leg
pelota ball
peluquero/a hairstylist (15)
pendiente *m.* earring
península peninsula
pensar (pienso) (en) to think (about) (4); **pensar + inf.** to intend/plan to (*do something*) (4)
pensión *f.* boardinghouse (18); **media pensión** room with breakfast and one other meal (18); **pensión completa** room and full board (18)
penúltimo/a next-to-last
peor worse (5); **ir de mal en peor** to go from bad to worse
pequeño/a small (2)
percibir to perceive
perder (pierdo) to lose (4); to miss (*a function*) (4)
pérdida loss
perdón pardon me, excuse me (PP)
perdonar to forgive
perejil *m.* parsley
perezoso/a lazy (2)
perfecto/a perfect
perfil *m.* profile
perfume *m.* perfume
periódico newspaper (2)
periodista *m., f.* journalist (16)
período period (*of time*)
perla pearl
permanecer (permanezco) to remain, stay
permanente permanent
permiso permission; permit; **con permiso** excuse me (PP)
permitir to permit, allow (12)
pero but (PP)
perro dog (2)
perseguir (*like* **seguir**) to chase; to pursue
persianas (window) shades, blinds
persona person (1)
personalidad *f.* personality

personalmente personally

perspectiva perspective

persuasivo/a persuasive

pertenecer (pertenezco) a to belong to

perturbar to bother, perturb

peruano/a *n., adj.* Peruvian

pesado/a heavy; difficult; boring (9)

pesar to weigh; **a pesar de** in spite of

pescado fish (*cooked*) (6)

pesimista *m., f.* pessimistic

peso weight; **tener exceso de peso** to be overweight

petróleo petroleum, oil

pez *m.* (*pl.* **peces**) fish (14)

picado/a chopped

picante hot, spicy (6)

Picis *m.* Pisces

picnic: hacer un picnic to go on a picnic (9)

pie foot (11); **a pie** on foot; **dedo del pie** toe (11); **levantarse con el pie izquierdo** to get up on the wrong side of the bed (11)

pierna leg (11)

Pilates *m. inv.:* **(método) Pilates** Pilates (10); **hacer (el método) Pilates** to do Pilates (10)

píldora pill

piloto pilot

pimienta pepper (6)

pingüino penguin

pino pine

pintar to paint (9); **pintar las paredes** to paint the walls (9)

pintor(a) painter (13)

pintoresco/a picturesque

pintura paint; painting (*general*) (13); painting (*piece of art*) (13)

pirámide *f.* pyramid

pirata *m., f.* pirate

Pirineos Pyrenees

piscina swimming pool (4)

piscolabis *m.* snack

piso floor (*of a building*) (12); apartment; **barrer el piso** to sweep the floor (9); **primer/segundo piso** second/third floor (12)

pizarra chalkboard (1)

pizzería pizza parlor

placer *m.* pleasure

plan *m.* plan (9); **hacer planes (para)** to make plans (to) (9)

planchar to iron (9)

planeta *m.* planet

plano *m.* map; blueprint

plano/a flat; **pantalla plana** flat screen (12); **tarifa plana** flat rate

planta plant; floor (*of a building*) (12); **planta baja** ground floor (12)

plantación *f.* plantation

plástico *n.* plastic

plata *n.* silver (3)

plato dish (*plate*) (4); dish (6); course (6); **lavar los platos** to wash dishes (9)

playa beach (5)

plazo deadline (11); **a plazos** in installments (16); **poner plazo** to set a deadline

plena *narrative musical form from the coasts of Puerto Rico*

plomero/a plumber (15)

pluma pen

pluscuamperfecto *gram.* pluperfect (*tense*)

población *f.* population (14)

poblado/a populated

pobre *n. m., f.* poor person; *adj.* poor (2)

pobreza poverty

poco *adv.* little (3); **dentro de poco** in a little while; **poco a poco** little by little; **un poco (de)** a little bit (of) (1)

poco/a *adj.* little, few (3)

poder *n. m.* power

poder to be able to, can (3)

poderoso/a powerful

poema *m.* poem

poesía poetry; **recital** (*m.*) **de poesía** poetry reading

poeta *m., f.* poet (13)

policía *m., f.* police officer (14); *f.* police (*force*); **mujer** (*f.*) **policía** policewoman

poliomielitis *f.* polio

política politics (17)

político/a *n.* politician (17); *adj.* political; **ciencias políticas** political science (1)

pollera *type of skirt made of various layers*

pollo chicken (6); **pollo asado** roast chicken (6); **pollo frito** fried chicken

polvo dust; **quitar el polvo** to dust

poner (*p.p.* **puesto**) to put, place (4); **poner la mesa** to set the table (9); **poner plazo** to set a deadline; **ponerle una inyección** to give (*someone*) a shot, injection (10); **ponerle una vacuna** to give (*someone*) a vaccination; **ponerse** to put on (*clothing*) (4); **ponerse** + *adj.* to get, become + *adj.* (8); **ponerse en contacto con** to get in touch with

pontificio/a pontifical

popularidad *f.* popularity

por *prep.* about (5); because of (5); by; for (7); through (7); during; along; by way of; **gracias por** thanks for (8); **por año** yearly, per year; **por ciento** percent; **por completo** completely; **por Dios** for heaven's sake (11); **por ejemplo** for example (11); **por eso** therefore (2); **por favor** please (PP); **por fin** at last (4); **por la mañana** in the morning (1); **por la noche** in the evening, at night (1); **por la tarde** in the afternoon (1); **por lo general** in general (4); **por lo menos** at least (11); **por medio de** by means of; **por otra parte** on the other hand; **por otro lado** on the other hand; **por primera vez** for the first time (11); **¿por qué?** why? (2); **por si acaso** just in case (11); **¡por supuesto!** of course! (11); **por todas partes** everywhere (11); **por última vez** for the last time (11); **por un lado** on the one hand

porcentaje *m.* percentage

porción *f.* portion

porque because (2)

portada entryway

portarse (bien/mal) to behave well/badly (8)

portátil portable; **computadora portátil** laptop; **radio portátil** (portable) radio (*apparatus*) (12); **televisor** (*m.*) **portátil** portable television

porteño/a *resident of Buenos Aires*

portero/a building manager (12); doorman (12)

portugués *m.* Portuguese (*language*)

portugués, portuguesa *n., adj.* Portuguese

posesión *f.* possession

posesivo/a possessive

posibilidad *f.* possibility

posible possible (2); **es posible que...** it's possible that . . .

posición *f.* position

positivo/a positive

postal: tarjeta postal postcard (7)

postre *m.* dessert (6)

postularse (a un cargo como candidato) to run (for office as a candidate) (17)

potencial *m.* potential

pozo well

práctica practice

practicar (qu) to practice (1); **practicar el alpinismo** to mountain climb; **practicar un deporte** to play, practice a sport

práctico/a practical

pradera prairie

preadolescencia preadolescence

precio (fijo) (fixed) price (3)

precioso/a precious

precipicio precipice

precipitado/a hasty

precisamente precisely

precolombino/a pre-Columbian

predicción *f.* prediction
preescolar *m., f.* preschooler
preferencia preference (PP)
preferible preferable; **es preferible que...** it's preferable that . . .
preferir (prefiero) (i) to prefer (3)
pregunta question (4); **hacer una pregunta** to ask a question (4)
preguntar to ask (*a question*) (6)
prehispánico/a pre-Hispanic
prematuro/a premature
premio award; prize
prenda article of clothing
prender to turn on (*lights or an appliance*)
prensa press (media) (17)
prensado/a pressed
preocupación *f.* worry
preocupado/a worried (5)
preocupante worrisome
preparación *f.* preparation
preparar to prepare (6)
preparativo preparation
preposición *f. gram.* preposition
presa capture
presencia presence
presentación *f.* introduction
presentar to present; to introduce
presente *m.* present (*time*); *gram.* present tense
preservación *f.* preservation
presidencia presidency
presidencial presidential
presidente/a president
presión *f.* pressure (11); **sufrir (muchas) presiones** to be under (a lot of) stress (11)
prestado/a: pedir prestado/a to borrow (16)
préstamo loan (16)
prestar to loan (7)
prestigio prestige
presupuesto budget (16)
pretérito *gram.* preterite (*tense*)
primario/a primary; **bosque** (*m.*) **primario** old-growth forest; **escuela primaria** elementary school
primavera spring (5)
primer, primero/a *adj.* first (4); **a primera vista** at first sight (15); **de primera** first-class; **el primero de** the first of (*month*) (5); **por primera vez** for the first time ; **primer piso** second floor (12); **primer ministro / primera ministra** prime minister; **primera clase** first class (7); **primera comunión** first communion
primero *adj.* first (4)
primo/a cousin (2)
principal main, principle
príncipe *m.* prince

principio beginning (16); **al principio** in the beginning, at first; **al principio de** at the beginning of (16)
prisa hurry (3); **tener prisa** to be in a hurry (3)
privado/a private
privilegio privilege
probabilidad *f.* probability
probable probable (13); **es probable que...** it's probable, likely that . . . (13)
probar (pruebo) to try, taste
problema *m.* problem
procesión *f.* procession
proceso process
producción *f.* production
producir (*like* conducir) to produce
producto product
profesión *f.* profession
profesor(a) professor (1)
profundidad *f.* depth
programa *m.* program
programación *f.* programming
programador(a) programmer (15)
progresivo *gram.* progressive
prohibir (prohíbo) to prohibit (12)
promedio average
prometer to promise (7)
pronombre *m. gram.* pronoun (1); **pronombre personal** personal pronoun (1)
pronominal *adj.* pronoun
pronto soon; **hasta pronto** see you soon; **tan pronto como** as soon as (16)
pronunciación *f.* pronunciation
pronunciar to pronounce
propiedad *f.* property
propina tip (18)
propio/a *adj.* own
propósito purpose
prórroga extension
próspero/a prosperous
protección *f.* protection
proteger (protejo) to protect (14)
protesta protest
protestar to protest
proveer (*like* ver) to provide
provenir (*like* venir) to come from
proverbio proverb
providencia providence
provincia province
provocar (qu) to provoke
provocativo/a provocative
próximo/a next (4); **el próximo año** next year; **el próximo martes** next Tuesday (4)
proyecto project
prudente *m., adj.* prudent
prueba quiz (11); test (11)
publicación *f.* publication
publicar (qu) to publish

publicidad *f.* publicity
publicitario/a: anuncio publicitario commercial, ad
público/a public (14)
pueblo town
puente *m.* bridge
puerco pig
puerta door (1)
puerto port (7)
puertorriqueño/a *n., adj.* Puerto Rican
pues *conj.* since, because, for; *adv.* then, well, all right
puesto job; position; place (*in line*) (7); **guardar (un puesto)** to save (*a place*) [in line] (7)
puesto/a (*p.p. of* **poner**) put, placed; set
pulgada inch
pulgar *m.* thumb
pulmón *m.* lung (10)
pulóver *m.* sweater (*Arg.*)
punta point, tip
punto point; **en punto** on the dot (*time*) (PP); **punto cardinal** cardinal direction (5); **punto de partida** starting point, point of departure; **punto de vista** point of view
puntual punctual
purista *m., f.* purist
puro *n.* cigar
puro/a pure (14); **aire** (*m.*) **puro** clean air

Q

que that (2); which; who (2); **así que** therefore, consequently, so; **hasta que** *conj.* until (16); **hay que + *inf.*** it's necessary to (*do something*) (13); **lo que** what, that which (4); **más... que** more . . . than (5); **menos... que** less . . . than (5)
¿qué? what? (PP); which? (PP); **¿por qué?** why? **¿qué día es hoy?** what day is today? (4); **¿qué fecha es hoy?** what's today's date? (5); **¿qué hora es?** what time is it? (PP); **¿qué onda?** what's new/ happening?; **¿qué tal?** how are you? (PP); **¿qué tiempo hace?** what's the weather like? (5)
¡qué... ! what . . . !; **¡qué + *adj.*!** how . . . + *adj.*! (11); **¡qué barbaridad!** how awful!; **¡qué chévere!** cool!; **¡qué extraño que... !** how strange that . . . ! (13); **¡qué ganga!** what a bargain!; **¡qué lástima que... !** what a shame that . . . ! (13); **¡qué mala suerte!** what bad luck!; **¡qué torpe!** how clumsy!
quebrar(se) ([me] quiebro) to break

quechua *m.* Quechua (*indigenous South American language*)

quedar to remain, be left (11); to be situated; **quedarse** to stay, remain (*in a place*) (5)

quehacer *m.* chore; **quehacer doméstico** household chore (9)

quejarse (de) to complain (about) (7)

quemar to burn

quena *South American panpipe*

querer to want (3); **quererse** to love each other (10); to be fond of each other (10); **eso quiere decir…** that means . . . (10); **fue sin querer** it was unintentional (11)

querido/a dear (5)

queso cheese (6)

quien(es) who, whom

¿quién(es)? who? (1); whom? (1); **¿de quién?** whose? (2)

quijongo *instrument consisting of a single-string bow with a gourd resonator*

química chemistry (1)

quince fifteen (PP); **menos quince** fifteen till (*the hour*) (PP); **y quince** fifteen past (*the hour*) (PP)

quinceañera *young woman's fifteenth birthday party*

quinientos/as five hundred (3)

quinto/a fifth (13)

quiosco kiosk (18)

quitar to remove; **quitar la mesa** to clear the table (9); **quitar el polvo** to dust; **quitarse** to take off (*clothing*) (4)

quizás perhaps

R

rabino/a rabbi

radical *m. gram.* stem

radio *m.* radius; **radio (portátil)** (portable) radio (*apparatus*) (12); *f.* radio (*medium*) (17); **estación** (*f.*) **de radio** radio station

radioyente *m., f.* radio listener; *m., pl.* radio audience

raíz *f.* (*pl.* **raíces**) root

rana frog

ranchero/a *adj.* ranch; **música ranchera** *traditional music of Mexico sung by mariachis*

rancho ranch

rápido *adv.* quickly

rápido/a fast; **comida rápida** fast food

rascacielos *m. inv.* skyscraper (14)

rato *n.* while, short time; **ratos libres** spare (free) time (9)

ratón *m.* mouse (12)

raya: de rayas striped (3)

raza race; **Día** (*m.*) **de la Raza** Columbus Day (Hispanic Awareness Day)

razón *f.* reason; **no tener razón** to be wrong (3); **tener razón** to be right (3)

reacción *f.* reaction

reaccionar to react

real real; royal; **pavo real** peacock

realidad *f.* reality

realista *m., f.* realist; *adj.* realistic

rebaja sale, reduction (3); **estar en rebaja** to be on sale

rebajar to lower

rebelde *n. m., f.* rebel; *adj.* rebellious

rebelión *f.* rebellion

recado written note

recámara bedroom

recepción *f.* front desk (18)

recepcionista *m., f.* receptionist

receptor *m.* receptor

receta recipe (6); prescription (10)

recetar to prescribe

recibir to receive (2)

recibo receipt

reciclaje *m.* recycling (1)

reciclar to recycle (14)

recién *adv.* newly, recently; **recién casado/a (con)** newlywed (to) (15)

reciente recent

recíproco/a reciprocal

recital (*m.*) **de poesía** poetry reading

reclinado/a reclined

recoger (recojo) to collect (11); to pick up (11)

recomendable recommendable

recomendación *f.* recommendation; **carta de recomendación** letter of recommendation

recomendar (recomiendo) to recommend (7)

reconquista reconquest

recordar (recuerdo) to remember (8)

recorrer to cross; to go through

recreo recess

rector(a) university president

recuerdo memory; souvenir

recuperación *f.* recuperation

recuperar to recuperate

recurso resource (14); **recurso natural** natural resource (14)

Red *f.* Internet; Net (12); **navegar (gu) la Red** to surf the Internet (12)

reducción *f.* reduction

referencia reference

referirse (refiero) (i) (a) to refer (to)

refinar to refine

refinería refinery

reflejar to reflect

reflexivo/a reflexive

refrán *m.* saying, proverb

refresco soft drink (6)

refrigerador *m.* refrigerator (9)

refugiarse to take refuge

refugio refuge

regalar to give as a gift (7)

regalo gift (2)

regatear to barter (3)

región *f.* region

registrar to search, examine (18)

regla rule

regresar to return (*to a place*) (1); **regresar a casa** to go home (1)

regulador (*m.*) **termómetro** thermostat

regular so-so, OK (PP)

reina queen (17)

reír(se) (río) (i) de to laugh (at) (8)

relación *f.* relation; relationship (15); **con relación a** regarding

relacionarse con to be related to

relajante relaxing

relajarse to relax

relativo/a relative

religión *f.* religion

religioso/a religious

rellenar to fill

relleno/a full, filled

reloj *m.* watch (3)

remedio remedy

remolcar (qu) to tow

remoto/a remote; **control** (*m.*) **remoto** remote control (12)

renombrado/a renowned

renovar to renovate

renunciar (a) to resign (from) (16)

reparar to repair (14)

repaso review

repente: de repente suddenly (10)

repetición *f.* repetition

repetir (repito) (i) to repeat

repetitivo/a repetitive

repique: tambor (*m.*) **repique** *typical drum of Uruguay (used in Candombe music)*

réplica replica

reportaje *m.* report

reportero/a journalist (17); **reportero/a deportivo/a** sports reporter

repostería confectioner's, cake shop

represa dam

representación *f.* representation

representante *n. m., f.* representative

representativo/a *adj.* representative

república republic

republicano/a Republican

requerir (requiero) (i) to require

requisito requirement

res *f.* beast, animal

reserva reserve; reservation (*Sp.*); **hacer reserva** to make a reservation

reservación *f.* reservation (18); **hacer una reservación** to make a reservation

resfriado *n.* cold (*illness*) (10)

resfriado/a *adj.* congested, stuffed up (10)

resfriarse (me resfrío) to get a cold (10)

residencia dormitory (1)

residencial residential

residente *m., f.* resident

resistir to resist

resolver (resuelvo) (*p.p.* **resuelto**) to resolve (14)

respectivo/a respective

respecto: (con) respecto a with regard to, with respect to

respetar to respect

respeto respect

respiración *f.* breath

respirar to breathe (10)

responder to respond

responsabilidad *f.* responsibility (17)

responsable responsible

respuesta answer (5)

restaurado/a restored

restaurante *m.* restaurant (4)

resto rest; *pl.* remains

restricción *f.* restriction

resucitar to resuscitate

resuelto/a (*p.p. of* **resolver**) resolved

resultar to result

resumen *m.* summary; **en resumen** in summary

retirarse to retire

retrato portrait

retumbar to resound, thunder

reunión *f.* reunion

reunirse (me reúno) (con) to get together (with) (8)

reverenciado/a revered

revés: al revés backward

revisar to check (14); **revisar el aceite** to check the oil (14)

revista magazine (2)

revolución *f.* revolution

rey *m.* king (17); **Día** (*m.*) **de los Reyes Magos** Day of the Magi (Three Kings)

rezar (c) to pray

Ricitos de Oro Goldilocks

rico/a rich (2); delicious (6)

ridículo/a ridiculous

rima rhyme

rinoceronte *m.* rhinoceros

río river (14)

riqueza wealth

ritmo rhythm (14)

robar to rob, steal

robo theft

robot *m.* robot

rocoso/a rocky

rodaja slice

rodear to surround

rojo/a red (3); **Caperucita Roja** Little Red Ridinghood

rollo de película roll of film

Roma Rome

romano/a *n., adj.* Roman

romántico/a romantic

romper(se) (*p.p.* **roto**) to break (11); **romper con** to break up with (15)

rondalla *group of serenaders or minstrels*

ropa clothes, clothing (3); **ropa interior** underwear (3); **planchar la ropa** to iron clothing (9)

rosado/a pink (3)

roto/a (*p.p. of* **romper**) broken

rubio/a blond(e) (2)

rueda de molino treadmill (10)

ruido noise (4)

ruidoso/a noisy

ruina ruin (13)

ruso Russian (*language*)

ruso/a *n., adj.* Russian

rutina routine (14); **rutina diaria** daily routine (4)

rutinario/a *adj.* routine

S

sábado Saturday (4)

sábana sheet (18)

saber to know (6); **saber** + *inf.* to know how to (*do something*) (6)

sabiduría wisdom

sabor *m.* taste; flavor

sabroso/a tasty

sacar (qu) to withdraw, take out (*money*)(16); to take (*photos*) (7); to get (*grades*) (11); to extract; **sacar buenas/malas notas** to get good/bad grades (11); **sacar dinero** to withdraw money; **sacar fotos** to take pictures (7); **sacar la basura** to take out the garbage (9); **sacar la lengua** to stick out one's tongue (10); **sacar un diente / una muela** to pull a tooth (10)

sacerdote *m.* priest

sacrificio sacrifice

sacudir los muebles to dust the furniture (9)

safari: ir de safari to go on a safari

Sagitario Sagittarius

sagrado/a sacred

sal *f.* salt (6)

sala room; living room (4); **sala de clase** classroom; **sala de emergencias/urgencia** emergency room (10); **sala de espera** waiting room (7); **sala de fumar/ fumadores** smoking area (7)

salado/a: agua (*f. but* **el agua**) **salada** saltwater

salar *m.* salt mine

salario pay, wages (16)

salchicha sausage (6)

salida departure (7)

salir (de) to leave (*a place*) (4); **salir bien/mal** to turn/come out well/ badly (4); **salir con** to go out with (4); **salir de vacaciones** to leave on vacation (7); **salir para** to leave for (*a place*) (4)

salmón *m.* salmon (6)

salón *m.* room; **salón de baile** ballroom; **salón de clase** classroom (1); **baile** (*m.*) **de salón** ballroom dance

salsa sauce; salsa (*music*)

salto waterfall

salud *f.* health (10)

saludable healthy; **llevar una vida saludable** to lead a healthy life

saludarse to greet each other (10)

saludo greeting (PP)

salvadoreño/a *n., adj.* Salvadoran

salvaje: animal (*m.*) **salvaje** wild animal (14)

san, santo/a *n.* saint; **Día** (*m.*) **de San Patricio** St. Patrick's Day; **Día** (*m.*) **de San Valentín** St. Valentine's Day; **Día** (*m.*) **de Todos los Santos** All Saints' Day

sandalias sandals (3)

sándwich *m.* sandwich (6)

sangre *f.* blood (10)

sanitario/a sanitary

sano/a healthy (10); **comer comidas sanas** to eat healthy food; **llevar una vida sana** to lead a healthy life (10)

santo/a holy; **Semana Santa** Holy Week

sardana *traditional dance of the region of Catalonia, Spain*

satélite *m.* satellite

satisfacción *f.* satisfaction

satisfacer (*like* **hacer**) to satisfy

satisfactorio/a satisfactory

Saudita: Arabia Saudita Saudi Arabia

sazonador(a) *adj.* seasoning

secadora clothes dryer (9)

sección *f.* section

seco/a dry; **limpiar en seco** to dry clean

secretario/a secretary (1)

secreto secret; **guardar en secreto** to keep as a secret

secuencia sequence

secundario/a secondary; **escuela secundaria** high school

sed *f.* thirst; **tener (mucha) sed** to be (very) thirsty (6)

seda silk (3); **es de seda** it's (made of) silk (3)

seguida: en seguida right away (10)

seguir (sigo) (i) to keep on going (14); to continue (5)

según according to (2)

segundo/a second (13); **segundo piso** third floor (12)

seguridad *f.* security (17); **pasar por el control de la seguridad** to go through security (7)

seguro/a *adj.* sure, certain (5); **es seguro que...** it's a sure thing that . . . (13); **(no) estar seguro/a (de)** to be (un)sure (of)

seguro/a *n.* insurance; **seguro social** social security

seis six (PP)

seiscientos/as six hundred (3)

selección *f.* selection

seleccionar to select

selva jungle; **selva tropical** tropical jungle; **Selva Amazonas** Amazon Jungle; **Selva Amazónica** Amazon Jungle

semáforo traffic signal (14)

semana week (4); **día** (*m.*) **de semana** weekday; **fin** (*m.*) **de semana** weekend (1); **la semana que viene** next week (4); **Semana Santa** Holy Week; **una vez a la semana** once a week (2)

semejante similar

semejanza similarity

semestre *m.* semester

semillero nursery; hot-bed

senador(a) senator

sencillo/a simple

sendero path

sensación *f.* sensation

sensible sensitive

sentado/a seated, sitting

sentarse (me siento) to sit down (4)

sentido meaning; sense

sentimental sentimental (15)

sentimiento feeling

sentir (siento) (i) to regret (13); to feel sorry (13); **¡lo siento (mucho)!** I'm (very) sorry! (11); **sentirse** to feel (*an emotion*) (8); **sentirse mal** to feel badly; to feel ill

señor (Sr.) *m.* man; Mr.; sir (PP)

señora (Sra.) woman; Mrs.; ma'am (PP)

señorita (Srta.) young woman; Miss; Ms. (PP)

separación *f.* separation (15)

separado/a separate

separar to separate; **separarse (de)** to separate (from) (15)

septiembre *m.* September (5)

séptimo/a seventh (13)

ser (*m.*) **humano** human being

ser to be (2); **ser** + *profession* to be a/an (*profession*); **ser aburrido/a** to be boring (9); **ser aficionado/a (a)** to be a fan (of) (9); **ser alérgico/a (a)** to be allergic (to); **ser divertido/a** to be fun (9); **ser en** + *place* to take place in/at (*a place*) (8); **¿cuál es**

la fecha de hoy? what is today's date? (5); **¿cuánto es?** how mucho is it? (3); **¿de qué color es?** what color is it? (3); **¿qué hora es?** what time is it? (PP); **es** he/she/it is (PP); **eres** you (*fam. s.*) are (PP); **es de algodón/cuero/lana/oro/ plata/seda** it's (made of) cotton/ leather/wool/gold/silver/silk (3); **es absurdo que...** it's absurd that . . . (13); **es cierto que...** it's true that . . . (13); **es de...** it is made of . . . (13); **es extraño que...** it's strange that . . . (13); **es hora de** + *inf.* it's time to (*do something*); **es (im) posible que...** it's impossible that . . . (13); **es improbable que...** it's unlikely that . . . (13); **es increíble que...** it's incredible that . . . (13); **es la una** it's one o'clock (PP); **es preferible que...** it's preferable that . . . (13); **es seguro que...** it's a sure thing that . . . (13); **es terrible que...** it's terrible that . . . (13); **es urgente que...** it's urgent that . . . (13); **es una lástima que...** it's a shame that . . . (13); **ayer fue (miércoles...)** yesterday was (Wednesday . . .) (4); **fue sin querer** it was unintentional (11); **llegar (gu) a ser** to become; **son las...** it's . . . o'clock (PP); **soy** I am (PP)

serie *f.* series

serio/a serious

servicio service (14); **servicio de cuartos** room service (18); **servicio militar** military service (17); **servicios públicos** public services

servilleta napkin

servir (sirvo) (i) to serve (4)

sesenta sixty (2)

sesión *f.* session

setecientos/as seven hundred (3)

setenta seventy (2)

sevillano/a *n.* person from Seville; *adj.* of/from Seville

sevillista *n.* person from Seville; *adj.* of/ from Seville

sexo sex

sexto/a sixth (13)

si if (2); **por si acaso** just in case (11)

sí yes (PP); **sí, me gusta...** yes, I like . . . (PP)

sicoanálisis *m. inv.* psychoanalysis

sicología psychology (1)

sicólogo/a psychologist (16)

siempre always (2)

sierra mountain

siesta nap (4); **dormir (duermo) (u) la siesta** to take a nap (4); **echarse una siesta** to take a nap

siete seven (PP)

siglo century

significado meaning

significar (qu) to mean

signo sign

siguiente *adj.* following (4)

sílaba syllable

silencio silence

silenciosamente silently

silla chair (1)

sillón *m.* armchair (4)

simbólico/a symbolic

símbolo symbol

simpático/a nice, likeable (2)

simular to simulate

sin without (4); **sin duda** without a doubt; **sin embargo** nevertheless (5); **sin hogar** homeless; **fue sin querer** it was unintentional (11)

sinceridad *f.* sincerity

sincero/a sincere

sino but (rather); **sino que** *conj.* but (rather)

sinónimo synonym

sintético/a synthetic

síntoma *m.* symptom (10)

siquiatra *m., f.* psychiatrist (16)

sistema *m.* system; **sistema GPS** GPS; **sistema inmunológico** immune system; **sistema solar** solar system; **analista** (*m., f.*) **de sistemas** systems analyst (16)

sitio place, location; room (*space*); **sitio Web** website

situación *f.* situation; **situación de urgencia** emergency

situado/a situated

sobre *n. m.* envelope (18); *prep.* on; on top of; over; about; **sobre todo** especially; above all

sobrepoblación *f.* overpopulation

sobreponer (*like* **poner**) to superimpose

sobrino/a nephew/niece (2)

social social; **seguro social** social security; **asistente** (*m., f.*) **social** social worker; **trabajador(a) social** social worker (16)

sociedad *f.* society

sociología sociology (1)

socorro help, aid

sofá *m.* sofa (4)

sofisticado/a sophisticated

software *m.* software

sol *m.* sun; **hace (mucho) sol** it's (very) sunny (5); **tomar el sol** to sunbathe (7)

solamente only

solar solar; **energía solar** solar energy; **sistema** (*m.*) **solar** solar system

solas: a solas alone

soldado soldier (16); **mujer** (*f.*) **soldado** female soldier (16)

soleado/a sunny

solicitado/a requested
solicitar to request; to apply for
solicitud *f.* application (*form*) (16); **llenar una solicitud** to fill out an application (16)
sólo *adv.* only (1)
solo/a *adj.* alone (4); single
soltero/a single, unmarried (2)
solución *f.* solution
solucionar to solve
sombrero hat (3); **sombrero hongo** bowler hat, derby
sonar (sueno) to ring (9); to sound (9)
sonido sound
sonreír(se) (*like* **reír**) to smile (8)
soñar (sueño) (con) to dream (about)
sopa soup (6)
sorprender to surprise; **me (te, le...) sorprende que...** it surprises me (you, him . . .) that (13)
sorpresa surprise (8); **fiesta de sorpresa** surprise party
sostener (*like* **tener**) to sustain
soy I am (PP); **yo soy de** I am from (PP)
Sr.: señor *m.* man; Mr.; sir (PP)
Sra.: señora woman; Mrs.; ma'am (PP)
Srta.: señorita young woman; Miss; Ms. (PP)
su(s) *poss. adj.* his, her, its, your (*form. s.*); their, your (*form. pl.*) (2)
subir (a) to climb; to go up (7); to get in/on (*a vehicle*) (7); to take, carry up
subjuntivo/a *gram.* subjunctive
subordinado/a *gram.* subordinate
subrayar to underline
substancialmente substantially
subtítulo subtitle
suburbios slums
suceso happening
sucio/a dirty (5)
sudadera sweatshirt (3)
Sudáfrica South Africa
Sudamérica South America
sudamericano/a *n., adj.* South American
sudoeste *m.* southwest
Suecia Sweden
suegro/a father-in-law / mother-in-law
sueldo salary (12); **aumento de sueldo** raise (*in salary*) (12)
suelo floor
sueño dream; **tener sueño** to be tired (3); **viaje** (*m.*) **de sueños** dream trip (18)
suerte *f.* luck (11); **¡qué mala suerte!** what bad luck!; **tener buena/mala suerte** to have good/bad luck (11)
suéter *m.* sweater (3)
suficiente enough, sufficient; **dormir (duermo) (u) lo suficiente** to sleep enough (10); **lo suficiente** enough (10)

sufijo *gram.* suffix
sufrir to suffer (11); **sufrir (muchas) presiones** to be under (a lot of) stress (11)
sugerencia suggestion
sugerir (sugiero) (i) to suggest (8)
Suiza Switzerland
sujeto subject
sultán *m.* sultan
suma sum
Superhombre *m.* Superman
superior higher; **escuela superior** high school
superlativo *n. gram.* superlative
supermercado supermarket
supervisión *f.* supervision
supervisor(a) supervisor
supuesto: ¡por supuesto! of course! (11)
sur *m.* south (5)
sureño/a southern
surfing: hacer surfing to surf
surgir (surjo) to arise
suroeste *m.* southwest
surrealista *adj. m., f.* surrealistic
suscripción *f.* subscription
suspender to suspend
sustantivo *gram.* noun (1)
sustituir (*like* **construir**) to substitute
SUV *m.* SUV (14)

T

tabacalero/a *adj.* pertaining to tobacco
tabaco tobacco
tabla table, chart
tabú *f.* taboo
Tailandia Thailand
taíno *pre-Columbian culture of the Caribbean*
tal such, such a; **con tal (de) que** *conj.* provided (that) (15); **¿qué tal?** how are you (doing)? (PP); **tal como** just as; **tal vez** perhaps
taladro drill
talento talent
tallado/a carved
taller *m.* (repair) shop (14)
talonario de cheques checkbook (*Sp.*)
tamal *m.* tamale
tamalada *get-together to make and eat tamales*
tamaño size
también also (PP)
tambor *m.* drum; **tambor repique** *typical drum of Uruguay (used in Candombe music)*
tampoco neither, not either (6)
tan *adv.* so; as; **tan... como** as . . . as (5); **tan pronto como** as soon as (16)
tango *dance of Argentina*
tanque *m.* tank (14)

tanto *adv.* so much; **tanto como** as much as (5)
tanto: estar al tanto to be up to date
tanto/a *adj.* as much, so much; such a; *pl.* so many; as many; **tanto/a(s)... como** as much/many . . . as (5)
tapa appetizer (*Sp.*) (8)
tarde *adv.* late (1)
tarde *n., f.* afternoon (PP); **buenas tardes** good afternoon (PP); **de la tarde** in the afternoon (PP); **por la tarde** in the afternoon (1); *adv.* late
tarea homework (4); chore
tarifa plana flat rate
tarjeta card (6); **tarjeta bancaria** debit card (16); **tarjeta de cobro automático** debit card; **tarjeta de crédito** credit card (6); **tarjeta de cumpleaños** birthday card; **tarjeta de embarque** boarding pass; **tarjeta de identificación** identification card (11); **tarjeta Internet móvil** wireless Internet card; **tarjeta postal** postcard (7)
tarta (de cumpleaños) (birthday) cake
tatuaje *m.* tattoo
Tauro Taurus
taxi *m.* taxi
taza cup (11)
te *d.o. pron. s.* you (*fam.*); *i.o. pron. s.* to/for you (*fam.*); *refl. pron. s.* yourself (*fam.*); **¿cómo te llamas?** what's your (*fam.*) name? (PP); **¿te gusta...?** do you (*fam.*) like . . . ? (PP)
té *m.* tea (6)
teatral theatrical; **obra teatral** play
teatro theater (9); **ir al teatro** to go to the theater (9); **obra de teatro** play (13)
teclado keyboard
técnico/a *n.* technician (16); *adj.* technical
tecnológico/a technological
tejer to weave (13)
tejidos woven goods (13)
tela cloth
tele *f.* T.V.; **mirar la tele** to watch television (2)
telefonear to call on the telephone
telefónico/a *adj.* telephone; **guía telefónica** telephone book; **llamada telefónica** phone call; **mensaje** (*m.*) **telefónico** phone message
teléfono (celular/móvil) (cellular) telephone (12); **hablar por teléfono** to talk on the phone (1); **número de teléfono** phone number
telegrama *m.* telegram
telenovela soap opera
televidente *m., f.* television viewer

televisión *f.* television (2); **mirar la tele(visión)** to watch television (2)

televisor *m.* television set

tema *m.* subject, topic

temer to fear (13)

temperatura temperature (10); **tomarle la temperatura** to take someone's temperature (10)

templo temple

temprano *adv.* early

temprano/a *adj.* early

tendencia tendency

tender (tiendo) a to tend to, be inclined to; **tender la cama** to make the bed

tengo I have (2)

tener to have (3); **tener alergia a** to be allergic to; **tener… años** to be . . . years old (2); **tener buena suerte** to have good luck (11); **tener (mucho) calor/frío** to be (very) warm, hot/cold (5); **tener cuidado** to be careful; **tener derecho a** to have the right to; **tener dolor de** to have a pain in (10); **tener en común** to have in common; **tener exceso de peso** to be overweight; **tener éxito** to be successful; **tener fiebre** to have a fever; **tener ganas de** + *inf.* to feel like (*doing something*) (3); **tener (mucha) hambre/sed** to be (very) hungry/thirsty (6); **tener la culpa** to be guilty; **tener lugar** to take place; **tener miedo (de)** to be afraid (of) (3); **tener que** + *inf.* to have to (*do something*) (3); **(no) tener razón** to be right (wrong) (3); **tener sueño** to be tired (3)

tenis *m.* tennis (9); **jugar (juego) (gu) al tenis** to play tennis; **zapato de tenis** tennis shoe (3)

tensión *f.* tension

tentación *f.* temptation

tentempié *m.* snack

teoría theory

tepui *m.* flat mountain top

tequila *m.* tequila

terapia therapy

tercer, tercero/a *adj.* third (13)

tercio *n.* third

termal thermal

terminación *f.* ending

terminar to end

término term

termómetro: regulador (*m.*) **de termómetro** thermostat

termostato thermostat

terraza terrace

terremoto earthquake

terrestre terrestrial

terrible terrible (13); **es terrible que…** it's terrible that . . . (13)

territorio territory

terrorismo terrorism (17)

terrorista *n., adj. m., f.* terrorist (17); **ataque** (*m.*) **terrorista** terrorist attack (17)

tesoro treasure

testigo *m., f.* witness (17)

testimonio testimony

texto text; **libro de texto** textbook

ti *obj.* (*of prep.*) you (*fam. s.*) (5)

tibio: huevo tibio por agua poached egg

tiburón *m.* shark

tiempo time (5); weather (5); *gram.* tense; **a tiempo** on time (7); **¿cuánto tiempo hace que… ?** how long has it been since . . . ?; **de tiempo completo/parcial** full-time/part-time (11); **hace (muy) buen/mal tiempo** it's (very) good/bad weather (5); **llegar (gu) a tiempo** to arrive on time; **pasar tiempo (con)** to spend time (with); **¿qué tiempo hace hoy?** what's the weather like today? (5); **tiempo libre** free time

tienda shop, store (3); **tienda (de campaña)** tent (7)

tiene he/she has, you (*form. s.*) have (2)

tienes you (*fam. s.*) have (2)

tierra land; Earth (*planet*); soil

tigre *m.* tiger

timbre *m.* stamp (*Sp.*); doorbell

tímido/a shy

tinto/a: vino tinto red wine (6)

tío/a uncle/aunt (2); *m. pl.* aunts and uncles

típico/a typical

tipo type (*coll.*); character, person, guy, dude

tira cómica comic strip

tirar to throw

tiritar to chatter (*teeth*)

títere *m.* puppet

titular to (en)title

título degree

toalla towel (18)

toallero towel rack

tocar (qu) to touch; to play (*a musical instrument*) (1); **tocarle a uno** to be someone's turn to (*do something*) (9)

todavía yet; still (5)

todo *adv.* entirely, completely; **de todo** everything (3)

todo/a *n.* whole; all, everything; *adj.* all (2); every (2); each; *m. pl.* everybody, all; **a toda velocidad** at full speed; **ante todo** above all; first of all; **de todas formas** anyway; **Día** (*m.*) **de Todos los Santos** All Saints' Day; **por todas partes** everywhere (11); **sobre todo**

especially; above all; **todo derecho** straight ahead (14); **todo el año** all year; **todo el día** all day; **todos los días** everyday (7) **venden de todo** they sell (have) everything

todoterreno/a all-terrain (14)

tolerante tolerant

tolteca *n., adj. m., f.* Toltec

tomar to take (1); to drink (1); **tomar el sol** to sunbathe (7); **tomar en cuenta** to take into account; **tomar una copa** to have a drink; **tomarle el pelo** to pull someone's leg; **tomarle la temperatura** to take someone's temperature (10)

tomate *m.* tomato (6)

tonelada ton

tono tone

tonto/a silly, foolish (2)

tope: fecha tope deadline

toreo bullfighting

torero/a bullfighter, matador

torneo tournament

toro bull (14); **corrida de toros** bullfight

torpe clumsy (11); **¡qué torpe!** how clumsy!

torre *f.* tower

tortilla potato omelet (*Sp.*); *thin unleavened cornmeal or flour pancake* (*Mex.*)

tortuga turtle

tos *f.* cough (10)

toser to cough (10)

tostado/a toasted (6); **pan** (*m.*) **tostado** toast (6)

tostadora toaster (9)

total: en total as a whole

tóxico/a toxic

trabajador(a) worker (16); **trabajador(a) social** social worker (16); *adj.* hard-working (2)

trabajar to work (1)

trabajo job, work (11); report (11); (piece of) work (11); **compañero(a) de trabajo** co-worker; **trabajo de tiempo completo/parcial** full-time / part-time job (11)

trabalenguas *m. inv.* tongue twister

tractor *m.* tractor

tradición *f.* tradition

tradicional traditional

traducir (*like* **conducir**) to translate

traductor(a) translator (16)

traer to bring (4)

traficar (qu) en drogas to traffic in / deal drugs

tráfico traffic (14); **embotellamiento/lío de tráfico** traffic jam

tragedia tragedy

trágico/a tragic

trago drink (*alcoholic*) (18)

traje *m.* suit (3); **traje de baño** bathing suit (3)

tranquilidad *f.* quiet, calm

tranquilo/a calm, quiet (10); **llevar una vida tranquila** to lead a quiet life (10)

transbordador (*m.*) **espacial** space shuttle

transición *f.* transition

tránsito traffic (14)

transmitir to transmit

transportación *f.* transportation

transportar to transport

transporte *m.* (*means of*) transportation (7); **transporte público** public transportation; **medio de transporte** means of transportation (7)

tratado treaty

tratamiento treatment (10)

tratar to treat; to deal with (*a subject*); **se trata de** it's a question of; **tratar de** + *inf.* to try to (*do something*) (13)

través: a través de across; through; throughout

travesía prank, joke

travieso/a mischievous

trece thirteen (PP)

treinta thirty (PP); **y treinta** half-past / 30 minutes past (*the hour*) (PP)

tremendo/a tremendous

tren *m.* train (7); **choque** (*m.*) **de trenes** train wreck; **ir en tren** to go/travel by train (7)

trepidar to shake; to vibrate

tres three (PP)

trescientos/as three hundred (3)

tribu *f.* tribe

trimestre *m.* trimester

triste sad (5)

triunfar to triumph

triunfo triumph, victory

trofeo trophy

tropical tropical; **selva tropical** tropical jungle

tropiezo mistake

trozo piece

trucha trout

tú *sub. pron.* you (*fam. s.*) (1); **¿y tú?** and you (*fam. s.*)? (PP)

tu(s) *poss. adj.* your (*fam. s.*) (2)

tubería plumbing

tumba tomb

túnel *m.* tunnel

turbio/a turbulent

turismo tourism

turista *n. m., f.* tourist

turístico/a *adj.* tourist; **clase** (*f.*) **turística** tourist class (7)

turnarse to take turns

turno turn

tuyo/a(s) *poss. adj.* your (*fam. s.*)

txistu *m. flute-type instrument of the Basque region*

U

u or (*used instead of* **o** *before words beginning with* **o** *or* **ho**)

ubicación *f.* placement; location

Ud.: usted *sub. pron.* you (*form. s.*) (1); *obj.* (*of prep.*) you (*form. s.*)

Uds.: ustedes *sub. pron.* you (*form. pl.*) (1); *obj.* (*of prep.*) you (*form. pl.*)

último/a last, final (11); latest; **de los últimos años** in recent years; **de última moda** trendy (hot) (3); **por última vez** for the last time (11)

un, uno/a one (PP); *ind. art.* a, an; **un poco (de)** a little bit (of) (1); **una vez** once; **una vez a la semana** once a week (1)

unánimemente unanimously

único/a *adj.* only; unique

unidad *f.* unit

unido/a united; **Estados Unidos** United States; **Naciones** (*f.*) **Unidas** United Nations

unión *f.* union

unir to join (together); to unite

universidad *f.* university (1)

universitario/a (of the) university (11)

unos/as *ind. art.* some, a few

urbanización *f.* urbanization

urbano/a urban

urgencia: situación (*f.*) **de urgencia** emergency; **sala de urgencia** emergency room (10)

urgente urgent (13); **es urgente que...** it's urgent that . . . (13)

uruguayo/a *n., adj.* Uruguayan

usar to use (3); to wear (3)

uso use

usted (Ud., Vd.) *sub. pron.* you (*form. s.*) (1); *obj.* (*of prep.*) you (*form. s.*); **¿cómo se llama usted?** what's your (*form. s.*) name? (PP); **¿y usted?** and you (*form. s.*)? (PP)

ustedes (Uds., Vds.) *sub. pron.* you (*form. pl.*) (1); *obj.* (*of prep.*) you (*form. pl.*)

útil useful

utilizar (**c**) to use, utilize

uva grape

¡uy! *interj.* oops!

V

vaca cow (14)

vacaciones *f. pl.* vacation; **de vacaciones** on vacation (7); **estar de vacaciones** to be on vacation (7); **ir de vacaciones a...** to go on vacation to . . . (7); **pasar las vacaciones en...** to spend one's vacation in . . . (7); **salir de vacaciones** to leave on vacation (7); **tomar unas vacaciones** to take a vacation (7); **vacaciones de primavera** spring break

vacuna vaccine; **ponerle una vacuna** to give a vaccination

vainilla vanilla

Valentín: Día (*m.*) **de San Valentín** St. Valentine's Day

valiente brave

valija valise, suitcase

valle *m.* valley

vallenato *folk music of Colombia*

valor *m.* value; courage, bravery

vals *m.* waltz

vaquero/a cowboy/cowgirl

variación *f.* variation

variar (varío) to vary

variedad *f.* variety

varios/as several

vasco/a *n., adj.* Basque

vaso glass

vecindad *f.* neighborhood (12)

vecino/a *n.* neighbor (12); *adj.* neighboring

vegetal *adj.* vegetable

vegetariano/a vegetarian

vehículo vehicle

veinte twenty (PP)

veinticinco twenty-five (PP)

veinticuatro twenty-four (PP)

veintidós twenty-two (PP)

veintinueve twenty-nine (PP)

veintiocho twenty-eight (PP)

veintiséis twenty-six (PP)

veintisiete twenty-seven (PP)

veintitrés twenty-three (PP)

veintiún, veintiuno/a twenty-one (PP)

vejez *f.* old age (15)

vela candle

velludo/a hairy

velocidad *f.* speed; **a toda velocidad** at full speed; **límite** (*m.*) **de velocidad** speed limit (14)

vendedor(a) salesperson (16)

vender to sell (2); **venden de todo** they sell (have) everything

venerar to venerate

venezolano/a *n., adj.* Venezuelan

venir to come (3); **el año que viene** next year; **la semana que viene** next week (4); **venga** come on

venta sale

ventaja advantage

ventana window (1); **lavar las ventanas** to wash windows

ventanilla small window (*on a plane*) (7); **asiento de ventanilla** window seat

ver (*p.p.* **visto**) to see (4); **a ver** let's see; **ir a ver una película** to go to the movies; **nos vemos** see you around (PP)

verano summer (5)

verbo *gram.* verb (PP)

verdad *f.* truth; **¿verdad?** right? (3)

verdadero/a true; real

verde green (3)

verdura vegetable (6)

verificar (qu) to verify

versión *f.* version

vestido dress (3); **vestido de novia** wedding gown

vestir (visto) (i) to dress; **vestirse** to get dressed (4)

veterinario/a veterinarian (16)

vez *f.* (*pl.* **veces**) time; **a veces** sometimes, at times (2); **a la vez** at the same time; **alguna vez** once; ever; **cada vez más** increasingly; **de vez en cuando** once in a while; **dos veces** twice (10); **en vez de** instead of; **érase una vez** once upon a time; **otra vez** again; **por primera/última vez** for the first/last time (11); **tal vez** perhaps; **un par de veces** a couple of times; **una vez** once (2); **una vez a la semana** once a week (2)

vía roadway (14); **de doble vía** two-way (14)

viajar to travel (7); **viajar al / en el extranjero** to travel abroad

viaje *m.* trip (4); **viaje de sueños** dream trip (18); **agencia de viajes** travel agency (7); **agente** (*m., f.*) **de viajes** travel agent (7); **compañero/a de viaje** traveling companion; **de viaje** on a trip (7); **hacer un viaje** to take a trip (4)

viajero/a *n., adj.* traveler (18); **cheque** (*m.*) **de viajero** traveler's check

vicepresidente/a vice president

víctima *f.* victim (17)

vida life (10); **llevar una vida saludable/sana** to lead a healthy life (10)

vídeo video; **cámara de vídeo** video camera (12)

videocasetera videocassette recorder (VCR) (12)

videojuego videogame; **jugar (juego) (gu) a videojuegos** to play videogames

vidrio glass

viejo/a *n.* old person; *adj.* old (2); **Noche** (*f.*) **Vieja** New Year's Eve (8)

viento wind; **hace (mucho) viento** it's (very) windy (5)

viernes *m. inv.* Friday (4)

vietnamita *n., adj.* Vietnamese

villancico Christmas carol

vino (blanco, tinto) (white, red) wine (6)

viñedo vineyard

violencia violence (14)

violento/a violent

violeta: de color violeta violet

violín *m.* violin

virgen *n. f.* virgin

visado visa

visión *f.* vision

visita visit

visitante *m., f.* visitor

visitar to visit (9); **visitar un museo** to visit a museum (9)

víspera eve

vista view (12); **a primera vista** at first sight (15); **punto de vista** point of view

visto/a (*p.p. of* **ver**) seen

viudo/a widower/widow (15)

vivienda housing (12)

vivir to live (2); **vivir en paz** to live in peace

vivo/a alive

vocabulario vocabulary

vocación *f.* vocation

vocal *n. f.* vowel

volante: objeto volante no identificado (OVNI) unidentified flying object (UFO)

volar (vuelo) to fly; **volar en avión** to fly, go by plane (7)

volcán *m.* volcano

volcánico/a volcanic

voleibol *m.* volleyball (9); **jugar (juego) (gu) al voleibol** to play volleyball

volumen *m.* volume

voluntario/a *n.* volunteer

volver (vuelvo) (*p.p.* **vuelto**) to return (*to a place*) (4); **volver a** + *inf.* to (*do something*) again (4)

vos *subj. pron.* you (*fam. s. Arg., Uru., C.A.*); *obj.* (*of prep.*) you (*fam. s. Arg., Uru., C.A.*)

vosotros/as *subj. pron.* you (*fam. pl. Sp.*) (1); *obj.* (*of prep.*) you (*fam. pl. Sp.*)

votante *m., f.* voter

votar to vote (17)

voz *f.* (*pl.* **voces**) voice; **en voz alta** aloud; **hablar en voz baja** to speak softly

vuelo flight (7); **asistente** (*m., f.*) **de vuelo** flight attendant (7)

vuelta: de ida y vuelta round-trip (7); **billete** (*m.*)/**boleto de ida y vuelta** round-trip ticket (7); **darse la vuelta** to turn oneself around; **de vuelta** returned

vuestro/a *poss. adj.* your (*fam. pl. Sp.*) (2)

W

Web *m.* Web; **sitio Web** website

Y

y and (PP); **y cuarto** a quarter (fifteen minutes) after (*the hour*) (PP); **y media (treinta)** half past / 30 minutes past (*the hour*) (PP); **¿y tú?** and you (*fam. s.*)? (PP); **¿y usted?** and you (*form. s.*)? (PP)

ya already (8); **ya no** no longer; **ya que** since

yerno son-in-law

yo *sub. pron.* I (1); **yo soy (de)** I am (from) (PP)

yoga *m.* yoga (10); **hacer (el) yoga** to do yoga (10)

yogur *m.* yogurt (6)

York: Nueva York New York

yoruba *n., adj.* (*West African ethnic group*)

Z

zampona *South American panpipe*

zanahoria carrot (6)

zapatería shoe store

zapato shoe (3); **zapato de tenis** tennis shoe (3)

zócalo central plaza (*Mex.*)

zona zone, area (12)

zoológico zoo

English-Spanish Vocabulary

A

able: to be able **poder** (3)
about **por** (5)
abroad **extranjero** *n.* (18)
absence **falta** (14)
absent: to be absent (from) **faltar (a)** (8)
absentminded **distraído/a** (11)
accelerated **acelerado/a** (14)
according to **según** (2)
account **cuenta** (16); checking account **cuenta corriente** (16); savings account **cuenta de ahorros** (16)
accountant **contador(a)** (16)
ache *v.* **doler (duele)** (10); *n.* **dolor** *m.* (10)
acquainted: to be acquainted with **conocer (conozco)** (6)
actor **actor** *m.* (13)
actress **actriz** *f.* (*pl.* **actrices**) (13)
additional **adicional** (PP)
address **dirección** *f.* (6)
adjective **adjetivo** *gram.* (2)
administration: business administration **administración** (*f.*) **de empresas** (1)
adolescence **adolescencia** (15)
advice (piece of) **consejo** (6)
advisor **consejero/a** (1)
aerobic: to do aerobics **hacer ejercicios aeróbicos** (10)
affectionate **cariñoso/a** (5)
afraid: to be afraid (of) **tener miedo (de)** (3)
after *prep.* **después de** (4); *conj.* **después (de) que** (16)
afternoon **tarde** *f.* (1); good afternoon **buenas tardes** (PP); afternoon **muy buenas** (PP); (*a time*) in the afternoon **de la tarde** (PP); in the afternoon **por la tarde** (1)
afterward **luego** (4)
age: old age **vejez** *f.* (15)
agency: travel agency **agencia de viajes** (7)
agent: travel agent **agente** (*m., f.*) **de viajes** (7)
agree: I (don't) agree **(no) estoy de acuerdo** (2)
ahead of time **con anticipación** (18); straight ahead **todo derecho** (14)
air **aire** *m.* (14)
airplane **avión** *m.* (7)
airport **aeropuerto** (7)
alarm clock **despertador** *m.* (11)
all **todo(s)/a(s)** *adj.* (2); all terrain **todoterreno** *inv.* (14)
allow **permitir** (12)
almost never **casi nunca** (2)
alone **solo/a** *adj.* (4)

alongside of **al lado de** (5)
already **ya** (8)
also **también** (PP)
always **siempre** (2)
American (*from the United States*) **estadounidense** (2)
among **entre** (5)
amusement **diversión** *f.,* **pasatiempo** (9)
analyst: systems analyst **analista** (*m., f.*) **de sistemas** (16)
and **y** (PP); and you? **¿y tú?** *fam.,* **¿y usted?** *form.* (PP)
angry **furioso/a** (5); to get angry (at) **enojarse (con)** (8)
animal **animal** *m.* (14); domesticated animal **animal doméstico** (14); wild animal **animal salvaje** (14)
announce **anunciar** (7)
annoyed **molesto/a** (5)
another **otro/a** (2)
answer *n.* **respuesta** (5); *v.* **contestar** (6)
answering machine **contestador** (*m.*) **automático** (12)
antibiotic **antibiótico** (10)
any **algún, alguno/a** (6)
anyone **alguien** (6)
anything **algo** (3)
apartment **apartamento** (1); apartment building **edificio de apartamentos** (12)
apologize **pedir disculpas** (11)
apple **manzana** (6)
appliance: home appliance **aparato doméstico** (9)
applicant **aspirante** *m., f.* (16)
application (form) **solicitud** *f.* (16)
appointment **cita** (10)
April **abril** *m.* (5)
architect **arquitecto/a** (13)
architecture **arquitectura** (13)
area **zona** (12)
argue (about) (with) **discutir (sobre) (con)** (8)
arm **brazo** (11)
armchair **sillón** *m.* (4)
army **ejército** (17)
arrival **llegada** (7)
arrive **llegar (gu)** (2)
art **arte** *f.* (*but* **el arte**) (1); fine arts **las artes** (13); work of art **obra de arte** (13)
artist **artista** *m., f.* (13)
arts and crafts **artesanía** (13)
as . . . as **tan... como** (5); as much/many as **tanto/a... como** (5); as soon as **tan pronto como** *conj.* (16); **en cuanto** *conj.* (16)

ashamed **avergonzado/a** (8)
ask: to ask for **pedir** (4); to ask a question **hacer una pregunta** (4); **preguntar** (6)
asparagus **espárragos** *pl.* (6)
assassination **asesinato** (17)
astronaut **astronauta** *m., f.* (16)
at **en** (PP); **a** (*with time*) (PP); at . . . (hour) **a la(s)...** (PP); at home **en casa** (1); at last **por fin** (4); at least **por lo menos** (11); at night **de la noche** (PP); **por la noche** (1); at the beginning of **al principio de** (16); at times **a veces** (2)
ATM **cajero automático** (16)
attack: terrorist attack **ataque** (*m.*) **terrorista** (17)
attend (*a function*) **asistir (a)** (2)
attendant: flight attendant **asistente** (*m., f.*) **de vuelo** (7)
attract **atraer** (*like* **traer**) (13)
August **agosto** (5)
aunt **tía** (2)
automatic teller machine **cajero automático** (16)
autumn **otoño** (5)
avenue **avenida** (12)
avoid **evitar** (14)
away: right away **en seguida** (10)
awful: an awful lot **muchísimo** (7)

B

baby-sitter **niñero/a** (9)
backpack **mochila** (1)
bad **mal** *adv.* (1); **mal, malo/a** *adj.* (2); it's bad weather **hace mal tiempo** (5); the bad thing, news **lo malo** (10)
baggage **equipaje** *m.* (7)
ballet **ballet** *m.* (13)
banana **banana** (6)
bank **banco** (16); (bank) check **cheque** *m.* (16)
bar **bar** *m.* (9)
barbeque **barbacoa** (6)
bargain *n.* **ganga** (3); *v.* **regatear** (3)
baseball **béisbol** *m.* (9)
basketball **basquetbol** *m.* (9)
bath: to take a bath **bañarse** (4)
bathing suit **traje** (*m.*) **de baño** (3)
bathroom **baño** (4)
bathtub **bañera** (4)
battery **batería** (14)
be **estar** (1); **ser** (2); to be (feel) (very) warm, hot **tener (mucho) calor** (5); to be (very) hungry **tener (mucha) hambre** (6); to be . . . years old **tener... años** (2); to be a

fan (of) **ser aficionado/a (a)** (9); to be able **poder** (3); to be afraid (of) **tener miedo (de)** (3); to be boring **ser aburrido/a** (9); to be (very) cold **tener (mucho) frío** (5); to be comfortable (*temperature*) **estar bien** (5); to be flexible **ser flexible** (11); to be fun **ser divertido/a** (9); to be in a hurry **tener prisa** (3); to be late **estar atrasado/a** (7); to be lucky/unlucky **tener buena/mala suerte** (11); to be on a diet **estar a dieta** (6); to be right **tener razón** (3); to be sleepy **tener sueño** (3); to be (very) thirsty **tener (mucha) sed** (6); to be wrong **no tener razón** (3); to be wrong (about) **equivocarse (qu) (de)** (11); to be, take place in/at (*place*) **ser en +** *place* (8)
beach **playa** (5)
bean **frijol** *m.* (6)
beautiful **bello/a** (14)
because **porque** (2); because of **por** (5)
become + *adj.* **ponerse** + *adj.* (8)
bed **cama** (4); to make the bed **hacer la cama** (9); to stay in bed **guardar cama** (10)
bedroom **alcoba** (4)
beer **cerveza** (6)
before *conj.* **antes (de) que** (15); *prep.* **antes de** (4)
begin **empezar (empiezo) (c)** (4); to begin to (*do something*) **empezar a + inf.** (4)
beginning: at the beginning of **al principio de** (16)
behave well/badly **portarse bien/mal** (8)
behind *prep.* **detrás de** (5)
believe (in) **creer (en)** (2)
bellhop **mozo, botones** *m. inv.* (18)
below *prep.* **debajo de** (5)
belt **cinturón** *m.* (3)
best **mejor** (5)
better **mejor** (5)
between *prep.* **entre** (5)
beverage **bebida** (4)
bicycle **bicicleta** (12); (mountain) bicycle **bicicleta (de montaña)** (12); to ride a bicycle **pasear en bicicleta** (9)
bicycling **ciclismo** (9)
big **gran, grande** (2)
bill (*for service*) **cuenta** (6); **factura** (16); (*money*) **billete** (16)
bird **pájaro** (2)
birthday **cumpleaños** *m. inv.* (5); birthday cake **pastel** (*m.*) **de cumpleaños** (8); to have a birthday **cumplir años** (8)
black **negro/a** (3)
blanket **manta** (18)

blog **blog** *m.* (17)
blond(e) *n., adj.* **rubio/a** (2)
blood **sangre** *f.* (10)
blouse **blusa** (3)
blue **azul** (3)
boardinghouse **pensión** *f.* (18); room and full board **pensión completa** (18); room with breakfast and one other meal **media pensión** (18)
boat **barco** (7)
body **cuerpo** (10)
book **libro** (1); textbook **libro de texto** (1)
bomb **bomba** (17)
bookshelf **estante** *m.* (4)
bookstore **librería** (1)
boot **bota** (3)
border **frontera** (18)
bore **aburrir** (13)
bored **aburrido/a** (5); to bore **aburrir** (13); to get bored **aburrirse** (9)
boring **pesado/a**; to be boring **ser aburrido/a** (9)
born: to be born **nacer (nazco)** (15)
borrow **pedir prestado/a** (16)
boss **jefe/a** (12)
bother: it bothers me (you, him, . . .) that **me (te, le…) molesta que** (13)
boy **niño** (2)
boyfriend **novio** (5)
brain **cerebro** (10)
brakes **frenos** (14)
bread **pan** *m.* (6)
break **romperse** (*p.p.* **roto/a**) (11); to break up (with) **romper (con)** (15)
breakfast **desayuno** (4); to have breakfast **desayunar** (6)
breathe **respirar** (10)
bride **novia** (15)
bring **traer** (4)
brother **hermano** (2)
brown **(de) color café** (3)
brunet(te) *n., adj.* **moreno/a** (2)
brush one's teeth **cepillarse los dientes** (4)
budget **presupuesto** (16)
build **construir** (14)
building *n.* **edificio** (1); building manager **portero/a** (12)
bull **toro** (14)
bump into, against **pegarse (gu) en/ con/contra** (11); **chocar (qu) con/ contra** (11)
bureau (*furniture*) **cómoda** (4)
bus **autobús** *m.* (7); bus station **estación** (*f.*) **de autobuses** (7); bus stop **parada del autobús** (18)
business **empresa** (16); business administration **administración** (*f.*) **de empresas** (1)
businessperson **hombre** (*m.*)/**mujer** (*f.*) **de negocios** (16)

busy **ocupado/a** (5)
but *conj.* **pero** (PP)
butter **mantequilla** (6)
buy **comprar** (1)
by *prep.* **por** (11); in the morning (afternoon, evening) **por la mañana (tarde, noche)** (1); by check **con cheque** (16)

C

cabin (*on a ship*) **cabina** (7)
café **café** *m.* (18)
cafeteria **cafetería** (1)
cake **pastel** *m.* (6); birthday cake **pastel de cumpleaños** (8)
calculator **calculadora** (1)
calendar **calendario** (11)
call *v.* **llamar** (6); to be called **llamarse** (4)
calm **tranquilo/a** (10)
camera **cámara** (12); digital/video **cámara digital/de vídeo** (12)
campground **camping** *m.* (7)
camping: to go camping **hacer camping** (7)
campus **campus** *m.* (12)
can *v.* **poder** (3)
candidate (*for a job*) **aspirante** *m., f.* (16); (*political*) **candidato/a** (17)
candy **dulces** *m. pl.* (6)
cap **gorra** (3)
capital city **capital** *f.* (5)
car **coche** *m.* (2); convertible car **carro/ coche descapotable** (12)
card: credit card **tarjeta de crédito** (6); debit card **tarjeta bancaria** (16); identification card **tarjeta de identificación** (11); postcard **tarjeta (postal)** (7) to play cards **jugar (juego) (gu) a las cartas** (9)
cardinal directions **puntos cardinales** (5)
carrot **zanahoria** (6)
carry **llevar** (3)
case: in case **en caso de que** (15); just in case **por si acaso** (11)
cash (*a check*) **cobrar** (16); *n.* **el efectivo** (16); in cash **en efectivo** (16)
cashier **cajero/a** (16); cashier window **caja** (16)
cat **gato/a** (2)
catch a cold **resfriarse (me resfrío)** (10)
CD **disco compacto, CD** *m.* (12)
CD-ROM **CD-ROM** *m.* (12)
celebrate **celebrar** (5)
cellular telephone **teléfono celular** (12)
ceramics **cerámicas** *pl.* (13)
cereal **cereal** *m.* (6)
certain *adj.* **seguro/a** (5); **cierto/a** (13); it's certain that **es cierto que** (13)

chair **silla** (1); armchair **sillón** *m.* (4)

chalkboard **pizarra** (1)

change *v.* **cambiar (de)** (12)

channel **canal** *m.* (12)

charge (*to an account*) **cargar (gu)** (16); (*someone for an item or service*) **cobrar** (16)

check (*bank*) **cheque** *m.* (16); by check **con cheque** (16); to check (the oil) **revisar (el aceite)** (14); to check baggage **facturar el equipaje** (7)

checking account **cuenta corriente** (16)

checkup **chequeo** (10)

cheese **queso** (6)

chef **cocinero/a** (16)

chemistry **química** (1)

chess **ajedrez** *m.* (9); to play chess **jugar (juego) (gu) al ajedrez** (9)

chicken (roast) **pollo (asado)** (6)

chief **jefe/a** (12)

child **niño/a** (2); as a child **de niño/a** (9)

childhood **niñez** *f.* (*pl.* **niñeces**) (9)

children **hijos** *m. pl.* (2)

chop: pork chop **chuleta de cerdo** (6)

chore: household chore **quehacer** (*m.*) **doméstico**

Christmas **Navidad** *f.* (8); Christmas Eve **Nochebuena** (8)

citizen **ciudadano/a** (17)

city **ciudad** *f.* (2)

civic **cívico/a** (17)

class **clase** *f.* (1); first class **primera clase** (7); tourist class **clase turística** (7)

classic(al) **clásico/a** (13)

classmate **compañero/a de clase** (1)

classroom **salón** (*m.*) **de clase** (1)

clean *adj.* **limpio/a** (5)

clean *v.* **limpiar** (9); to clean the (whole) house **limpiar la casa (entera)** (9)

clear the table **quitar la mesa** (9)

clerk **dependiente/a** (1)

clever **listo/a** (2)

client **cliente/a** (1)

climate **clima** *m.* (5)

close **cerrar (cierro)** (4)

close to **cerca de** (5)

closed **cerrado/a** (5)

closet **armario** (4)

clothes dryer **secadora** (9)

clothing **ropa** (3); to wear (*clothing*) **llevar, usar** (3)

cloudy: it's (very) cloudy, overcast **está (muy) nublado** (5)

clumsy **torpe** (11)

coffee **café** *m.* (1)

coffee pot **cafetera** (9)

coin **moneda** (16)

cold (*illness*) **resfriado** (10); it's (very) cold (*weather*) **hace (mucho)**

frío (5); to be (very) cold **tener (mucho) frío** (5); very cold, frozen **congelado/a** (5)

collect **recoger (recojo)** (11)

collision **choque** *m.* (17)

color **color** *m.* (3)

comb one's hair **peinarse** (4)

come **venir** (3)

comedy **comedia** (13)

comfortable **cómodo/a** (3); to be comfortable (*temperature*) **estar bien** (5)

command **mandato** (6)

communicate (with) **comunicarse (qu) (con)** (17)

communication (*major*) **comunicaciones** *f.* (1); means of communication **medios de comunicación** (17)

community **comunidad** *f.* (12)

compact disc **disco compacto** (12)

comparison **comparación** *f.* (5)

complain (about) **quejarse (de)** (8)

composer **compositor(a)** (13)

computer **computadora** (*L.A.*) (1); **ordenador** *m.* (*Sp:*) (12); computer disc **disco de computadora** (12); computer file **archivo** (12); computer science **computación** *f.* (1)

concert **concierto** (9); to go to a concert **ir a un concierto** (9)

confirm **confirmar** (18)

congested **resfriado/a** (10)

congratulations **felicitaciones** *f. pl.* (8)

conserve **conservar** (14)

contact lenses **lentes** (*m. pl.*) **de contacto** (10)

content *adj.* **contento/a** (5)

continue **continuar (continúo)** (5); **seguir** (14)

control: remote control **control** (*m.*) **remoto** (12)

convertible (*car*) **carro/coche** (*m.*) **descapotable** (12)

cook *v.* **cocinar** (6); *n.* **cocinero/a** (16)

cookie **galleta** (6)

cool: it's cool (*weather*) **hace fresco** (5)

copy **copia** (12); to copy **copiar, hacer una copia** (12)

corner (street) **esquina** (14)

corporation **empresa** (16)

cotton **algodón** *m.* (3); it is made of cotton **es de algodón** (3)

cough **tos** *f.* (10); to cough **toser** (10); cough syrup **jarabe** *m.* (10)

country **país** *m.* (2)

country(side) **campo** (12)

couple (*married*) **pareja** (15)

course (*of a meal*) **plato** (6); of course **por supuesto** (11)

courtesy: greetings and expressions of courtesy **saludos y expresiones** (*f.*) **de cortesía** (PP)

cousin **primo/a** (2)

cover **cubrir** (*pp.* **cubierto/a**) (14)

cow **vaca** (14)

crash *n.* (*vehicular*) **choque** *m.* (17); *v.* (*computer*) **fallar** (12)

crazy **loco/a** (5)

create **crear** (13)

credit card **tarjeta de crédito** (6)

crime **delito** (14)

cross **cruzar (c)** (18)

cruise(ship) **crucero** (7)

cry **llorar** (8)

cuisine **cocina** (6)

cup **taza** (11)

currently **en la actualidad** (9)

custard: baked custard **flan** *m.* (6)

customs (*border*) **aduana** *s.* (18)

D

dad **papá** *m.* (2)

daily routine **rutina diaria** (4)

dance **baile** *m.* (13); **danza** (13); to dance **bailar** (1)

dancer **bailarín, bailarina** (13)

date (*calendar*) **fecha** (5); (*social*) **cita** (15); what's today's date? **¿cuál es la fecha de hoy?, ¿qué fecha es hoy?** (5)

daughter **hija** (2)

day **día** *m.* (1); what day is today? **¿qué día es hoy?** (4); day after tomorrow **pasado mañana** (4); the day before yesterday **anteayer** (10); every day **todos los días** (1)

deadline **plazo** (11)

dear *n., adj.* **querido/a** (5)

death **muerte** *f.* (15)

debit card **tarjeta bancaria** (16)

December **diciembre** *m.* (5)

delay *n.* **demora** (7)

delighted **encantado/a** (PP)

demonstration **demostración** *f.* (17)

dense **denso/a** (14)

dentist **dentista** *m., f.* (16)

deny **negar (niego) (gu)** (13)

department store **almacén** *m.* (3)

departure **salida** (7)

deposit **depositar** (16)

desk **escritorio** (1)

dessert **postre** *m.* (6)

destroy **destruir** (*like* **construir**) (14)

develop **desarrollar** (14)

dictator **dictador(a)** (17)

dictatorship **dictadura** (17)

dictionary **diccionario** (1)

die **morirse (me muero) (u)** (*p.p.* **muerto/a**) (8)

diet: to be on a diet **estar a dieta** (6)

difficult **difícil** (5); **pesado/a** (9)

digital camera **cámara digital** (12)

dining room **comedor** *m.* (4)

dinner **cena** (6); to have dinner **cenar** (6)

directions: cardinal directions **puntos cardinales** (5)

director **director(a)** (13)

dirty **sucio/a** (5)

disaster **desastre** *m.* (17)

disc: compact disc **disco compacto, CD** *m.* (12); computer disc **disco de computadora** (12)

disco: to go to a disco **ir a una discoteca** (9)

discover **descubrir** (*p.p.* **descubierto/a**) (14)

discrimination **discriminación** *f.* (17)

dish (*plate*) **plato** (4); (*course*) **plato** (6)

dishwasher **lavaplatos** *m. inv.* (9)

divorce **divorcio** (15)

divorced **divorciado/a** (15); to get divorced (from) **divorciarse (de)** (15)

dizzy **mareado/a** (10)

do **hacer** (4); (*do something*) again **volver a** + *inf.* (4); to do aerobics **hacer ejercicios aeróbicos** (10); to do exercise **hacer ejercicio** (4); to do Pilates **hacer (el método) Pilates** (10); to do well/poorly **salir bien/mal** (4)

doctor (*medical*) **médico/a** (2)

dog **perro/a** (2)

domesticated animal **animal** (*m.*) **doméstico** (14)

door **puerta** (1)

doorman **portero/a** (12)

dormitory **residencia** (1)

double room (18) **habitación** (*f.*) **doble**

doubt **dudar** (12)

downtown **centro** (3)

drama **drama** *m.* (13)

draw **dibujar** (13); draw, attract **atraer** (*like* **traer**) (13)

dress **vestido** (3)

dressed: to get dressed **vestirse (me visto) (i)** (4)

dresser (*furniture*) **cómoda** (4)

drink **bebida** (4); **copa, trago** (*alcoholic*) (18); to drink **tomar** (1); **beber** (2)

drive (*a vehicle*) **conducir** (14); **manejar** (12)

driver **conductor(a)** (14); driver's license **licencia de manejar/ conducir** (14)

dryer (*for clothes*) **secadora** (9)

during **durante** (4); **por** (4)

dust the furniture **sacudir los muebles** (9)

DVD **DVD-ROM** *m.* (12)

DVD player **lector** (*m.*) **de DVD** (12)

E

e-mail **correo electrónico** (12), **e-mail** *m.* (12)

each **cada** *inv.* (4)

ear (inner) **oído** (10); (outer) **oreja** (10)

early *adv.* **temprano** (1)

earn **ganar** (16)

earring **arete** *m.* (3)

east **este** *m.* (5)

Easter **Pascua** (8)

easy **fácil** (5)

eat **comer** (2); eat breakfast **desayunar** (6); eat dinner, supper **cenar** (6)

economics **economía** (1)

economize **economizar (c)** (16)

egg **huevo** (6)

eight **ocho** (PP); eight hundred **ochocientos/as** (3)

eighteen **dieciocho** (PP)

eighth **octavo/a** *adj.* (13)

eighty **ochenta** (2)

electric **eléctrico/a** (14)

electrician **electricista** *m., f.* (16)

electricity **luz** *f.* (*pl.* **luces**) (11)

electronic equipment **electrónica** (12)

elephant **elefante** *m.* (14)

eleven **once** (PP)

embrace **abrazarse (c)** (10)

embarrassed **avergonzado/a** (8)

emergency room **sala de emergencias/ urgencia** (10)

emotion **emoción** *f.* (8)

emotional state **estado afectivo** (8)

energy **energía** (14)

engagement **noviazgo** (15)

engineer **ingeniero/a** (16)

English (*language*) **inglés** *m.* (1); *n., adj.* **inglés, inglesa** (2)

enjoy oneself, have a good time **divertirse (me divierto) (i)** (4)

enough *adv.* **bastante** (15); **lo suficiente** (10)

entertainment **diversión** *f.* (9)

envelope **sobre** *m.* (18)

environment **medio ambiente** (14)

equality **igualdad** *f.* (17)

equipment **equipo** (9)

era **época** (9)

eruption **erupción** *f.* (17)

evening: good evening **buenas tardes** (PP); evening **muy buenas** (PP); in the afternoon, evening **de la tarde** (PP); in the evening **por la tarde** (1)

event **acontecimiento, evento** (17); **hecho** (8)

every **cada** *inv.* (4); *adj.* **todo(s)/a(s)** (2); every day **todos los días** (1)

everything **de todo** (3)

everywhere **por todas partes** (11)

exactly, on the dot (*time*) **en punto** (PP)

exam **examen** *m.* (3)

examine **examinar** (10); **registrar** (18)

excuse me **con permiso** (PP); **perdón** (PP); **discúlpeme** (11)

exercise **ejercicio** (4); to exercise **hacer ejercicio** (4)

expect **esperar** (6)

expense **gasto** (12)

expensive **caro/a** (3)

explain **explicar (qu)** (7)

expressions: greetings and expressions of courtesy **saludos y expresiones** (*f.*) **de cortesía** (PP)

extract **sacar (qu)** (10); extract a tooth/ molar **sacar un diente / una muela** (10)

eye **ojo** (10)

eyeglasses **gafas** (10)

F

fact **hecho** *n.* (8)

factory **fábrica** (14)

faithful **fiel** (2)

fall (*season*) **otoño** (5); *v.* **caer** (11); to fall asleep **dormirse** (4); to fall down **caerse** (11); to fall in love (with) **enamorarse (de)** (15)

family **familia** (2)

fan: to be a fan (of) **ser aficionado/a (a)** (9)

far from **lejos de** (5)

fare (*transportation*) **pasaje** *m.* (7)

farm **finca** (14); farm worker **campesino/a** (14)

farmer **agricultor(a)** (14)

fascinate **fascinar** (13)

fast **acelerado/a** (14)

fat **gordo/a** (2)

father **papá** *m.*, **padre** *m.* (2)

fax **fax** *m.* (12)

fear: to fear **temer** (13)

February **febrero** (5)

feel (*an emotion*) **sentirse** (8); to feel like (*doing something*) **tener ganas de** + *inf.* (3); to feel sorry **sentir, lamentar** (13)

female soldier **mujer** (*f.*) **soldado** (16)

fever **fiebre** *f.* (10); have a fever **tener fiebre** (10)

fiancé(e) **novio/a** (15)

field (*agricultural*) **campo** (14)

fifteen **quince** (PP); a quarter (fifteen minutes) to (*the hour*) **menos cuarto/quince** (PP); a quarter (fifteen minutes) past (*the hour*) **y cuarto/quince** (PP)

fifth *adj.* **quinto/a** (13)

fifty **cincuenta** (2)

fight *n.* **lucha** (17); *v.* **luchar** (17), **pelear** (9)

file: computer file **archivo** (12)

fill (up) **llenar** (14); to fill out an application **llenar una solicitud** (16)

finally **por fin** (4)

find **encontrar (encuentro)** (8); to find out (about) **enterarse (de)** (17)

fine **muy bien** (PP)

finger **dedo (de la mano)** (11)

finish **acabar** (11)

first *adv.* **primero** (4); *adj.* **primer, primero/a** (13); at first sight **a primera vista** (15); first floor **planta baja** (12); first of (month) **el primero de (mes)** (5); first class **primera clase** (7)

fish (*cooked*) **pescado** (6); (*animal*) **pez** *m.* (*pl.* **peces**) (14)

five **cinco** (PP); five hundred **quinientos/as** (3)

fix **arreglar** (12)

fixed price **precio fijo** (3)

flat: flat tire **llanta desinflada** (14); flat screen **pantalla grande** (12)

flexible **flexible** (11)

flight **vuelo** (7); flight attendant **asistente** (*m., f.*) **de vuelo** (7)

flip-flops **chanclas** (3)

floor (*of a building*) **piso** (12); ground floor **planta baja** (12); second floor **primer piso** (12); third floor **segundo piso** (12); to sweep the floor **barrer el piso** (9)

flower **flor** *f.* (7)

flu **gripe** *f.* (10)

fly **volar (vuelo) en avión** (7)

folkloric **folclórico/a** (13)

following *adj.* **siguiente** (4)

fond: to be fond of each other **quererse** (10)

food **comida** (6)

foolish **tonto/a** (2)

foot **pie** *m.* (11)

football **fútbol** (*m.*) **americano** (9)

for **por** (7); **para** (2); for example **por ejemplo** (11); for that reason **por eso** (2); for heaven's sake **por Dios** (11); for the first/last time **por primera/última vez** (11); for (*a period of time*) **hace... que** (11); for what purpose? **¿para qué?** (15)

forbid **prohibir (prohíbo)** (12)

foreign languages **lenguas extranjeras** (1)

foreigner **extranjero/a** *n.* (1)

forest **bosque** *m.* (14)

forget (about) **olvidarse (de)** (8)

form (*to fill out*) **formulario** (18)

forty **cuarenta** (2)

four **cuatro** (PP); four hundred **cuatrocientos/as** (3)

fourteen **catorce** (PP)

fourth **cuarto/a** *adj.* (13)

freeway **autopista** (14)

freezer **congelador** *m.* (9)

French (*language*) **francés** *n. m.* (1); (French fried) potato **papa/patata (frita)** (6)

frequently **con frecuencia** (1)

fresh **fresco/a** (6)

Friday **viernes** *m. inv.* (4)

fried **frito/a** (6); **papa/patata frita** French fried potato (6)

friend **amigo/a** (1)

friendly **amistoso/a** (15)

friendship **amistad** *f.* (15)

from **de** (PP); from the **del** (*contraction of* **de** + **el**) (2)

front desk **recepción** *f.* (18)

front: in front of **delante de** (5)

frozen **congelado/a** (5)

fruit **fruta** (6); **jugo de fruta** fruit juice (6)

full (no vacancy) **completo/a** (18)

full-time **de tiempo completo** (16); full-time job **trabajo de tiempo completo** (16)

fun: to be fun **ser divertido/a** (9)

function **funcionar** (12)

furious **furioso/a** (5)

furniture **muebles** *m. pl.* (4); to dust the furniture **sacudir los muebles** (9)

G

game **partido** (9)

garage **garaje** *m.* (4)

garbage **basura** (9)

garden **jardín** *m.* (4)

gas (*not for cars*) **gas** *m.* (12); gas station **estación** (*f.*) **de gasolina, gasolinera** (14)

gasoline **gasolina** (14)

generally **por lo general** (4)

German (*language*) **alemán** *m.* (1); *n., adj.* **alemán, alemana** (2)

get **sacar (qu)** (11); **obtener** (*like* **tener**) (12); to get along well/ poorly (with) **llevarse bien/mal (con)** (15); to get down (from) **bajarse (de)** (7); to get good/ bad grades **sacar (qu) buenas/ malas notas** (11); to get off (of) **bajarse (de)** (7); to get (on/in) (*a vehicle*) **subir (a)** (7); to get tired **cansarse** (10); to get together (with) **reunirse (me reúno) (con)** (8); to get up **levantarse** (4); to get up on the wrong side of the bed **levantarse con el pie izquierdo** (11); to get, obtain **conseguir** (*like* **seguir**) (8); to get (*a job*) **conseguir** (*like* **seguir**) (16)

gift **regalo** (2)

girl **niña** (2)

girlfriend **novia** (5)

give **dar** (7); to give (*as a gift*) **regalar** (7); to give (someone) a shot, injection **poner(le)** (*irreg.*) **una inyección** (10); give a party **dar/ hacer una fiesta** (8)

go **ir** (3); to be going to (*do something*) **ir a** + *inf.* (3); to go (to) (*a function*) **asistir (a)** (2); to go by (train/ airplane/ bus/boat) **ir en (tren/ avión/ autobús/ barco)** (7); to go home **regresar a casa** (1); to go shopping **ir de compras** (3); to go out with **salir con** (4); to go through security (check) **pasar por el control de la seguridad** (7); to go to bed **acostarse (me acuesto)** (4); to go up **subir** (7)

gold **oro** (3); it is made of gold **es de oro** (3)

golf **golf** *m.* (9)

gorilla **gorila** *m.* (14)

good **buen, bueno/a** *adj.* (2); good afternoon **buenas tardes** (PP); good morning **buenos días** (PP); good night **buenas noches** (PP); the good thing, news **lo bueno** (10)

good-bye **adiós** (PP)

good-looking **guapo/a** (2)

government **gobierno** (14)

grade (*in a course*) **nota** (11); (*level*) **grado** (9)

graduate (from) **graduarse (me gradúo) (en)** (16)

granddaughter **nieta** (2)

grandfather **abuelo** (2)

grandmother **abuela** (2)

grandparents **abuelos** *pl.* (2)

grandson **nieto** (2)

gray **gris** (3)

great **gran, grande** (2)

green **verde** (3); green pea **arveja** (6)

greet each other **saludarse** (10)

greeting: greetings and expressions of courtesy **saludos y expresiones** (*f.*) **de cortesía** (PP)

groceries **comestibles** *m.* (6)

groom **novio** (15)

ground floor **planta baja** (12)

grow **crecer (crezco)** (15)

guest **invitado/a** *n.* (8); (*in a hotel*) **huésped(a)** (18)

guide **guía** *m., f.* (13)

H

hairstylist **peluquero(a)** (16)

half-past (*the hour*) **y media/treinta** (PP)

ham **jamón** *m.* (6)

hamburger **hamburguesa** (6)

hand **mano** *f.* (11); hand in **entregar (gu)** (11)

handbag **cartera** (3)

handsome **guapo/a** (2)

happen **pasar** (5)

happening **acontecimiento, evento** (17)

happy **alegre** (5); **feliz** (*pl.* **felices**) (8); **contento/a** (5); to be happy (about) **alegrarse (de)** (12)

hard **difícil** (5); hard drive **disco duro** (12)

hardworking **trabajador(a)** (2)

hat **sombrero** (3)

hate **odiar** (7)

have **tener** (3); **haber** (*inf. of* **hay** there is/are) *auxiliary* (12); to have a good/bad time **pasarlo bien/mal** (8); to have breakfast **desayunar** (6); to have dinner, supper **cenar** (6); to have lunch **almorzar (almuerzo) (c)** (6); to have a snack **merendar (meriendo)** (6); to have just (*done something*) **acabar de** + *inf.* (6); to have to (*do something*) **tener que** + *inf.* (3)

he **él** (1); he is **es** (PP)

head **cabeza** (10)

health **salud** *f.* (10)

healthy **sano/a** (10)

hear **oír** (4)

heart **corazón** *m.* (10)

heat **calor** *m.* (5); **gas** *m.* (12)

heating **calefacción** *f.* (12)

hello **¡hola!** (PP)

help *n.* **ayuda** (6); *v.* **ayudar** (6)

her *poss.* **su(s)** (2)

here **aquí** (1)

highway **carretera** (14)

his *poss.* **su(s)** (2)

history **historia** (1)

hit **pegar (gu)** (9)

hobby **pasatiempo, afición** *f.* (9)

hockey **hockey** *m.* (9)

holiday **día** (*m.*) **festivo** (8)

home **casa** (2); at home **en casa** (1)

homework **tarea** (4)

honeymoon **luna de miel** (15)

honk **tocar (qu) la bocina** (14)

hope **esperanza** (17); to hope **esperar** (12); I hope, (that) **ojalá (que)** (13)

horn (*car*) **bocina** (14)

hors d'oeuvres **botanas, tapas** (8)

horse **caballo** (9); to ride a horse **montar a caballo** (9)

host **anfitrión** *m.* (8)

hostess **anfitriona** (8)

hot (*spicy*) **picante** (6); (*temperature*) **caliente** (6); (*trendy*) **de (última) moda** (3); hot dog **salchicha** (6); it's (very) hot **hace (mucho) calor** (5); to be (feel) (very) hot **tener (mucho) calor** (5)

hotel **hotel** *m.* (18); luxury hotel **hotel de lujo** (18) two- (three-, four-, five-) star hotel **hotel de 2 (3, 4, 5)**

estrellas (18); hotel guest **huésped(a)** (18)

house **casa** (2)

household chore **quehacer** (*m.*) **doméstico** (9)

housing **vivienda** (12)

housekeeper **amo/a** (**ama** *f. but* **el ama**) **de casa** (16)

how + *adj.*! **¡qué** + *adj.*! (11)

how? what? **¿cómo?** (PP); how are you doing? **¿qué tal?** (PP); how are you? **¿cómo está(s)?** (PP); how many? **¿cuántos/as?** (1); how much does it/do they cost? **¿cuánto cuesta(n)?** (3); how do you get to . . . **¿cómo se llega a...?** (14) how often? **¿con qué frecuencia?** (2); how much? **¿cuánto?** (1)

human **humano/a** (10)

humanities **humanidades** *f.* (1)

hungry: to be (very) hungry **tener (mucha) hambre** (6)

hurry: to be in a hurry **tener prisa** (3)

hurt **doler (duelo)** (10)

hurt oneself **hacerse daño** (11)

husband **esposo** (2); **marido** (15)

hybrid **híbrido/a** (14)

I

I **yo** (1); I am **soy** (PP); I am from **soy de** (PP); I didn't mean it **fue sin querer** (11); I'm sorry **discúlpeme** (11); I'm (very) sorry **lo siento (mucho)**; I'm called **me llamo** (PP); I hope (that) **ojalá (que)** (13) (11)

ice cream **helado** (6)

identification card **tarjeta de identificación** (11)

if **si** (2)

improbable: it's improbable that . . . **es improbable que…** (13)

in **en** (PP); (*the morning, evening, etc.*) **por** (1); in case **en caso de que** (15); in cash **en efectivo** (16); in order to **para** (2)

incredible: it's incredible **es increíble** (13)

inequality **desigualdad** *f.* (17)

inexpensive **barato/a** (3)

infancy **infancia** (15)

inflexible **inflexible** (11)

inform **informar** (17)

injection: to give (someone) an injection **ponerle una inyección** *f.* (10)

insist (on) **insistir (en)** (12)

inspector **inspector(a)** (18)

install **instalar** (12)

installment: to pay in installments **pagar (gu) a plazos** (16)

intelligent **inteligente** (2)

intend to (*do something*) **pensar (pienso)** + *inf.* (4)

intended for **para** (2)

Internet **Internet** (17)

interest (*v.*) **interesar** (7); *n.* **interés** *m.* (16)

interview (*n.*) **entrevista** (16)

interviewer **entrevistador/a** (16)

interrogative **interrogativo/a** (PP)

invite **invitar** (6)

iPod **iPod** *m.* (12)

iron clothes **planchar la ropa** (9)

island **isla** (5)

Italian (*language*) **italiano** *m.* (1)

its *poss.* **su(s)** (2)

J

jacket **chaqueta** (3)

January **enero** (5)

jeans **jeans** *m. pl.* (3)

job **empleo** (16); **trabajo** (11); full-time/part-time job **trabajo de tiempo completo/parcial** (11)

joke **chiste** *m.* (7)

journalist **periodista** *m., f.* (16)

juice **jugo** (6); fruit juice **jugo de fruta** (6)

July **julio** (5)

June **junio** (5)

just in case **por si acaso** (11)

K

keep (*documents*) **guardar** (12); **mantener** (*like* tener) (17); to keep on going **seguir (sigo) (i)** (14)

key **llave** *n. f.* (4); key in **escribir a computadora** (16)

kill **matar** (17)

kind *adj.* **amable** (2)

king **rey** *m.* (17)

kiosk **quiosco** (18)

kiss each other **besarse** (10)

kitchen **cocina** (4)

know **conocer (conozco)** (6); to know (how) **saber** (6)

L

laborer **obrero/a** (16)

lack **falta** (14)

lady **señora (Sra.)** (PP)

lake **lago** (14)

lamp **lámpara** (4)

landlady **dueña** (12)

landlord **dueño** (12)

language **lengua** (1); foreign languages **lenguas extranjeras** (1)

large **gran, grande** (2)

last **último/a** (11); last night **anoche** (10); to last **durar** (17) late **tarde** *adv.* (1); to be late **estar atrasado/a** (7)

later: see you later **hasta luego** (PP)

laugh (about) **reír(se) (de)** (8)

law **ley** *f.* (17)

lawyer **abogado/a** (16)

lazy **perezoso/a** (2)

lead a healthy/calm life **llevar una vida sana/tranquila** (10)

learn **aprender** (2); to learn (about) **enterarse (de)** (17); to learn how (*to do something*) **aprender a** + *inf.* (2)

least **menos** (5); at least **por lo menos** (8)

leather **cuero** (3); it is made of leather **es de cuero** (3)

leave (from) **salir (de)** (4); (for) **salir para** (4); (behind) (in [*a place*]) **dejar (en)** (9)

left: to the left (of) **a la izquierda (de)** (5); to be left **quedar(se)** (11)

leg **pierna** (11)

lend **prestar** (7)

lenses: contact lenses **lentes** (*m. pl.*) **de contacto** (10)

less . . . than **menos... que** (5)

letter **carta** (2)

lettuce **lechuga** (6)

librarian **bibliotecario/a** (1)

library **biblioteca** (1)

license **licencia** (14); driver's license **licencia de manejar/conducir** (14)

lie **mentira** (12)

life **vida** (10); to lead a healthy/calm life **llevar una vida sana/tranquila** (10)

light **luz** *f.* (*pl.* **luces**) (11); *adj.* light (not heavy) **ligero/a** (6)

like **gusto** (PP); **gustar** (7); do you (*form.*) like . . . ? **¿le gusta... ?** (PP); do you (*fam.*) like . . . ? **¿te gusta... ?** (PP); I (don't) like . . . **(no) me gusta(n)...** (PP); I would like . . . **me gustaría...** (7); to like very much **encantar** (7)

likeable **simpático/a** (2)

likely: it's likely that . . . **es probable que...** (13)

likewise **igualmente** (PP)

limit: speed limit **límite** (*m.*) **de velocidad** *f.* (14)

line (*of people*) **cola** (7); to stand in line **hacer cola** (7)

listen (to) **escuchar** (1)

literature **literatura** (1)

little *adj.* **poco/a** (3); *adv.* **poco** (1); a little bit (of) **un poco (de)** (1)

live **vivir** (2)

loan **préstamo** (16)

lobster **langosta** (6)

lodging **alojamiento** (18)

long **largo/a** (2)

look at **mirar** (2); to look for **buscar (qu)** (1)

lose **perder (pierdo)** (4)

lot: a lot *adv.* **mucho** (1); a lot (of) **mucho/ a** (2); an awful lot **muchísimo** (7)

love *v.* **amar** (15); **encantar** (7); **quererse** (15); *n.* **amor** *m.* (15); in love (with) **enamorado/a (de)** (15); to fall in love (with) **enamorarse (de)** (15)

luck **suerte** *f.* (11)

lucky: to be lucky **tener suerte** (11)

luggage **equipaje** *m.* (7)

lunch **almuerzo** (6); to have lunch **almorzar (almuerzo) (c)** (4)

lung **pulmón** *m.* (10)

luxury *n.* **lujo** (12); luxury hotel **hotel** (*m.*) **de lujo** (18)

-ly *adv. ending* -**mente** (11)

lyrics (*song*) **letra** *s.* (6)

M

machine: answering machine **contestador** (*m.*) **automático** (12)

magazine **revista** (2)

maid **criada** (18)

mail **correo** (18); e-mail **correo electrónico** (12), **e-mail** *m.* (12)

maintain **mantener** (*like* **tener**) (17)

make **hacer** (4); to make a mistake (about) **equivocarse (qu)** (11); to make plans to (*do something*) **hacer planes para** + *inf.* (9); to make stops **hacer escalas/paradas** (7); to make the bed **hacer la cama** (9)

mall: shopping mall **centro comercial** (3)

man **hombre** *m.* (1); **señor (Sr.)** *m.* (PP); businessman **hombre de negocios** (16)

manager **gerente** *m., f.* (16)

many **muchos/as** (2); how many? **¿cuántos/as?** (1)

march **demostración** *f.* (17)

March **marzo** (5)

market(place) **mercado** (3)

marriage **matrimonio** (15)

married **casado/a** (2); married couple **pareja** (15)

marry **casarse (con)** (15)

masterpiece **obra maestra** (13)

match (*for lighting things*) **fósforo** (18)

material **material** *n. m.* (3)

mathematics **matemáticas** *pl.* (1)

May **mayo** (5)

me *d.o., i.o.* **me**; *obj. (of prep.)* **mí** (5)

meal **comida** (6)

means: that means **eso quiere decir** (10)

means: means of communication **medios de comunicación** (17); means of transportation **medio de transporte** (7)

meat **carne** *f.* (6)

mechanic **mecánico/a** (14)

medical **médico/a** (2); medical office **consultorio** (10)

medicine **medicina** (10)

meet (*a person*) **conocerse (conozco)** (15); (*someone somewhere*) **encontrarse (encuentro) (con)** (10)

memory **memoria** (12)

menu **menú** *m.* (6)

message **mensaje** (12)

messy **desordenado/a** (5)

metro stop **estación** (*f.*) **del metro** (18)

Mexican *n., adj.* **mexicano/a** (2)

microwave oven **horno de microondas** (9)

middle age **madurez** *f.* (15)

midnight **medianoche** *f.* (8)

military service **servicio militar** (17)

milk **leche** *f.* (6)

milkshake **batido** (18)

million **millón** (*m.*) (**de**) (3)

mineral water **agua** *f.* (*but* **el agua**) **mineral** (6)

miss (*a function, bus, plane, and so on*) **perder (pierdo)** (4)

Miss **señorita (Srta.)** (PP)

mistake: to make a mistake (about) **equivocarse (qu) (de)** (11)

modem **módem** *m.* (12)

modern **moderno/a** (13)

molar **muela** (10)

mom **mamá** (2)

Monday **lunes** *m. inv.* (4)

money **dinero** (1)

month **mes** *m.* (5)

moped **moto(cicleta)** *f.* (12)

more *adv.* **más** (1); more . . . than (5) **más... que**

morning: in the morning **de la mañana** (PP); **por la mañana** (1); good morning **buenos días** (PP)

mother **mamá, madre** *f.* (2)

motorcycle **moto(cicleta)** *f.* (12)

mountain **montaña** (7)

mouse **ratón** *m.* (12)

mouth **boca** (10)

movie **película** (4); movies **cine** *m. s.* (4); movie theater **cine** *m.* (4)

Mr. **señor (Sr.)** *m.* (PP)

Mrs. **señora (Sra.)** (PP)

much *adv.* **mucho** (1); how much does it do they cost? **¿cuánto cuesta(n)?** (3); too much *adv.* **demasiado** (9)

museum: to visit a museum **visitar un museo** (9)

mushroom **champiñón** *m.* (6)

music **música** (13)

musician **músico/a** *n. m., f.* (13)
must (*do something*) **deber** + *inf.* (2)
my *poss.* **mi(s)** (2); my

N

name **nombre** *m.* (6); what's your
  (*form.*) name? **¿cómo se llama
  usted?** (PP); what's your (*fam.*)
  name? **¿cómo te llamas?** (PP); my
  name is . . . **me llamo…** (PP)
nap: to take a nap **dormir (4) la siesta**
  (4)
nationality **nacionalidad** *f.* (2)
natural resources **recursos naturales**
  (14)
nature **naturaleza** (14)
nauseated **mareado/a** (10)
neat **ordenado/a** (5)
necessary **necesario/a** (2); it is
  necessary to (*do something*) **hay que**
  + *inf.* (13)
need *v.* **necesitar** (1)
neighbor **vecino/a** (12)
neighborhood **barrio, vecindad** *f.* (12)
neither, not either **tampoco** (6)
nephew **sobrino** (2)
nervous **nervioso/a** (5)
Net **Red** *f.* (12); to surf the Net **navegar
  (gu) la Red** (12)
never **nunca** (2); **jamás** (6); almost
  never **casi nunca** (2)
new **nuevo/a** (2); New Year's Eve
  Noche (*f.*) **Vieja** (8)
news **noticias** *pl.* (17); news media
  prensa (17)
newscast **noticiero** (17)
newspaper **periódico** (2)
next *adv.* **luego** (4); *adj.* **próximo/a** (4);
  next to **al lado de** (5); next week
  la semana que viene (4)
nice **amable** (2), **simpático/a** (2)
niece **sobrina** (2)
night: at night **de la noche** (PP); **por
  la noche** (1); good night **buenas
  noches** (PP); last night **anoche**
  (10), tonight **esta noche** (5)
nine **nueve** (PP); nine hundred
  novecientos/as (3)
nineteen **diecinueve** (PP)
ninety **noventa** (2)
ninth **noveno/a** (13)
no **no** (PP)
nobody, not anybody, no one **nadie** (6)
noise **ruido** (4)
none, not any **ningún, ninguno/a** (6)
north **norte** *m.* (5)
nose **nariz** *f.* (10)
not **no** (PP); not anything **nada** (6);
  not either **tampoco** (6); not ever
  nunca, jamás (6)
notes (*academic*) **apuntes** *m.* (11)
notebook **cuaderno** (1)

nothing **nada** (6)
noun **sustantivo** *gram.* (1)
November **noviembre** *m.* (5)
now **ahora** (1)
nowadays **hoy (en) día** (17)
nuclear **nuclear** (14)
number **número** (PP)
nurse **enfermero/a** (10)

O

obey **obedecer (obedezco)** (14)
object **objeto** (1)
obligation **deber** *m.* (17)
obtain **obtener** (*like* **tener**) (12)
ocean **océano** (7)
October **octubre** *m.* (5)
of **de** (PP); of the **del** (*contraction of* **de**
  + **el**) (2); of course **por supuesto**
  (11)
off: to turn off **apagar (gu)** (11)
offer *v.* **ofrecer (ofrezco)** (7)
office **oficina** (1); doctor's office
  consultorio (10); political office
  cargo (17); post office **oficina de
  correos** (18)
oil **aceite** *m.* (6)
OK *adj.* **regular** (PP)
old *adj.* **viejo/a** (2); old age **vejez** *f.* (15)
older **mayor** (5)
on **en** (PP); on top of **encima de** *prep.*
  (5)
once a week **una vez a la semana** (2)
one **uno** (PP); one hundred **cien,
  ciento** (2); one thousand **mil** (3)
one-way (*ticket*) **de ida** (7)
only **sólo** *adv.* (1)
open **abierto/a** (5); to open **abrir** (*p.p.*
  abierto/a) (2)
opera **ópera** (13)
operate (*a machine*) **manejar** (12)
or **o** (PP)
oral report **informe** (*m.*) **oral** (11)
orange (*color*) **anaranjado/a** *adj.* (3);
  orange (*fruit*) **naranja** (6)
orchestra **orquesta** (13)
order (*in a restaurant*) **pedir** (4);
  (*someone to do something*) **mandar**
  (12)
other **otro/a** (2); *pl.* **los/las demás** (12)
ought to (*do something*) **deber** + *inf.* (2)
our *poss.* **nuestro/a(s)** (2)
outdoors *adv.* **afuera** (5)
outskirts **afueras** *n. pl.* (12)
oven: microwave oven **horno de
  microondas** (9)
overcoat **abrigo** (3)
owner **dueño/a** (6)
ozone layer **capa de ozono** (14)

P

pace **ritmo** (14)

pack one's suitcase(s) **hacer la(s)
  maleta(s)** (7)
package **paquete** *m.* (18)
pain **dolor** (*m.*) **(de)** (10); to have a
  pain (in) **tener dolor (de)** (10)
paint (the walls) **pintar (las paredes)**
  (9)
painter **pintor(a)** (13)
painting **cuadro, pintura** (13)
pair **par** *m.* (3)
pants **pantalones** *m.* (3)
paper **papel** *m.* (1)
pardon me **con permiso, perdón** (PP);
  discúlpeme (11)
parents **padres** *m. pl.* (2)
park **estacionar** (11)
parking place/lot **estacionamiento** (14)
part **parte** *f.* (4)
partner (*married*) **pareja** (15)
part-time **de tiempo parcial** (16);
  part-time job **trabajo de tiempo
  parcial** (16)
party **fiesta** (1); to have a party **dar/
  hacer una fiesta** (8)
pass through security (check) **pasar por
  el control de la seguridad** (7)
passenger **pasajero/a** *n.* (7)
passport **pasaporte** *m.* (18)
past *adj.* **pasado/a** (10)
pastime **pasatiempo** (9)
pastry **pastel** *m.* (18); small pastry
  pastelito (18); pastry shop
  pastelería (18)
patio **patio** (4)
pay *n.* **salario** (16); *v.* **pagar (gu)** (1); to
  pay cash **pagar en efectivo** (16); to
  pay in installments **pagar a plazos**
  (16)
PDA *PDA* *m.* (12)
pea: green pea **arveja** (6)
peace **paz** *f.* (*pl.* **paces**) (17)
peasant **campesino/a** (14)
pen **bolígrafo** (1)
pencil **lápiz** *m.* (*pl.* **lápices**) (1)
people **gente** *f. s.* (12)
pepper **pimienta** (6)
permit **permitir** (12)
person **persona** (1)
personal pronoun **pronombre** (*m.*)
  personal (1) *gram.*
pet **mascota** (2)
pharmacist **farmacéutico/a** (10)
pharmacy **farmacia** (10)
phase **etapa** (15)
philosophy **filosofía** (1)
phone: to talk on the phone **hablar por
  teléfono** (1)
photo(graph) **foto(grafía)** *f.* (7)
photographer **fotógrafo/a** (16)
photography **fotografía** (13)
photos: to take photos **sacar (qu) fotos**
  (7)
physics **física** (1)

pick up **recoger (recojo)** (11)

picnic: to have a picnic **hacer** un *picnic* (9)

pie **pastel** *m.* (6)

Pilates (**el método**) **Pilates** (10); to do Pilates **hacer** (**el método**) **Pilates** (10)

pill **pastilla** (10)

pillow **almohada** (18)

pink **rosado/a** (3)

place *n.* (*in line*) **puesto** (7); *v.* **poner** (4)

plaid **de cuadros** (3)

plans: to make plans to (*do something*) **hacer planes para** + *inf.* (9)

plate **plato** (6)

play *n.* (*dramatic*) **obra de teatro** (13); *v.* play (*a game, sport*) **jugar (juego) (a, al) (gu)** (4); to play chess **jugar al ajedrez** (9); to play cards **jugar a las cartas** (9); to play (*a musical instrument*) **tocar (qu)** (1)

player **jugador(a)** (9)

playwright **dramaturgo/a** (13)

please **por favor** (PP)

pleased to meet you **encantado/a** (PP), **mucho gusto** (PP)

pleasing: to be pleasing **gustar** (7)

plumber **plomero/a** (16)

poet **poeta** *m., f.* (13)

police officer **policía** *m., f.* (14)

policy **política** (17)

politician **político/a** (17)

politics **política** *s.* (17)

polka dot **de lunares** (3)

pollute **contaminar** (14)

pollution: there's (lots of) pollution **hay (mucha) contaminación** *f.* (5)

political office **cargo** (17)

poor **pobre** (2)

poorly **mal** (1)

population **población** *f.* (14)

pork chop **chuleta de cerdo** (6)

port **puerto** (7)

porter **maletero** (7)

possible **posible** (2)

post office **oficina de correos** (18)

postcard **tarjeta postal** (7)

potato **papa** (*L.A.*), **patata** (*Sp.*) (6); French fried potato **papa/patata frita** (6)

pottery **cerámica** (13)

practice **entrenar** (9); **practicar (qu)** (1)

prefer **preferir (prefiero) (i)** (3)

preference **preferencia** (PP)

prepare **preparar** (6)

prescription **receta** (10)

present (*gift*) **regalo** *n.* (2)

press *n.* **prensa** (17)

pressure: to be under (a lot of) pressure **sufrir (muchas) presiones** (11)

pretty **bonito/a** (2)

price **precio** (3); fixed, set price **precio fijo** (3); (*of a transportation ticket*) **pasaje** *m.* (7)

print **imprimir** (12)

printer **impresora** (12)

probable: its probable that . . . **es probable que...** (13)

profession **profesión** *f.* (16)

professor **profesor(a)** (1)

programmer **programador(a)** (16)

prohibit **prohibir (prohíbo)** (12)

promise *v.* **prometer** (7)

pronoun: personal pronoun **pronombre** (*m.*) **personal** (1) *gram.*

protect **proteger (protejo)** (14)

provided (that) **con tal (de) que** (15)

psychiatrist **siquiatra** *m., f.* (16)

psychologist **sicólogo/a** (16)

psychology **sicología** (1)

public *adj.* **público/a** (14)

pure **puro/a** (14)

purple **morado/a** (3)

purse **bolsa** (3)

put **poner** (4); to put on (*clothing*) **ponerse** (4)

Q

quarter after (*hour*) **y cuarto/quince** (PP); quarter till **menos cuarto/ quince** (PP)

queen **reina** (17)

question **pregunta** (4); (*matter*) **cuestión** *f.* (16); to ask (a question) **hacer una pregunta** (4); **preguntar** (6)

quit **dejar** (16); (*doing something*) **dejar de** + *inf.* (10)

quiz **prueba** (11)

R

radio (*apparatus*) (12) **radio** *m.*; (*medium*) **radio** *f.* (17); portable radio **radio portátil** (12)

rain **llover (llueve)** (5); it's raining **llueve** (5)

raincoat **impermeable** *m.* (3)

raise **aumento** (12)

rather *adv.* **bastante** (15)

read **leer** (*like* **creer**) (2)

reason: for that reason **por eso** (2)

receive **recibir** (2)

recently married to **recién casado/a con** (15)

recipe **receta** (6)

recommend **recomendar (recomiendo)** (7)

record **grabar** (12)

recorder (tape) **grabadora** (12)

recycle **reciclar** (14)

red **rojo/a** (3); red wine **vino tinto** (6)

reduction **rebaja** (3)

refrigerator **refrigerador** *m.* (9)

regret **sentir** (13); **lamentar** (13)

relationship **relación** (15)

relative **pariente** *m., f.* (2)

remain (*in a place*) **quedar(se)** (5); (*be left*) **quedar** (11)

remember **recordar (recuerdo)** (8); **acordarse (me acuerdo) (de)** (11)

remote control **control** (*m.*) **remoto** (12)

rent **alquiler** *m.* (12); to rent **alquilar** (12)

renter **inquilino/a** (12)

repair **arreglar, reparar** (14); (repair) shop **taller** *m.* (14)

report **informe** (*m.*) (11), **trabajo** (11)

reporter **reportero/a** (17)

reservation **reservación** *f.* (18)

resign (from) **renunciar (a)** (16)

resolve **resolver** (*like* **volver**) (*p.p.* **resuelto/a**) (14)

resource **recurso** (14); natural resources **recursos naturales** (14)

responsibility **responsabilidad** *f.* (17), **deber** *m.* (17)

rest **descansar** (4)

restaurant **restaurante** *m.* (4)

résumé **currículum** *m.* (16)

retire **jubilarse** (16)

return (*to a place*) **regresar** (1); **volver** (*p.p.* **vuelto/a**) (4); to return home **regresar a casa** (1); (*something*) **devolver** (*like* **volver**) (*pp.* **devuelto/a**) (16)

rhythm **ritmo** (14)

rice **arroz** *m.* (*pl.* **arroces**) (6)

rich (*wealthy*) **rico/a** (2); (*tasty*) **rico/a** (6)

ride a bicycle **pasear en bicicleta** (9); to ride a horse **montar a caballo** (9)

right (*legal*) **derecho** *n.* (17); right? **¿no?, ¿verdad?** (3); right away **en seguida** (10); right now **ahora mismo** (5), **en la actualidad** (9) to the right (of) **a la derecha (de)** (5); to be right **tener razón** (3)

ring **sonar (suena)** (9)

river **río** (14)

roadway **vía** (14)

roasted **asado/a** (6)

role **papel** *m.* (13)

roller skates **patines** *m. pl.* (12)

rollerblade *v.* **patinar en línea** (9)

room **cuarto** (1); room (*in a hotel*) **habitación** *f.* (18); classroom **salón** (*m.*) **de clase** (1); double room **habitación** (*f.*) **doble** (18); emergency room **sala de emergencias/urgencia** (10); living room **sala** (4); room and full board (all meals) **pensión** (*f.*) **completa** (18); room service **servicio de cuartos** (18); room with(out) bath/

shower **habitación** (*f.*) **con/sin baño/ducha** (18); single room **habitación** (*f.*) **individual** (18); waiting room **sala de espera** (7)

roommate **compañero/a de cuarto** (1)

round-trip ticket **billete** (*m.*)**/boleto de ida y vuelta** (7)

route **vía** (14)

routine: daily routine **rutina diaria** (4)

rug **alfombra** (4)

ruin *n.* **ruina** (13)

run **correr** (9); (*machines*) **funcionar** (12); to run into/against **pegarse (gu) en/con/contra** (11), **chocar (qu) (con/contra)** (11); to run out (of) **acabar** (11); to run for political office **postularse a un cargo como candidato** (17)

S

sad **triste** (5)

salad **ensalada** (6)

salary **sueldo** (12)

sale **rebaja** (3)

salesperson **vendedor(a)** (16)

salmon **salmón** *m.* (6)

same **mismo/a** (5); same here **igualmente** (PP)

sandals **sandalias** (3)

sandwich **sándwich** *m.* (6)

Saturday **sábado** (4)

sausage **salchicha** (6)

save **conservar** (14); (*documents*) **almacenar** (12); (*money*) **ahorrar** (16); (*a place*) **guardar un puesto** (7)

savings **ahorros** *pl.*; savings account **cuenta de ahorros** (16)

say **decir** (7); to say good-bye (to) **despedirse** (*like* **pedir**) **(de)** (8)

schedule **horario** (11)

school **escuela** (9)

schoolteacher **maestro/a (de escuela)** (16)

science **ciencia** (1); computer science **computación** *f.* (1); natural/ political/social sciences **ciencias naturales/políticas/sociales** (1)

screen **pantalla** (12); flat/big screen **pantalla plana/grande** (12)

script **guión** *m.* (13)

sculpt **esculpir** (13)

sculptor **escultor(a)** (13)

sculpture **escultura** (13)

sea **mar** *m.* (7)

seafood **mariscos** *pl.* (6)

seaport **puerto** (7)

search **registrar** (18)

season **estación** *f.* (5)

seat **asiento** (7)

second *adj.* **segundo/a** (13)

secretary **secretario/a** (1)

security check **control** (*m.*) **de la seguridad** (7)

see **ver** (4); see you around **nos vemos** (PP); see you later **hasta luego** (PP); see you tomorrow **hasta mañana** (PP)

sell **vender** (2)

send **mandar** (7)

sentimental **sentimental** (15)

separate *v.* (from) **separarse (de)** (15)

separation **separación** *f.* (15)

September **septiembre** *m.* (5)

serve **servir (sirvo) (i)** (4)

service: military service **servicio militar** (17); room service **servicio de cuartos** (18)

set price *n.* **precio fijo** (3)

set the table **poner la mesa** (9)

seven **siete** (PP); seven hundred **setecientos/as** (3)

seventeen **diecisiete** (PP)

seventh *adj.* **séptimo/a** (13)

seventy **setenta** (2)

shake hands **darse la mano** (10)

shame **lástima** (13); it is a shame **es una lástima** (13); what a shame that . . . ! **¡qué lástima que… !** (13)

shampoo **champú** *m.* (18)

share **compartir** (16)

shave oneself **afeitarse** (4)

she **ella** (1); she is **es** (PP)

sheet **sábana** (18)

shellfish **marisco** (6)

ship **barco** (7); cruise ship **crucero** (7)

shirt **camisa** (3)

shoe **zapato** (3); tennis shoe **zapato de tenis** (3)

shop (repair) **taller** *m.* (14)

shopping **de compras** (3); shopping mall **centro comercial** (3); to go shopping **ir de compras** (3)

short (*in height*) **bajo/a** (2); (*in length*) **corto/a** (2)

shot: to give (someone) a shot **ponerle una inyección** *f.* (10)

should (*do something*) **deber** + *inf.* (2)

show *v.* **mostrar (muestro)** (7); *n.* **espectáculo** (13)

shower: room with attached shower **habitación** (*f.*) **con ducha** (18); to take a shower **ducharse** (4)

shrimp **camarón** *m.* (6)

sick *adj.* **enfermo/a** (5); to get sick **enfermarse** (8)

sickness **enfermedad** *f.* (10)

sidewalk **acera** (14)

sight: at first sight **a primera vista** (15)

silk **seda** (3); it is made of silk **es de seda** (3)

silly **tonto/a** (2)

silver **plata** (3); it is made of silver **es de plata** (3)

sing **cantar** (1)

singer **cantante** *m., f.* (13)

single (*not married*) **soltero/a** (2); single room **habitación** (*f.*) **individual** (18)

sink (*bathroom*) **lavabo** (4)

sir **señor (Sr.)** *m.* (PP)

sister **hermana** (2)

sit down **sentarse (me siento)** (4)

six **seis** (PP); six hundred **seiscientos/as** (3)

sixteen **dieciséis** (PP)

sixth *adj.* **sexto/a** (13)

sixty **sesenta** (2)

skate **patinar** (9); skates **patines** *m.* (12)

skateboard **monopatín** *m.* (12)

ski **esquiar (esquío)** (9)

skirt **falda** (3)

skyscraper **rascacielos** *m. s.* (14)

sleep **dormir (duermo) (u)** (4)

sleepy: to be sleepy **tener sueño** (3)

slender **delgado/a** (2)

small **pequeño/a** (2); small window (*on a plane*) **ventanilla** (7)

smart **listo/a** (2)

smile **sonreír (se)** (*like* **reír**) (8)

smoke **fumar** (7)

smoking area **sala de fumar/de fumadores** (7)

snow **nevar (nieva)** (5); it's snowing **nieva** (5)

so that **para que** (15)

so-so **regular** (PP)

soap **jabón** *m.* (18)

soccer **fútbol** *m.* (9)

social worker **trabajador(a) social** (16)

sociology **sociología** (1)

socks **calcetines** *m. pl.* (3)

sofa **sofá** *m.* (4)

soft drink **refresco** (6)

solar **solar** (14)

soldier **soldado**; female soldier **mujer** (*f.*) **soldado** (16)

solve **resolver** (*like* **volver**) (*p.p.* **resuelto/a**) (14)

some **algún, alguno/a** (6)

someone **alguien** (6)

something **algo** (3)

sometimes **a veces** (2)

son **hijo** (2)

song **canción** *f.* (13)

soon: as soon as **tan pronto como** (16); *conj.* **en cuanto** (16)

sorry: I'm (very) sorry. **Lo siento (mucho).** (11)

sound *v.* **sonar (sueno)** (9)

soup **sopa** (6)

south **sur** *m.* (5)

Spanish (*language*) **español** *m.* (1); *n., adj.* **español(a)** (2)

speak **hablar** (1)

species **especie** *f.* (14); endangered species **especie en peligro de extinción** (14)

speed: speed limit **límite** (*m.*) **de velocidad** (14)

spend (*money*) **gastar** (8); (*time*) **pasar** (5)

spicy **picante** (6)

sport **deporte** *m.* (9)

sports *adj.* **deportivo/a** (9)

spring **primavera** (5)

stage **escenario** (13); (*phase*) **etapa** (15)

stamp (*postage*) **estampilla** (18)

stand in line **hacer cola** (7); to stand up **levantarse** (4)

start up (*a car*) **arrancar (qu)** (14)

state **estado** (2)

station **estación** *f.* (7); bus station **estación de autobuses** (7); gas station **estación de gasolina, gasolinera** (14); train station **estación del tren** (7); station wagon **camioneta** (7)

stationery **papel** (*m.*) **para cartas** (18); stationery store **papelería** (18)

stay *n.* (*in a hotel*) **estancia** (18); to stay (*in a place*) **quedar(se)** (5), **alojarse** (18); to stay in bed **guardar cama** (10)

steak **bistec** *m.* (6)

stereo **estéreo** (12)

stick out one's tongue **sacar (qu) la lengua** (10)

still **todavía** (5)

stockings **medias** *pl.* (3)

stomach **estómago** (10)

stop **parar** (14); (*doing something*) **dejar de** + *inf.* (10); to make stops **hacer escalas/paradas** (7); bus stop **parada del autobús** (18)

store **tienda** (3); to store (*documents*) **almacenar** (12)

stove **estufa** (9)

straight ahead **todo derecho** (14)

strange **raro/a** (8); **extraño/a** (13); it's strange **es extraño** (13)

street **calle** *f.* (12)

stress **estrés** *m.* (11)

stressed out **estresado/a** (11)

strike (*labor*) **huelga** (17)

striped **de rayas** (2)

student **estudiante** *m., f.* (1); *adj.*, of students **estudiantil** (11)

study **estudiar** (1)

stuffed up **resfriado/a** (10)

subject (*school*) **materia** (1)

suburb **afueras** *pl.* (12)

subway stop **estación** (*f.*) **del metro** (18)

succeed in (*doing something*) **conseguir** (*like* **seguir**) + *inf.* (8)

suddenly **de repente** (10)

suffer **sufrir** (11)

sufficiently **bastante** (15)

sugar **azúcar** *m.* (6)

suggest **sugerir (sugiero) (i)** (8)

suit **traje** *m.* (3); bathing suit **traje de baño** (3)

suitcase **maleta** (7); to pack one's suitcase(s) **hacer la(s) maleta(s)** (7)

summer **verano** (5)

sunny: it's (very) sunny **hace (mucho) sol** (5); sunbathe **tomar el sol** (7)

Sunday **domingo** (4)

supper **cena** (6); to have (eat) supper **cenar** (6)

sure *adj.* **seguro/a** (5); it's a sure thing that **es seguro que** (13)

surf the Net **navegar (gu) la Red** (12)

surprise **sorpresa** (8) it surprises me (you, him, . . .) **me (te, le,...) sorprende** (13)

SUV **SUV** (14)

sweater **suéter** *m.* (3)

sweatshirt **sudadera** (3)

sweep (the floor) **barrer (el piso)** (9); (*vacuum*) **pasar la aspiradora** (9)

sweets **dulces** *m. pl.* (6)

swim **nadar** (7)

swimming **natación** *f.* (9); swimming pool **piscina** (4)

symptom **síntoma** *m.* (10)

systems analyst **analista** (*m., f.*) **de sistemas** (16)

T

T-shirt **camiseta** (3)

table **mesa** (1); (end) table **mesita** (4)

take **tomar** (1); **llevar** (3); to take (photos) **sacar (qu) (fotos)** (7); to take a nap **dormir la siesta** (4); to take a trip **hacer un viaje** (4); to take care of oneself **cuidar(se)** (10); to take leave (of) **despedirse** (*like* **pedir**) **(de)** (8); to take off (*clothing*) **quitarse** (4); to take out (*withdraw money*) **sacar (qu)** (16); to take out the trash **sacar (qu) la basura** (9); to take place in **ser en** (8); to take someone's temperature **tomarle la temperatura** (10)

talk **hablar** (1); to talk on the phone **hablar por teléfono** (1)

tall **alto/a** (2)

tank **tanque** *m.* (14)

tape **cinta** (12); to tape **grabar** (12); tape recorder/player **grabadora** (12)

tea **té** *m.* (6)

teach **enseñar** (1)

technician **técnico/a** *n.* (16)

telephone **teléfono** (1); cell/mobile telephone **teléfono celular/móvil** (12)

television **televisión** *f.* (2); to watch television **mirar la tele(visión)** (2)

tell **decir** (7); **contar (cuento)** (7)

teller **cajero/a** (16); automatic teller machine **cajero automático** (16)

temperature **temperatura** (10); to take someone's temperature **tomarle la temperatura** (10)

ten **diez** (PP)

tenant **inquilino/a** (12)

tennis **tenis** *m. s.* (9); tennis shoe **zapato de tenis** (3)

tent **tienda de campaña** (7)

tenth **décimo/a** (13)

terrible: it's terrible that . . . **es terrible que...** (13)

terrorism **terrorismo** (17)

terrorist **terrorista** *m., f.* (17); terrorist attack **ataque** (*m.*) **terrorista** (17)

test **examen** *m.* (3); **prueba** (11)

textbook **libro de texto** (1)

thank you **gracias** (PP); thank you very much **muchas gracias** (PP); thanks for **gracias por** (8)

that **que** (2); that which **lo que** (4); that *adj.*, that one *pron.* **ese, esa** (3); that *adj.*, that one *pron.* (*over there*) **aquel, aquella** (3); that *pron.* **eso** (3); that *pron.* (*over there*) **aquello** (3); *conj.* **que** (2) that means **eso quiere decir** (10)

theater: to go to the theater **ir al teatro** (9)

their *poss.* **sus** (2)

then **luego** (4)

there is (not), there are (not) **(no) hay** (PP); **haber** (12)

there: (over) there **allí** (3); way over there **allá** (3)

therefore **por eso** (2)

these *adj., pron.* **estos/as** (2)

they **ellos/as** (1)

thin **delgado/a** (2)

thing **cosa** (4)

think **creer** (2); to think (*about*) **pensar (en)** (4)

third **tercer, tercero/a** *adj.* (13)

thirsty: to be (very) thirsty **tener (mucha) sed** (6)

thirteen **trece** (PP)

thirty **treinta** (PP); thirty, half-past (*the hour*) **y media, y treinta** (PP)

this *adj.*, this one *pron.* **este, esta** (2); this *pron.* **esto** (2)

those *adj.*, those (ones) *pron.* **esos/as** (3); those *adj.* (*over there*), those (ones) *pron.* (*over there*) **aquellos/as** (3)

three **tres** (PP); three hundred **trescientos/as** (3)

throat **garganta** (10)

through **por** *prep.* (7)

Thursday **jueves** *m. inv.* (4)

ticket **boleto, billete** *m.* (7); one-way ticket **billete/boleto de ida** (7); round-trip ticket **billete/boleto de ida y vuelta** (7)

tie **corbata** (3)

time: (at) what time? **¿a qué hora?** (PP); what time is it? **¿qué hora es?** (PP); (*period*) **época** (9); ahead of time **con anticipación** (18); on time **a tiempo** (7); spare time **ratos** (*pl.*) **libres** (9); full/part-time job **trabajo de tiempo completo/ parcial** (16)

tip (*to an employee*) **propina** (18)

tire *n.* **llanta** (14); flat tire **llanta desinflada** (14)

tired **cansado/a** (5)

to the **al** (*contraction of* **a** + **el**) (3)

toast **pan** (*m.*) **tostado** (6)

toasted **tostado/a** (6)

toaster **tostadora** (9)

tobacco stand/shop **estanco** (18)

today **hoy** (PP); what's today's date? **¿cuál es la fecha de hoy?, ¿qué fecha es hoy?** (5)

toe **dedo del pie** (11)

together **juntos/as** (7)

tomato **tomate** *m.* (6)

tomorrow **mañana** *adv.* (PP); see you tomorrow **hasta mañana** (PP); day after tomorrow **pasado mañana** (4)

tongue **lengua;** to stick out one's tongue **sacar (qu) la lengua** (10)

tonight **esta noche** (5)

too **también** (PP); too much **demasiado** *adv.* (9)

tooth **diente** *m.* (10); back tooth, molar **muela** (10)

toothpaste **pasta dental** (18)

tourist *adj.* **turístico/a** (7); tourist class **clase** (*f.*) **turística** (7)

towel **toalla** (18)

trade **oficio** (16)

traffic **tráfico, tránsito** (14); traffic signal **semáforo** (14)

train **tren** *m.* (7); train station **estación** (*f.*) **del tren** (7); to go by train **ir en tren** (7); to train **entrenar** (9)

translator **traductor(a)** (16)

transportation: means of transportation **medio de transporte** (7)

trash: to take out the trash **sacar (qu) la basura** (9)

travel **viajar** (7); travel agency **agencia de viajes** (7); travel agent **agente** (*m. f.*) **de viajes** (7)

traveler **viajero/a** (18)

traveling **de viaje** (7)

treadmill **rueda de molino** (10)

treatment **tratamiento** (10)

tree **árbol** *m.* (14)

trendy **es de última moda, está de moda** (3)

trip **viaje** *m.* (7); on a trip **de viaje** (7); round-trip ticket **billete** (*m.*)/ **boleto de ida y vuelta** (7); to take a trip **hacer un viaje** (4); dream trip **viaje de sueños**

try to (*do something*) **tratar de** + *inf.* (13)

Tuesday **martes** *m. inv.* (4)

tuition **matrícula** (1)

tuna **atún** *m.* (6)

turkey **pavo** (6)

turn **doblar** (14); to turn in **entregar (gu)** (7); to turn off **apagar (gu)** (11); to be someone's turn **tocarle (qu) a uno** (9); to turn out well/ badly **salir bien/mal** (4)

twelve **doce** (PP)

twenty **veinte** (PP)

twice **dos veces** (10)

two **dos** (PP); two-way **de doble vía** (14); two hundred **doscientos/as** (3)

type *v.* **escribir** (*p.p.* **escrito/a**) **a computadora** (16)

U

ugly **feo/a** (2)

unbelievable **increíble** (13)

uncle **tío** (2)

understand **comprender** (2); **entender (entiendo)** (4)

underwear **ropa interior** (3)

unfortunately **desgraciadamente** (10)

unlucky: to be unlucky **tener mala suerte** (11)

unintentional: it was unintentional **fue sin querer** (11)

university **universidad** *f.* (1); (of the) university **universitario/a** (11); university campus *campus* *m.* (12)

unless **a menos que** (15)

unlikely: it's unlikely that . . . **es improbable que…** (13)

unoccupied **desocupado/a** (18)

unpleasant **antipático/a** (2)

until *prep.* **hasta** (4); *conj.* **hasta que** (16); until (see you) tomorrow **hasta mañana** (PP); until later **hasta luego** (PP)

urgent **urgente** (13); it's urgent that **es urgente que** (13)

us *d.o.* **nos;** to/for us *i.o.* **nos** (PP)

U.S. *adj.* **estadounidense** (2)

use **usar** (3); **gastar** (8)

V

vacant **desocupado/a** (18)

vacation: to be on vacation **estar de vacaciones** (7); to go on vacation **ir de vacaciones** (7); to spend one's vacation in . . . **pasar las vacaciones en…** (7); to leave on vacation **salir de vacaciones** (7); to take a vacation **tomar unas vacaciones** (7)

vacuum *v.* **pasar la aspiradora** (9); vacuum cleaner **aspiradora** (9)

vegetable **verdura** (6)

vehicle **vehículo** (12)

verb **verbo** *gram.* (PP)

very **muy** (1); very very **-ísimo/a** (8); very well **muy bien** (PP)

veterinarian **veterinario/a** (16)

victim **víctima** (17)

video camera **cámara de vídeo** (12)

videocassette recorder (VCR) **videocasetera** (12)

view **vista** (12)

violence **violencia** (14)

visit a museum **visitar un museo** (9)

volleyball **voleibol** *m.* (9)

vote **votar**

W

wages **salario** (16)

wait (for) **esperar** (6)

waiter **camarero** (6)

waiting room **sala de espera** (7)

waitress **camarera** (6)

wake up **despertarse (me despierto)** (4)

walk **caminar** (9); to take a walk **dar un paseo** (9)

wall **pared** *f.* (4)

wallet **cartera** (3)

want **desear** (1); **querer** (3)

war **guerra** (17)

warm: to be/feel (very) warm/hot **tener (mucho) calor** (5)

wash: to wash (the windows, the dishes, clothes) **lavar (las ventanas, los platos, la ropa)** (9)

washing machine **lavadora** (9)

watch **reloj** *m.* (3); to watch **mirar** (2); to watch television **mirar la televisión** (2)

water **agua** *f.* (*but* **el agua**) (6); mineral water **agua mineral** (6)

we **nosotros/as** (1)

wear (*clothing*) **llevar, usar** (3)

weather **tiempo** (5); it's good/bad weather **hace buen/mal tiempo** (5); what's the weather like? **¿qué tiempo hace?** (5)

weave **tejer** (13)

wedding **boda** (15)

Wednesday **miércoles** *m. inv.* (4)

week **semana** (4); next week **la semana que viene** (4); once a week **una vez a la semana** (2)

weekday **día** (*m.*) **de la semana** (4)

weekend **fin** (*m.*) **de semana** (1)

welcome: you're welcome **de nada, no hay de qué** (PP)

well *adv.* **bien** (PP); *interj.* well . . . **bueno...** (2); well paid **bien pagado** (16)

well-being **bienestar** *m.* (10)

west **oeste** *m.* (5)

whale **ballena** (14)

what **lo que** (4)

what . . . ! **¡qué... !**; what a shame! **¡qué lástima!** (13)

what? **¿qué?** (PP), **¿cuál(es)?** (1); what are you like? **¿cómo eres / es usted?** (PP); what's the date today? **¿cuál es la fecha de hoy?, ¿qué fecha es hoy?** (5); what time is it? **¿qué hora es?** (PP); at what time? **¿a qué hora?** (PP); what's your name? **¿cómo te llamas?, ¿cómo se llama usted?** (PP); what for? **¿para qué?** (15)

when? **¿cuándo?** (1)

where? **¿dónde?** (PP); where (to)? **¿adónde?** (3); where are you from? **¿de dónde eres/es Ud.?** (PP)

which **que** (2); that which **lo que** (4)

which? **¿qué?** (PP); **¿cuál(es)?** (1)

while **mientras** *conj.* (9)

white **blanco/a** (3); white wine **vino blanco** (6)

who **que** (2)

who? whom? **¿quién(es)?** (1)

whole **entero/a** (9); to clean the whole house **limpiar la casa entera** (9)

whose? **¿de quién?** (2)

why? **¿por qué?** (2)

widow **viuda** (15)

widower **viudo** (15)

wife **esposa** (2); **mujer** *f.* (15)

wild animal **animal** (*m.*) **salvaje** (14)

win **ganar** (9)

windy: it's (very) windy **hace (mucho) viento** (5)

window **ventana** (1); small window (on a plane) **ventanilla** (7)

windshield **parabrisas** *m. inv.* (14)

wine (white, red) **vino (blanco, tinto)** (6)

winter **invierno** (5)

wish **deseo** (8); **esperanza** (17)

with **con** (1) with me **conmigo** (5); with you (*fam.*) **contigo** (5)

without **sin** (4)

witness **testigo** *m., f.* (17)

woman **señora (Sra.)** (PP); **mujer** *f.* (1); business woman **mujer de negocios** (16) woman soldier **mujer soldado** (16)

wool **lana** (3); it is made of wool **es de lana** (3)

word **palabra** (PP)

work (labor) **trabajo** (11); work (of art) **obra (de arte)** (13); (*person*) to work **trabajar** (1); (*machine*) **funcionar** (12)

worker **obrero/a** (16); farm worker **campesino/a** (14); social worker **trabajador(a) social** (16)

world **mundo** (7)

worried **preocupado/a** (5)

worse **peor** (5)

woven goods **tejidos** (13)

write **escribir** (*p.p.* **escrito/a**) (2)

writer **escritor(a)** (13)

written *p.p.* **escrito/a** (11); written report **informe** (*m.*) **escrito** (11)

wrong: to be wrong **no tener razón** (3); to be wrong (about) **equivocarse (qu) (de)** (11)

Y

yard **patio** (4)

year **año** (5); (*in school*) **grado** (9); to be . . . years old **tener... años** (2)

yellow **amarillo/a** (3)

yes **sí** (PP)

yesterday **ayer** (4); the day before yesterday **anteayer** (10)

yet **todavía** (5)

yoga **yoga** *m.* (10); to do yoga **hacer yoga** (10)

yogurt **yogur** *m.* (6)

you *sub. pron.* **tú** *fam. s.* (1); **usted (Ud.)** *form. s.* (1); **vosotros/as** (*fam. pl., Sp.*) (1); **ustedes (Uds.)** *pl.* (1); *d.o.* **te, os, lo/la, los, las**; to/for you *i.o.* **te, os, le, les**; *obj.* (*of prep.*) **ti** (5), **Ud., Uds., vosotros/as** you (*fam.*) are **eres** (PP); you (*form.*) are **es** (PP)

you're welcome **de nada, no hay de qué** (PP)

young woman **señorita (Srta.)** (PP)

younger **menor** (5)

your *poss.* **tu(s)** *fam.* (2); **su(s)** *form.* (2); **vuestro/a(s)** *fam. pl. Sp.* (2); **vuestro/a(s)** (17)

young *adj.* **joven** (2)

youth **juventud** *f.* (15); as a youth **de joven** (9)

Z

zero **cero** (PP)

zone **zona** (12)

Credits

Photo Credits

Note: In this edition, the appendix materials are found online.

G

gender
  of adjectives, 61
  of adverbs, 103
  of nouns, 33–35, 49
  of pronouns, 41–42
  See also Appendix 1 (*online*)
generalizations (impersonal
  expressions), 67, 341, 366
geography of the Hispanic
  world, 20–21
gerundios, 148
gerunds, with other verbs, 151
getting information, 88
government and civic
  responsibility, 436–437,
  447
gran(de), 63
greetings, 4–5, 22
Guatemala, 84, 91, 94, 104
gustar, 16, 212–213, 216, 226,
  350
  with indirect object
    pronouns, 212–213, 226
  verbs like, 216, 350
gustaría, 213, 456

H

haber, 237, 259, 382–383,
  418n, 457n
  See also Appendix 4 (*online*)
hablar, 43, 259
hacer, 119, 140, 220, 226, 378
  idioms, 120
  with weather expressions,
    140
  See also Appendix 4 (*online*)
hay, 15, 418n
health and physical well-being,
  276, 278, 296–297
Hispanic last names, 56
Hispanics in the United States,
  40
hobbies and fun activities, 252,
  272
holidays and celebrations,
  230–232, 231, 247
Honduras, 94, 104
horoscope signs, 143
house, items in and parts of,
  114–115, 136–137, 254,
  262, 273
houses in the Hispanic world,
  115
housing, 325, 345

I

idioms
  definition, 100
  followed by infinitive, 101
  with **hacer,** 120
  with **tener,** 57, 100–101,
    109, 141, 171, 256, 260
immigration, 455
imperative. *See* commands
imperfect indicative, 258–260
  conditional versus, 457
  forms of, 259

irregular, 259
  preterite versus, 282–285
  regular, 259
  summary of uses, 282–285,
    296
  words and expressions
    associated with, 285
  See also Appendix 1 (*online*)
imperfect subjunctive. *See* past
  subjunctive
impersonal expressions, 67,
  341, 366
  with subjunctive, 361, 366
  See also Appendix 1 (*online*)
impersonal **se,** 143n
Inca culture, 339, 343
indefinite and nonexistent
  antecedents, 397–398,
  407
indefinite articles, 35, 49
  definition, 34
indefinite words, 184–185, 195
indicative, 119–121, 329n, 333,
  423
  after conjunctions of time,
    423–424, 429
  See also Appendix 3 (*online*)
indirect object pronouns,
  207–209, 213, 226
  expressions of emotion
    with, 355
  placement, 208
  with prepositional phrase,
    213
  usage with **se** in unplanned
    events, 306–307
  with **gustar,** 213
infinitive, 44, 46, 75
  definition, 16
  ir + a + infinitive, 105, 108
  + prepositions, 116–117
  as singular subject, 213
  See also Appendix 1 (*online*)
infinitive commands, 395
informal commands
  with **tú,** 328–330, 344
  with **vosotros/as,** 330
interrogative, definition, 29
interrogative words, 69,
  268–269, 272
  + **ir,** 105, 108
  list of, 29, 50
  + stem-changing verbs, 126
  written accents, 93
ir + a + infinitive, 105, 108
ir (*irregular*), 105, 108, 148n,
  220, 226, 259, 272
  See also Appendix 4 (*online*)
-ir verbs, 75–76, 82, 148, 192,
  241, 329, 335, 344, 457
  See also Appendix 4 (*online*)
-ísimo/a, 234
-ista, professions with, 68n

J

jamás, 185
jobs and professions
  (*vocabulary*), 410–412,
  429
jugar, 125n

L

la, 33–35
languages
  European, 50, 62
  gender of, 62
last names, Hispanic, 56
Latin American universities, 28
le
  becomes **se,** 245
  for **lo,** 180n
Lectura (*reading*)
  animal weight graph, 92
  apartment ads, 326
  furniture ad, 116
  geography of the Hispanic
    world, 20–21
  graphic design ad, 122
  guessing meaning from
    context, 20
  Hispanic scholarships ad,
    332
  Internet access ad, 427
  jewelry ad, 163
  language courses ad, 37
  newspaper headlines, 442
  nonprofit ad, 315
  oil company ad, 372
  rental car ad, 13
  restaurant ad, 268
  text messaging ad, 324
  travel ads, 205, 212
  travel cartoon, 223
  university ad, 30
  voting ad, 439
likes and dislikes, expressing,
  213, 216, 350
linking, and diphthongs, 31, 93
ll, pronunciation of, 7n, 140
llevar, 276
lo, 180
  with singular masculine
    adjective (for general
    characteristics), 279
  See also Appendix 2 (*online*)

M

mal(o/a), 63, 162
maps
  Colombia, 257, 258
  Costa Rica, 146
  El Salvador, 118
  Guatemala, 94
  Honduras, 94
  Mexico, 60
  Nicaragua, 118
  Panamá, 177
  Peru, 327
  República Dominicana, 206
  South American countries
    and capitals, 145
  Spanish-speaking world, 10
  Venezuela, 281
masculine, 279
más de, 264
más (...) que, 160
mayor, 162
medicine in Hispanic countries,
  280
mejor, 265

menor, 162
menos de, 264
menos (...) que, 160
-mente, 304
México, 60, 71, 159
mi, mí, 144
money. *See* banking
months of the year, 142
mood of verbs, 329n
  See also Appendix 1 (*online*)
morir (past participle), 378,
  388
mucho, 103

N

nada, 185
nadie, 185
nationalities, 62, 64, 83
  See also adjectives, of
    nationality
negation, negative commands,
  191
negation, verbs and, 44
negative sentences, 44
negative **tú** commands, 329
negative words, 184–185, 195
  double negative, 185
neuter
  demonstrative, 63
  lo, 180
neuter demonstrative
  pronouns, 97, 108
news, the (*vocabulary*), 434,
  447
Nicaragua, 110, 118, 129, 135
ningún, ninguno/a, 185
no, 44
¿**no?,** 88
Notas comunicativas.
  See communication
  strategies
Notas culturales. *See* cultural
  notes
nouns
  + adjectives, 63
    See also Appendix 2
      (*online*)
  + articles, 33–34
  definition, 14
  gender of, 33–35, 49
  plural, 37–38, 49
  singular, 33–35, 49
  See also Appendix 1 (*online*)
numbers, 14, 56, 83, 91, 142,
  352, 366
  See also Appendix 1 (*online*)
nunca, 185

O

object
  direct object pronouns, 180,
    195, 208
  double object pronouns,
    244–245, 248
  indirect object pronouns,
    207–209, 213, 226,
    306–307
  pronouns objects of
    prepositions, 245